The Heart of Development

The Heart of Development

Gestalt Approaches to Working with Children, Adolescents and Their Worlds

Volume I: Childhood

Edited by
Gordon Wheeler & Mark McConville

Routledge
Taylor & Francis Group
LONDON AND NEW YORK

First published 2002 by GestaltPress

Published 2014 by Routledge
2 Park Square, Milton Park, Abingdon, Oxfordshire OX14 4RN
711 Third Avenue, New York, NY 10017, USA

First issued in paperback 2015

Routledge is an imprint of the Taylor & Francis Group, an informa business

Library of Congress Cataloging-in-Publishing Data

ISBN 13: 978-1-138-14193-3 (hbk)
ISBN 13: 978-0-88163-340-5 (pbk)

Table of Contents

Preface
Violet Oaklander 9

Introduction
Gordon Wheeler 18

Part I: Theory

Chapter 1. The Developing Field: Toward a Gestalt Developmental Model
Gordon Wheeler 37

Part II: Applications

Chapter 2. The Therapeutic Process with Children and Adolescents: A Gestalt Therapy Perspective
Violet Oaklander 85

Chapter 3. Physical Process Work with Children and Adolescents
Denise Tervo 113

Chapter 4. Integrating Gestalt in Children's Groups
Keith Tudor 147

Table of Contents

Chapter 5. Compulsion and Curiosity: A Gestalt Approach to OCD
Gordon Wheeler 165

Chapter 6. Janet Lederman and the Gazebo School
Eduardo Eizner 183

Chapter 7. ADD: A Gestalt Perspective
Jay Kent-Ferraro & Gordon Wheeler 199

Chapter 8. Healing Young, Wounded Hearts: Gestalt Group Therapy with Children of Divorce
Cynthia Reynolds & Ansel Woldt 239

Part III: Perspectives and New Directions

Chapter 9. Between Parent and Child: The Power of Shame
Gordon Wheeler 265

Chapter 10. Confluent/Constructivist Treatment of Children with Learning/Behavior Disorders
Joan Benevento 285

Chapter 11. A Development Model with Applications for Working with Young Children
Steven S. Wexberg 311

Chapter 12. The Pinocchio Syndrome: Path to Wholeness: Gestalt therapy with Children and Adolescents
Felicia Carroll 331

To my children:

Alexander, Sarah, Rebekah, Jon, Ben, Mariam, Jennifer, Elizabeth, and Rolf–my teachers and my inspiration–and to my first teacher, Ben Kerr Wheeler, who always knew how to play with children.

With love and gratitude –

Gordon Wheeler

Preface

Violet Oaklander

I am honored to write the preface for Volume One of Heart of Development. This book is an outgrowth of the first International Conference on Gestalt Therapy With Children and Adolescents. This was a landmark conference--the recognition that Gestalt Therapy holds an important place in work with children. Imagine a whole conference on Gestalt Therapy with children and adolescents! It actually did happen, much to my gratification and delight. This conference represented a culmination of a lonely journey of mine that lasted for thirty years.

This preface may appear to be taking the form of a autobiographical sketch. As I contemplate this, I realize that this part of my life actually represents the history of Gestalt therapy with children.

I became interested in applying Gestalt therapy to my work with children in 1970. I started working with severely emotional disturbed children in the schools in 1967 without much preparation. I had been teaching in a designated "culturally deprived" school for two and a half years before that, and, because of my innovative, unusual (and successful) approaches, I knew I would be denied tenure. The principal of the school actually suggested that maybe I'd be better off in the field of recreation, since, when she would come into my room (often), the children would be working in noisy groups, laughing uproariously at my funny spelling test sentences, or singing with gusto Pete Seeger and Woody Guthrie songs to my guitar playing. The school counselor suggested I look into teaching severely emotionally disturbed children.

I read everything I could find about working with these very difficult children. There was very little to be found, and after struggling on my own for about four years. I decided to go back to school to get a Master's Degree in Special Education, with emphasis in emotional disturbance. Like the Tin Man in *The Wizard of Oz*, I thought such a degree would give me the knowledge I so desperately yearned for. I wanted to find a dynamic, effective, humanistic approach to working with these troubled children. However, I continued to feel frustrated since the program just didn't meet my needs. After a certain amount of protest, I was granted some independent study time, and embarked on a search by visiting existing programs for disturbed children throughout Southern California. Behavior modification was in vogue, and I was mortified by the rigid, mechanistic methods I witnessed. It began to dawn on me through these visits, and the various child therapy books I read, that I might be pursuing an illusion.

It was about this time that the Los Angeles Gestalt Therapy Institute initiated its first training program, and, because of a transformational experience I had at Esalen Institute with Jim Simkin in the Fall of 1969 related to the illness and death of my almost 15-year-old son, Michael, I decided to enter the program. I began perusing the Gestalt Literature and found nothing written about children. In 1969 and 1971, two books were published about Gestalt work with children: Janet Lederman's *Anger and the Rocking Chair* (1969), a poignant lyrical account of her experiences with difficult children in a school setting, and George Brown's *Human Teaching for Human Learning* (1971), a wonderful description of the use of Gestalt awareness techniques in confluent educational classrooms. However, nothing was to be found in the traditional Gestalt therapy literature focusing on psychotherapy with children.

I spent much time experimenting with the children in my class, at first with techniques and then applying theoretical concepts to my interactions with them. As my theoretical rationale expanded, the response of the children amplified. The results were nothing short of miraculous; (this principal actually called me a 'miracle worker').

Subsequently, I left the school setting, got another degree in psychological counseling, and started a private practice working with many children, individually and in groups, from various situations and cultures. My Gestalt therapy oriented approach, combined with the use of many expressive and projective techniques, expanded and developed. I was giving many workshops and classes for professionals during this time, and found that people who worked with children from a variety of disciplines and in diverse settings were craving help and guidance. "What do you do with the kid?" was a common refrain, as these therapists begged for more enlightenment. The attitude of these people struck a familiar note in me as it became more and more apparent that there was a serious dearth of information and training regarding effective psychotherapy with children and adolescents.

It finally dawned on me that the elusive book that I perpetually searched for would have to be written by me. I eventually entered a Ph.D. program and after three more years of intense struggle, I completed my dissertation, a two-volume tome, out of which emerged the book, *Windows To*

Preface

Our Children: A Gestalt Therapy Approach to Children and Adolescents (1978/1988).

After the book was published, I expected that there would be many such books appearing on the market, as happens with many kinds of subject matter relating to psychotherapy and self-help. This phenomenon did not occur. The book, without much publicity, moved underground in a kind of grass roots movement throughout the world. This amazing happening served to accentuate the intense need child and adolescent therapists had for direction. I began to receive invitations to do workshops all over the country and outside the country and thus began my traveling life. I started my own two-week summer training program in 1980 that continues to attract therapists from everywhere. The response to my work was exhilarating and heart-warming to me, but nevertheless the journey continued to be a solitary endeavor.

I decided from the beginning that my work could not be exclusive to Gestaltists. People who work with children are desperate for direction and support and the children they work with need these clinicians' full involvement in assisting them back onto their rightful path of health and growth. The healthy development of children is naturally attuned to Gestalt therapy philosophy and theory. Many people who have come to my training programs and workshops have gone on to take Gestalt training; however, the approach is effective without that training and thousands of people can attest to this. Not only have many, many children benefited from this approach, but also many people have shared this work with other practitioners in agencies, hospitals, schools, institutions and other places where the lives of children are involved.

Happily, my journey is no longer steeped in solitude; this was effectively manifested by the Heart of Development conference in Cleveland. A new generation is carrying on this work. In this book you will find a rich and varied wealth of material describing the use of Gestalt Therapy philosophy, theory and practice with children. Each contribution brings the author's own unique and creative style and interpretation of the Gestalt approach to his or her work, and each contribution affirms the potent effectiveness of each approach. If you live or work with children, you will be enriched after reading this book.

Violet Oaklander
Santa Barbara, CA

References

Brown, G. (1971, 1990). *Human teaching for human learning*. New York, NY: Viking Press; also The Gestalt Journal Press.

Lederman, J. (1969). *Anger and the rocking chair*. New York, NY: McGraw-Hill.

Oaklander, V. (1978, 1988). *Windows to our children*. New York, NY: Real People Press; also The Gestalt Journal Press.

The Editors

Gordon Wheeler has written extensively on the Gestalt model as the basis of a new integration of evolutionary psychology, developmental constructivism, and intersubjective understanding. In particular his writings in the field have focused on self and developmental theory, intimacy and relationship, shame and support, narrative theory, gender studies, men's issues, and child and adolescent therapy. A longtime member of the teaching faculty of the Gestalt Institute of Cleveland, Gestalt International Study Group, the Esalen Institute, and a number of training institutes overseas, he also serves as Director and Editor of GestaltPress, where he has overseen the editing and production of some twenty-five books on Gestalt topics by other authors. He is the father of five children and three stepchildren, and together with his wife Nancy Lunney Wheeler, divides his time between Cambridge, Massachusetts and Big Sur, California. His recent books in the Gestalt field include *Beyond Individualism: Toward a New Understanding of Self, Relationship & Experience* (GestaltPress/The Analytic Press, 2000) and *Reading Paul Goodman: Gestalt Therapy, Essays & Commentary* (in press).

Mark McConville, Ph.D. is a clinical psychologist in private practice in Shaker Heights, Ohio specializing in adolescent and family psychology. He is a senior faculty member at the Gestalt Institute of Cleveland, and has lectured widely on the subjects of child development, parenting, and counseling methodology. In addition to his practice, Mark consults regularly with Hathaway Brown School and University School, both in the Cleveland area. His book, *Adolescence: Psychotherapy and the Emergent Self* (Jossey-Bass, 1995) was awarded the Nevis Prize for Outstanding Contribution to Gestalt Therapy Theory. Together with other faculty members at the Gestalt Institute of Cleveland, Mark is involved in the development of a post-graduate training program in Gestalt approaches to working with children and adolescents.

The Contributors

Joan Benevento, Ph.D. is a special educator, school psychologist, and guidance counselor, specializing in working with children with learning/behavior disorders. Her training in Gestalt therapy was at the New York Institute for Gestalt Therapy. Longtime coordinator of the graduate Special Education program at St. John's University in New York, she developed and taught graduate courses in which she presented a synthesis of Gestalt therapy theoretical concepts and Piaget's model of cognitive development.

Felicia Carroll, MA, MEd. is a child and adolescent therapist in private practice in Santa Barbara, California. She has credentials in educational psychology, child development, and counseling psychology. She is a certified play therapist, supervisor, and trainer, and teaches nationally and internationally. A trainer with the Violet Oaklander Institute, she has written several chapters about Gestalt therapy with children.

Eduardo Eizner, MA, MFCC is a bicultural/bilingual, licensed psychotherapist born and raised in Argentina. He holds Master's degrees in psychology from both Belgrano University in Buenos Aires and Chapman University in California. He has worked with individuals and groups for many years at the Esalen Institute in Big Sur, California, where he has also served as Director of the Gazebo Park School. He is the father of two children.

Jay Kent-Ferraro, Ph.D.,LPC, DAPA, NCP is an authority in optimal performance coaching and leadership development and founder of Empowerment Technologies, a consulting company offering executive coaching and specialty human resource consultation. He works with clients ranging from Fortune 500 executives and front-line managers to government agencies to both profit and not-for-profit companies in a broad range of industrial, professional, and service-related industries. He is also a full-time associate of Jeff Magee International and Vice President of Curriculum Development for Perfectuniversity.com, an interactive, e-based training company.

Iris Fodor, Ph.D. is Professor of Applied Psychology at New York University where she trains graduate students in School Psychology and

Cognitive, Gestalt, and Integrative Therapy. She has given workshops and written extensively about the integration of Cognitive and Gestalt therapy and theory. Her recent writings include "A Woman and Her Body: Cycles of Pride and Shame" in *The Voice of Shame: Silence and Connection in Psychotherapy* (1996).

Violet Oaklander, Ph.D. is author of the book, *Windows to Our Children: A Gestalt Therapy Approach to Children and Adolescents*, as well as a number of articles and book chapters, and audio and video tapes on psychotherapeutic work with children. She teaches her approach, which combines Gestalt therapy theory, practice and philosophy with a variety of expressive techniques, widely throughout the world. She is Director of the Violet Oaklander Institue in Santa Barbara, California, devoted to the training of professionals who work with children and adolescents. Her book is considered a classic in the field, and her contributions tof mental health work have been recognized with a number of awards.

Cynthia Reynolds, Ph.D. is Assistant Professor in Counselor Education at the University of Akron. Her dissertation, directed by Dr. Ansel Woldt, focused on the coping styles of children of divorce from a Gestalt perspective. She is a licensed professional clinical counselor and licensed psychologist. In addition, she spent fifteen years as a school counselor where she gained considerable experience in facilitating groups for children of divorce. She maintains a private practice in play therapy in Kent, Ohio.

Denise Tervo, Ph.D. is a licensed psychologist, supervisor, and trainer in private practice in Pittsburgh, Pennsylvania. She works with children, adolescents, adults, families, and clinical supervision groups. She completed her Gestalt training at the Gestalt Institute of Cleveland and at the Violet Oaklander Institute. She is a member of the senior teaching faculty at the Gestalt Institute of Cleveland and Co-Chair of the advanced Third Year Track, Working with Physical Process.

Keith Tudor, MA, MSc, CQSW, Dip.Psychotherapy, PTSTA, MAHPP is a director of Temenos in Sheffield, England, and of its Person-Centred Psychotherapy and Counselling, Supervision, and other postgraduate courses. He currently runs a specialist supervision and training group, supporting practitioners working with children and young people. He is an Honorary Lecturer at Liverpool John Moores University, has written extensively in the field of mental health, counselling and therapy, and is the author of three books: *Mental Health Promotion*, *Group Counselling*, and with Tony Merry, *Dictionary of Person-Centred Psychology*. He edited *Transactional Analysis Approaches to Brief Therapy*, and is the editor of a series Advancing Theory in Therapy (to be published by Brunner/Routledge).

Steven Wexberg, M.D. has a practice in general pediatrics in Cleveland, Ohio, and is Senior Clinical Instructor in Pediatrics at Case Western Reserve University School of Medicine. His training in Gestalt therapy was at the Gestalt Institute of Cleveland, where he is a member of the visiting faculty. He also works as a psychotherapist with adults, couples, and groups, and has a special interest in supporting parents' exploration of the spiritual dimensions of parenting.

Ansel Woldt, Ed.D. is Professor Emeritus at Kent State University, where he directed thirty-six doctoral dissertations on Gestalt therapy, and continues to teach counseling courses while also serving as Gestalt Archivist. He is Founding Secretary, Archivist, and Continuing Education Officer for the Association for the Advancement of Gestalt Theray (AAGT), and an Associate Editor of the *Gestalt Review*. He maintains a private practice in Kent, Ohio, where he lives with his wife, Nancy Woldt.

Introduction

Gordon Wheeler

Gestalt therapy and related work under a Gestalt model with children, adolescents, and families is at one and the same time a young field, and one with deep roots and a long history. It was as early as 1925 that Kurt Koffka, one of the original founders of the German Gestalt school of cognitive and perceptual psychology published *The Growth of the Mind* in English translation, the first book-length treatment of child development from a Gestalt psychology point of view. In contrast to the then-dominant models of childhood–the psychoanalytic and the behaviorist–Koffka's perspective on child development emphasized the characteristic Gestalt themes of holism and contact, the unity of affect and communication, perception as the active configuration of meaningful wholes and relationships, the figure-ground relationship in mental process, the primacy of perspective and context, the integrity of experience, and the necessity of approaching the whole subject from the child's own subjective point of view. Of two other themes emphasized by the author, one will be familiar to students of Gestalt over the past couple of generations, while the other is only now becoming fully "figural," as Koffka himself would have put it. The first of these is the positioning of Gestalt as an integrative perspective, resolving and clarifying the problems and contradictions of both the "inner" (dynamic/subjective) and "outer" (behaviorist) schools. The second is his firm location of the Gestalt model in the evolutionary tradition, as the psychological system best able to answer the challenges of the Darwinian revolution. (Indeed, the Gestalt psychology model itself may be understood as belonging to what we now would call evolutionary psychology, in the broad sense of beginning to articulate a model of mind that could describe and account for how we survive and thrive as individuals and as a species, as problem-solving animals in a complex and demanding social/environmental field).

These same concerns, which Paul Goodman sometimes liked to refer to by the more homely phrase "getting along in the world" (1951, 1994), were then to be taken up by a group collecting around Fritz and Laura Perls in New York in the years immediately following World War II, including Goodman, Paul Weisz, and the reform educator Elliot Shapiro, as they met to articulate a new approach they called Gestalt therapy (see Stoehr, 1994). The Perlses, who had been exposed to the Gestalt psychology revolution in the course of their own graduate and professional training in Germany, had made an attempt to include some Gestalt ideas in their first book, *Ego, Hunger & Aggression* (1947, later subtitled *The Beginnings of Gestalt Therapy*)–chiefly the idea of the holistic construction and deconstruction (or "destructuring") of meaning in perception, cognition, and action–themes which were to become dominant in models of brain, mind, and culture in the second half of the twentieth century. To Fritz Perls in particular, the accent of the approach would always be on the deconstructive side of the process, the necessity of thinking and feeling "autonomously" for oneself, destroying and metabolizing whatever cultural beliefs and values one might have been "fed" in infancy and childhood, in favor of independence and self-definition (F. Perls, 1969, 1973). Laura Perls (1991), with her background in movement and dance, was more concerned with the development of support for movement and action; but in practice this support turned out to mean essentially "self-supports"–grounding, posture, breathing, and the like–not inderdependence on the support of others and with the social surround. Thus, both the Perlses remained in many ways grounded in the strong individualism of the Freudian model in which they had been schooled, with its privileging of firm self-boundaries, mature autonomy, and self-determination.

At the same time, the ironies and contradictions of the Oedipal model, in which a seemingly autonomous maturity is achieved by simply internalizing (Perls would have said "introjecting") the societal values of the father, were not lost on either of the Perlses, who were both cultural radicals and themselves victims of the totalitarianism sweeping Europe, and then later the rise of fascism in South Africa, their first home-in-exile (see F. Perls, 1969). Indeed, these contradictions were exactly what they hoped to mitigate or resolve, by a revaluing and reemphasis of the role of healthy aggression and self-assertion in child development. (Fritz's own view of early childhood, like Freud's, remained an oddly fatalist one: the nursling, as he begins to develop teeth, begins naturally to "cannibalize" the breast–which leads in turn to an inevitably too-early, forced weaning. Thus self-assertion is always at the price of intimate connection, and thus perhaps too the lifelong flavor of Fritz Perls's clinical work and personal life, in both of which he showed sharp reactivity to any hint of "confluence" or relaxation of a rather rigid, "mature" self-boundary; see Perls, 1969).

Meanwhile, Paul Goodman, likewise an admirer of Freud as well as a critic of Oedipal theory, brought his own concerns and his own spin to the model: specifically a much greater emphasis on the relational and the communal, growing out of his anarchistic politics, his interpretation and experience of Eros, and not least, his years of working with children of various ages (Stoehr, 1994). If childhood to Freud (and to Fritz Perls) was a sort of dangerous affliction to be recovered from, to Goodman something like the reverse was true: it was childhood and a childlike spirit of spontaneity and play that were to be valued, over a rigid, solemn, unerotic and self-contained "maturity," which seemed to Goodman the opposite of everything lively and desirable in life, relationships, art, work, and politics (which should all be one and the same thing, to Goodman). And perhaps it was this very valuing of spontaneity and open creativity that made Goodman, like both Perlses, dispositionally averse to codifying these general philosophical ideas on development into anything remotely like a formal system, much less a schematized linear stage model like so many others offered to us down through the whole century of developmental models since Freud's time (a brief comparative selection of these models is given in Chapter One ahead). In any case, since it was Paul Goodman writing these ideas up for the second, theoretical volume of their joint book, but in some indeterminate manner on the basis of the Perlses' and others' ideas as well as his own, it was perhaps inevitable that the result would show a number of stress lines of unclarity or even irresolvable contradiction between and among these varying emphases and concerns (see discussion in Wheeler, 1991).

Given all this, it is not surprising either if the ideas of many Gestaltists remained rudimentary at best, or else just muddled, when it came to questions of childhood and human development. After all, many of us were drawn to Gestalt in the first place because of our dissatisfaction with the linear rigidities and programmatic unreality of the dominant models on just these topics: contact, growth, creativity, relationship, social and political context, and what Goodman called the "false dichotomies" of the mainstream culture, in which "childish vs. mature" figured prominently (to which we could add "individual vs. social," "personal vs. political," "self vs. relationship" or "self vs. other," and so on–none of which correspond very well to the felt experience of real living; see Goodman, 1951; also Wheeler, 2000). Thus many of us rejected the traditions we were schooled in, without anything very clear to put in their place.

In the face of all these contradictions and concerns, some simply took refuge in Perls's more simplistic slogans on the subject–in particular the often-cited one that holds that development is pretty well summed up as the (linear) progress from need for others to "self-support" (leaving that old Perlsian/Freudian bugaboo, dependency, in its familiar position as the feared and shamed negative/regressive pole of the system). Meanwhile, as long as Gestalt therapy itself was understood to mean some kind of highly confrontive, more or less psychodramatic encounter in which self-reliance and self-expression (as opposed to, say, intimate connection, listening and dialogue, empathic intersubjectivity, and mutual support) were the only coin of the realm, then the idea of Gestalt work with children must have seemed almost oxymoronic in any case. The imagined, ideal "autonomy" of the client just couldn't have seemed all that applicable to the position of the child, who is by nature and by situation so visibly engaged in that most fundamental and real developmental process, the working out of the integrative possibilities and range for the exploration, expression, and definition of self-in-relationship (and not self as-opposed-to-relationship, as both Perls and Freud often seem to suggest). For Freud, these tensions are resolved, more or less, into a sort of uneasy, long-term truce as the outcome of the Oedipal conflict (a kind of Versailles Treaty of the mind, like that pact by which World War I was halted, more or less, without ever being resolved). For Perls, at times it seemed that the whole rest of life after that harsh, precocious weaning has the character of one long, deathly resistance against regressive yearnings for commitment, connection, and intimacy. For Freud, the picture of post-Oedipal development often looks and sounds as drearily life-denying as Goodman found it to be: stiff, unplayful, uncreative, "masculine" in the worst sense, and above all, unerotic.

Thus those who were still interested in charting the development and clinical treatment of the child and adolescent probably mostly turned to other models (or in many cases no models at all; many or most child clinical workers have long put more trust in on-the-job clinical wisdom and lore, over the menu of available systems and maps, which like the Freudian, often seem to have been drawn up somewhere far from the lives and experience of any actual children). Those who were drawn to Gestalt often seemed to see no particular interest, and perhaps no real possibility, of applying the model to work with children, at least in its more Perlsian forms. Gestalt work went on, without any clearly articulated picture or map of human development, particularly in the childhood years.

For this we all suffered, and the model suffered. First of all, by making or accepting this "false dichotomy" between Gestalt work and developmental perspectives, we effectively deracinated the model itself. The contextual, figure-ground model, after all, is a "nested" picture: old figure has generated old ground, which gives interactive rise to new figure, new figure-ground resolution, in the new situation and the "new self." Thus our history is always contained in our present–not as a "dead hand" (at least, not in the healthy case), but as a dynamic, informing ground out of which and against which present meaning works, in creative, lively exchange. If we have no clear picture of who we once were and how we got from there to here, no meaningful "story," then we really don't know who it is we are dealing with, or for that matter who we ourselves are, in living process terms. And this is still true, no matter how much we may fear the tyranny of the old linear developmental models, which seemed and often were prescriptive, constrictive, and frankly deadening (indeed, Perls and even Goodman sometimes seemed to fear the power of dynamically structured ground, in the form of "introjected" ideas, to the point of denying its crucial existence and process role–a denial which makes no sense under the terms of the Gestalt model itself; see Goodman, 1951; also Wheeler, 1991).

Secondly, we suffered in a subtler way, from this denial of the importance of an understanding of development. The fact is, we all do have ideas of development–just as we all carry notions of human nature, how human process works, and what healthy living looks like, personally and socially. These ideas, which may be explicit or implicit, aware or out of awareness, are embodied, encoded, and expressed in what the deconstructivists call a "practice:" that is, all the gestures and processes and encounters of ordinary living, as we go about our day, coping with the people and the exigencies of our own lives. This practice is there, "in the ground," by the very terms of our gestalt-making model. To deny that we have and embody such preconceptions (as the deconstructivists have also warned us about; see e.g. Foucault, 1980), is just to sweep those preconceptions off the table and under the rug, where they are not available for dialogue and deconstruction themselves–but where they are still exercising an all the more controlling effect on contact and relationship.

Thus we become like some therapists of an earlier era (including, alas, some Gestaltists, who of all people should know better), claiming a superhuman ability to meet the client in some "pure" encounter or contact, freed from all personal or cultural blinders like gender or sexual orientation, ethnicity and race, class, and so on. Surely in today's global community we are all past the point of imagining self-indulgent and domineering absurdities of this kind, which were a wishful fiction when they were first articulated by Husserl (1983), in the context of the dominant European culture of a century and more ago–and are a dangerous fiction now, because of the way they disempower the client, blocking dialogue or challenge to us about all those preconceptions which we may want to deny we have, carry, and "practice." If we insist that we don't have and don't need notions of development or theories of human nature to be "in contact" with self and others, we are just misunderstanding the constructive dynamic of contact and experience themselves, and of our own nature–which is after all what the Gestalt model is all about.

And yet–there were always revisionist voices, under and around the dominance of a certain spin on the Perlsian model (which was and is itself a crucial revisionist voice under and around the dominant culture, with its familiar ruling triad of conformist materialism, militarism, and imperialism, as active or more today as it was half a century ago, when Perls and Goodman were first writing in the field). First of all was Perls himself, in his late-late incarnation as communal explorer, in his last months in experimental community at Lake Cowichan, Canada. Then there was Goodman, first, last, and always, with his radical insistence on decentralized communal forms, personal relations, school reform, and not least, the radical deconstructive power of the erotic, to subvert the boundaries that block relationship and intimacy (see discussion in Stoehr, 1994). And if Laura Perls's work emphasized self-supports over social supports, still it introduced the crucial notion of the dynamic role of support in contact and development. At the Gestalt Institute of Cleveland (always at the forefront of Gestalt work beyond the individual), Richard Wallen and Edwin Nevis were early in extending Gestalt insights to organizational systems; Sonia Nevis, the late Bill Warner, and Joseph Zinker were early and active in taking up the questions of intimacy, couples' relationships, and family life; Erv Polster worked with community groups from the early 1960s in best Goodman tradition; Elaine Kepner and many others were developing a Gestalt theory of group work, beyond the hot-seat-plus-audience model popularized by Fritz Perls (for discussion of all these and related developments, see Wheeler, 1991). In California, Gary Yontef was emphasizing dialogue, while George Brown was developing the model for "confluent education" (1971) which would aim at integration of cognitive and affective development (or rather, at the removal of their false separation, since we know now that cognition is always organized and mediated by affect; see Damazio, 1994). Judith Brown (1998/1979) was likewise working with and writing about couples, and creating innovative approaches to the use of narrative in therapy, long before that was the current fashion, And from the 1970s onward, there has been

Violet Oaklander, defying and cutting through the developmental muddle described above, to create and craft her own magic in working with children through a Gestalt model. In a real sense, Violet Oaklander, as much as any one person, is the founder of Gestalt work with children: thus all of us in the field today are in a sense her grateful children, even as we go on learning and growing from her writings and her training today.

Today, as I write even these few names, it is a real pleasure to note how many of them (and many others) could be carried forward in a fairly direct vector toward the material and the insights of one or more chapters in this collection, which build on and extend their earlier work. Thus again new figure is created and yielded out of old ground, in dynamic, constructivist interaction with the felt realities and urgencies of our present moment. This is how theory renews itself, and how we renew ourselves as well, avoiding the twin extremes of a rigid adherence to past doctrine (the fundamentalism of fixed ground) and an equally rigid fixation on the present moment only (the equally dead anomie of figure fixation in the moment, without the rootedness in context and purpose that gives it life and meaning). (Certainly in making up any rapid list of this kind, inevitably one omits more significant contributors than one includes. For this I apologize in advance, and hasten to add that the list is meant to be suggestive and personal, not inclusive or exhaustive by any means.)

To continue in this line, my own work (e.g., 1990, 1991, 1995, 1996) has been very much concerned over the years with pointing out how uneasily the hyperindividualistic bent of Gestalt work in some hands sits with the actual theoretical bases and implications of the model, which are inherently intersubjective, relational, and social-constructionist. Building on these insights and concerns, I have tried in Chapter One in this collection, "Toward a Gestalt Developmental Model," to take up all this work, the "mainstream" of Gestalt and its creative revisionism alike, steeped as it all is in a deep theoretical and personal/clinical appreciation of the centrality of relationship in human living, and build on it in the direction, at least, of a developmental/field perspective and model that would be fully "Gestalt." That is to say, a direction fully congruent with the lived experience and felt truth of our lives as we live and know them, and of the basic terms and requirements of our human nature-in-the-world (always remembering that the world of the human being is first, last, and always a world of other human beings).

In the process, what emerges in this chapter is not so much a new set of labels for the same familiar developmental "stages" (which are essentially sociobiological at least up through puberty, for all that they are given different labels in different systems, always according to the particular lens of that particular lens-grinder)–but rather a different perspective on all the other models, as well as a basis for evaluating them and understanding them from the inside. This after all is part of the theoretical use of the Gestalt model: the way it contextualizes and relates one system, one approach to another, by understanding each of them from the inside in relation to the awarenesses and felt needs that went into that particular creative form at a given time, with a given population. This is the comparative constructivism opened up to us by Gestalt–the basic idea that we are born to create meaningful whole pictures we can use to deal with our world, which is the legacy of a hundred years of Gestalt research and practice, and still a fresh and contentious idea today. My hope is that this chapter will be the first of many on the subject, from many voices, all of us serving together to reroute and re-root our own model in a necessary, and long missing, developmental. ground.

Preceding and following that theoretical chapter, we are honored indeed to have Violet Oaklander's voice not once but twice in this volume: first in the Foreword, where she recounts from a personal perspective some of this same history and progression, in terms of her own journey from the fringes to the very center of the Gestalt world. Surely there cannot be any Gestaltists in the world today who are not familiar with the name Violet Oaklander; and given her indefatigable training and travels, there cannot be many child/adolescent clinicians in the world of any school or persuasion, who have not heard of her moving and quietly revolutionary work with children. The reader has only to turn to Chapter Two, "The Therapeutic Process with Children and Adolescents: A Gestalt Therapy Perspective," to see why this is the case. The magic of Oaklander's work with children comes off the page. This chapter is meant by the author to serve as a base in some form for a book-length work she is currently at work on (following her classic 1978 volume, *Windows to Our Children*). Pending that happy event, we gladly present it in this form here.

With Chapter Three, "Physical Process Work with Children and Adolescents," Denise Tervo takes up the work of many earlier Gestaltists (Laura Perls and James Kepner [1994] come to mind, soon to be joined with a new book by Ruella Frank [2001]), and extends and develops it for work with children. In the process, Tervo comes up with insights and clinical interventions that will serve every "body" therapist, whatever the age of their clients–and every child and adolescent therapist, whether or not they regard themselves as "body-oriented" (or Gestalt-oriented, for that matter). All experience is embodied (at least in this lifetime): Tervo inspires and guides us all to be more adept in working with that crucial experiential dimension.

Group work has been central to Gestalt practice since the beginning, and yet the literature on Gestalt groups is still meager, while that on Gestalt group work with children is almost nonexistent. Keith Tudor's Chapter Four, "Integrating Gestalt in Children's Groups," was an early, happy exception, and it is with special pleasure that we reprint it here (it was first published in *The Gestalt Journa*l, Vol. XIV, in 1991). Tudor's creative range and deep respect for the felt experience of the child continue to offer all of us new ideas and new inspiration in our clinical and other work with children in group settings.

Chapter Five, "Compulsion and Curiosity: A Gestalt Approach to OCD," has likewise appeared before, in the *British Gestalt Journal* (Vol. 3, 1994). Writing up a case is its own particular genre of storytelling, and its own particular form of theory exposition. My own hope with this article was first of all that the person and personality of a remarkably intelligent, sensitive, and deep-hearted boy might come alive on the page. Secondly, I hope to illustrate for the reader something of what those of us who work with the Gestalt model know so well: namely, how the real contact between therapist and client is the locus and the agent of change, and how that "contact between" then acts in some way to rebalance and recalibrate the "contact within" that client–much as pharmacological intervention is increasingly relied on to do today.

To want to illustrate this is not to be "against" psychopharmacology with children and adolescents. Most of us who work with children (or adults) would agree that used wisely and in the context of therapeutic relationship, the panoply of biochemical agents available for use today can offer valuable, at times essential support for the work (a point that will come up again in Chapter Seven). But psychotropic medications should be a subsidiary or secondary intervention. Unfortunately, as we know in these days of penny-wise, pound-foolish "managed (i.e., rationed) care," they are increasingly the primary or only intervention.

But contact and relationship are themselves biochemical events, with strong biochemical consequences, as an overwhelming body of research now amply demonstrates (see e.g., van der Kolk, et al., 1996). It is time and past time for us to move beyond one of the deepest "false dichotomies" of our materialistic culture: the old scientistic canard of "nature vs. nurture." For the human being, as Paul Ehrlich (2000) points out in his excellent summary of evolutionary thinking, nature is nurture. Our human nature is to be born highly social and highly immature–and then to spend the rest of our lives working out social patterning, which in turn becomes to a very large extent the patterning of the brain, on a biochemical and oftentimes a structural level. This after all is why psychotherapy works and why a developmental model which does not encompass consideration of the social field remains largely irrelevant and unusable in our work with children.

And "work with children" of course means much, much more than work that is explicitly clinical, or even self-consciously therapeutic. The application of Gestalt ideas to an educational setting in early childhood is illustrated in the next article, Chapter Six, "The Gazebo School Park," by Eduardo Eizner. Eizner was the long-time director of the experimental pre-school at the Esalen Institute in Big Sur, California, an experiment founded by Janet Lederman some three decades ago, and like Esalen itself, still going strong. In this warm and "hands-on" chapter we can see clearly the essential function of experimental or lab institutions such as Esalen and Gazebo: to explore and push at the received ideas and conventional wisdom about who we are, and what is possible in our human potential. Obviously, the form of Gazebo itself doesn't translate directly to every educational setting (though many of the ideas and insights do). But you can't help feeling that many of our abandoned generations of out-of-control or lost-self adolescents and young adults would be different people today, with different lives, if they had had something very like Gazebo in their own preschool years.

Meanwhile, from pre-school through teen years the most frequently-diagnosed "disorder" or label assigned to children and adolescents today is "ADD"–"Attention Deficit Disorder," usually further qualified as "with or without hyperactivity," already suggesting the non-specific sweep of the category. In our view, this is another one of those diagnoses, like "OCD," that should probably always be written in quotation marks, to remind us that what we are dealing with is really a broad range of developmental difficulties that comprise a complex interactive mix of the predispositional, the early relational (and its impact on brain patterning, a neglected research area), the familial, the educational, and the sociopolitical, in both their causes and their dynamic implications. With Chapter Seven, Jay Kent-Ferraro and I present vignettes and discussion from a diverse range of young patients who have picked up this label somewhere along their troubled developmental journeys, as parents, teachers, clinicians and other caretakers have struggled to help them deal with their distress, and the distress they often cause others. It is far from clear to us exactly what we or they gain by reifying such a complexly interactive picture into a single diagnostic pigeonhole–rather as if we were to collect all cases of school difficulty, say, or marital breakdown, under single, catchall diagnoses like "School Failure Disorder," or "Marital Difficulty Syndrome," which would serve more to obscure the real and varied dynamics of each case than to clarify any common features among them. What we do believe strongly, here as in the other chapters in this collection, is that an approach that is flexible and multilevel, spanning the range from the pharmacological to the environmental, and above all relational and dynamically contextual–in a word, Gestalt-based–is the most productive in supporting this varied population (and their families, teachers, and others) to move toward more productive, more satisfying lives and relationships. This approach is powerfully exemplified in the strong, caring, and sensitively intelligent work of Jay Kent-Ferraro; thus it is a real pleasure to welcome and introduce this valued colleague and friend into print with this collaborative piece.

Divorce is a fact of life and of working with children and adolescents today. With Chapter Eight, "Healing Young Wounded Hearts: Gestalt Group Therapy with Children of Divorce," Cynthia Reynolds and Ansel Woldt take us into a direct and sobering confrontation with why this is so, what the costs often are, and how we as clinicians and others working with children can address those costs. In the process, they illustrate once more the most central point of Chapter One on the issues and theory of a Gestalt developmental model: that the single most crucial and reparative "field support" for development and growth is the availability of an "intimate witness" to the child's own world, and the child's own experience. It is the presence of that witness function in the living, intersubjective field that makes the difference between creative adjustment that is rigid, constricted, and closed to new experience, and the kind of creative growth that serves as ground for restoration and realization of self. This sense of shared reality is what Reynolds and Woldt aim to provide in their children's groups, not only from the therapists but from and among the other children themselves.

With Part III–Perspectives and New Directions–we turn to considerations of Gestalt work with children that are not necessarily limited to application with some particular group (though as for that, in true Gestalt spirit there are theory, applications, and wider considerations in every chapter, and really almost any chapter in the book might have been placed in one of the other two sections). Both Robert Lee and I have presented our collaborative work on shame and self in Gestalt field perspective in many venues, both live and in print (Lee & Wheeler, 1996). Lee shares further clinical applications and insights from this work in Volume Two of this series, as I do as well, with particular emphasis on father/son relations and the intergenerational transmission of shame. Here, what I have tried to do in Chapter Nine, "Between Parent and Child: The Power of Shame," is to give a new statement of Lee's and my joint work in today's perspective with particular focus on the role and experience of the parent. Shame, as Lee and I have often argued in print, is the key clinical and developmental affect in any social-field or intersubjective perspective, such as Gestalt. Understanding shame dynamics, and how to heal shame wounds, turns out to be one of the prime clinical gifts of Gestalt, to us and to students and practitioners of other models as well.

With Chapter Ten, "Confluent/Constructivist Treatment of Children with Learning/Behavior Disorders," Joan Benevento, a clinician and an academic who has made a long and deep study of Piaget's model of children's cognition, integrates that work with the Gestalt model's insights about the inseparability of affect from cognitive process. As the dust settles from the psychological battles of the past century, Piaget is already coming to stand, perhaps along with James and Lewin and a few others, over and above much or all of Freud, as one of those thinkers whose concepts made a lasting difference in our understanding of human nature and human process. His developmental model is incomplete (see Chapter One), and has been productively challenged by Wilber (2000) and others; but the main tenets (again including the Gestalt idea of nested sequences) have held up. That, together with the many points of parallel thinking between the two models, makes it all the more worthwhile to integrate them here.

Chapter Eleven, "A Gestalt Developmental Model with Applications for Working with Young Children," by Steven Wexberg, a pediatrician and Gestalt therapist, would seem on the face of it to be one of those "applications" chapters that could as well go back in the second section–and would, but for Wexberg's reflections on general issues and dynamics of a lifespan model of human development. The taking-off-point here is that homeliest of child raising examples: toilet-training. The implications, in the hands and mind of this wonderfully sensitive, eminently sensible clinician, extend much further.

Chapter Twelve, "The Pinocchio Syndrome–Path to Wholeness: Gestalt Therapy with Children and Adolescents," takes up another neglected Gestalt topic: narrative work with children and adults. Here Felicia Carroll takes us on a wonderful ride through the literary fairy tale of the boy who wanted to become real–dissecting it and building on it as a metaphor and a ground for examining both child therapy and child development in general. Like Chapter Two, this one is intended eventually by the author to serve as the basis in some way for a book-length treatment of the topic. It promises to be a wonderful book, of relevance to parents, clinicians, and all who live and work with children and adolescents.

This then is the collection, Volume One. Volume Two, under the lead editorship of Mark McConville, takes up where we leave off here, with adolescence and beyond. Mark McConville is one of those rare developmentalists who can talk stages without losing focus on the real child/adolescent her or himself, giving us "at last... a developmental stages model (of adolescence) that is not linear and can account for the fits and starts and repeats of real life" (in the words of Iris Fodor, psychotherapist and Professor of Applied Psychology at New York University, commenting on his wonderful earlier book, *Adolescence: Psychotherapy and the Emergent Self*). It has been a pleasure and an honor working with this valued colleague and friend on these first Gestalt collections on therapy and related work with children, adolescents, and their worlds. This rich "texturality" then pervades the other contributions to Volume Two in this series as well. I recommend it to the reader, even the reader who thinks she/he is "only" interested in childhood, not the looming risks and stakes of the period ahead–in the same way as I recommend child clinical training (and reading) to all psychotherapists, as part of our essential training in understanding our clients of all ages, and ourselves. (And Mark's brief account, in that earlier book, of his sudden leap-by-default into that scarier clinical/adolescent world that "nobody else wants" is both hilarious and sobering).

And yet every celebration must also carry regrets. Along with feelings of appreciation and warm collegiality in presenting this rich and stimulating mix of authors and subjects, goes regret at the absence of others, whose fine work wasn't available within the time frame, or just couldn't be squeezed into the publisher's confines of this volume. Their valuable work, and that of others, will surely find a place in future volumes. Even more I deeply regret and apologize for the scarcity–amounting to a relative absence–of minority voices in this first volume (a lack which both Mark and I have labored to make up, in very small part, in Volume Two). There can never be a real excuse for important absences of this kind; the only compensatory value can come from renewed commitment on my part, and on all our parts, not to let this happen again, in future volumes and elsewhere.

For now, enjoy, engage, let the authors know your comments and challenges–and take heart and spirit from the voices that are here, for the difficulties, pleasures, and above all the importance of the work.

In recent writings (e.g., 2000) I have expressed my indebtedness and gratitude to a wide array of sources, teachers and mentors, colleagues, students, clients, friends and family, whose vibrant and generous gifts of self and spirit have informed and interpenetrated with my own work, and my own life. To all those names I would add and single out here in particular all those children and families I have worked with over the years at Beaverbrook Guidance Clinic, at a number of schools and other settings, as well as in my own practice–students and patients and clients of all ages, but particularly the younger ones (eleven months and up!), who have taught me so much.

No creative activity goes on without support. I find that support in many, many places: first of all from my wife, Nancy Lunney Wheeler, and my family, but also including especially the Gestalt International Study Center (and its annual Writers' Conferences over the past decade and more), the New England Gestalt Study Group (also known as the Boston Writers and Eaters–sometimes Eaters and Writers), the Field Theory Circle, and the Esalen Institute, with its wonderfully overlapping community of teachers, students, residents, and seekers of all ages.

Over the years I've often gotten the remark, familiar no doubt to others who work clinically with children: "Oh, you're a child psychologist? That must be so helpful to you as a parent!" Of course, every clinician/parent knows that the very opposite is the case (or as my kids would say, "Not...."). Clinical training, unchecked, is likely to make you artificial and unrealistic as you try to deal with the real exigencies of real living with children and adolescents (like those hapless fathers in movies and sitcoms of a generation or so back, who had to take over with the kids for a day or a week or so for some reason, and found all their Ideas and Theories about order and method put through the meat grinder, and handed back to them as sausage).

On the other hand, having and raising five children of my own, and then acquiring three stepchildren as well in mid-life, have been the greatest joys and the greatest challenges of my life–and the source of my greatest learnings, both as a person and as a clinician and student of child development, human nature, and family life. These children have been my teachers, clinically and personally; to them I owe the greater part of everything I know and of whatever gifts I may bring to the business and pleasure of therapeutic work with children (as well as the correction or at any rate improvement of many of the deficits and confusions I bring to the table as well). Moreover, to my wonder and delight, all eight of them (plus my son-in-law, who makes nine and counting), in addition to their other boundless gifts of heart, mind, and humor, show remarkable talent for relationship and work and play with children, and share with me an immense and spontaneous enjoyment of children of all ages. If they get some of that enjoyment and that satisfaction from me in some sense, then I am enormously gratified. I know I come by much of it myself directly from my own father, a born teacher, a born tease, and a man who lived for his children and grandchildren. To all of them I dedicate my work as lead editor of this collection.

It was Winnicott who first said that in order for the child's play to be of use therapeutically, it must first be real play–a sentence that could have come straight out of Goodman. Given the constraints of his time and his inherited model, he did not go on to emphasize (as Goodman did) that this means the engagement and the play must also be real for the therapist. Thus the essential first gift for anyone who works with children and adolescents has to be play itself, that capacity for enjoyment of and with the young which brings the interaction and the work to life. As Goodman also emphasized (1951, 1994), this capacity, this gift for finding the playful child within ourselves and in each other, is one of the essential hallmarks–along with qualities of heart, intelligence, and integrity–of the fully human being, and the full life.

Both Mark McConville and I join in hoping that some of this capacity for play and the sheer enjoyment of children (along with something of the other essential capacities) comes through for you, as it does for us, in the chapters ahead.

Gordon Wheeler
Big Sur, California
Spring 2001

References

Brown, G. (1971). *Human teaching for human learning: An introduction to confluent education*. New York, NY: Viking.

Brown, J. (1998). *Back to the beanstalk: Enchantment and reality for couples*. Cambridge, MA: GestaltPress.

Damasio, A. (1994). *Descartes's error: Emotion, reason, and the human brain*. New York, NY: Putnam.

Ehrlich, P. (2000). *Human natures: Genes, cultures, and the human prospect*. Washington, DC: Island Press.

Foucault, M. (1980). *Power and knowledge*. New York, NY: Pantheon.

Goodman, P. (1951). *Novelty, excitement & growth* (Vol. 2 in Perls, F., Hefferline, R., & Goodman, P., *Gestalt therapy: Excitement and growth in the human personality*). New York, NY: Julian Press.

Goodman, P. (1994). *Crazy hope and finite experience: Final essays of Paul Goodman*. T. Stoehr (Ed.). San Francisco, CA: Jossey-Bass.

Husserl, E. (1983). *Ideas pertaining to a pure phenomenology and to a phenomenological philosophy*. Dordrecht, Netherlands: Kluwer.

Kepner, J. (1994). *Body process: A gestalt approach to working with the body in psychotherapy*. San Francisco, CA: Jossey-Bass.

Koffka, K. (1925). *The growth of mind: An introduction to child psychology*. R.M. Ogden (Trans.). New York, NY: Harcourt, Brace.

Lee, R., & Wheeler, G. (1996). *The voice of shame: Silence and connection in psychotherapy*. San Francisco, CA: Jossey-Bass.

McConville, M. (1995). *Adolescence: Psychotherapy and the emergent self*. San Francisco, CA: Jossey-Bass.

Perls, L. (1991). *Living at the boundary*. Highland, NY: Gestalt Journal Press.

Perls, P. (1947). *Ego, hunger & aggression*. London: Allen & Unwin.

Perls, P. (1969). *In and out the garbage pail*. Moab, UT: Real People Press.

Perls, P. (1973). *The gestalt approach and eye witness to therapy*. Palo Alto, CA: Science and Behavior Books.

Stoehr, T. (1994). *Here, now, next: Paul Goodman and the origins of gestalt therapy*. San Francisco, CA: Jossey-Bass.

van der Kolk, B., Weisaeth, L., & McFarland, A. (Eds.) (1996). *Traumatic stress: The effects of overwhelming experience on mind, body, and society*. New York, NY: Guilford.

Wheeler, G. (1990). Gestalt ethics. In E. Nevis (Ed.), *Gestalt therapy: Perspectives & Applications*, (pp. 113-128). Hillsdale, NJ: GestaltPress/The Analytic Press.

Wheeler, G. (1991). *Gestalt reconsidered: A new approach to working with contact and resistance*. Hillsdale, NJ: GestaltPress/The Analytic Press.

Wheeler, G. (1994). The tasks of intimacy: Reflections on a gestalt approach to working with couples. In G. Wheeler & S. Backman, (Eds.), *On intimate ground: Gestalt approaches to working with couples*, (pp. 31-59). San Francisco, CA: Jossey-Bass.

Wheeler, G. (1996). Self and shame: A new paradigm for psychotherapy. In R. Lee & G. Wheeler (Eds.), *The voice of shame: Silence and connection in psychotherapy*, (pp. 23-58). San Fransico, CA: Jossey-Bass.

Wheeler, G. (2000). *Beyond individualism: Toward a new understanding of self, relationship & experience*. Hillsdale, NJ: GestaltPress/The Analytic Press.

Wilber, K. (2000). *A theory of everything*. Boston, MA: Shambhala.

Winnicott, D. (1986). *Holding and interpretation*. New York, NY: Grove Press.

Yontef, G. (1993). *Awareness, process, and dialogue*. Highland, NY: Gestalt Journal.

Part I:

Theory

1

The Developing Field: Toward a Gestalt Developmental Model

Gordon Wheeler

Revisioning the Self-and-Other[1]

Gestalt work with children and adolescents, like all Gestalt work with people, rests ultimately on a radically re-visioned understanding of self, self-experience, and human nature and process, which underlies and then unifies a great variety of approaches, applications and methods under the Gestalt model. This view, which contrasts strongly with much of our common legacy of clinical and psychological training, is what we may call a field model of self and experience–an approach which is subtly but crucially different from the individualistic self and developmental models that have long dominated our clinical traditions, and the culture at large. In place of models which start with the individual self in isolation, and then view development from an outside, objective/mechanical point of view, we have here a model that attempts to look at experience from a subjective viewpoint, but at the same time to place that experience in its dynamic context of constant interaction and mutual influence with other subjective selves. Such a synthesis is both needed and deeply welcome, we believe, in a world that is struggling for relationship and meaning on every level, from the personal/developmental to the ecological/political–and at the same time is deeply confused about the relationship between self-development and other people, the individual and the social, autonomy and interdependence–which is to say all the questions of development in the broadest sense.

All these are the "part-whole" or gestalt relationship questions of our individual lives and our living social field; and all of them are much clarified by the articulation of a developmental model that is constructivist and phenomenological, relational and intersubjective, and holistic in the sense of taking in and unifying the full domain of living, from the body/affective/cognitive to the relational, community and spiritual dimensions of experience. We do unify all these dimensions of experience in our own development and in our ordinary life, at least as best we can. We have to try to do this, to live and make sense of our lives; and in fact some integration of this kind is probably close to a definition for most of us of healthy self-development in full human living. Yet these domains are widely separated in most of our received clinical models, and in much of the Western cultural tradition we are all a part of–the individual from the relational, the affective from the cognitive, the personal from the political, the bodily from the spiritual, and so on–with destructive results that we can see everywhere in the world around us, including of course our clinical and other work with. children, adolescents, and the worlds they live in.

Putting these dimensions back together, we believe, will give us a theoretical model that can encompass and clarify both the "interiority" of self-experience and the dynamic mutual shaping of self and self-process in and with the social field–two perspectives on development and behavior that again have long been separated in much of our inherited clinical discourse. And as the Gestaltist Kurt Lewin pointed out long ago, there is nothing so practical as a good theory–because it is our theoretical model that orients and supports us to know when to do what in our work with children and others, and what part of the child's world to intervene on, and how: her world of internal experience and "structure," her behavior and behavioral contingencies, her family, her wider social systems, and so on. All of us who work with children do intervene at all these levels, of course; but we often have to do it without the support of–even in defiance of–our received developmental and self-models, which generally point us to one or another separate domain of the child's living, and leave it to us (and the child) to integrate them as best we can. A Gestalt field model of self and development provides us that support and that orientation–things we've almost forgotten that a model is supposed to provide us, and that a theory is supposedly for.

These are large promises, and important practical hopes. To see how such an integrated developmental viewpoint can itself be developed out of the premises of the Gestalt self model, and then how such a model can make a supportive difference in our work with children, adolescents, and their worlds, we will first discuss the need for a new model, and then move to a consideration of some of the types of developmental models that are already available for us to pick from, and already in use in various settings. From there we will move on to the beginnings at least of articulation of an integrated Gestalt field model of self and development, which we will argue is much closer both to our own lived and felt experience, and to the living problems and potentials of our work with children, adolescents, and their worlds of living. Finally, we will discuss applications of this model, to see what practical difference it can make and how it may support us in the interventions we need to make every day as therapists, counselors, teachers, parents and other adults in the lives of children.

The Need for a New Approach: A Consideration of Developmental Models

Most of us who work with children and adolescents have long been uncomfortable, at best, with the application of many of our inherited clinical and developmental models to any actual living children we work with, and to their families and life problems. When we look at "internal" or "depth" models, principally those growing out of the broad psychoanalytic tradition, we often have a sense that the developing child is being viewed far too much in isolation, as if human development were something purely "inner" or biologically-driven, something like the development of an acorn into an oak, with only the external provision of some bare minimum of biological conditions from the environment: sun, water, soil nutrients, and so forth. By a metaphorical stretch we could liken the social context of development to a physical environment of this kind, and certainly this has been done in many models; but in the end the stretch is simply too great, and the metaphor breaks down. Such a reductionistic picture, the "environment as background," does violence in particular to the intersubjective nature of our social world, which is populated not by "objects," resources and targets only, but by other subjective beings whose behavior is mediated by their own inner experience and self-process, like our own. This means that as we go about our life business of organizing our world to meet our needs and goals (and avoid the dangers and risks we perceive around us), the inner lives and self-process of other people are significant parts of our own experiential field, influencing and influenced by our own self-process and construction of meaning, in ways that the behavioral and drive models of self and development cannot handle or account for. This kind of objection applies not only to the classic Freudian model and its derivatives, with their language of drive, cathexis and object, but even to a sweeping revision like Erik Erikson's (1951, 1963) influential attempt to move beyond the limiting terms of his own Freudian legacy, and include family and culture in the developmental picture. Erikson's ambitious synthesis of psychoanalysis and anthropology, which dominated much developmental thinking at least in the English-speaking world for a generation, is probably as far as anyone can go in trying to integrate Western individualism with broader social and cultural perspectives; but ultimately the attempt is limited by the terms of the individualist, separate-self model he inherits from Freud and is then trying to stretch to fit the newer anthropological data. For example, the idea that separate identity is and must be formed and solidified before intimate intersubjective relationship can start, as Erikson's model implies, is simply too far from our lived, recursive experience to be helpful–and too far as well from the intervening two generations of infant research and feminist and other critiques of our established developmental models, critiques which emphasize the development of relationality from the earliest days of life.[2] Rather, our sense of self and sense of other–identity and relationship–are not separate stages but back-and-forth or recursive developmental processes which both run all through life, each giving rise to the other in ways that a self-in-isolation model cannot very well address or help us with. How and why this must be so will be clearer when we present a Gestalt field model of development in the pages ahead.

Also in this "internal" camp are important cognitive models such as Piaget's (1947), or Kohlberg's (1981) moral development scales, each of which lays out roughly parallel maps of inherent developmental progress from primitive or infantile to mature stages in a sort of natural unfolding of our inborn potential. Both models emphasize that the stages have a biological clock component and cannot be much accelerated: a child cannot reach the Piagetian stage of concrete operations, say, or the Kohlberg stage of social-conformity ethics, much before the age of "latency" because these stages are dependent on the development of symbols and a certain type of abstract thinking of which younger children are physically/cognitively incapable. (And notice how the use of the word "latency" illustrates how far the Freudian model has permeated our discussions of development, even when we think we have rejected its basic terms). On the other hand, the stages can plainly be retarded–something that Kohlberg at least recognizes even if he gives little attention to what social conditions might promote or retard moral progress from stage to stage. Some people never get to the Piagetian cognitive stage of full symbolic operations, for example–the manipulation of abstract ideas in terms of each other,–which would seem to be necessary for the kind of abstract standards of justice which Kohlberg associates with the highest levels of ethical reasoning and judgment. And certainly it is only too tragically obvious in the world that many, many people never reach what we would recognize, along with all the major religious traditions of the world, as a high or good standard of ethical behavior and moral decision-making. But again, why they don't get there, or what kinds of developmental conditions beyond the individual would be necessary to support this kind of growth and movement, are simply not much addressed in the literature of these models. Thus these perspectives remain focused on the individual in isolation, implicitly assuming that "self" is something deeply internal and mostly autonomous, and end up being not so much wrong as just unhelpful, when we turn to real children, real problems, and real lives.

These three–Erikson, Piaget, and Kohlberg together with Kohut (e.g., 1971)–probably represent the most important and influential of all the developmental models offered roughly at mid-century, which is to say up to around a generation ago, and all of them still remain broadly influential today.[3] At the other extreme, seemingly, are all the social-psychological theories and models that do talk about system, culture, and the interpersonal world. Clinically we have all the systemic schools of thought, now branching out and deepening more and more into narrative and self-organizational models and complexity theory (Kaplan & Kaplan, 1994; Kaufman, 1994; Maturana & Varela, 1987; White & Epston, 1991). These talk about the self-organizational properties of individuals, families, and other interpersonal systems but still generally leave a gap between this discussion and the implications of variously ordered systems for individual development. And then in social philosophy we have the explicit consideration of the social and systemic context for the "good life"–some notion of which must be embedded somewhere in our clinical ideas about health and dysfunction–but still without the developmental time dimension of individual/life span developmental models.[4]

But just as working with children inherently undermines our cultural bias toward viewing people and problems in isolation from context, so it also makes it glaringly obvious that however much we may feel that we work "with the present moment" in therapy or counseling, or "where the client is" without any theoretical blinders, in fact we are never navigating without some implicit map, however deeply buried or unspoken. With adults we may forget our implicit theoretical assumptions and beliefs about development (while still being guided and constrained by them). With children, no one can approach a four-year-old, say, as she would approach a fourteen-year-old; treat a preverbal child the same as a verbal child; fail to take note of puberty, and so on. These two crucial and related points–contextualism and developmentalism–are gifts of clinical perspective forced on the child worker by the nature of the child–and of us all. Gifts, because they are important truths that the person who works only with adults may easily lose sight of in our individualistically biased culture. These truths can reorient and sharpen our work with children and adults as well, if only we can find a model that can do justice to both these points at the same time.

The trouble comes when so many of our received developmental models, as we have seen, seem to one degree or another to neglect that crucial first point–contextualism–or all the ways in which we are dynamically embedded in and arise out of a relational field from our earliest beginnings of or as self–while most of the perspectives that do address relationship, social context, culture and so forth are not developmental. To begin to construct a developmental model that can do both things–that is, help us think developmentally without losing sight of the interactive social context of that development–requires a level of thinking, and a model of self and self-process, at a new order of complexity. Let us turn, then, to a self model that does reflect the complexity and contextuality of subjective experience, and thus can handle both poles of self-experience–the "inner" and "outer" worlds–as dynamic aspects of an integrated whole of lifelong self-experience and development. This is the Gestalt field model of self and self-process drawn in particular from the provocative suggestions of Paul Goodman (Perls, Hefferline, & Goodman, 1951) and the subsequent half-century of infant and cognitive research–and very much based as well on the earlier insights and perspectives of the Gestaltists Kurt Lewin and Kurt Goldstein, and the philosophical works of James, Ricoeur, and Quine, among others.

For example, think of an array of developmental models widely in use today, underlying and guiding interventions in clinical, educational, and related settings. Broadly, these models may be grouped in line with the three major traditions of clinical study and practice across the past century: psychoanalytic, cognitive/behavioral, and "existential/humanistic"–the three great streams which can be usefully integrated and contextualized, we are proposing here, by the Gestalt approach (see also discussion in Wheeler, 1994a). With Freud we have the familiar oral-anal-phallic stages, paralleled in Erikson by trust-autonomy-industry, and by Kohlberg's moral development scale, of punishment, conformity, and rules/principles (and, somewhat more derivatively, by Kohut's stages of mirroring, idealizing, and twinship). With Piaget we have a different view based on perceptual/cognitive processes: sensorimotor, preoperational, concrete operations, and so forth. Among the humanistic models we have the familiar Maslowian (Maslow, 1954) hierarchy of needs, from security up through self-actualization, which could also be conceived developmentally, with each life stage characterized by a dominant class of needs (assuming the previous stages are resolved). Thomas Kegan (1984) focuses on meaning-making, which is much closer to our Gestalt understanding of human process, and lists progressive "stylistic" stages like incorporative, impulsive, imperial, interpersonal, and so on. Within a Gestalt traditon, we likewise might derive an implicit developmental table from Perls's ideas on oral aggression (Perls, Hefferline, & Goodman, 1951), with life task stages based on stages of contact, either as elaborated by Goodman (1951) in their joint work, or as refined in the "Cycle" model moving from sensation and awareness through action to contact or resolution.

Looked at in this way, the Perlsian perspective on development would fall somewhere between the Freudian (with oral aggression substituting for Eros and Thanatos) and the Maslowian, moving as the Freudian does from the supposedly passive dependency of the infant to an ideal of fully autonomous, self-reliant adult maturity. In all these cases, the content of the identified stages and, to a lesser extent, the exact placement of the boundaries between stages, shifts; what remains fairly constant is the notion of a more or less linear sequence of more or less discrete stages, in the ideal case at least, from age to age and stage to stage. Moreover, many of these models are implicitly unidirectional: to Perls as to Freud, it is "infantile," and thus shameful, to go back to dependency (or "polymorphous perversion," in the Freudian lexicon). We simply "get over" our "infantile" needs, as we become firmly individuated and non-dependent adults. (Among the Freudians, Kohut [1977] for one recognized that life and development simply don't work this way, and that theory must be adjusted to recognize the legitimacy crucial role of lifelong needs for empathic mirroring, ideals, and the interdependent relationship).

In all fairness, Erikson certainly attempts to ground internal factors (in his case, Freudian drive theory) in a social/cultural field, through the crucial mediating process of child-rearing practices. The failure of the attempt, ultimately, lies in the contradiction of grafting social factors onto a self-model that is actually asocial or antisocial by definition: in the end, culture is still no more than an external constraint on natural development, in his model. The same general objection applies to Kohut's (1971) self-theory model, with its "self-object" language, where other people become a sort of external crutch, propping up the various self-functions of cohesion, stability, continuity in time and space, sense of self-worth, and so on. These are crucial processes, and Kohut contributes greatly to our understanding of them; but we believe relations with others are something more than all that, and that the inner self-field is itself relational by its very nature, in ways the various psychodynamically-derived models cannot in the end describe or account for.

The Gestalt Model of Self and Self-Process

Traditionally in Western culture, and thus in most of our inherited clinical and psychological models, when we talk about "self" and "self-experience," we are speaking of something we imagine as deeply private and inward-looking, the "innermost nature" of an individual person, that which makes him or her uniquely him or herself and no other, apart from whatever is going on interactively "around" that self–which is to say, outside it. This is the doctrine of individualism in psychology and philosophy (and in developmental models)–a doctrine that is rooted in Western culture, in a dominant line that reaches back to prehistory and the oral tradition of Homeric and Biblical tales at least.[5] This position rests on the assumption that something called "self"–or the essential individuality of a person–already exists in a real way prior to and apart from relationships and development in a relational field. So deep is this underlying assumption about our nature and our self-experience that it amounts to a dominant cultural paradigm in our thinking and attitudes about ourselves and others; an implicit belief system that colors our language and our experience itself in ways of which we are not at all always fully aware. Thus it seems natural to us to speak of "self and other," or even "self versus other," where something called "self-needs" is seen as other than, or even opposed to, relationship considerations and the needs of other people. We can find this language at times even in models that are trying to address relational needs specifically, such as the Self-in-Relation model of the Stone Center.[6]

In our work with children, and indeed in our lives in general, we sense intuitively that there is something wrong with this picture, some way in which the assumption of "self before relationship" misses our self-experience of being constituted in and by relationship. To be sure, we have (and we see in our clients and others around us, children and adults alike) some clear sense of being a unique locus or synthesis of experience; and certainly that uniqueness is in some way related to our ideas and our sense of self. At the same time we know, as McConville (1996) points out, that the family field is not just similar to, but in a real sense is the "unconscious" of the developing child; the "unthought known" that we all carry, coloring our sense of both self and the world, and the interactive/integrative processes between them that we know as living itself (the phrase comes from revisionist psychoanalyst Christopher Bollas [1989]). We know too that the field that the child internalizes is not one of "objects" at all, but is deeply intersubjective from a very early age, perhaps from the very beginning, in a sense which the Gestalt self model will make more clear shortly. Consider for example the way a child of under one year old will try to get the caretaker's attention, even reaching physically to turn the other person's head in the right direction, to see not just the child but *what the child sees.* When you think about it, this implies an enormous degree of what we call intersubjectivity–the ongoing assumption, here on the part of the still preverbal infant, that there is another person "in there," one with some kind of inner attentional process like the child's own (Stern, 1986). Likewise for the supposed stage of "infantile autism" (Mahler, 1993)–an early withdrawn period of infant non-responsiveness (which may well have been a medical artifact of the use of ether in childbirth)–or the old child-rearing dictum that two-year-olds are only capable of "parallel play" rather than true interaction. These traditional modern beliefs about development just don't hold up when we observe any actual infants or two-year-olds in the play situation. The latter rule, which amounted to a seat-of-the-pants law of development and was long cited as an argument against daycare and even play groups before the age of at least three, now looks more like a kind of cultural blind spot, a place in the field where the terms of the prevailing individualist assumptions clouded our view of the child's behavior and experience. At the same time, the belief that the toddler is too much a separate individual by nature to play cooperatively tends to harmonize with and even justify the living arrangements of the separate nuclear family, isolated from other families and a wider community of toddlers and older children, which in turn becomes a self-fulfilling prophecy, since small children raised in that relative isolation may indeed tend to show a delayed capacity to play interactively and intersubjectively. Again, what we see and do depends on the meaningful map or underlying whole-field gestalt that we bring with us into the observation situation–and then take away again with us, either modified and reorganized by the new observations and experience, or else preserved as it was, sacrificing the potential new learning and development for the sake of conservation of the given paradigm, the given structure of belief and understanding.

But then how can we ever take up a different view of self and development if the one we have now, and the very language we express it in, are enclosed in deeply-held assumptions about human nature that are in part out of our awareness yet firmly embedded in culture? Goodman (Perls, Hefferline, & Goodman, 1951) sketched out the beginnings of an answer that destabilizes this firm paradigm–not by challenging the uniqueness of our self-experience (which after all is something most of us do sense and value out of the Western tradition, in some sense)–but rather by *relocating* the self-function out of the deep private recesses of the individual and toward some overarching position as the integrator of experience. This was an idea that was current at the time in various formulations such as in the works of Kohut (1971), Winnicott (1988), and phenomenological philosophers such as Paul Ricoeur. Goodman's particular communitarian spin on the concept was to point out that if self is understood not as the "little man in the machine," but as the process function of synthesizing all the various dimensions of perception, desire, experience, and value, then we do better to picture self-process not in the hidden center of the person but "at the boundary" between person and environment; actively poised to resolve the worlds one thinks of as "outer" and "inner" into some workable, livable whole (Perls, Hefferline, & Goodman, 1951).

The implications of this shift of vision, from "inner self" to "whole-field self," are subtle yet extremely far-reaching for self-experience and for developmental perspectives as well. If self-process is to be found not just in the innermost recesses of the private world, but in the "contact," or gestalt resolution of that private world with the outer or "public" world of events and environment, then "self" itself becomes something both private and shared, something "given in contact" (Perls, Hefferline, & Goodman, 1951, p. 256). It becomes an experiential process that is found and comes to life in the encounter with the world at large. This is the living activity which Goodman called "creative adjustment," by which he means to emphasize the dual or boundary nature of self-process: me acting creatively on my environment and my environment acting on, constraining, and informing me (adjustment).

But then we would argue that the most crucial feature of this picture–and one often left out of even interactive or contextual models–is the fact that that field of self-experience is not for the most part a field of "objects" at all, but rather is a world of other people. They are other subjective selves like me and who, like me, are the locus or vantage point of organizing that field–our field–into their own meaningful wholes of understanding and action from their own distinct points of view. And in a deep sense this insight and perspective–that the people in my field have experiences and perceptions of their own–is not some later developmental achievement, which comes (if ever) only after the achievement of my cohesive individual identity and self-process. Rather, from a very early age there is no successful, satisfying "creative adjustment" which is not based on the dawning at least of this perspective, which has its roots in our earliest preverbal sensings of ourselves, as ourselves, sensings which are developmentally inseparable from our dawning awareness of other selves as themselves. In an experiential field which is intersubjective from the beginning, we argue that my very capacity to know myself as myself arises in an inseparably interactive way with my capacity to know yourself as yourself; each supports, informs, and also limits the other.[7] Thus, in a Gestalt perspective, the line of development of intersubjectivity is the course of development itself. It is far from being a late stage in the progress of individual identity-formation, as the individualist models would have it. Self and relationship are not opposed terms in a field perspective, with the one given in advance and the other added on later. They are poles of experience in dynamic figure-ground relationship, each one the context or ground for the other, each one developing mutually, or else becoming arrested or distorted together.

Thus, our selves both remain distinct and unique–since no one else organizes the experiential field from the same point of view, which is to say in terms of the same subjective stock of needs, perceptions, desires, beliefs and memories–and at the same time interpenetrate one another in a way that completely contradicts and subverts the old individualist way of thinking. This is not only because we are all in some sense organizing and acting on and in the "same territory," but even more than this, because the inner subjective worlds of other people are crucially part of the experiential field I want and need to organize and integrate with my own. I am "wired" to do this, as we will be discussing below. I must do it to interact successfully, survive, and develop my own self-process. As the long and rich body of work in the research area of attribution psychology has demonstrated, only in the direst cases do we actually react to other people's behavior *per se*–which is to say to other people as if they were "objects" or things. Rather, we mostly react to them in the way that enables us to "map our field" meaningfully and predictively–which is to say, in terms of our understanding or imagination of *their* motivations, which give us a better guess about what they will likely do *next.* To imagine the inner state or motivational world of another person is nothing more than another way of saying "intersubjective" in practical, experiential terms. To be sure, the inner life of other people is often a part of my field that is relatively unknown to me, or at times hard to know; but again, getting to know it is not something other than or opposed to my own self-process. It is a crucial part of that process itself.

Implications for a Gestalt Model of Development

First of all, it is important to recognize that however much we may welcome the idea of a whole-field approach to self and development, one that takes in both the inner world and the context of experience, it still takes some time to get used to a different language of self. Such a language includes the outer world of the child (or of ourselves) not just as the setting of self-process, but as an equal pole or dimension of self-experience. The idea that my "self" is not some purely private protected nugget within my inborn core, but rather is, in some real sense, "out there," exposed to the environment, acting, reacting, and interacting in the dynamic processes of managing life, may at first feel alarmingly de-centering. As with the Copernican shift of vision from a stable earth in the center of the universe to a shifting spinning ball in space or the Darwinian revolution in seeing ourselves as a moment in biological development rather than a fixed and final act of creation, this parallel shift in psychology–from an individualist to a whole-field/phenomenological view–may at first seem to threaten our sense of self as a stable given and a fixed reference point for our own construction of experience.

As it sinks in, however, isn't this language for self and self-process much closer, descriptively, to the feel of my own lived experience? Am I not always occupied, in just this kind of sense, in looking, assessing, evaluating, predicting, and generally trying to manage the world "out there"–or else reflecting on all these processes, just experiencing and taking it all in–and doing all this at the same time in the service of meeting some need, reaching some sense of satisfaction and resolution "in here" out of the realm of my own desires? And isn't this active, dynamic process what we mean and feel by aliveness itself, by being or "having" a self in the first place, the ongoing organization of a whole field of experience? By the same token, we speak of "losing ourselves" in meditation or other states of intense concentration or passion, meaning that we lose the sense of the boundary, the awareness of doing anything, and enter a state we call "being," the state of "no-self." How can we reduce this complexity to a simpler order, such as "inner" experience alone, and call that one pole of field-experience "self," without losing the very essence of what we are talking about when we discuss self and development themselves? Neither realm, after all–"inner" or "outer" experience–makes any living sense except as it relates to and is informed by the other. Needs take us toward the outside world, while our perceptions of that world, as Lewin observed in 1926, organize the chaos of that world into *usable wholes of meaning.* Lewin and subsequent cognitive psychologists have called this process "mapping" to emphasize the pragmatic origins of our evolutionary nature. This is why, as the Gestalt model insists, there is no perception without evaluation–and no "data" at all, internal or external–except as it is integrated into a whole picture of significance and organized complexity. This whole picture of significance serves as the basis for understanding, and thus predicting, and as the potential ground for action to satisfy our needs by integrating our inner and outer worlds.

In other words, we are "wired" for meaning, and the self viewed in this subjective or phenomenological way is the agent–or better, the process itself–of that constructive activity ("agent" from the Latin, meaning literally the acting or doing). Development, from this perspective, is the elaboration of successively more complex, more highly organized wholes of meaning. These wholes evolve potentially throughout life, from the first dawning organization of the experiential field into "me/you," through the integration and evaluation of wider and wider fields of perception and activity, and on to include, ultimately, the meaning of the imaginable cosmos. This is the "direction of development," to use Montague's (1955) phrase, a direction given by the terms of our human nature and evolutionarily constructed equipment, that process which by our nature we *cannot not* do, and which mediates and organizes our behavior and experience at each developmental age and stage.[8]

This way of grounding our definition of development in a whole-field model of self-process and self-experience has a number of implications when thinking more concretely about the developmental stages and milestones of childhood and adolescence and of the life span as a whole from a Gestalt perspective. First of all, it implies that the most central organizing dimension of our developmental process is the interpersonal–or as we would prefer to say, intersubjective–a dimension which is separated out or overlooked in many perspectives, even by those which do try to discuss contact "with the environment." As human animals, our environment is first, last, and always a social environment, with even our most physical needs and appetites (as well as our thoughts, feelings, and memories themselves) being mediated and co-constructed in and by our social experience. Likewise in this view the spiritual perspective or dimension of life, which is often much neglected in our work with children, is not some realm apart from everyday living, but is a natural extension of our process of gestalt-formation or meaning-making, and is significant throughout life.

Most importantly for our purposes here, if we take a whole-field view of self and experience, then we are supported to see that development always and *necessarily means the development of a whole field.* Not just development in a field or context, but development of that context. If healthy adulthood and healthy living are to be supported, achieved and sustained over time, the outer realm of the child's self-experience must also undergo development, as much as the inner or "structural" realm that we are used to talking about in clinical models. The outer field or environment that is integrated into the child's evolving self-process–not just as the setting of that process, but as a dynamic pole of ongoing integration–must itself evolve over time, in some organized harmony with the biological/experiential growth of the child, if the child's development is to cohere and make sense. At the simplest level, the parents the four-year-old needs–or the twelve-year-old or, for that matter, the twenty-year-old–are different parents from the ones that the child needed as an infant. They themselves must grow and develop so as to present different selves to meet the evolving self-process of the child. As the world widens, the community, the school, and the society the child needs–or sadly, needs to be protected from–become increasingly significant, again not just as the environment of the child's self, but as the dynamic material which is being integrated in and by the self-process of the child. Thus political and social conditions and structure as well become something more than the background or even the necessary supports for development, but rather are integrated into the self-structure, the process patterns and dynamics, of the developing subjective person.

These essential observations do not take the place of the kind of concrete map of milestones and stages we are accustomed to thinking about as developmental theories and models–nor do they make our available models necessarily wrong or even not useful. What they do–and what the Gestalt model in general can do for us, in relation to other perspectives and schools–is to contextualize and integrate the other models, so that we know better what we are talking about when we think developmentally. They show us which particular models are useful for what kinds of situations and problems. They inform us what is included or left out of a given developmental map and what the implications of this may be for our understanding of a particular child in a particular situation.

What we are looking for in taking up a Gestalt developmental perspective is not so much a new list or new labels for the significant stages of childhood, but rather a new way of viewing the child's developmental field as a whole. It gives us a fresh understanding when using the various models we hold as lenses on particular problems and interventions, without losing sight of the whole field.[9] With this in mind, let us turn to a consideration (see Figure 1) of some of the particular models that are widely available in the field, to see how they may look different when we are beginning with a different idea of self, experience, and the developmental field.

Current Developmental Models Compared

The table begins with the familiar Freudian model–oral, anal, phallic, and so on. The Freudian model is then echoed and expanded in the Eriksonian version that casts each stage not just as a phase change in biological drive, which is key to Freud's understanding (e.g., 1933/1999), but as critical periods for a certain component of character. This is Erikson's (1951) attempt to account for how the physiological drive is transformed through the mediation of cultural child-rearing practices into personality and character styles, both individual and culture-wide. As we discussed briefly above, this is Erikson's effort to marry the individual/biological with the cultural or family environment with the goal of explaining how it is that certain patterns–certain *styles of contact,* as we would say in Gestalt language–become preferred and dominant in certain cultural contexts. Without giving up the basic terms of the Freudian individualistic conception of self as something essentially separate and bounded off from the field, as we talked about above, Erikson nonetheless finds a way of at least locating this individual self in a social setting–which, from our point of view, is a considerable step beyond the classical drive model of self.

The Kohlberg model, also briefly mentioned above, takes up the developmental line of moral thinking and judgment, focusing on the question of how we approach and evaluate a moral/ethical problem. This model, which has been widely influential in American education in particular over the past generation, has come under heavy fire in more recent years from a point of view which very much bears on our discussion here (e.g., Gilligan, 1982). A problem which had plagued Kohlberg's research from the beginning was the odd fact that women tended to score lower than men on the

Figure 1. Comparative Array of Some of the Available Developmental Models

	0-1 year	1-3 years	3-6 years	7-11 years	12-17 years	18 years
Freud	Oral Phase	Anal Phase	Phallic Phase	Latency	<<<<< Genital Phase >>>>>	
Erikson	Trust/Mistrust	Autonomy/ Shame	Initiative/ Guilt	Industry/ Inferiority	Identity/ Diffusion	Intimacy-Generativity
Piaget	Sensorimotor	<<<< Preoperational >>>>		Concrete Operations	Early Formal Operations	Full Formal Operations
Maslow	<<<< Physical Survival >>>>		Safety	Love/Affiliation	Self-Esteem	Self-Actualization
Kohut	Self-Regulating	Empathic Mirroring	Idealizing	Twinship	<<< Emergence of Mature Self Objects >>>	
Kegan	Incorporative	Impulsive	Imperial	Interpersonal	Institutional	Intersubjective
Perls	Introjection/ Resistance	Autonomy/ Confluence	Projection/ Inhibition	Concentration/ Deflection	Expression/ Retroflection	Orgasmic/ Egotistical
McConville	<<<<<<<<<< Embedded Self Period >>>>>>>>>>				<< Disembedded Self Period >> *Differentiating – Interiorizing – Integrating*	

moral reasoning scales generated under the model, a model purported to assess the degree of the person's progress toward the highest level of moral development. This kind of result seemed plainly to fly in the face of common sense and everyday experience, to say nothing of a sweeping array of statistics on attachment, violent crime, and a whole range of familiar pro- and anti-social behaviors, none of which seem to suggest any moral deficiency in women (though an argument might be made the other way around!) How to account for such an apparently glaring discrepancy? To be sure, Kohlberg's findings were uncomfortably close to the Victorian assumptions of the moral inferiority of women. For lack of a full-blown Oedipal threat and crisis, in Freud's view, women never fully internalize the parental/paternal superego, and thus remain always morally immature. Kohlberg, to his credit, was long uncomfortable with these questions and endorsed Gilligan's critique of his own work.

Gilligan's answer to this problem was to point out that Kohlberg essentially followed what we would call self-in-isolation thinking–the same perspective that Gilligan tends to label as "masculine." That is, he arbitrarily assigns the highest developmental ranking to a kind of abstract moral judgment independent of the particular situation or field. Consequently, Kohlberg's model is rule-based or principled rather than people- or needs-based. Ethical solutions to the problems in Kohlberg's tests which were more situationally based, more concerned with taking care of everybody in the field (even at the expense, at times, of logical consistency), scored just slightly lower. And it is true that in this culture at least, males are somewhat more likely to make appeal to rule-based explanations of their own moral positions, while females, at least on these measures, are likely to offer justifications somewhat more based on the attempt not to leave anybody out, and less on the abstract moral principle involved. Both genders do use both kinds of explanation, but this difference has held, across a considerable body of work inspired by Kohlberg and then confirmed by Gilligan. In other words, Gilligan argued, gender bias is built into the scale itself that quite arbitrarily values "lone judgment," arrived at (or at least justified after the fact) by logical deduction from a set of abstract principles over and above a kind of whole-field perspective and concern. (For further discussion, see Wheeler & Jones, 1996). Thus, Gilligan's work has important parallels to the questions we are raising about self and development here from a Gestalt perspective, parallels which will be developed further below in the discussion of gender issues in development in general.

Maslow's (1954) model, which derives from his "hierarchy of

needs" schema of safety-affiliation-achievement-self realization is included here because of the close affinities between his conception of self-as-creative agent, or self-growth as an inherent goal of living, with the contact model of self and process offered by Goodman and Perls some years before; indeed, Perls was inclined to feel that Maslow had borrowed from his and Goodman's work extensively and without due credit. Likewise, Thomas Kegan's (1982) model of self-as-meaning-maker has important parallels with the developmental language we are looking for and constructing here. A Gestalt understanding of self and self-process necessarily emphasizes meaning making, which is another way of saying contact, as the essential self activity. What differs, again, is that Kegan remains in the individual or more purely interior self tradition, while our intent, following Goodman, is to offer something more radical, a notion of self that is not just located in a field, but rather partakes of the field, constructs and is constructed out of a field, making the traditional boundary between "me" and "other" or "environment" into the arena of self-activity itself–rather than a place of disjunction or separation, as in self-versus-other models.

The Perlsian model suggested here is not directly given by Perls (1947; also Perls, Hefferline, & Goodman, 1951), but is the kind of developmental picture that might be drawn from his thinking about contact and resistance, and implies the progressive move as he saw it out of infantile dependency (characterized by confluence and introjection, or "no boundary" between self and environment) and on toward mature autonomy or "self-supports" (see Perls, 1969). But note, again, that this picture of an unbounded and passive infant self, drinking in the world without any clear capacity for active/aggressive self-structuring, is not at all supported by the subsequent half-century of infant research (see again Stern, 1986).

In contrast to this Perlsian picture is the more whole-field Gestalt model offered by Mark McConville (1996). McConville focuses specifically on developmental stages in adolescence, within an overarching developmental frame that characterizes the adolescent process as one of "disembedding the self" from the family context of childhood, and repositioning the developmental process within a wider social field. The result of this stage, in McConville's view, is not or not necessarily the sharp break with family implied by more individualistic models of adolescence, but rather a new, more complex, articulated relational process, a reconnection that is itself the new adolescent self. Useful implications of McConville's approach include particularly the way he characterizes "stages" not so much along a rigid time line, but rather as a dynamically interrelated set of tasks which take place recursively, with the relative accomplishment of any given task serving as ground for the figure of the other or "next" tasks, in a sequence which will recur and vary with each individual case and context. By recursive in this kind of model we mean not just that the tasks can be (indeed, must be, like all important life tasks) worked on over and over–but also that work on the particular task that is figural at the moment is supported by and grounded in the relative progress on all the other tasks, whether we think of them as developmentally earlier or later. Thus for example the first adolescent task in the model, differentiating or "disembedding" itself, which involves making a new kind of boundary between family and a more protected or autonomous private self-world, is both the ground for and in some ways the result of using this more private inner space as the location of the "next" task, innerness or "interiority." Some degree of new boundary is needed, in order to permit a freer experimentation with a new complexity of inner life, which in turn permits and supports the assertion of more boundary or differentiated self-definition, based on the new complexity of that protected inner space. And so on, until enough complexity and solidity have been achieved that both of these things can serve as ground for the new stage of integration, which then supports new boundary complexity, new interiority and new connections with others, and new movement out into an adult world.

With this model we can begin to see some of the potential of a Gestalt whole-field approach to developmental questions, in the support the Gestalt self-model offers to thinking in this figure-ground or recursive way, as opposed to the straight-line progression often implied in individualist models, which can make them so difficult to apply to actual cases. To look now at other, even more fundamental implications of Gestalt perspectives for developmental thinking, let us pull back and consider the array of models in Figure 1 as a whole, with a view to seeing what stands out for us now from contemporary and past developmental thinking in general, and what kind of ground that thinking offers us for constructing a more holistic, more experience-near framework for understanding children, adolescents, and adults–both our clients and ourselves.

Toward a Gestalt Developmental Model

What are the implications of the kind of comparative focus we have been taking, for the articulation of a new model here? We can start by observing that all the models in Figure 1 share a perception of discontinuous stages in child/adolescent development, periods of growth that are qualitatively different from the periods before and after. These stages are bounded by phase shifts, discontinuous moments in living when the self reorganizes around a new capacity, and integrates/responds to a new field. The transitional moment itself may be somewhat diffuse and extended; still, the field of experience before and after is organized differently, by and as a different self. Birth itself can be looked at as the most radical of these phase/field transitions; puberty is another such a moment, when the field of self undergoes a dramatic shift, triggered by physiology but by no means limited to the biological dimension of the field.

Both of these are plainly biologically discontinuous moments or periods–from umbilical oxygenation to breathing, or from pre-reproductive to sexually mature. But other moments or periods, which may be less obviously biologically driven, still involve and demand an organizational shift in the whole field, both inner and outer. Consider, for example, the transition from pre-ambulatory to ambulatory that roughly coincides in most toddlers with the somewhat more extended transition from pre-verbal to verbal. This transition means not just a new environment of experience with new skills and opportunities, but also an entirely different field of living; a new terrain of experience (the landscape I can see and walk to or the new timescape that is language itself). It means qualitatively different inner and outer fields and literally a new self.

The presence of temperament does remain, and much research has shown temperament to be a relatively stable element in development at least through childhood.[10] But temperament viewed in isolation, from the point of view of individualist models, means something different from temperament in our field perspective (in much the same way as we will talk about voice below). Take the case of a very active, somewhat restless, perhaps even irritable infant. With the advent of walking and talking, this high energy level, which may be in part inborn or "temperamental," suddenly has whole new worlds for expression and use. What may have been a frustration, and at times an irritant for infant and caretakers alike, now can serve as the physiological grounding for an active, exploring, amazed, and amazing toddler "coming into her own," but only if the outer field (parents and other caretakers, neighbors and community, as well as environmental safety) receives, supports, and validates this energy and these new contact capacities.

But, what if this doesn't happen? What if the child's physiological tendency toward a certain level of motoric activity is received as wrong, unwelcome, shameful or even dangerous? What if the child is the "wrong gender" for such a high activity level? Or the environment is chaotic or physically unsafe? Or the caretakers are made anxious, alarmed, or otherwise disturbed by so much activity? Then what might have been a happy resolution into a new phase of expression and exploration may become instead a downward cycle of resistance, friction, emotional rejection, loneliness and shame. And the "innate temperament" of the child may then shift from active, motoric, curious, assertive to jerky, sullen, impulsive, depressed. Temperament, far from being a purely physiological predisposition (though such predispositions do of course exist), becomes a meaningful concept in development only in dynamic field interaction of the kind our new model is describing and addressing.

Or, backing up further in infant development, what of the bonding process in the earliest neonatal period? This is a process emerging more and more in current research as a key to all subsequent cognitive/affective/social development, just as our new model would predict.[11] Plainly the infant is born "prewired" to bond. Visual focal distance and gazing, prepotency of a human facial gestalt, "molding," capacity to discriminate smell and emit sounds that signal differences of mood state–all these things and many more indicate our enormous inborn readiness, in the vast majority of cases, to receive stimulation from and respond to a primary caretaker-infant bonding relationship. This relationship will, in turn, become the template for future relational patterns and no doubt much future attentional and cognitive/affective patterning as well.[12] But again, the very notion of bonding implies a "bonding field," a person or persons receiving this readiness, responding to it, and interacting with it. This responsive interaction transforms a set of physiologically, evolutionarily preferred pathways into living patterns of interaction and learning–a field of self where the innate contact directions and capacities of the infant are met dynamically with corresponding contact capacities and responses on the part of other people. The self, as Winnicott (1988) observes poetically, "first exists in the eye of the mother" (or as we would prefer to say today, the caretaker, male or female). Likewise, says Winnicott, in a remark pregnant with promise of a field perspective, there is "no such thing as a baby" because there is only a baby with a caretaker. In a field perspective, again, the relevant unit is not the individual, but the *relational field* or, at the least, that part of the relational field that is significant and presenting at the moment (Winnicott, 1988).[13]

And again, what if this is not the case? What if the inborn activity level–the "squirmy" motoric baby pattern–interferes with the bonding capacities of the caretaker (who may feel hurt, rejected, ashamed or angry with the apparent "failure" to achieve some imagined baby-parent fusion)? To reverse the gender-dystonic case above, what if the baby is placid and "dreamy" but again is the "wrong gender" for such "passivity?" Contrariwise, what if the caretaker is overly busy, easily distracted, or slightly depressed, in which cases the active, "demanding" baby may fare better, with the quieter child of either gender slipping more easily into a pattern of isolation and depression him or herself?

Or what if the child is in the normal range temperamentally, but still at the short-attention span, more impulsive/distractible end of that range? And, to go further, what if the environment is chaotic, the caretaking is undependable and irregular while increased bids for attention by the infant do not lead to increased attention (positive or negative) in any reliable way? Isn't this a developmental formula for pushing a pre-dispositionally marginal infant over the line into the familiar "attention deficit disorder (ADD)," a diagnostic category that is rapidly becoming the most frequent diagnosis in schools and child clinics?[14] Doesn't this child learn quite normally to "grab what comes by" and then let the attentional figure go again easily? Isn't that a behavioral/phenomenological description of what we mean by ADD? After all, attentional and related cognitive processes are quite plastic through the first year of life at least–a time of life which is emerging more and more as the critical period for cognitive development and problem-solving, as well as emotional and relational development. It is more than plausible that those early bonding experiences of long caretaker-child gazing and cooing are the prototypes and the catalyst for attentional patterning in general and quite resistant to restructuring in later life.

In all these examples, our question is this: what do all these individualistic models have to offer us as we study and address the interactive nature and challenges of actual children developing in and with their actual worlds–which is to say, the whole relevant field of child development itself? Perhaps the most striking feature of all our developmental tableau is the absence of any clear reference at all to environmental conditions, much less to full dynamic field interaction and integration of the field as the essential activity of self and the relevant topic of developmental thinking. Again, development has to mean development of a whole field. We know this from our work with children and adolescents and from the way that work informs and transforms our work with adults as well; (a point which makes a good argument for the inclusion of a child rotation as a requirement in the training and certification of all clinicians, including those who do not plan on future work with children or adolescents). But all too often the models available to us do not support these experiences and intuitions, as we try to orient developmentally to make practical interventions in response to the needs of children.

This is not to say that any or all of these models are useless. As Goodman said in speaking of the different schools of therapy, if all of us are looking at the "same animal," then we expect to find and do find extensive cross-correspondences and useful cross application between and among the different models (Perls, Hefferline, & Goodman, 1951). The issue is not right and wrong, but rather which perspective, which language, gives us the best picture for supporting effective interventions in our work with children and adolescents. Our argument here is that all these models are problematic by being incomplete; thus they can be of limited use or even harmful unless and until we contextualize them with the kind of whole-field perspective we are developing here. Despite the attempts of many of them–especially Erikson's and other neo-psychodynamic models such as those of the Object Relations school–to address context or relationship in some way, they all have varying degrees of difficulties in accounting for the whole relevant field of the child's living and with helping us see the interactive, integrative nature of that field.[15] Since the external dimension of this field (i.e., external phenomenologically from the point of view of the child's subjective experience) is the relevant arena for many of our interventions with children and adolescents, these are serious difficulties indeed.

To see more of what our developmental picture looks like when we do contextualize in this way, let us turn now to consideration of a number of general themes of development, still with the idea that everything will necessarily look somewhat different (and we believe, somewhat clearer) when we start with a self-model closer to our own experience of living as well as that of the children and adolescents with whom we work. The first of these themes, (1) intersubjectivity and intimacy, has already been touched on above. Here we will try to articulate more of what intersubjectivity means in a field perspective, and what that means for developmental thinking. In particular this will involve the question of how we come to know ourselves and others over time as a developmental process. We aren't born knowing the inner field or the outer field of experience, after all, or even necessarily born knowing how to learn these things. Again, these are points and processes that emerge as crucially central in a field model, but are in some way ignored or taken for granted by most of the available individualist models of development.[16]

The rest of the discussion will then be organized under the further thematic headings of (2) support and shame (the polar counterpart of support, we will be arguing, in a field perspective), (3) gender and identity, and finally (4) narrative and voice. This last topic will be an integrative theme of development that will round out the discussion for now and lead us to our conclusions. Each of these themes can be viewed as having a developmental line of its own, and each supports and interacts with the others, in ways that, again, a Gestalt field model can help us see with new clarity and usefulness.

1. Intersubjectivity and Intimacy

Our central and ongoing task in life, from the point of view of a field/phenomenological or experiential model, is the mapping and manipulating of the full field of experience into an integrated whole or gestalt which combines enough elements of inner needs and outer conditions to support our living and growing and generally moving on. We call this "generally moving on" process development. Again, this is a process and a point of view that bring evolutionary thinking, psychological process, and what we call "meaning-making" together into a coherent perspective. As Lewin (1926, 1935) pointed out, all thinking/feeling, all body/mind activity, is potentially of the nature of what we think of as "problem-solving," by mapping out a situation with a view to managing it toward a certain end. (To be sure, "passive" or incidental learning exists, but to Lewin as to us this is something like the idling state of a great machine, maintaining readiness for the next challenge.) This has to be true, by nature of our being physically vulnerable, low instinct, and thus highly social animals in a complex and shifting problem-solving field. We are "wired" to operate this way, because if we weren't, we wouldn't have survived this far. "Meaning-making" in this view is the natural extension of our innate gestalt-formation process. It's our capacity and necessity for forming and energizing a "figure of interest," something to work on, cope with, or think about from and within an organized background of relational patterns. The organized background itself gives predictability to our world and significance to the focus of interest itself. This is our nature, and the elaboration of these meaningful wholes is, in a real sense, development itself.

But, "highly social animals" means that we are doing this integrative process–the process we are calling "self"–in a field of other people who are doing the same kind of thing. Their behavior, like ours, is not governed directly by "what happens," but rather is mediated like ours by their "maps," their own understanding and estimation of predictions and promises and risks in their field. Which means in turn that their inner worlds are crucially significant parts of our relevant field, and must be taken into account as we organize a useful and meaningful map of understanding to guide our own action and growth in a field which we all share. We do not and cannot relate to each other as "objects" only, because that will lead us to a chaotic and unpredictable field (as any parent, politician, boss or other planner knows well, from any and every attempt to regulate other people's behavior by means of external stimuli/rewards alone, in isolation from any understanding of their own inner worlds). All this–and this is the crucial implication of a Gestalt field perspective on self and development–has been stated in various ways throughout this discussion and is repeated here for emphasis. We repeat it not because the points are so subtle or difficult but rather because they are so obvious, and at the same time so strikingly absent from most treatments of the twin subjects of development and self.

But how do I know your inner world? Plainly the methods I use for knowing the physical world–mostly observation and inference and what we call "projection" when it comes to understanding the motivations of others–while still relevant here, are not a complete method for learning in this area. For that matter, how do I know my own inner world? As clinicians, teachers and others working with children and adults we know all too well how deficient many children and adults are in this kind of knowing, and how debilitating these deficiencies are (for example, see discussion in Chapter 5 in this volume). And more than just the contents, how do I learn how to go about learning skills and knowledge of this kind? Increasingly in schools today, as knowledge explodes and lifelong skills learning is more and more key in Western culture, the educational emphasis shifts from learning particular subject areas to *learning how to learn,* how to approach a new subject area or, perhaps best, doing both at the same time. This means developing a meta-awareness or meta-perspective on how I am going about learning a particular area as I am studying and learning that area. What is the analogy, when it comes to knowing the inner realms of experience; my own and those of others?

The answer is that we learn these skills and meta-skills *intersubjectively.* Which is to say, in a bonded relationship with another person who presents as a self, models and exposes her/his own self-process in some way, and relates to us as a subjective being with an active self-process like his or her own. This is something we know directly from experience–from our own and from that of our patients and others. The intersubjective caretaker talks to the child about what is going on interpersonally. It is no surprise, again from our field perspective, that this early talking about and talking to is now emerging as a crucial field process in early and later cognitive development, right in the first, so-called "preverbal" year of life. Interestingly, this "baby talk" is often presented in a sort of fused dialogue form, with the caretaker providing all the voices, speaking now of himself in the third-person (as if from the baby's experience), now for the baby in the first-person, and then perhaps as a fused "we" in fluid interchange of roles:

> "*Oops, Daddy's sorry, Daddy's so tired this morning, we almost fell down, didn't we! Here we go, now just let Daddy find this diaper cream, there, this will just take a second and then you're going to feel so much better.*"

And then a moment later (speaking as if for the baby now, giving the baby voice):

> "*Oh, I don't like that cold cream, do I, that's freezing me, Daddy, there, now, that's better.*"

This kind of discourse is spoken from or with a relaxed self-boundary (self-boundary here meaning not the outer shell of the individualist/isolated self, but rather the place of self-definition or voice in the field), and as such is perhaps inherently vulnerable or "undressed." Thus it can be somewhat embarrassing to be overheard in this mode, which may strike us as "silly" or "babyish"–and yet it makes perfect sense when we think of it as crucial training in intersubjectivity and dialogue.

We may be tempted to say that it is only the caretaker's tone of voice that is soothing here while the words themselves are not understood. Yet something more is going on as well, something that we might call a subjective or intersubjective *orientation*, giving a kind of readiness training or attitude preparation for full verbal intersubjectivity later on. The intersubjective sequencing goes like this: the baby's distress is generally met first with body contact, and then with a kind of pause or question which includes looking or scanning discriminatively ("projectively," if you will) for clues to an interpretation of the child's inner experience. This is so as to adjust the response to the cause, since without some useful estimation of the other person's inner state the response we offer will itself be unhelpful or wrong. "Hmm, you're not wet–you know what? I think you're hungry." And, then another moment later, "*That's it, Daddy. I was starving, that's all. Daddy understands me. Daddy knew the whole time,*" and so on in that vein, shifting fluidly from voice to voice and, in a sense, from self to self. The words are lost on the child, to be sure, but we may assume from the developmental results that the attitude is in some way noted, internalized, and then used. And, by "attitude," we mean intersubjective meta-skills and patterns such as:

- *pause and scan to check for inner need state of the other;*
- *self-expression is a signal of some inner state (in both people);*
- *feelings are information, and even have names;*
- *expression leads to response in the field, and expression can be tailored and targeted to modulate the* other's *response in the field, making it more to our liking.*

Again, the "building blocks" for all these things are inborn and prewired, in the ways touched on above in the discussion of bonding. The integration of them into habits, skills, and perspectives for successful intersubjective mapping of a multiple-selves field is learned. And that learning begins at birth, with essential consequences for lifelong development.

Moreover, that learning takes place in an intersubjective field that includes another person who has a sense of her/his own inner world, and takes an interest in ours. This process of making my inner world known and getting to know the inner world of the other is what we call intimacy. It is also known as *inside knowing* and is distinguished from how we know the more public or physical field (Wheeler, 1994). In this field/developmental perspective, intimacy as a process then emerges as the *necessary arena and developmental ground for learning how to know the self,* a process that we can now see more clearly as inseparable from learning how to know the inner reality of another person. Developmentally, we begin not with a separate, isolated self, gradually freeing itself from infantile dependency, but rather with a field of relationship out of which a sense of self-boundary–of "me" and "you" as not the same–begins to take on dynamic shape and cohesiveness. Only to the extent that that relational field is a field of intimacy–which is to say a field of subject relating to subject, not a field of "object relations"–does a full experience of subjectivity arise. Subjectivity, as a developmental progression and achievement, depends on intimacy in this sense. This dependent intimacy first occurs in infancy, and then to a considerable extent remains with us throughout life, although preferably on ever more sophisticated levels of exchange and meaning. Thus we never lose our need for intimate relationship, in the sense of a person or persons who take an interest in, see, and receive the expression of our inner worlds, thus supporting more articulation in that expression itself. And ongoingly, through life, our full sense of self and fully subjective sense of others go hand in hand, each of them both supporting and constraining the other.

2. Support and Shame

But, what if that support and that reception are not there, early in infant development and then crucially at other times? In an individualist model of development the self develops out of an inner drive–again, the acorn-to-oak metaphor–more or less on its own impulse with only the provision of some minimal standard of environmental input and stability in the very early years. The presumption and the goal state of many of these models is *maximum autonomy of self;* and development is seen, as we have discussed, particularly in the Freudian-derived systems, as the progress from infantile dependence to mature independence, or as Perls (1969) put it, from "environmental supports to self-supports." In these kinds of models, based as they are on assumptions of this type, the idea itself of support is associated with weakness and poor character (we should be "self-reliant"), and always at least potentially charged with shame.

The picture is entirely different in a field model. If we start with the field and think of the self as organizing the whole relevant field, then it follows that whatever happens, happens with support from somewhere in the field. This support may be from inside or outside the self-boundary, or both, or both in dynamic interaction, but it has to come from somewhere. This means that in place of thinking of "self-supports" as mature and good, versus "support from others" as immature and compromising, we scan the whole field of the child's living to mobilize and integrate a coherent whole picture of support for the intervention and the developmental direction the child needs. This after all is what a healthy and appropriate developmental field should be doing all the time: organizing an integrated, coherent set of outer supports that mesh with and themselves support the evolving capacities and skills (the "inner supports" and resources) of the child–and doing it in a way that itself evolves over time to match the changing potential abilities of the growing child. The healthy field presents the "right amount" of scope and challenge (which is the same thing as the "right amount" of support) to foster and stretch the child at a given developmental moment. Again, here we see how the field itself must develop, and to assess a child we must assess the developmental change of that field.

Note too that this does not mean developing unidirectionally in a steady linear progression from more to less environmental support over time. Rather, the movement is fluid, recursive, and situational. The secure and independent nursery-school child may well need more outside support, not less, as he moves to kindergarten with all its social and academic challenges. In the same way, many children need more support from the outside at the end of "latency," which is typically a moment when they get vastly less of it. This is especially so during the transition to middle school or junior high when they leave a familiar/familial neighborhood primary school, a stable peer group, and oftentimes the security of a single-classroom teacher.[17]

We can see how this integrated perspective on support plays out in our own lives when we undertake any important new challenge. Think for example of any life project or plan: typical life decisions are the decision to take on a particular job, to couple and raise a family, perhaps to undertake a degree or training program. A major reorganization of the whole field is required in each case and is what any large life project entails. This means not a greater "field-independence" but rather a demand for considerably increased support from both the inner *and* outer realms of self-experience and living. In the case of a higher educational degree, for example, the project can usually only be accomplished by the organization and sustaining of enormously complex interactive support systems over and through the space/time of living activity. First comes making the plan. For this I will probably need an exploratory stage: What do I want? What are my goals (in interaction with my partner's goals, perhaps my children's needs)? What's out there? Which program suits my needs, requirements, and resources as well as the needs of others I am identifying with and including in the decision? Plainly the support of a well-developed inner process of self-knowing and self-scanning is crucial here, as well as many less visible processes such as holding and evaluating information, making priorities and choices, managing multiple needs and variables (supporting a family through the process, finding a place to live, etc.). Moreover, if the decision is to be a good one which is well supported by significant others in my personal world, then I need the skills and support of feedback from them and dialogue with them. Without these, the plan itself may end up undermined by divorce or other relational crises, or some other kind of relational stress and strain.

Then there's the program itself: time has to be set aside and protected, which generally means the cooperation at least of other people, and the negotiation that produces that cooperation. Perhaps my aging parents want to help financially but have limited means. In this case, I will need skills for mobilizing and negotiating that support in a way that protects them and facilitates my plan. Perhaps the best solution is for a parent to move in or nearby, both to help with the children and to gain long-term security. At this point the question of whether we are talking about a "self-support" or an "environmental support" becomes murky to the point of being moot. The point is that here the self-skills demanded are not a simple, linear matter of "self-support" in an isolated sense. Certainly time management, study schedule, and the like involve important private or partly private self-dimensions such as those we call "will-power" or "perseverance." But the skills I need to live out this decision well are not simply those of greater effort and self-reliance. Rather, what is involved is the mature interactive ability to mobilize *a whole field of support*, both inner and outer, which will serve both to sustain this project and to then integrate it into other life needs and projects. For this kind of developmental challenge in real living neither realm of support–the inner or the outer–can possibly be sufficient on its own:

In other words, we view support in a field model not just as an environmental transaction, much less as a state or sign of immaturity or dependency, but as a *field condition*; a dynamic aspect of my field of living, as one that I myself can influence and co-construct. Indeed, the whole course of development from infancy through adulthood, which we have already characterized as a progressive elaboration of more and more complex and well-articulated wholes of understanding or meaning, could equally well be characterized as the increasingly complex and integrated whole-field organization of support. The questions in a field model are thus never ones of simply "support versus autonomy," but rather *what kinds of field support* are active or potential? What is supported or not supported in this particular field and from the point of view of this particular child or adult? And what are the sources of that support, inner and outer? Again, what we have here is a point that is deeply familiar to clinicians and others who work with children, but is not well supported by many of our available developmental theories.

This way of looking at the developmental picture has a number of further implications. For one thing, it provides a useful link between "dynamic" and "systemic" views of the child. These two ways of looking often seem to take us in different or opposite directions, but their relationship is subtler. "System" in psychotherapy refers to the notion of a set of social patterns or rules that will come into play in a social group, often the family, and have the effect of shaping or constraining behavior. System members of any age usually know the "rules of the game" of the systems in which they are living. They thus tend to modulate their behavior in some way in anticipation of effects and reactions around them. If the child doesn't know this, then plainly the therapy or other intervention has to start there. The starting point would be either working with the child to become more aware or working with the environment to become more consistent and informative. We know the child (or the adult for that matter) cannot navigate without a usable map of this kind, which means we are instinctively making and using the kind of field-organizational assumptions about self and experience that are being presented here.

But then the "system" I am in is effectively *that map of what is supported or unsupported* (punished, shamed, or just not received and validated) in my relevant world. Subjectively speaking, "system" means a map of perceived supports in this sense. Of course, my map may be crude, or poorly articulated, or just plain wrong in some points. But again, in all of these cases therapy or another kind of input may well need to begin at one of several starting points. One place could be the psycho-educational question of "What are the rules?" Another could be the environmental question of whether any stable system at all is in place in this sense. Yet another is the more process-therapeutic question of how and why it is that I am not constructing that map well? Or how and why am I not making good use of it? In this last case, my behavior, even if it is self-assertive or aggressive/oppositional behavior, will have a quality of randomness or self-destruction.

The intervention needed may be dialogic, as in the case of a child who has developed new capacities and need for independence. In this case, the family field has not kept up and is still reacting as if to a younger child. Another case would be of a family field that has become more functional, (for example when parents are in recovery from a substance problem), while the child has moved "ahead" into precocious self-reliance and caretaking, and now needs and can afford to experiment with dependency.

Or, take the case of an adolescent's emerging sexuality that may be perceived by the young person (rightly or wrongly) as unacceptable to the parents–either because it is the "wrong kind" of sexuality or just because it is sexuality *per se*. Either way, we know from experience (and from the terms of a Gestalt self-organizational model of development) that any phobic avoidance tends to be self-sustaining, while allowing little room for experiment and new information. That is, avoiding talking about something, to the extent that it lessens anxiety about a bad outcome, just leads to more avoidance and more not talking. In dialogue, the child may discover that she has underestimated the understanding of the parents, or the parents may find their own attitudes evolving through the dialogic process itself.

And even beyond the interpersonal question, there is the question of the development of self-experience. We understand from a field model how it is that the parts of the self that are not articulated dialogically tend to remain not just hidden or secret, but also underdeveloped, less experienced, and less incorporated into the integrated and integrating self. This is a central point that will be developed more below in the discussion of self-narrative and voice.

Another implication of this view of support has to do with our understanding from a field perspective of notions like will, self-effort, and choice. The answer to any life challenge by an individualist model inherently tends to be along the lines of "try harder." We admonish, or perhaps try to inspire the child, often making appeal to a significant relationship that we think the child values. This itself is a move to consideration of the whole field that is not well supported by the individualistic picture. With adults, including ourselves, we may tend to apply the same thinking: the person should just "make more of an effort" because we can't help someone who won't "help himself." This is true, of course, but the either-or flavor of the "self-or-other" model then makes it hard to see how it is that the person can ever begin "helping himself," if he isn't already doing that now. And thus we wait for him to "touch bottom," "hit the wall," or somehow otherwise become inspired to make or experience a large transformation.

There is a place and a reality to all this in life and in development, but what the field model does that is helpful here is to break this large-scale either-or down. It does so by redirecting our attention to the whole field. Take the serious example of an adolescent who is caught up in a destructive pattern of drinking and drugging. Certainly at some point the person has to "make a choice;" and certainly choice always retains some element of mystery, some dimension that at times can feel like grace. But which choice? In practice, the choice not to drug, to say "No" at the party where everyone else seems to be getting high and taking risks, may well just be beyond the capacities of the adolescent at that moment. But the choice not to go to that party, even to associate with different friends in the first place; the choice to work out, say, instead of "hang out" after school; the choice of enrolling in a tutoring program–all of these may be within the felt choiceful realm for that teenager.

These choices themselves are still deeply interactive, even here. For the adolescent to associate with different friends we may need to organize placement in a different school. In order for the distractible child to "get down to" her homework, we may need to organize the home and the evening differently–or if the home can't be influenced, provide the support of an after-school tutoring resource. In all these cases what we are doing is scanning the whole field for the relevant and practical choice points, and mobilizing the whole field in support of the manageable, doable choice. Thus the therapeutic processes of teaching and learning the skills of rehearsal, sequencing, and imagining outcome will all go hand in hand with the modification and mobilization of environmental supports. These environmental supports will, in turn, bring about a reorganization of the whole field of supports as they bear on particular moments of choice. We are no longer concerned with the question of "will power" in this kind of integrated view. We are no longer affected by the isolated, heroic (or shaming and blaming) sense that such moments of choice tend to take on in the culture at large. We welcome and admire "heroic" moments of choice when our patients and students and other children and adolescents can make them, but we recognize all too well that a field and a plan that rely on heroic choice in this sense are a field and a plan already in deep trouble.

This in turn brings us to consideration of the other pole or counterpart of support in a field model: shame as a developmental issue. Again, in an individualist perspective, shame is a feeling of personal weakness and inadequacy. This means among other things that shame itself is shameful, as a kind of confession of the truth of the self-perception, and thus best kept hidden and unexpressed. Shame after all is a feeling of field-connectedness and in a sense field-dependence; it's a needing and not getting some reaction or validation or other support from others. And in an individualist perspective, it is that very field-dependence that development is supposed to lead away from. In other words, to the extent that I am still reactive to your acceptance (or lack of it), I am in a state of weakness and immaturity (and femininity).[18] The hiding of shame issues and the difficulty in addressing them thus issue clearly from the older models.

In a field model, once again, all of this looks entirely different. If the purpose and activity of the self is to unify the whole field, then we are never in a state of not needing support from some place in the field. To be sure, the more support we have from "inside," the more flexible and free we can be in choicefully building our supports "outside." In this way we make them fit while bettering our interaction with our developmental needs and our inner support system in the way of the extended example above. But again, this is quite different from saying that the child, adolescent, or adult should be moving away from external supports in the simplistic, all-or-nothing way sometimes implied by the older models.

But what happens if the outer field "pulls away" from some important felt need or part of the inner self? We mean by "pulls away" not just opposition or resistance but non-reception, the kind of reaction that threatens or breaks the relationship itself. We know experientially that these are the process antecedents of the feelings we know as shame, and always arise originally in important relationship when that relationship itself is threatened. After all, to the infant the caretaking relationship is the dominant field. The developing child senses from the beginning what parts of the inner self are not acceptable, cannot be received, or provoke a pulling away of the field in this sense even before the verbal period.

Thus, shame in a field model, like support, is something more than just an individual feeling or experience. It is that, of course, but it is also a field condition. Or, perhaps better, it is a sign giving *information about the conditions of the relevant field.* As information, shame tells us when the field is too deeply split for the self to integrate it wholly. If the threatened relationship is important enough, and the split deep, and long-lasting enough, then the result will be a kind of self-integration which excludes or diminishes significant aspects and dimensions of the felt inner world. That is, if shame is early enough and pervasive enough, then development follows the kind of course that Winnicott called the "false self" (Guntrip, 1971). That is, it will show the kind of field/self integration that is overwhelmingly constituted by the outer pole of field experience to the neglect of the exploration and articulation of the felt inner world.

And so it is that shame emerges as the key affect in a field/self model, which tells us when the key processes of self are under threat and possibly not well enough supported to be maintained on some present course. In this way, shame takes the role in the field model that anxiety held in the individualistic model: where Freud's "signal anxiety" was a kind of alarm signal that the inner drives were pushing against the bounds of safety and support, "signal shame" serves a parallel purpose in a whole-field picture as the sign that integrative self-process itself is under threat (see Freud, 1933/1999).

Indeed, we would say in this perspective that much of the anxiety Freud points to–and locates as an internal tension between the "metapsychological" functions of id, ego, and superego–*is anxiety over the apprehension of shame*. (That is to say the feeling or anticipation of a loss of field connection that is so serious as to threaten the integrating self-process itself). This threat to self-process itself is the real power of shame and is nearly impossible to account for under the terms of a strict individualist model.

Again, if the nature and function of the self is to integrate the whole field, then when that integration is impossible in some important way, the result is not just discomfort, but this kind of potential threat to self-cohesion at a deep level. Thus it is that a field perspective enables us to see how and why extreme shame experiences may be catastrophic, internally and externally, and why it is that extreme shame can be directly associated with rage, substance abuse, violence toward others, and suicide. In the final analysis, *the self must integrate*–and for that process must draw on whole-field support. In cases of drastic, sustained failure of that support, the self moves in some way to self-destruct.[19]

3. Gender and Identity

How do we come to know and anticipate which behaviors and experiences, which aspects of the internal world, can and will be met in the outer field in a way that promises livable field integration? To be sure, there are many cues, clues, and cultural and other systems through which we may internalize values, basic belief sets, and other organized systems of opinion, working hypotheses, and knowledge. But at all times in all human cultures–and particularly strongly in our own Western culture–our deepest and most developmentally pervasive organizing rubric for sorting our way through the complex field of self-process is the set of beliefs, values and behavioral clusters we know as gender. Gender, that is, in the systems/phenomenological terms we have been developing all through this paper, *is a map of the field.* It's a chart that sorts and organizes the developing child or adolescent's world into what is or is not "doable," into what is or is not supported in the whole field. To be sure, a child (and we) can do things that go against widely prevailing gender norms, but to do so always requires "local" support in the field–support from family, peers, other role models, literature, and so forth. It requires "internal support" as well, which means for the child drawing on inner strength which itself comes directly from other earlier or ongoing interpersonal support in the immediate field.

The child begins to express gendered self-awareness at the verbal level generally by the beginning of the third year at least (Money, 1985), but long before this moment gender difference is already dynamically present and active in the field. Much research shows this dynamic differential in the neonate's world as parents and other caretakers handle and respond differently to children from birth according to their gender. Boys, for instance, are typically stimulated more but allowed to cry longer than girls before being comforted–a complex set of differential field responses that have complex effects on the developing male or female self, to the detriment, we would argue, of both groups in different ways. This holds true whether the caretaker is a man or a woman. So strong and deep is this gendered field-orientation that typically the first question from any new caretaker or stranger about an infant, no matter how young, is an inquiry about gender itself. The question is asked almost automatically as if we would not know how to take up relationship even with an infant without that knowledge. Indeed, in experimental situations where the subject is asked to hold a swaddled infant for a moment and that inquiry is purposely deflected or left unanswered, the subjects typically show considerable uncertainty and even discomfort about handling the child at all (handling it "correctly" we are tempted to presume).

We have no reason to think that self-process per se, as we understand it, is in any way inherently a gendered thing–except for the fact that the field we are born into, and integrate into our developing selves, is itself a *gendered field*. And this means, by the terms of our field/self model, that the self we develop (or the self that "develops us") is then by definition a gendered self. We may step outside gendered norms, of course–but we leave them *as* a man or *as* a woman, leaving the norms of our own gender, and we do this always and only with some special sub-field support (internal and/or locally external), in the way discussed above. Similarly, we may have intense experiences we call transpersonal or spiritual, or other "peak" experiences of a variety of types which take us "beyond" gender, but there again, these experiences require new and unusual supports if they are to be sustained and integrated. The word "beyond" itself suggests how deeply these experiences depart from the norms of our lives. Indeed, experiences that are "beyond gender" are often those we would call "beyond self" in some sense, and would once again show how closely our experiences of self and gender overlap–and have to overlap–in a deeply gendered field.

But, if gender is a field map as well as a social code for support and non-support, how are that map and that code held in place? What are the enforcers that maintain the boundaries of these categories dynamically in the face of all the constructive and deconstructive pressures in the inner and outer field? Our answer in a field model of development, and one that integrates many of the themes we have been developing here is that the map of the gendered field is energized and held in place by the threat of shame, and of course by active shaming as well. When we think of experiences we've had or might have that diverge sharply and seriously from gender norms, we can often capture a sense of active discomfort or even outright shame just thinking about them.

Similarly, when we recall our most deeply shaming experiences from our own developmental history, very often we can see, on reflection, a strong element of gender-norm violation in the scenario contributing to and heightening the experience of shame. (Indeed, it is a useful and instructive exercise to think back on any past experience of shame and shaming and view it with a gender lens). Thus, gender, to restate the definition in these terms, *is a field map and a social code of support and shame*, which are themselves polar complements in a field model (shame being the affect of non-support in the field). Shame holds the contours and boundaries of the map in place, and countering or deconstructing the gender map and code requires that amount and quality of extra support needed to compensate that break in the field–just as any deep shame experience is ultimately healed and overcome, either at that developmental stage or later in life, through the de-shaming effects of connections with others in the field.

All this means that what we call "identity"–the *who-I-am-in-myself-and-in-the-world* as a kind of bridge or boundary experience and concept which has always tended to nudge the individualist models in a social field direction–is likewise a deeply gendered notion and process in a field perspective. This is again for the same reason. The field of identity development and identity formation is a gendered field. Identity, in our model much as in individualist models, is a matter of what I identify with and where I "find myself" in the field. The difference in our perspective is that rather than starting with a separate "I" and then looking for where that self can fit in a wider environment (in the way of the Eriksonian model, for example, as was discussed above), here the self finds and becomes itself as it interacts and integrates living processes in the field. This is not to say that the "inner self" has no meaning or that our identity, the "who we are," has no interior component. On the contrary, in our view here, "inner-self-experience" is real and is crucial; but it is dynamic, not fixed or developmentally prior to relational experience, and it is one pole of integrative self-experience rather than the whole process.

And thus in a field perspective we do not need to see any inherent split between identity and relationship or, for that matter, between relationship and self. The field we are born into–"thrown into" in Heidegger's phrase–and which it is our life task to make sense of and give meaning to, *is a relational field*–and a gendered field as well. In a field model, aspects and dynamics of the field are aspects and dynamics of the self.

4. Voice and Narrative

And how does self-process then come together in taking up its position, place, and action in the field? How is all this coherent resolution and integrative process that we have been talking about expressed? In a dynamic field model, the self, rather than being a formed entity "thrown into" an environment, as some existential philosophers have it, is rather a developing position or locus in and of that field. Self in this perspective can be well conceived as a point of view in (and on) the field we all share (in much the same spirit as Goodman's when he speaks of the "self-boundary" as a "place" where things happen, rather than a thing in itself).

As a "point of view," self is both individual and unique–*and an integral part of that common field*, constructed in and out of the same common elements and dimensions, and along the same dynamic principles, as other selves. To mature and achieve full human development, in this sense, is the same as achieving and giving voice to that coherent, connected point of view. Thus, "voice," like other key concepts we have touched on here (self, support, shame, development, intimacy, gender, and so on), emerges as quite a different notion and one more dynamically alive and connected, from the way the concept is developed in an individualist model. In older models, "voice" and "capacity to speak your mind" would be thought of as internal characteristics of the individual person–and thus to be treated, as in cases of underdevelopment, basically with various forms of "assertiveness training." Assertion and training for robust self-expression certainly are crucial elements of treatment and healthy functioning, but they too look different in a new model. Here, we would view "voice" and "capacity to give voice" first and always as characteristics of a field. In a field where one person or one group of persons has the "right to speak" and others have diminished rights or no rights in some areas, no one really has a voice and no one person can achieve full voice. This is because the achievement of full voice, the fully articulated and elaborated expression of an unfettered self-process, *is utterly dependent on a developmental field of other voices*, other selves who can first lead and then engage ongoingly in the kind of intersubjective dialogue which is essential to evoke and support self-development. To "have a voice," which in this perspective is the same as "having experience" in a full sense, is thus a matter of inner capacity and of the receptive conditions in the field. One's voice begins to emerge, at least potentially, somewhere beginning in one's developmental history or during later corrective relationships. This means that the relevant unit for developmental study in a field perspective is not "voice" alone, but *"voice-and-listener."* The area of study will include the field itself in which voice is given and in which it makes sense to give voice to anything at all. This begins crucially in childhood where the absence of any important listener leads to atrophy and diminishment in the development of voice, and thus of self in our sense of the term.

And how is voice then organized? How do we know where and when to reach out into the outer field, giving voice to our position and experience in that particular moment? What grounds that position and that moment in larger contexts of meaning so that voice connects and makes sense to ourselves and to others? Remember here that in a Gestalt developmental view we start with Gestalt process/organizational notions about what our own cognitive/affective/perceptual/valuing processes are, by our nature, and what the purpose is of all this elaborate constructivist nature. As we discussed above, the thrust and effect of our inborn perceptual nature, which is to select and invest energy in figures of interest embedded in a whole picture or gestalt of understanding, is to be able to sense and judge practically what is going to happen *next* in relation to where we want and need to go. That is, our developmental/evolutionary nature as high-learning, low-instinct social animals is our remarkably developed ability to learn and make predictions in the service of survival and growth in an ever-changing field. So far at least, to use Goodman's term, our capacity for creative adjustment (which is Goodman's most salient definition of the elusive word "contact," with the accent on the term creative) has enabled us as an animal species to survive and adapt, more or less well, to an enormous range of environments while other more ecologically specific species have fallen by the evolutionary wayside. In other words, in a very real sense in Gestalt we understand our nature as fundamentally future-oriented (with the very notion of "development" certainly being a prime example of that orientation). We are "wired," to repeat this thought in somewhat varied terms, to think and perceive in temporally-linked sequences of meaning–" first this, then that," or "that means/leads to this." When we speak of the child learning in development to know and understand the world, inner and outer, it is associations and sequences of this kind raised developmentally to elaborately complex interactive levels of which we are thinking.

But, "temporally linked sequences of meaning, raised to complex interactive levels" is a close working definition of story; the "recounting" of how one thing leads or has led to another, and what that means. This is why we can say, in Gestalt, that the human being "is the story-telling animal" (see discussion in Wheeler, 1993). We understand ourselves and others–which means connect ourselves meaningfully to each other and to other contextual wholes–in terms of story; and we do this not just out of tradition or culture, but also by the very terms of our perceptual/cognitive/developmental nature. In this sense, we did not and do not invent our self-stories so much as our self-stories invent us. Again, we do not first exist as individuals, then know ourselves, then form a self-story, and finally tell it to another. Rather, we find and create our story in the telling of it to another person, and that act is the same as the creative construction of the self. Again, to be sure, that self-story can then be continued internally in what we call "monologue," but this happens if and only to the extent that monologue grows developmentally out of dialogue in all the ways discussed above.

The self that acts creatively to unify the field into wholes of meaning and action, the self that is itself a developmental achievement, integrating all the other developmental field lines and themes we have been discussing in these new terms, is itself a narrative self, a story-maker and a story, by its very Gestalt nature. In this way, finally, development can be viewed as the narrative therapies view it: as the development of a coherent, meaningful, contextualized self-and-life-story: one that has clear boundaries, clear relatedness, meaningful inter- and intraconnections and articulation, one that leads somewhere, has energy for both presence and carrying forward in time and space into more inclusive and cohesively meaningful wholes of understanding. "Here and now *and next*," was Goodman's phrase (1994) for it, and indeed all these properties of good story form and of the developmentally mature self are none other than the characteristics described by Köhler, Koffka and others as the inherent properties of "good form" or "good gestalt."[20] These properties include brightness, liveliness, energy, clarity, boundaries, internal structure and cohesiveness, connectedness to the field, and pragnanz–that basic dynamic quality of our essential Gestalt nature, of going somewhere in a purposive, meaningful way, which is development itself.

Conclusion

The self that develops is both the result and the goal of development, but is not an *individual* itself in the way we have been used to conceptualizing it. Rather, it is a coherent integrative process that unifies the whole field out of and into an individual point of view, resolving the inner and outer realms of experience into ever-new wholes of meaning and action.

These new meaningful wholes of understanding then change each of those realms in turn, the interior and the exterior domains. This movement creates the new ground for further self-construction, new resolutions of the whole field, and new levels of meaning. In this way, self-process is the engine of its own growth by virtue of our inherent drive to organize the field (which Goldstein [1939] called the "single drive" of our human nature). This is development; and this means, in turn, that the field in and out of which development takes place *is itself a developing field*. It must be viewed in this way if we are to assess an individual child or adolescent meaningfully and usefully or, for that matter, take up any developmental topic or theme.

This developing field must itself be actively intersubjective for individual development to be supported and full. The interior pole of self-experience can never develop fully at all without this. Without this intersubjective dimension, what we have then is not a human agent of any developmental age and stage but only a reactor, empty at best, and dangerously destructive to self and others at worst. Thus, *intersubjective bonding and reception emerge as the first key field criteria and characteristics for full human development*. This need for intersubjective reception and reflection (including the support of differentiation and challenge) is developmentally crucial not only in childhood, but ongoingly throughout life: a theme and a process which we have discussed here as a field understanding of the dynamics of intimacy in development. Our ongoing development in this sense is then constrained and channeled by the interpersonal process we feel and know as *shame*–again a familiar theme that is considerably clarified by being viewed in field perspective. Much of the differential support and shame to which we are subject developmentally is then encoded as gender, which we can also view in field perspective as a map for negotiating our social world which itself is a deeply gendered field. The dynamic relation of that developing sense of self to the whole-field context is a field definition of *identity*, while the dynamic concept of *voice* unifies and actualizes the exercise of self-organization and self-process in the field. We find and make ourselves by giving voice in relationship, thereby both articulating and, at the same time, constructing our interior experience, and in the process build our own characteristic point of view that is the essence of self in field perspective.

Finally, *narrative* organizes our developing self and sense of self. It locates us in the space/time of our field, giving meaning to our inner and outer fields together, including the world we share with and in other people. The development of self through childhood and adolescence and on throughout the life span is the construction and articulation of a meaningful self-narrative, by which we mean a story that locates us meaningfully in the field. Coming full circle with our Gestalt perspective on self and development we can then say that the development of self, at any moment of growth or ongoingly through life, is the same as the emergence of the properties of "good gestalt" in the self-narrative, and in the observed and observing, integrated and integrating self.

All this comprises the beginnings at least of a fully Gestalt field/phenomenological perspective on development, developmental themes and issues, and the developing self of the child in all its field implications. The use of a model of this kind, we believe, puts us in a significantly better position to organize our own phenomenological reality to construct an understanding of the child in the field. It enables us then to choose and apply interventions at any or all domains of that field, the inner and outer worlds of the child's developing self-process. And it allows us to maintain a clear sense of the dynamic interaction of all these domains–interior experience, family, peer and adult relations, school, community, politics and culture–during the process of our interventions.

Ultimately, our concern in working with children is a concern with their worlds. The interior world of the child is not only woven of imagination, creativity, and developing thoughts and feelings, but also includes the outer world of political and social realities, economic conditions, and cultural practices and values. It includes particularly those values and cultural patterns that would teach us, following the ideology of the old individualist paradigm and model, that the children of our world are not all of our children. The myth that the old ideology maintains is that the children of others are "their" responsibility–not ours–and that the conditions of support and shame, bonding and rupture, reception and rejection in the field which are integrated into and as the developing selves of children, are ultimately not our concern. Rather, in a Gestalt developmental model we are supported to understand and apply what we already know deep within: that every part of the field is a part of each of us, that all the children of the world are the particular charge and concern of us all, and that the conditions of their development, which will become integrated as and into their very selves, are the conditions of our own selves as well. We are unique, but never separate. We are deeply part of each other and in our belongingness, to each other and to the field that we share, lies our full humanity, and our fullest individual development of self.

Footnotes

1. For the ideas about a Gestalt field approach to development in this essay, I am very much indebted to a sustained exchange on these topics with Mary Ann Kraus. For the discussion of shame below, as always, I draw on extensive collaboration with Robert Lee; see Lee & Wheeler (1996).

2. See for example Stern (1986); Belenky, et al., (1986); also see discussion in Wheeler (1994).

3. See discussion in Wheeler (2000).

4. See for example extensive discussion of the work of Rawls, Taylor, Sanders, and other social/philosophical thinkers about the self in Alford (1991).

5. See discussion in Wheeler (1995, 1996, 2000).

6. See for example Miller (1976).

7. See also discussion of this point from a Gestalt developmental perspective in Wheeler (1994).

8. See the discussion of the "drive to organize" in Goldstein (1939, 1940).

9. This is especially so given that the most relevant and organizing dynamics or factors in the child's life and self-process at a given time may lie outside the focus of one particular model or another. This is the problem with models that fail to take a whole-field perspective.

10. See for example Kagan (1984).

11. See e.g., Ferraro & Wheeler in this volume.

12. See e.g., Stern (1986) and Fantz (1963).

13. See also discussion in Khan (1991).

14. See Ferraro & Wheeler in this volume.

15. See discussion in Wheeler (2000).

16. See also Wheeler (1995, 2000).

17. Note that this corresponds with the modal presenting patient at child clinics. A typical example would be a 10 to 11-year-old boy with some behavioral disorder and carrying a modal diag nosis of "ADD," which is after all a kind of difficulty in organizing a changing field.

18. See Wheeler & Jones (1996) and Wheeler (1996) for further discussion of the gender ideology of the individualist model.

19. See Lee (1995); Lee & Wheeler (1996); and Wheeler (1997) for further discussion.

20. See discussion in Zinker (1994) as well as Wheeler (1991).

References

Alford, J. (1991). *The self in social theory*. New Haven, CT: Yale University Press.

Bollas, C. (1989). *The shadow of the object.* New York, NY: Columbia University Press.

Belenky, M., Clinchy, B., Goldberger, N., & Tarule, J. (1986). *Women's ways of knowing.* New York, NY: Basic Books.

Erikson, E. (1951). *Childhood and society*. New York, NY: Norton.

Erikson, E. (1963). *Identity, youth & crisis.* Cambridge, MA: Harvard University Press.

Fantz, R. (1963). Patterns of vision in newborn infants. *Science,* 140, 296-297.

Ferraro, J., & Wheeler, G. (2001). Attention deficit disorder: A gestalt perspective. In M. McConville & G. Wheeler (Eds.), *The heart of development: Gestalt approaches to working with children, adolescents, & their worlds: Volume two: Adolescence*, (pp. 195-233). Hillsdale, NJ: GestaltPress/The Analytic Press.

Freud, S. (1933/1999). *The complete psychological works of Sigmund Freud: The standard edition.* New York, NY: Norton.

Gilligan, C. (1982). *In a different voice.* Cambridge, MA: Harvard University Press.

Goldstein, K. (1939). *The organism.* Boston, MA: American Book Co.

Goldstein, K. (1940). *Human nature in the light of psychopathology.* Cambridge, MA: Harvard University Press.

Goodman, P. (1951). Novelty, excitement & growth. In F. Perls, R. Hefferline, & P. Goodman, *Gestalt therapy: Excitement and growth in the human personality*. New York, NY: Janus Press.

Goodman, P. (1994). *Crazy hope and finite experience*. San Francisco, CA: Jossey-Bass.

Guntrip, H. (1971). *Psychoanalytic theory, therapy, and the self.* New York, NY: Basic Books.

Kagan, J. (1984). *The nature of the child.* New York, NY: Basic Books.
Kaplan, N., & Kaplan, M. (1994). Processes of experiential organization in couple and family systems. In G. Wheeler & S. Backman (Eds.), *On intimate ground: A gestalt approach to working with couples,* (pp. 109-127). San Francisco, CA: Jossey-Bass.
Kaufmann, S. (1991). *Understanding complexity.* New York, NY: Basic Books.
Kegan, R. (1982). *The evolving self.* Cambridge, MA: Harvard University Press.
Khan, M. (1991). Foreword. In D. Winnicott, *Holding and interpretation.* New York, NY: Grove/Atlantic.
Kohlberg, L. (1981). *The philosophy of moral development.* San Francisco, CA: Harper & Row.
Kohut, H. (1977). *The restoration of self.* New York, NY: International Universities Press.
Lee, R. (1995). Gestalt and Shame. *British Gestalt Journal, 4*(1).
Lee, R., & Wheeler, G., (Eds.). (1996). *The voice of shame: Silence and connection in psychotherapy.* San Francisco, CA: Jossey-Bass.
Lewin, K. (1926). Intention, will, and need *(Vorsatz, Wille, Bedürfnis). Psychologische Forschung, 7,* 330-85.
Lewin, K. (1935). *A dynamic theory of personality.* New York, NY: McGraw-Hill.
Mahler, M. (1993). *On human symbiosis and the vicissitudes of individuation.* New York, NY: International Universities Press.
Maslow, A. (1954). *Motivation and personality.* New York, NY: Harper.
Maturana, V., & Varela, F. (1987). *Tree of knowledge: The bio logical roots of human understanding.* Boston, MA: Shambala.
McConville, M. (1995). *Adolescence: Psychotherapy and the emergent self.* San Francisco, CA: Jossey-Bass.
Miller, J. (1976). *Toward a new psychology of women.* Boston, MA: Beacon Press.
Money, J. (1985). *Straight, gay & in between.* New York, NY: Basic Books.
Montague, A. (1955). *The direction of human development.* New York, NY: Harper & Row.
Perls, F. (1947). *Ego, hunger & aggression.* London: Allen & Unwin.
Perls, F. (1969). *In and out the garbage pail.* Moab, UT: Real People Press.
F. Perls, R. Hefferline, & P. Goodman (1951). *Gestalt therapy: Excitement and growth in the human personality.* New York, NY: Janus Press.

Piaget, J. (1947). *Intelligence.* New York, NY: Basic Books.

Stern, D. (1985). *The interpersonal world of the infant.* New York, NY: Basic Books.

Wheeler, G. (1991). *Gestalt reconsidered: A new approach to contact and resistance.* New York, NY: Gardner Press.

Wheeler, G. (1993). Translator's introduction. In B. Heimannsberg & C. Schmidt (Eds.); C. Harris & G. Wheeler (Trans.). *The collective silence: German families and the legacy of shame,* (pp. xv-xxviii). San Francisco, CA: Jossey-Bass.

Wheeler, G. (1994a). Introduction: Why gestalt? In G. Wheeler & S. Backman (Eds.), *On intimate ground: A gestalt approach to working with couples* (pp.1-30). San Francisco, CA: Jossey-Bass.

Wheeler, G. (1994b). The tasks of intimacy. In G. Wheeler & S. Backman (Eds.), *On intimate ground: A gestalt approach to working with couples,* (pp. 31-59). San Francisco, CA: Jossey-Bass.

Wheeler, G. (1995). Self and shame. *British Gestalt Journal, 4*(2), 29-36.

Wheeler, G. (1998). Tell me a story. In J. Brown (Ed.), *Back to the beanstalk.* Cambridge, MA: GestaltPress.

Wheeler, G., & Jones, D. (1996). Finding our sons: A male-male gestalt. In R. Lee & G. Wheeler (Eds.), *The voice of shame: Silence and connection in psychotherapy,* (pp. 61-99). San Francsico, CA: Jossey-Bass.

Wheeler, G. (1998). Toward a gestalt developmental model. *British Gestalt Journal, 7*(2), 115-125.

Wheeler, G. (2000). *Beyond individualism: Toward a new understanding of self, relationship, and experience.* Hillsdale, NJ: GestaltPress/The Analytic Press.

White, M. & Epston, D. (1990). *Narrative means to therapeuetic ends.* New York, NY: Norton.

Winnicott, D. (1988). *Human nature.* London: Free Association Books.

Zinker, J. (1994). *In search of good form: A gestalt approach to working with couples and families.* San Francisco, CA: Jossey-Bass.

Part II:

Applications

2

The Therapeutic Process with Children and Adolescents: A Gestalt Therapy Perspective

Violet Oaklander

I have noticed that there appears to be a natural progression in my therapeutic work with children that I call the therapy process. From a certain perspective, it may look as if nothing much is going on, that we're playing around when in actuality there is a very definite process, a sequence, if you will, in the therapy encounter with children. In spite of the fact that the word sequence implies a progression from one thing to another, this process is not always linear, though the relationship does come first. However, with subsequent aspects of the therapeutic process, I tend to go back and forth as I assess the child's needs. Most people assume that my work consists of using a variety of expressive, projective techniques. Although this is true to some extent, there is much more that requires attention before these techniques are used.

Relationship

Nothing happens without at least a thread of a relationship. The relationship is a tenuous thing that takes careful nurturing. It is the foundation of the therapeutic process and can, in of itself, be powerfully therapeutic. This I/Thou relationship, based on the writings of Buber (1958), has certain fundamental principles that are highly significant in work with children. We meet each other as two separate individuals, one not superior to the other. It is my responsibility to hold this stance. I am as authentic as I know how to be–I am myself. I don't use a teacher voice or a patronizing voice. I will not manipulate nor judge. Although I am perpetually optimistic regarding the healthy potential of the child that I meet in my office, I will not place expectations upon her. I will accept her as she is, in whatever way she presents herself to me. I will respect her rhythm and, in fact, attempt to join her in that rhythm; I will be present and contactful. In this way our relationship flourishes.

Transference generally enters into any relationship; however I do not encourage it. The child may react to me as a parent figure; however, I am not her parent. I have my own point of view, my own limits and boundaries, my own way of responding. In relating to my client as a separate being, I give her the opportunity to experience her own *self*, her own boundaries–to perhaps experience herself in a new way. I am not hopelessly enmeshed with her, as a parent might be. As I maintain my own integrity as a separate person, I give the client the opportunity to experience more of her own self, thus enhancing her sense of self and improving and strengthening her contact· skills.

Further, I have a responsibility to be aware of any "buttons" pressed in me that may not be genuine emotional responses to the contextual situation, and to explore these counter-transference responses to eliminate their detriment to the client. I am true to myself as well. I am not afraid of my own feelings and responses, and I know my own limits. I honor what's important to me. We begin on time and end on time. I pace the session so that there is time for the child to help me clean up (except sand tray scenes). In this way, closure is clearly evident.

Once the initial resistance is overcome, I can begin to feel that thread of relationship with most children. However, there are some children who cannot form a relationship, at least for some time. These are children who have been severely injured emotionally at a very early age, or perhaps at birth. Trust eludes them. For these children, the focus of the therapy becomes the relationship. Of course honoring and respecting the child's resistance is vital, for it is the one way that the child has learned to protect herself. Finding creative, non-threatening ways to reach the child is the task of the therapist.

Contact

The next issue that I address in the therapeutic process is that of contact. Contact involves having the ability to be fully present in a particular situation with all of the aspects of the organism–senses, body, emotional expression, and intellect–ready and available for use. Is the child able to make and sustain good contact? Or does he move in and out of contact, or have difficulty making contact at all. In every session together, contact is a vital, existential issue. Nothing much happens without some contact present. What happens outside the session may be similar or different, and I can only work with what we have together. Sometimes a child has so much difficulty sustaining contact with me that the focus of the therapy becomes one of helping the child feel comfortable with making and sustaining contact. Children who have troubles, who are worried and anxious, frightened, grieving, or angry, will armor and restrict themselves, pull themselves in, cut parts of themselves off, inhibit healthful expression. When the senses and the body are restricted, emotional expression and a strong sense of self will be negligible.

Good contact also involves the ability to withdraw appropriately rather than to become rigidified in a supposedly contactful space. When this happens it is no longer contact, but a phony attempt to stay in contact. An example of this is the child who never stops talking, or who can never play alone and needs to be with people at all times.

We speak of contact skills–the how of contact. These skills involve touching, looking and seeing, listening and hearing, tasting, smelling, speaking, sound, gesture and language, moving in the environment. Sometimes in our therapeutic journey it is necessary to give children many experiences to open the pathways to contact. Children who have been abused particularly desensitize themselves, as do most children who have experienced some kind of trauma.

Sometimes, I will notice that a child who generally has the capacity to make good contact will come into the session, and appear to be distracted. I will know immediately that something amiss has happened prior to this time. I might casually ask the child to tell me something that happened at school that he didn't like, or something that happened on the way to my office. I need to assess the child's contact level at each meeting.

Resistance

Children evidence a variety of behavioral manifestations, often called resistances, as their way of attempting to cope and survive and make contact with the world as best they can. Sometimes it works–but more often children do not get what they need as they engage in these behaviors. They are considered inappropriate by others, and only make things worse. Since they have little awareness of cause and effect, they try harder, generally by accelerating the behaviors, but their efforts fail them, and life is far from satisfying. As they gain more self-support through a stronger sense of self, the unsuccessful behaviors drop away and are replaced by more satisfying, effective ways of contacting the world.

Most every child will be resistant–self-protecting–to some degree. If there is no resistance whatsoever, I know that this child's self is so fragile that she must do whatever she is told to do in order to feel that she can survive. I want to help this child strengthen herself so that she can feel some resistance, to have enough support to pause and consider.

Resistance is the child's ally; it is the way she takes care of herself. I expect resistance and I respect that resistance. I am more often surprised when it is not there, than when it is. In some situations, I articulate it for the child, "I know you probably don't want to do this drawing, but I want you to do it anyway. Whatever you do, I don't want you to do your best. We just don't have time for that." I want to help the child soften somewhat, and go through the resistance to some degree for a little while. The very fact that I will accept the child's resistance often helps her take the risk to do something new. As the child begins to feel safe in our sessions, she will drop the resistance for a time. However, when she has experienced or divulged as much as she can handle, as much as she has inside support for, the resistance will come up again. In this way, resistance surfaces over and over again, and each time it must be honored. We cannot force the child to go beyond her capabilities. Resistance is also a sign that beyond this place of defense, there is highly significant material to be explored and worked through. The child seems to know on some intuitive, visceral level when she can handle such material, and I have learned to trust this process. As we work with self-expression and emotional expression activities, the issues emerge again and again. The therapeutic work with the child is accomplished in small segments.

I see resistance as a manifestation of energy as well as an indication of the contact level of the child. As the child engages with me or some activity or technique, there suddenly may be a perceivable drop in energy, and contact shifts away from me or away from the task at hand. I can often see this manifestation before the child's own awareness, by observing his body response at that moment. I may say, "Let's stop this for now and play a game" to the great relief of the child (obvious through the body). He is back in contact with me. Some children show their resistance is passive ways; that is, they will ignore, act distracted, seemingly not hear what I say, or begin to, without response, do something other than what I have suggested. If that child finally comes to a place where she can say clearly, "No, I don't want to do that," I will quickly reinforce that direct, contactful statement by immediately honoring it.

Senses

To enhance tactile sensation I might encourage the child to fingerpaint or work with pottery clay, using lots of water. We might sit at the sand tray running our hands through the sand as we talk. I might bring in a variety of textures to touch and compare, or we might examine various textures right in the office. We might listen to sounds in and outside the office or the sounds of music or drum. We might look at flowers, colors, pictures, light, shadow, objects, each other. Books on early childhood education provide a wealth of ideas for activities to enhance the senses, and are effective with people of all ages. In my book, *Windows to Our Children* (Oaklander, 1978/1988), I describe how I made use of the Orange Exercise to open and enhance the senses. I gave each child in a group an orange. Slowly we investigated every aspect of the orange–examining it, smelling it, weighing it, feeling its temperature and texture, licking it. We peeled off the skin and examined it very carefully, biting and tasting it. We peeled the fibrous layer and examined this. We marveled at the shiny, protective layer over the orange, noting that it had no taste. We divided each orange into segments, took a segment and very carefully went through the examination procedure. We then traded segments with everyone in the group, discovering in amazement that each segment was different in taste and texture, though all delicious. One twelve-year-old year old girl remarked later, "I can never eat an orange, or any fruit, the way I used to anymore. Now I really know it." This child was referring to her enhanced awareness and sharpened sensory capabilities.

When children feel safe in my office, they will often regress and allow themselves to have experiences that one may deem more appropriate for a younger child. When this happens, I celebrate inside myself. Children who live in dysfunctional families, or have been traumatized in some way, tend to grow up too fast. They skip over many important developmental steps. Some children will pour lots of water on the clay, unconsciously replicating mud play. Others will use water in fairly creative ways. A twelve-year-old boy, after learning that he had to help me clean up, insisted on washing all the clay tools. I told him that I usually don't wash them, but he insisted. As I watched him at the sink, I was reminded of my three-year-old daughter standing on a stool at the sink washing her toy dishes. This boy did not need a stool, but he was involved in the washing much as my daughter had been. He was giving himself an experience that he needed; this was evident by his relaxed body and smiling face.

The Body

Our next focus is the body. Every emotion has a body connection. Notice how your body reacts the next time you feel angry or joyous. Notice the constriction of your head when you hold in your anger. Notice the tightening of the throat and chest you as fend off tears, the hunching of the shoulders when you feel anxious or frightened. Children develop body patterns at an early age, often creating at that time the defects in posture that we usually see more clearly in adolescents and adulthood.

Children who are troubled restrict their bodies and become disconnected from them. I want to help them unblock, loosen up, breathe deeply, know their own bodies, feel proud of that body, feel the power that lies within that body. Often we begin with the breath. Children, and adults, when anxious and fearful, restrict the breath, thus cutting themselves off further from themselves. We invent games that involve breathing. We do breathing exercises. We blow up balloons and move them through the air with our breath to see who can keep the balloon up the longest. We do relaxation, meditative exercises involving the breath. We blow cotton balls across a table to see whose will reach the end first. We play games involving making sounds, singing, and screaming. Adolescents in particular are fascinated by the power of the breath. Over and over again they will tell me how they remembered to breathe deeply, imagining the breath bathing the body and the brain, during school examinations and how helpful this was to them. The secondary gain of feeling power over one's life, rather than a victim of it, is immeasurable.

We do many exercises involving the body. We might dance around the room, throw a Nerf ball, fall on pillows, have a Bataca fight, and play a hand-wrestling game. Hyperactive children particularly benefit from controlled body experiments such as yoga, or body movement games when they can experience body control with movement. Bed-wetters benefit greatly from bodywork since they are generally quite disconnected from their bodies. Creative dramatics, particularly pantomime, is a tremendous aid for helping children know their bodies. Each movement must be exaggerated in order to get the idea across. We play many games involving mime.

We don't necessarily spend a whole session doing sensory, breathing and body activities. If it appears indicated, I will suggest an activity that the child may or may not be willing to do. Much depends on my own enthusiasm and willingness to involve myself in these activities with the child, as well as my skill in presenting them. We may spend five minutes or a whole session with these activities. We may need to negotiate and compromise, spending part of the time with what the child wants to do, and part with what I suggest. Once the child allows himself to be involved in these experiences, he generally enjoys them greatly. Therapy with children is like a dance: sometimes I lead and sometimes the child leads.

Strengthening the Self

Helping the child develop a strong sense of self is a major prerequisite in helping him express buried emotions. Further, the child begins to feel a sense of well-being as well as a positive feeling about himself. Let me remind you that these steps as outlined in this discussion of the therapeutic process are not at all consecutive. We go back and forth as needed. We may be focusing on sensory work, and while the child is enjoying the tactile sensation of wet clay, for example, along with the kinesthetic experience inherent in working with pottery clay, he may feel an increased sense of self. This heightened feeling of self will often spontaneously evoke emotional expression.

Strengthening the self involves, besides sensory and body experiences, defining the self by:

- experiencing some power and control;
- making choices;
- experiencing mastery;
- owning projections;
- the setting of boundaries and limits;
- being playful and using the imagination;
- contacting one's own aggressive energy.

Defining the Self

To empower the self one must know the self. Many experience are provided to help children make "self" statements. The child is encouraged to talk about herself through drawing, collage, clay, puppets, creative dramatics, music, metaphors, dreams–any technique that will help the child focus on herself. "This is who I am" and "This is who I am not" is what the child is learning and integrating into her awareness. I make lists that the child dictates to me of foods she likes and foods she hates, things she doesn't like about school and things she does like, if any. The child might draw a picture of all the things she wishes for, or what makes her happy or sad or angry or afraid, or all the things she likes to do. Or I might ask the child to make, out of clay, figures or abstract shapes to represent herself when she feels good and when she feels bad. Honoring the child's thoughts, opinions, ideas, suggestions is an important aspect of strengthening the self. Sometimes, with adolescents, I will use an astrology book, or the manual after giving them a projective test. I will read various sentences pertaining to their birth sign, or the manual's interpretation of the test and will then ask, "Does this fit for you? Each time the child can say, "Yes, this is how I am" or "No, I'm not like that" or even "Well, sometimes I'm like that and sometimes I'm not," she is establishing more of who she is. The more the child can be assisted to define herself, the stronger the self becomes and there is more opportunity for healthful growth.

Choices

Giving the child many opportunities to make choices is another way to provide inner strength. Many children are fearful of making even the most insignificant choices for fear of making a wrong one. So I will provide as many non-threatening choices as I can: "Do you want to sit on the couch or at the table? Do you want markers or pastels?" Later the choices become a bit more complicated: "Which size paper would you like? (3 choices) What would you like to do today?" A typical response may be, I don't know," or "I don't care," or "whatever you want me to." I smile and patiently insist that they make the choice, unless, of course, I see that it is just too painful to make such a decision at this time. I encourage parents to give their children the opportunity to make choices whenever possible.

Mastery

Children who live in dysfunctional families, alcoholic families, who have been abused, neglected or molested, often grow up too fast and skip over many important mastery experiences vital to healthy development. In some cases the parents may do too much for the child, thwarting his need to struggle; other parents are so rigid they don't allow the child to explore and experiment. Some parents have the belief that frustration improves staying power. Children *never* learn to accomplish tasks through frustration. There is a fine line between struggle and frustration and it is important to be sensitive to that point. The baby struggles to put the smaller size box into the larger one, but when frustration sets in he begins to cry. The older child loses energy–cuts off contact. Mastery experiences come in many forms. Some are planned, such as bringing in a new game and figuring it out together, building a structure out of Leggos or Lincoln Logs, or figuring out a puzzle. Some children, as they begin to feel safe with the therapist, create their own experiences, such as drowning the clay with water, or intently washing clay tools. These kinds of experiences are closely related to regression. The child herself creates opportunities to relive the kinds of experiences she may have missed, or needed more of.

Sometimes mastery experiences present themselves spontaneously. An eleven-year-old boy, for example, attempted to make a bird fly in a sand scene he was creating. He asked me for a stick and some string. I knew that the string wouldn't work, but wisely kept my mouth shut. He soon discovered, after many tries, that he couldn't tie the bird onto the top of the stick with string. His energy began to fade, his contact with the task was broken, and any minute I knew he would decide to stop working on his sand scene. Sensing the onset of frustration, I gently said, "I have an idea that might work. Would you like to hear my idea?" The boy nodded and I said, "Maybe wire would work, or even something like masking tape. I don't know–what do you think?" The boy opted for some picture wire–it worked–and his energy and smile and big sigh indicated to me his mastery experience. (I did not say, "Don't forget, that was my idea.")

Of course children who use many of the projective techniques experience mastery, not by my saying, "That's a beautiful picture, or a wonderful sand scene," but by their own intrinsic satisfaction. I caution parents to avoid overblown, general statements as "That's a beautiful drawing," or "You are a musical genius." Children generally turn such statements into negative introjects. More effective are statements as, "I like the colors of that picture," or "I like the way you cleaned your room," staying with the "I" message.

Owning Projections

Many of the techniques we use are projective in nature. When a child makes a sand scene, draws a picture, tells a story, he is tapping into his own individuality and experience. Often these expressions are metaphorical representations of his life. When he can own aspects of these projections, he is making a statement about himself and his process in life. His awareness of himself and his boundaries intensifies. When the child describes his "safe place" drawing to me, he feels heard and respected as I listen carefully. When I ask him to give me a statement about his place that I can write on his picture, he feels further validated. When we connect his statement to his life today, he begins to feel his own significance in the world.

From a 14-year-old's safe place drawing of an ice cave, I write as he dictates, "I am walking through my ice cave and I am thinking." I ask him what he is thinking about. "I am thinking about everything–school, my life." I ask if anyone else is there. "No, no one knows how to get here–I'm the only one that knows the way in and the way out." I ask how this place relates to the reality of his life. "I need a place like that. It's hard for me to think about anything when my brother is around." (He is an identical twin.)

He expands a bit about this situation and draws a picture representing how he feels when his brother is around–a tight mass of dark colored lines. He admits that he doesn't know how to feel free without finding an ice cave in which to hide. We have come one step further toward helping this boy find and own himself.

Boundaries and Limits

Good parenting involves clear limit-setting appropriate for the child's age level so that the child can know, experiment and test her boundaries. When a boundary is not available, the child tends to feel anxious and may flail around in search of this boundary. Her sense of self becomes amorphous. The parents need to know when it is appropriate to stretch the boundaries so that the child, at each developmental level, can find new areas of exploration. In our sessions my limits and boundaries are clear. We begin on time; we end on time. I do not answer the phone–in fact they notice that I generally turn it off. My desk is off-limits and we don't flick paint around the room. At the end of each session the child helps me clean up (except for sand tray scenes.) Closure of the session is made clear by this activity. I don't articulate these "rules;" they are dealt with naturally as they come up. I believe that my own self-respect and my limits free children to become more acquainted with themselves. Further, I am aware of my own limits in another way–I know, and sometimes learn in the process, what I can do or cannot do. If I am recovering from the flu, I will not engage in a Bataca fight with a child, for example. If I am required in a game to jump 100 times, I inform the child when I reach my limit. I can also respect the child's need to limit herself at times, and I need to be aware of my own unrealistic expectations.

Playfulness, Imagination and Humor

Young children naturally have a flair for playfulness and imagination and love to laugh at funny things. The have not restricted or inhibited themselves as yet. Imaginative play is an integral part of child development. Often these natural resources are stifled in children who are traumatized in some way. Providing many opportunities for imaginative play is a necessary component of child therapy and serves to free and enhance the self. The therapist needs to know how to play with the child; If this quality of life is obscured or lost, the therapist herself must find a way to regain this joyful behavior. Fortunately, I have never lost the capacity for play, and this attribute has served me well with my own children and with the many children with whom I've worked. Because there is so little opportunity in life to experience playfulness and imagination as an adult, I am very fortunate to have found my own avenues for these expressions. Many parents have difficulty allowing themselves to joyfully play with their children. When I am aware of this, we spend some time in my office just playing. I can be a good model for this activity.

Power and Control

As children begin to trust me and feel at home in my office, they begin to take over the sessions. This step is one of the most exciting parts of the therapy for me. When I see this happen, I know that there is progress. The children I work with (and actually most children) have no power over their lives. They might fight for control, engaging in power struggles, but actually these children feel a terrible lack of power. The kind of control that happens in the sessions is not the same as a fighting for power–it is a contactful interaction, but one where the child, in the play (and the child always knows it's play), has the experience of control. It is one of the most self-affirming actions that take place in our sessions.

Here is an example with a little bit of the child's story: (In child work it is essential for me to know the child's "story"–his history, the life he comes from, the life he is in now. Without this understanding of the child's field, the experience lacks connection and substance.) Joey was found in an abandoned car when he was about 5 years old. He was tied to the seat with ropes, and it was concluded that he had been tied often and not allowed to move much, since his body showed evidence of rope burns, and his muscles were quite atrophied. He was close to death when found. After a time in the hospital, and two foster homes, he was adopted. (His birth parents were never found.) His adoptive parents brought him to therapy when he was ten years old due to his extremely hyperactive behavior (in spite of medication), as well as severe bouts of explosive and destructive anger.

Joey spent the first four sessions running around the room, picking things up and throwing them down. In these sessions, my focus was to establish a relationship and to help Joey sustain contact with me or something in the room, and so I attempted to join him by running around the room with him, picking up each object he threw down, making a brief comment about it, and chasing after him to the next item. I noticed that at the second session, he paused for a second as I made my comment, and by the fourth session he had slowed down considerably, and was actually responding and interacting with me. The relationship flourished and we participated together in a number of sensory, contact enhancing activities. Musical instruments were a great favorite with Joey and we spent some time communicating without words through the drums and other percussion instruments. He spent one whole session looking through a kaleidoscope, finding interesting designs, inviting me to look at them, and then waiting for me to find something he could look at. (A contactful episode *par excellence.*) Suddenly everything changed and he began to take control of the sessions in a new way. He spotted a set of handcuffs and set the stage for an enactment. "You are a robber and I am the policeman. You steal this wallet (an old one on the shelf) and I come after you and catch you." So we played this game with great gusto with various new directions from Joey. He was clearly in charge. At the second session as we played out the scenario, he said, "I wish I had some rope so I could tie you up." I brought in some rope at the next session and he gleefully tied me up. Once or twice I came out of my role to tell him the rope was too tight for me, and he quickly loosened it. We enacted this scene–me grabbing the wallet, he chasing me and grabbing me, putting on the handcuffs and tying me up–for several sessions. Joey added various elements and new dialogue at each session. When he tired of this game, Joey decided to play "principal's office." He surrounded himself with the staple machine, toy telephone, and various office-like items. He directed me to be a therapist who called him for advice about various children in his school. Joey delighted in this game as well, and we played it many sessions. During this time his mother reported that he was a transformed child–happy, no longer destructive, calm.

In between other play scenes Joey invented, we began to work on various other aspects of the therapy process, engaging in self-defining activities and focusing on emotional expression, particularly anger. He was quite responsive, and in fact often advised me, when we played principal's office, to tell my troubled child (usually a large teddy bear) to draw pictures of his angry feelings as well as other activities he himself had attempted. I saw Joey weekly for about one and a half years, including his parents every few sessions. At our last session Joey brought in a music tape he liked and, at his request, we danced to it the whole session with much abandon and laughter!

It is tempting to interpret Joey's dramatic play–much of it is quite obvious. Interpretive words seem superficial in comparison with the depth of his experience. A final note about Joey: He asked his mother why he was seeing me. She replied, "When you were little, you never had a chance to play. Violet is giving you that chance now."

Aggressive Energy

The term "aggressive energy" offends some people for it reminds them of hostile and destructive behavior. One of the definitions given in my dictionary for the word "aggressive" is "marked by driving forceful energy or initiative." It is this definition that I refer to when I use this term. It is the energy one uses to bite an apple. It is the energy one needs to express a strong feeling. It is an energy that gives one a feeling of power. It is an energy that gives one the self-support needed to take action. Children are confused about this kind of energy, equating it with trouble for themselves. Children who are fearful, timid, withdrawn and appear to have a fragile self are obviously lacking aggressive energy. Children who hit, punch, have overt power struggles and generally act "aggressive" lack this kind of energy as well. They are acting beyond their boundaries and not from a solid place within themselves.

I provide many opportunities for a child to experience aggressive energy and to feel comfortable with it. The self-support children gain from these activities is a pre-requisite for expression of suppressed emotions. The child who has been traumatized needs help in expressing buried emotions in order to work through that trauma, be it illness, the death of a loved one, a loss of a pet, a divorce, abuse, witnessing violence, or molestation. Since the child takes everything personally as part of her normal developmental process, when she undergoes trauma she feels responsible and blames herself for that trauma. This self-blame severely diminishes the self and makes it very difficult for the child to fully express the emotions that need to be expressed to promote healing. Further, the child developmentally takes in many negative introjects, faulty beliefs about herself. These negative messages fragment the child, inhibit healthy growth and integration, and are the roots of her self-deprecating attitude, low self-esteem, and feelings of shame. A beginning in turning this disheartening process around is to help the child develop a strong sense of self, which in and of itself gives one a sense of well-being and positive feeling of self. Self-support activities are essential for this task.

The aggressive energy activities have several requirements to be effective. First, they must take place in contact with the therapist. Having the child engage in these experiences by herself at home, or as the therapist passively looks on, does not have the same impact as when the therapist is actively engaged with the child. This engagement is required in order for the child to feel comfortable with the internal force she may have feared. Second, these activities take place in a safe container. The child knows that the therapist is in charge and will not allow any harm to interfere with the experience. Third, there is a spirit of fun and playfulness in the interaction. Fourth, the play is exaggerated. Since the child has avoided this kind of energy (whether retroflecting or deflecting), she must go beyond the center point before she can come back to balance.

Aggressive energy activities can involve smashing clay, shooting dart guns, pounding drums, smashing figures or cars together, puppets eating each other, having a Bataca fight, and so forth. There are some games that promote this kind of energy, though unfortunately there aren't too many. Two games I have that were excellent aggressive energy games, but are no longer manufactured, are *Hawaiian Punch* and *Whack Attack*. A game called Splat, where play-do bugs are smashed, comes close. *Don't Break The Ice* is a game suitable for children who are fearful of demonstrating this energy at first. Hitting the "ice" with a small mallet is quite mild. Let me emphasize again that to experience aggressive energy in a therapeutic context requires involvement of the therapist with the child.

Janine was a ten-year-old girl who had suffered much trauma including physical and sexual abuse, and abandonment. She had been in several group and foster home placements, and finally was adopted into a new family. Her process was to be as good as possible and smile at all times. Before I could begin to help Janine express outwardly her myriad feelings, including anger and grief, I knew that she needed to gain a stronger sense of self and to feel her aggressive energy. The turning point came with the puppets. One day I asked her to pick any puppet, and uncharacteristically she picked an alligator with a big mouth– (her usual choice would be a cute kitten or bunny). I picked up another alligator and said, "Hello. You sure have a big mouth and lots of teeth. I bet you're going to bite me." "Oh, no!" Janine's puppet answered. "I am your friend. We can play together." "Oh yeah?" I said, as I inched my puppet closer to her mouth. "I know you're going to bite me." Janine backed her puppet away as I came closer, but soon my puppet was directly into her puppet's mouth. Almost involuntarily, Janine's alligator lightly closed onto my puppet. "Ow! Ow! You bit me!" I yelled as my puppet dramatically dropped to the floor. "Do that again! Do that again!" Janine shouted. And so we did, over and over, bringing in other "bad" puppets as the shark and the wolf for her to bite. Not quite midway into this play, Janine was biting my various puppets with great force and our puppets engaged in a great struggle before mine dropped to the floor. At the end of this session Janine was smiling broadly (not her usual forced smile), stood up straight and left with a flourish. In subsequent sessions we successfully began to deal with her suppressed emotions.

Danny, eight-years-old, had been witness to violence in his home until his mother fled, taking him with her and leaving behind all that he was familiar with, including his father. Danny appeared to have difficulty adjusting to his new environment: he was disruptive at school, bullied other children, and physically and verbally abused his mother. In my office Danny was terrified of any aggressive energy activities. He refused to have a Bataca fight with me, and would command me to cease and desist if my puppet spoke aggressively to his.

As Danny felt safer and more comfortable with me, he began tentatively to suggest some of the more energetic actions. Eventually, he initiated games of attack with me involving *He-Man* figures, shooting at a target with a rubber dart gun, and other similar games. Simultaneously, his behavior at school and at home dramatically improved.

Many therapists have argued that children who have witnessed violence, particularly in the home, should not be introduced to "violent" play in the therapist's office. These children are particularly restricted and cut off from themselves. They blame themselves for the chaos and family disruption. They feel guilty if they are angry at having to leave their homes, or feel sad to leave their fathers. At the same time, they want to protect their mothers. They are so confused, that the only recourse is to restrain themselves and push down their emotions. With Danny, the organism, in its quest for health, broke through his boundaries in unacceptable aggressive behavior. I believe that these children need opportunities to find the power within themselves in order that they may be freed from the constraints that inhibit their ability to accept and express their varied emotions, and to live freely and joyfully.

Emotional Expression

To help children unlock buried emotions and to learn healthy ways to express their emotions in daily life is not a simple matter. A variety of creative, expressive, projective techniques assist in this work. These techniques involve drawings, collage, clay, fantasy and imagery, creative dramatics, music, movement, storytelling, the sand tray, photography, the use of metaphors and a variety of games. Many of these techniques have been used for hundreds of years in many cultures for communication and self-expression. You might say we are giving back to children modes of expression that are inherently theirs. These modalities lend themselves to powerful projections that can evoke strong feelings. Everything the child creates is a projection of something inside of her, or at the very least, something that interests her. So if a child tells a story you can be sure that there is material in that story that reflects the child's life or who she is, and expresses some need, wish, want or feeling that the child has.

If a child creates a sand tray scene with the varied miniatures that are displayed on shelves, the very act of projecting this symbolic material is in and of itself therapeutic. Something within the child has been expressed. If the child tells a story about his scene, even more of himself is expressed on perhaps another level. If the child can own various aspects of the scene, integration takes place at a much quicker pace.

For example, Jimmy, who is seven, is very absorbed in making a sand scene. I can see as I watch him that all of his energy is devoted to his task. He is fully present and contactful with his task. I do not interrupt or talk, unless he asks me to help him find a certain object. I watch the clock so that I can pace the session in order to make sure he can make some kind of closure before the time is up. I may say, "You need to finish now," (although most children announce, "I'm done," with plenty of time to spare.) If we don't have time to talk about his scene, that will be fine. I can see by his energy level that whatever he is doing is very important to him and needs to be done. Now Jimmy looks at me and tells me his is finished. There are ten minutes left to the session. He says, "This is the best I've ever done!" Jimmy, who loves to do sand scenes, says this each time he does one, indicating to me his satisfaction and pleasure. He describes the scene to me. There are numerous monster-type figures in conflict encounters with each other. There is a cave with some crystals in it. There are many, many trees and hidden among the trees is a tiny green caterpillar. Jimmy looks at his scene with perspective and articulates what makes sense to him. (Most children will look at their scenes and attempt to make sense out of them. an important part of the integrative process. Children always try to make sense of what goes on in their lives, and feel frustrated and confused much of the time. They need to experience the satisfaction and power of making sense of their own creations, at least.)

Jimmy says that the monsters are fighting each other over the treasure in the cave, that he put lots of trees in because he likes trees so much, and that one can't always see things that are under them like the hidden caterpillar. I ask why the monsters are fighting and he answers that he doesn't know but maybe to get the treasure. "None of them will get the treasure because they are too busy fighting. But the caterpillar is safe because the monsters don't see him." (He is now developing a story/metaphor.) I then ask which figure or object is he and, after careful consideration, he says that he is the caterpillar. (If we had had more time I might have had a dialogue with the caterpillar.) "What about the caterpillar makes you want to be it?" I ask. Without hesitation he says, "Because it is hidden and safe." I then ask in a very soft voice, "Jimmy, do you wish you had a safe place like that in your life?" He lowers his head, looks at his feet, and says softly, "Yes, I need one." He then begins to chatter about my Polaroid camera and the picture I will take of his scene. I know that his resistance has surfaced, and he has turned his attention elsewhere. Whatever has happened is just about enough for him at this time.

There are many therapeutic levels in this piece of work. Jimmy has expressed his actual life metaphorically in this scene, something he would never be able to articulate at his age: the conflict, the danger, the goodness, and hope that is inaccessible, the feeling of being small and powerless, the need to be safe and hidden, his fears and his anger. Of course these are my interpretations, though probably fairly accurate since I know about Jimmy and his life. My interpretations are not therapeutic, however. What is healing is Jimmy's expression of what he needed to express in his scene–understood by him perhaps on a very deep intuitive level, the feeling of safety in my office, the easy relationship that we have developed, the acceptance and respect he feels from me, the knowledge that there are limits and boundaries that I set and take responsibility for (as, for example, time), and his feeling of control and power within those limits to do what he needed to do without interruption. What is also therapeutic is our interaction regarding his scene, my interest in it and my acceptance of it as a serious piece of work. I ask questions, but I do not push for more than he will give me. For me the most therapeutic aspect of this session was Jimmy's statement about needing a safe place of his own. His expression, which surfaced from deep within, is now fertile ground for us to explore at a later time, rather than a hidden feeling blocking healthy organismic functioning. The resistance that came up, evidenced by Jimmy changing the subject, told me that Jimmy reached his limit in this piece of work, and that he did not have enough support to go further. Time, too, may have added to this resistance, since he knew our time was just about up. In a sense he grounded himself.

Often when the time is up I may need to help children ground themselves by asking superficial questions, such as, "What do you think you're having for dinner tonight?" It is particularly essential to help children come back to earth if they become excited and high in the course of our sessions.

Assisting children in emotional expression often has a sequence of its own. Sometimes children have pushed their feelings down so far that they are completely disconnected from the whole concept. So when this becomes evident, we begin talking *about* feelings. What are feelings anyway? We explore, cognitively, all of the aspects of anger, grief, fear, and joy. One can feel mild annoyance, for example, or, at the other end of the continuum, blind rage. Then there are body states that often labeled as feelings, such as frustration, boredom, confusion, anxiety, impatience, and loneliness. We examine these states as well. We look at pictures, play games, make faces, move our bodies to drum beats, act out various feelings, use puppets, draw pictures, use clay, make lists, tell stories, read stories–all related to feelings and body states. Language plays an important role too. As children grow and develop mastery in language, they are much more able to be aware of and express the nuances of their feelings in a more satisfying way.

An eight-year-old girl who had been severely physically abused by her father was unable to express any feelings at all. It was as if she had no understanding of what feelings were. A game we played called *The Happy Face Game* mystified her. It consists of cards with various faces and no matter which card she picked, she said the same thing: "I feel happy when it's my birthday. I feel mad when it's my birthday. I feel sad when it's my birthday." Even though she listened with some interest to my statements when I picked a card, she continued her birthday statements. We played many games about feelings, as indicated above. One day we were playing school at her request, and as the teacher she told me to write something that made me sad, mad and happy. While I did this I noticed that she was busy writing her own sentences on the chalkboard on the wall. She wrote, "I am sad because my cat ran away and I don't know where she is. I am mad because my mother wouldn't let me watch TV last night. I am happy because my father doesn't hit me now."

Children don't always move from talking about feelings to expressing their own feelings. We may use projections as a forum for expression. The drawings, the stories, the sand tray scenes will be replete with material to draw from in helping the child own her own feelings. For example, Terri, a 13-year-old girl drew a snake in a desert after a fantasy exercise. I asked her to be the snake and describe her existence as that snake. Naturally, there was some resistance to this request. I said, "I know it's crazy but just say "I'm a snake." Imagine the snake is a puppet and you have to speak for it, give it a voice." So she said, "I'm a snake" (rolling her eyes.) I immediately engaged the snake in a dialogue, asking it questions as "where do you live? What do you do all day?" and so forth. Finally I said, "What's it like being out there in the desert by yourself, snake?" After some pause, she answered in a very low voice, head down, "Lonely." The change in her energy, body posture and voice quality told me that something inside of her was being left unsaid. So I said very softly, "Do you, as a girl, ever feel that way?" She looked up at me and as I held her gaze, she burst into tears. She continued at that point to describe her feelings of isolation and desperation.

I'd like to emphasize a few points here. First, it is very important for me to ask important questions in a very soft, almost casual manner. Second, I have learned that when children cry it is mortifying for them (especially for a 13-year-old). If I focus on the tears, as I might with an adult, I will probably facilitate the closing down process. So I keep on talking.

"Tell me about your loneliness, Terri," and she did. When the session was over, Terri drew a quick figure next to the snake. "That snake is really me, isn't it?" she said. Not all children will identify so readily with their projections. Often I need to say, "Is there anything about your story that fits for you?" or "Do you ever feel like you want to attack someone like the lion in your scene?"

Since emotions have a body counterpart, we spend some time helping children become more aware of their own body reactions. As children become attuned to their bodies, they can often use these responses as clues. For example, 16-year-old Susan, stated that she never felt angry. We did a fantasy experience where I asked her to imagine something that could make her or someone angry and to notice what she felt in her body. She then drew a picture of a cloud over a head. She labeled this "The cloud of confusion." I suggested that she use this as a clue–that whenever she felt confused to check to see if something was happening that she didn't like. ("Don't like" is a watered down, less threatening expression for some children.) If she could know she was angry, she could then choose an appropriate way of expressing it.

The child and I discuss at length various ways she might express angry feelings privately without bringing further trouble to herself. By this time I have hopefully convinced them of the organism's need to rid itself of this negative energy, rather than push it down. We make a list of these activities and practice them in the office. Some of the more popular methods include tearing magazines, drawing a face and jumping on it, hitting a designated pillow, screaming into a pillow, running or some other physical activity while focusing on the angry feeling, writing an unmailed letter to the object of the anger, and so forth. It is necessary for children to have outlets such as these. Direct expression is certainly ideal, but difficult for all of us and especially for children. When they attempt to directly tell a teacher or a parent what is making them angry, they are accused of having a bad attitude and often punished. Children do tend to speak in a louder voice when angry; they have not yet learned the art of diplomacy.

The child generally will go to great lengths to avoid dealing with deep feelings–feelings that are kept hidden, and interfere with healthy development. He very rarely says, "Today I'd like to work on my father." The child has so little support to deal with the intensity and weight of these feelings, that he will suppress them to such an extent that he actually has little awareness of them. However, his behavior and life process are greatly affected by these feelings, and helping children uncover them and express them is essential in therapeutic work.

Eleven-year-old John exhibited behaviors and symptoms that were interfering with his life. His grades were falling, he became forgetful, often had headaches and stomachaches. When I asked his mother when he began to have these symptoms, she vaguely stated that it had been going on for a couple of years, but actually had worsened lately. When I asked if anything had happened two years before, she said his brother had died, but she felt that they had all handled their grief quite well. I know that children need a lot of assistance to go through grief, and they are so good at pushing feelings down that they are often seen as doing well. Further, I know that changes in behavior and new symptoms appear gradually, and become accelerated as time goes by. A child does not say, "This is not working for me. I'll try something else." The behaviors and symptoms intensify and increase. At one of our sessions, I asked John to make a clay figure of his brother and to talk to him. He became quite agitated and refused. I gently asked, "What are you thinking about, John?" (I rarely ask children what they are feeling, since they usually say "fine" or "I don't know.") John shouted, "I *hate* those doctors!" I quickly put a lump of clay in front of him and handed him a clay mallet. "Give it to those doctors," I said. John began to smash the clay with the mallet. I became a sort of cheerleader, urging him on. (This is not a time for the therapist to stay quiet.) He smashed with lots of energy. "Yeah, give it to them. Tell them why you're mad at them." John began shouting, "I hate you. You wouldn't let me see my brother. I never saw him again. I hate you." After awhile I asked John to make a figure of his brother. He made a figure in the hospital bed. "If you could say anything you wanted to him, what would you say?" Tears came down his face has he told his brother how much he missed him. There was silence as he intently looked at his clay brother. He said softly, "Goodbye," picked up the figure and kissed it, gently laid it down, and said to me, "Do we have time for a game of Connect 4?" We spent a few more sessions focusing on his brother, and John's behavior dramatically changed. He is now a happy, productive, well-adjusted boy.

Self-Nurturing

A vital step in the therapeutic process is what I call self-nurturing work. In essence my goal is to help children be more accepting, caring and actively nurturing to themselves. This is a difficult task since children are brought up with the idea that it is selfish and wrong to care about the self. If a child says, "I'm very good at this," she may be accused of bragging. The children I work with have introjected, swallowed whole, taken in many faulty messages about themselves from a very early age at a time they did not have the maturity and cognitive ability to discriminate what fit for them or did not fit. These introjects cause children to restrict and inhibit aspects of the self and interfere with healthful growth. These negative self-messages tend to remain with them throughout life, and particularly emerge under stress. Children developmentally, in their egocentricity, blame themselves for the traumas that occur in their lives.

I find that even if parents change their manner of relating to and communicating with their children, their faulty belief system persists, often going underground to emerge at times of tension and pressure.

> Even a young child, particularly the disturbed child has a very well developed critical self. He develops powerful negative introjects and often does a better job of criticizing himself than his parents do. This judgmental stance, often well hidden from others, is detrimental to healthful growth. The child may say to himself, "I should be a better boy," but the enactment of this wish is beyond his power and comprehension. The will to "be better" enhances his despair. Self-acceptance of all of one's parts, even the most hateful, is a vital component of unimpaired, sound development (Oaklander, 1982, p. 74).

Fragmentation is a disastrous result of self-deprecation. Integration begins to take place when we can help the child begin to learn to accept the parts of herself that she hates, and to understand the function and purpose of those parts. Through this process, children acquire skills for treating themselves well.

This is a revolutionary concept for most children, since, as indicated above, they have learned that it is egotistical, self-centered and frowned upon to treat oneself well. They will then look to others to do this job, and feel let down when it doesn't happen, further reinforcing the negative introject. Adolescents feel guilty when they do nice things for themselves, which debilitates rather than strengthens.

The first part of the self-nurturing process involves digging out those hateful parts of self. Though fragmentation prevails, the child tends to identify herself totally with each hateful part. If the message is "I'm stupid," she feels that stupidity is her whole identity. Comprehending that the hateful part is only one aspect of herself is usually a new concept. Once a part is identified, the child may be asked to draw it, make it out clay, or find a puppet that represents that part. The part is fully described, portrayed, and exaggerated. The child is encouraged to talk to that part, and often critical, angry statements are directed at the hateful demon. In this way, she expresses her aggression outwardly, rather than turning it in toward the self. With this kind of outpouring of energy, she gains self-support for the next step that involves finding a nurturing component within the self. Sometimes the hateful part becomes a younger child, about four or five-years old, an age when children absorb many negative self-messages. The child then dialogues with this younger self. Realizing that the part is actually a belief from a much younger age often helps the child to develop a nurturing stance. Sometimes we use a projective technique such as a fairy godmother puppet that is loving, accepting, and nurturing to the hateful part. The child is then encouraged to repeat the fairy godmother's words to see how it feels to say them to himself.

Eleven-year-old Joseph expressed much anger and disgust at a drawing of the clumsy part of himself that he named "Mr. Klutz." Mr. Klutz couldn't do anything right and fell down and bumped into things all the time. As the fairy godmother puppet, he told Mr. Klutz after awhile, "At least you try things!." Joseph turned to me in wonderment and said, "That's right, I do try things!"

A piece of integration took place at that moment right before my eyes. I suggested to Joseph that he imagine his fairy godmother sitting on his shoulder each time he did something klutzy, and she told him that she liked him even when he fell or bumped into things, and she was glad he tried. Joseph reported in later sessions that he really wasn't as clumsy as he originally thought.

Seven-year-old Lisa thought she was stupid because she had trouble learning to read. Her fairy godmother puppet said, "You're pretty good in math, so you're not so dumb as you think." (These were Lisa's own projected words.) Lisa was able to say these words to the drawing of her dumb self, without the use of the puppet, with sincerity. She reported later that she was reading pretty well now.

Twelve-year-old Zachary admitted that deep down he felt he was a very bad person and deserved his abuse and abandonment. He made a figure of a four-year-old Zach, the age that he remembered his first beating. It was not difficult for him to see that this small figure of a small child had not deserved such treatment, and he was able to talk to his little boy self in a nurturing way. I asked Zachary to find something at home to represent this young child part of him, a pillow, a stuffed animal, a ball, and to talk to him every night before he went to sleep, telling him what a nice kid he was and that he did not deserve the beatings. I especially wanted him to tell this part that he would always be with him, that he would never leave him. We practiced this in the office after I explained that, even though this exercise seemed strange and weird, it was extremely important that he follow these directions. He did as directed, and exhibited a decided improvement in his demeanor.

Persistent Inappropriate Process

Generally the inappropriate behaviors that have brought children into therapy have diminished or completely disappeared by the time we have worked through the various components of the therapy process. After several months of therapy, Janine gradually grew to trust others and develop a strong sense of self. She began to express her emotions clearly and transformed herself from a meek, timid child into one who could comfortably stand up for herself. Joseph, who had presented himself as severely hyperactive, no longer needed to move incessantly in order to avoid contact. He now had good contact skills, and was calm and present in most situations. We were able to focus on the deeper emotions of anger and grief that lay within him.

There are times, however, when certain behaviors tend to persist, and it is at this time I focus on them. When a child initially comes into therapy, I do not confront the behaviors. I don't say, "Let's talk about your fighting." I might ask the child to describe the experience of fighting, paint his feelings during the fighting, or draw a picture of one of his fights. But we don't discuss the fighting with the intent of changing his behavior at that time. (I do confront trauma fairly early on, however.) I see the behavior as a symptom of something deeper. When the child does not appear to be happier, stronger and functioning well in his life, I need to first evaluate my work carefully. If the child and I have a good relationship, he is able to sustain contact, has been responsive, and has shown a fairly healthy process during our time together, then I know I need to focus on that behavior that is still causing concern and distress.

Since Gestalt therapy is a process-oriented therapy, rather than a content-focused therapy, helping children become aware of their particular process takes precedence over modifying the behavior through specific problem solving, rewards, lectures, or other types of interventions. It is through the awareness and experience of their actions that change begins to take place.

Change within this context is often paradoxical in nature. Beiser (1979) states, "Change occurs when one becomes what he is, not when he tries to become what he is not." Following this principle I will devise activities and experiments to direct the child's awareness toward his behavior. Prerequisite to these experiments is the child's new feelings of self-worth and self-support, as well as skills for appropriately expressing his feelings.

Twelve-year-old James was very shy. He lived in a large, chaotic family and somehow had been lost in this atmosphere. I worked with the family as well as James individually, and though much good work was accomplished, James remained painfully shy with other children. A therapeutic group would have been helpful, but one was not available. Together we delved deeper into his shyness. He made a clay sculpture representing his shy self, and one for the self he wished for. He discovered that his shy self was quite young and had some poignant dialogues with his little boy self. He discovered that he had had very good reason to be shy at that time as a way of coping and protecting himself.

I devised an experiment whereby he would approach a group of children at school at lunchtime, and pay full attention to the feelings in his body and the thoughts in his head. This was a painful experiment, but with his newly developed sense of self, he agreed to carry it through. At the next session he drew a picture of his feelings using different colors, and listed his thoughts: "They don't like me. I'm not good enough." James was surprised to recognize these thoughts as old messages about himself. A further experiment was suggested involving taking the younger James by the hand (figuratively) and talking to one boy in his class about an assignment. We talked about rejection, something he usually expected. And so with my support and with the idea that this was an experiment, James carried out the assignment with great success. Further such experiments along with their successes helped him realize that he could discard that old, shy self.

Ending of Therapy

I am often asked about how I know when it is time to stop the therapy. If the child is doing well in his life, and our work has taken on an aura of just hanging out together, it's time to stop. If the child, who once couldn't wait to come to the sessions, becomes very busy in her life with friends and activities and says she doesn't have time to come, it's probably time to stop. If the child is doing well in life and our sessions are still fruitful, it is

NOT time to stop. If nothing much is happening in our sessions and symptoms persist at home, it is time for me to take a good hard look at what I'm doing or not doing. If resistance comes up and persists, even though I know there is more work to be done, we sometimes have to stop for a while. This often happens with children who have undergone severe trauma, particularly molestation. The child can only work through certain aspects of the trauma at her specific developmental level. If a four-year-old has been traumatized in some way, she may work through her anxieties and feelings over that trauma, but only to the extent of her four-year-old cognitive and emotional abilities.

At various stages of her life, issues may present themselves related to that early trauma, causing inappropriate behaviors or symptoms to emerge, calling for further therapy suitable for her current developmental level. Further, children often reach a plateau in their work and need time to integrate what has been accomplished. Sometimes parents take their children out of therapy for a variety of reasons, such as financial and time constraints or insurance company limitations. When this happens I must respect the parents' wishes and leave the door open for subsequent work.

The length of time of therapy with a child is quite variable depending on many factors. Sometimes we work for a few sessions, sometimes three or four months or a school year, and sometimes for two years. Regardless of the length of time or the reason for ending, special attention is given to closure. Closure is not taken lightly–it is an important aspect of the therapeutic process. In a sense, therapy has been the foreground; a vital figure in the child's life, and the completion of this gestalt allows the child to move on to a new place. As needs are met, new masteries achieved, new discoveries made, blocked feelings expressed, there is a period of homeostasis and satisfaction. This is closure, and from this place, the child can grow and develop in healthy ways.

Our last session can represent a rite of passage. To honor this event, we pay homage to our sessions. We talk about all the various activities that have taken place. The child and I look at her folder together much as a photograph album, remembering the various drawings and sand scene photos. Depending on the child's age we decide on the final event. We may make goodbye cards for each other, or the child might choose a favorite game to play. We talk about endings and beginnings. I have asked adolescents to create a sand scene representing our time together, or the feelings accompanying the ending or one thing that stands out for them from our time together. Some children will draw pictures of their mixed feelings: sad to be leaving and happy to be leaving. Such drawings can relieve the confusion they feel ever having opposing feelings. What we do to honor our final meeting is a cooperative decision.

Parents and Families

The focus of this chapter has been the therapeutic process with children and adolescents. Working with parents and the family is certainly part of that process, though at a different level. I do, as a general rule, see the parents with the child at least every four to six weeks, if I am seeing the child individually. I will bring in other members of the family as necessary, sometimes seeing the child and his siblings without the parents. Occasionally, I have seen a child alone every other week and with her mother or both parents the alternate week.

Educating parents about the therapy process is essential. Unless parents understand and know what I am doing, they can easily sabotage the work. Parent education becomes a vital part of the therapy process and most parents are grateful for it. If the parents are hostile and angry, I must honor that resistance, offer my support and continue my attempt to establish a working relationship with them. I know that often the hostility is a mask for their own pain, anxiety and feelings of failure as parents. If parents refuse to participate at all, but continue to bring in their child because they must, as by court order, I will continue to work with the child, often addressing the issue of their parents' attitude with the child. Every session can give that child inner strength to cope with his family.

Even when parents willingly participate in sessions, there is a decided difference in family work and individual child work. Children are certainly relieved and happy when parents change dysfunctional ways of relating to them, but often the negative introjects are just buried deeper only to surface at a later time. The child does not automatically become emotionally healthy when his family begins to make changes. He still needs to gain a stronger sense of self, express buried emotions, learn how to get his needs met or to meet his own needs appropriately, learn to be self-accepting and self-nurturing, and begin to learn how to manage faulty messages of the self that have already become ingrained as part of his belief system about himself.

References

Buber, Martin (1958). *I and thou*. New York, NY: Scribner.

Fagan, J., & Shepherd, I. (1970). *Gestalt therapy now: Theory, techniques, applications*. New York, NY: Harper & Row.

Beiser, A. (1970). The paradoxical theory of change. In J. Fagan & I. Shepherd (Eds.), *Gestalt therapy now: Theory, techniques, applications*, (pp. 77-80). New York, NY: Harper & Row.

Oaklander, V. (1978/1988). *Windows to our children: A gestalt therapy approach to children and adolescents*. Highland, NY: The Gestalt Journal Press.

3

Physical Process Work with Children and Adolescents

Denise Tervo

Connie

Connie was a five-year-old child with large, brown, doe-like eyes, a huge heart, and a wounded body. She came to me because of her withdrawn behavior at the preschool that she attended three days a week. As a special needs consultant, my job was to work with the school's children and provide the individual psychotherapy that they needed above and beyond the therapeutic classroom where they resided day by day. Connie came as a wounded bird, but with all the mastery of a slippery fish in getting her way one way or another.

Connie's mother was blind and had not been able to take care of her properly. From the time she was three years old, it had been Connie 's responsibility to negotiate welfare, access transportation, and obtain special help from neighbors for her mother. While her mother loved Connie very much, Connie had been the caretaker most of the time. Thus their bond was strong, but not one that was especially healthy for either of them. Connie's mother was also concerned that her mother's second boyfriend may have sexually assaulted Connie. He was not Connie's father, and Connie had been terrified of him. Mother's present boyfriend did not want to have anything to do with Connie. Once again, because of her mother's immature affections, Connie was emotionally out of the picture in her family system.

Connie, at five years old, had been possibly sexually abused, displaced, and abandoned. It is no wonder that her large, doe-like eyes were constantly scanning the room. She was constantly vigilant underneath the outwardly calm exterior of a child who seemed much older than her years.

Connie's only outward signs of disturbance were found in her periodic masturbation, bed-wetting, and pseudo-mature stance in the world.

When we first met I felt as if I was talking to a twent- year-old in a five-year-old's body. She was pleasant, poised, and had a half smile on her face as she entered my room. I had observed her in the classroom several times, so I was not an unfamiliar face. Yet, her degree of comfort with me was out of proportion for most children her age when first meeting a stranger. She commented on the flowers on my table, and made herself at home. Connie sat perfectly still in the little chair while scanning all of the toys on the shelves with her eyes.

While she was appropriately sitting in a chair, being "a good girl" as she had been taught to do by her mother, Connie's energy had clearly shifted out through her eyes. Connie was drinking in all the specific details of the toys in the room in her repeated scanning of her environment. Of course, she was the daughter of a blind mother. Connie had clearly learned. to see for two people. In contrast, I was equally interested in the stillness, almost deadness of her body and physical frame as she sat erect in the chair. She looked like a little soldier in perfect "ladylike fashion." It was difficult to notice her breathing. When watching her I wondered if she had learned to sneak breaths, so as not to disturb her environment. I later learned that my curiosity had proved correct. When they had been living with the mother's physically violent second partner, both Connie and her mother had learned to be extremely quiet, so as not to wake the sleeping giant monster.

When using my eyes and "drinking her in" as she seemed to do with my room, I became aware of my own body, my movements, and tensions. While matching my body stance with hers and sitting as she did, I was able to gain some very interesting information about the way my body reacted. I experienced being in a very tight box with my skin as the frame. The box felt as if it was both a protective shell and a prison. All of my energy was flowing out of my eyes. I seemed to be drawing in information from my left, and watching the environment for any possible movements or sudden moves with my right eye.

When shuttling back to being an observer of Connie, I was able to notice subtleties in her physical frame as well. She was leaning slightly forward with her left side. Her head was forward as if trying to move closer to the toys, while continuing to remain seated as a "good girl." The right side of her body was perfectly erect, almost soldier-like. She sat in the position of attention, as if almost ready to be called into battle at any time. I became aware of her frequent quick glances at me out of the corner of her right eye.

How interesting to have a sentinel on guard at all times to watch me! Yet, she presented herself as this perfectly calm, poised, pseudo-adult who could ask me about the curios in my room. This was our first meeting, so I wanted to honor her boundaries and let her get acclimated in the room. I kept my observations to myself, to be used at a future date. Interestingly, my awareness of Connie's left/right body splits would go on to be a major focus in my work with her over the next several years. How Connie split herself into pieces to keep herself safe was her creative adjustment. It was a way of managing a violent, chaotic environment.

Over the next several months, Connie and I would go on to explore ways that she had split herself to keep herself alive inside while maintaining a cool exterior. Her terror and rage were submerged deep into her body, lest she express them and be hurt more. In addition, Connie maintained a left/right split that helped maintain her normal five-year-old curiosity and excitement of the world while also vigorously scanning to be aware of the next possible blows from her stepfather. Connie also maintained an upper body/lower body split. While she would be cognitively focused, curious, and active in her head, below her shoulders Connie seemed frozen into her soldier-like position of both submission and control. Her multiple body splits, or deadening and disowning parts of herself, are body processes that are frequently found when working with abuse survivors.

Using many expressive art materials, exaggerated breath, sound development, and large body movements with Connie, we were able to help her regain and rediscover the cut off, disowned parts of herself. Connie was a very sensitive, kinesthetic as well as visual learner. Over the next several sessions Connie and I joined in her visual and kinesthetic world. As we worked together with clay we squeezed it, and began putting sounds and words to our work. As I continued to talk about her body structure and report back to her how I felt or what I did, she became fascinated with my *seeing* of her, not just in her eyes seeing out. We began to play around with the disowned body splits and in a fun way began to reclaim parts of herself. My seeing her was a reorganization of her perceptual field from her blind mother.

Many months later Connie became more physically expressive in our sessions. Connie began verbalizing her fear of her previous abuser and aggressively began making penises out of clay and destroying them. We had developed a strong trusting relationship and Connie no longer had to visually keep tabs on me. Connie was able to discern when she needed her sentinel on guard, and when she could breath and move easily. Connie no longer had to split herself into parts She could focus all of her awareness and energy on her own needs. Within our safe environment Connie was finally able to express her rage and hurt over the violence and abuse in her life.

Introduction/Overview

The Gestalt approach emphasizes the way we organize our whole field of experiences. This field includes our internal feelings and experiences, external behavior, spiritual feelings, thoughts, relationships and our body self. This approach is holistic, which means that we believe that our organization of experiences is unitary, in some important sense the same, on all these levels. It is through this organized contact that we meet our needs, survive, learn and grow.

The previous scenario of Connie described above and the following descriptive case examples are intended to help the reader experience physical process work not only cognitively, but "in the flesh." Physical process work is not in addition to Gestalt practice, but a natural extension and enrichment of Gestalt's holistic attention to the client's embodied self. Even though several of these case examples have similar life stresses, such as the death or loss of a significant person or physical/sexual abuse, each client's experience of the field and their own physical process is different.

Gestalt Therapy/Gestalt Physical Process

The following is a brief description of Gestalt physical process theory and terminology to assist the reader in a smoother understanding of the case examples and physical process work with children and adolescents that is shared in this chapter.

Gestalt therapy with children/adolescents has frequently employed a more unified field approach of working with the child within the context of a larger system field (school, family, community). A child's experiences occur at all levels. Sometimes the child/adolescent is not able to make organized contact with either herself (intrapersonal issue) and/or her environment (interpersonal). Hence the child/adolescent must return to the self in a creative adaptation onto herself instead of the environment For example, it is not safe to express anger in a violent family system, so the child learns to creatively adapt and pull his own hair when angry (retroflection). Or, instead of taking a risk and feeling her mother's disappointment about her new Grunge boyfriend, the adolescent bites her tongue, tightens her neck muscles, and changes the subject (deflection). In both cases there is the environmental level that is impacting the child and the intrapersonal (within self) resolution or action by the child as a response to the environment.

In theory, many different therapeutic approaches share this belief of working with a child/adolescent within the context of a larger system. Yet, many of them neglect to focus on the body, on how children organize and give a concrete form to (embody) our experiences. And thus they may miss or neglect a powerful resource and knowledge bank for understanding people and for opening up learning and experimenting with change. They may overlook a source of knowledge about how we hold and organize ourselves physically and energetically in the world and how we can live differently.

In Gestalt physical process, we believe that no matter what body experience we focus on at a given moment, we are really attending to all dimensions of the child's experience as they are integrated at that moment within a living, dynamic whole. Thus, how I am holding my body at the moment has something to say about my relationships from the past, in the present, and possibly in the future. How I hold my body and move or breathe has something to say about my beliefs about my world and myself.

I believe that all relationships have some physical basis and expression. The child interacts with others and is in relationship to others through her body. There is nothing that does not happen physically. Speaking, breathing, expressing feelings, moving all occur in her body. A child/adolescent's creative ability is to manage to modulate what he/she is physically feeling and is able to express into his/her environment. The child's behavior and range of movement is modified based upon what the child knows, or believes, the field can tolerate. Tensions, holding breath, subtle body movements or "stuck or frozen" places of holding in her body are cues to ways the child may be embodying the conflict between her internal sensations and her experience of her field. The child/adolescent is in relationship to the others over time. She makes or is in the experience of self and other in the immediate moment. Contact is the relationship that occurs in and through the child's body. All our thoughts feelings and sensations are experienced in our body over time and in relationship to others. Thus, both child development and relationships are bodily events.

Gestalt Physical Process: Theoretical Overview

The purpose of Gestalt physical process is to increase the child/adolescent's depth and range of awareness. The goal is to broaden the range of the child's ability to support and ground his or her self (self-functions), and to increase his sense of choicefulness and capacity to make contact with his environment and his or her self.

Attention to body process affects ongoing contact in the environment. While working with a person, not on a body, the therapist helps the child make contact or awarely experience the disowned aspects of his or her self and learn to understand body tensions and stuck points or other "resistances" as part of the self, not as outside of the self boundary. With the therapist's assistance, the child /adolescent gains a more expansive understanding of his body as a support for his own ground (self support), as well as a support for making contact with his environment (school, family, peers). By assisting the child/adolescent in increasing her range of movement, releasing structural tension and holding awareness of disowned parts, the child/adolescent has a better range of choice and empowerment in the field.

Gestalt bodywork involves working with the "embodiment" or comprehensive essence of organization of the self, not just fixing the body. Gestalt theory focuses on the experiences of the child/adolescence's body as a way to experience herself as a physical, whole organism rather than split into parts (i.e., body and head, or feeling her left side, and being numb on the right side of her body.)

Physical process is a creative adaptation to support or maintain the child/adolescent within his environmental field. Gestalt physical process focuses on a variety of creative ways in which the child/adolescent learns to adjust his or her self to an environment that is not supportive for the whole child. These adjustments have been called resistances (Perls, Hefferline, & Goodman, 1951) or self-modulations (Wheeler, 1991). The child/adolescent may lose his or her bodily sensations (desensitization) and become numb or cut off from his body, as in the upcoming case of Erin. The body may become an "it" which is not claimed, and does not listen, or binge eats (projection). Gestalt physical process work may focus on ways in which a child/adolescent lacks definition of his body as a focus. In Gestalt therapy, we see this lack of definition as confluence or lack of figure formation. In other instances, the body functions are inhibited (retroflected) and a child/adolescent learns to contain and hold energy in his body, instead of acting out in the environment as in the case of Johnny and his dad. In the process of deflection body experiences may not be attended to because of seemingly more demanding themes or figures as in the case of Lisa. Introjection is the process by which the child internalizes the parents' feelings or beliefs about the child's body thereby loosing identification with his own felt experience.

Physical Process Work

Physical process work emphasizes bridging the mind/body split that has been supported in the past in Western culture and in the medical model (Kepner, 1987). Physical process work with children and adolescents enhances body and energy awareness within the framework of normal development and facilitates a more natural and fluid self-expression in relation to others. This phenomenological and experiential way of working with children/adolescents further enhances their contact with themselves and their environment. Their disowned and habitual body patterns are not as embedded as those of adults. Children and adolescents usually retain a more natural propensity for movement and expression. Thus they are able to discover "deadened" or "disowned" (inexperienced) parts of themselves (i.e., frozen shoulders, sadness, anger) and return to their more natural stance of self-management (orgasmic self-regulation).

How the child or adolescent organizes her body in order to negotiate the interpersonal field in which she is embedded is a key emphasis in my work with children/adolescents. This negotiation or contact style is the child's pattern of experiencing herself and others in the immediate moment. The therapist must be cognizant of the child and the child's interpersonal field in order to make meaning and gain understanding of her contact style. In the case of Connie, her creative adjustments to the stressful home environment and serving as her mother's eyes created multiple splits in her body awareness. It was crucial that Connie both deadened her breathing and affect as well as keeping a vigilant, hypersensitive "eye" to avoid her mom's volatile boyfriend and further abuse. These "creative adjustments" are examples of self-regulation and Connie's contact style. They were her attempt to support her own welfare in a threatening interpersonal field.

Using physical process observations, the therapist can gain a broader assessment of the client. This fuller and more holistic assessment can guide the child/adolescent therapist's interventions to more accurately attend to the client's self organization in the field. With Connie, my interventions were all made with consistent awareness of her creative adaptations in seeing for two, in desperately needing to be seen by a safe adult, and in being an abuse survivor.

Client/Therapist Interpersonal Field

The therapist and client create their own interpersonal field. The therapist and client each bring facets of themselves to the interpersonal field that they create.

The child brings normal developmental issues, genetic and constitutional issues, family system dynamics, and issues of trauma such as alcoholism, abuse, divorce, or adoption to the field. The child/adolescent is imbedded in a number of fields, including family, neighborhood, and peers. Sometimes there are struggles between fields, for example family versus peers (McConville, 1995).

The field in which the child/adolescent is imbedded is different from that of the adult. Since children or adolescents must continue to live with their families, their range of choices is restricted. They cannot just leave this house, job, or community as might an adult. They make many creative adjustments in order to adapt/adjust to their environment, and these limitations.

There are also physiological differences in the experience of the field between children/adolescents and adults. Physiological change is evolving more rapidly in children as growth and the hormonal changes of puberty occur. This evolution is sometimes marked by awkwardness, physical limitations, and an ever-increasing lack of identification with one's own changing body. One of the significant physiological aspects of the field for children is their size in relation to peers.

Children and adolescents continue to grow and develop along natural developmental pathways. Physiological, cognitive, and emotional changes continue as they progress through their natural stages of childhood. Impasses may occur that block the natural growth process. Developmentally, an eight year old's capacity for understanding what is fair and right is very different than a sixteen-year-old's. Consequently, it is imperative to understand normal developmental stages. The therapist must ascertain if his client's body reactions or beliefs may be creative adaptations to stress or merely part of the normal developmental process. The meaning making of a child/adolescent's words, "I hate you, and I'm going to kill you" is usually very different coming from a four year old than from an eighteen year old.

The therapist brings her own developmental issues, constitutional issues, issues of trauma, and dynamics from her family system. All these areas are part of the therapist's ground that she brings to the session. When using ourselves as an instrument in the therapeutic field, what we bring to the client is our own history and our repertoire. Our own self-awareness, grounding in Gestalt theory, ease and comfort in being an embodied presence are all part of the system.

As is true with all therapeutic relationships, it is important that a therapist work with physical process attention to her own physical and emotional issues both before and during work with children/adolescents. I must be able to discern which are my issues, and which are my child/adolescent client's? Is this my tightness in my chest, or the tightness I am mirroring from my client? How is she holding herself, her fears, or her tears? How do I hold my sadness that may be similar or different from my client's way? What have I done with my feelings related to my own childhood and adolescence?

The challenge of utilizing physical process work is that the awareness and techniques must be developed in the therapist. I can't teach what I haven't yet learned to embody myself. Therefore, physical process work enriches my natural flow and movement in working with any child or adolescent.

Therapeutic Field

As Oaklander (1978, 1982) so aptly describes, Gestalt work is different some other methods of working with children and adolescents. In Gestalt work it is the expression of the self and the self within an interpersonal field that is important. Movements, sounds, play, creative expression and expressive arts materials are used to assist the therapist and child/adolescent in their experimentation. The focus of the work is not in analyzing the meaning of what toys the child uses. Rather, process work is seen as experiments in movement or play that are developed as an avenue to acknowledge the client's present impasses and to help create new ways of being for the child/adolescent. How the client makes contact with toys, the room, and the therapist is just as important as the content of the picture, sand tray, story, or the specific colors used to draw pictures. How the adolescent approaches a task, his ability to make decisions about size of paper, choice of art materials, or how he moves through the room are all part of the Gestalt context. Hence, my clinical method involves numerous process observations rather than just the content the client brings to the session.

In Gestalt physical process work with children, I utilize all of the previous methods of working with children and adolescents, but emphasize the physical component. How the child/adolescent organizes his physical structure, the way he breathes, walks, and interacts with me or his environment is a primary part of my focus. For some children, helping them manage their anxiety and begin to feel enough self support to make their own decisions about materials to use in making a mask is the experiment or therapeutic work in our session. It is fine if they never finish the mask, as an example. Their journey may be one of dealing with their anxiety about doing it perfectly, or only as the adult wants it. Helping them stay with their discomfort in not yet knowing (the answer, the correct choice), breathing out their worry and anxiety, and taking a risk in making a choice is a huge piece of work. For another explosive, hyperactive child, my stance is to support the child to experience external and internal boundaries, and to help him or her contain or funnel energy more appropriately.

Gestalt physical process focuses on the child/adolescent's gaining awareness of his physical expressions and self-organization, and seeing how he embodies them and carries them into the future. Once children/adolescents gain awareness, they may choose to accept things as they are and continue with their current pattern of behaviors. Or, they may experience other behaviors that allow them to expand their repertoire of alternative ways to breathe, move, or deal with situations. As in a familiar restaurant, the child/adolescent may discover that there are other things to order from the menu besides pizza each time!

Range of Possible Techniques Used in Physical Process Work with Children and Adolescents

Zinker (1977) has described the therapist as needing to "be bold, like an improvisational jazz musician." As a dancer myself, this metaphor fits for me in using physical process work. As a therapist, I experience myself like an improvisational dancer. The dance between the child/adolescent client and myself supports the ebb and flow of our relationship and the development of the work. This intertwining of therapist and client enhances the client's growth and energetic charge as both of us learn to listen to her natural beat. With both of us in sync, the client's natural ways of organizing herself and meeting her own needs (orgasmic self-regulation) are unimpeded.

In order to work with a client in this way, I need to be in my body, feeling and sensing my own experience and movement. I need to attend to the phenomena of the client's experience rather than any theories I may have about her. I do not want to control the themes (figure) or direction of the work. Instead I try to work with the client to help her gain awareness of the ways she interacts with others and her ability to support herself (working the boundary of contact both intrapersonally and interpersonally). Like the LSM (long slow method) of marathon training, we as therapists must "stay with" the client, pacing her and seeing the path ahead. This path has edges, and our job is to help the client approach the edge in a different manner from before. If we avoid the edge, no change occurs. If the client falls into the edge without any options, she may be only re-enacting trauma. This edge is the client's impasse and the therapy session is the opportunity for her to experience this impasse and negotiate it differently.

Techniques and body process methods must be understood within the framework of Gestalt Theory. There is a wide range of techniques possible in physical process work with children and adolescents. Methods of work include: observation of body process by the therapist; attending to physical supports and structure; exaggerated movement and repetition of movements or gestures. Further directed awareness of body structure, framing client issues physically, working polarities through the body, energy work, and more expressive work are optional methods of working with children and adolescents.

The therapist can help the child/adolescent embody and gain awareness on a physical level of her stance in the world. By helping the child open up her natural pathways of embodied expression through breath, sounds, or movement, the child expands her repertoire of possible ways of connecting, experiencing others, and being in the world. From a Gestalt perspective, health is flexibility. Therefore, physical process work with children and adolescents enhances health through greater mobility, fluidity, and range of expression and experience.

While there are many types of physical process interventions that I use in my work, I never do any direct touch or "hands on" work with children, and only rarely with adolescents. Many children and adolescents have frequently experienced body boundary violations, large or small, and they have a preconceived sense that they must usually go along with adults and never say "no." Thus, in an effort to respect their boundaries and autonomy, I suggest directed touch experiments. The purpose of hands-on or directed touch is to increase body sensation and awareness, and to help loosen tight patterns in a child/adolescent's musculature or structural system. With directed touch the adolescent may place his own hand on the part of his or her body that feels tight, numb, or painful; but again, only if he feels comfortable in doing so. If the client does not, I suggest the child/adolescent hold his hand a few inches away from his body and attend to that area of his body area with his focus and his breath.

All experiments are collaborative. I am always joining and mirroring the experimental work. I frequently use humor, playfulness, and my own exaggeration of sounds, breathing or movements. If I am more extreme than they are, children/adolescents seem more willing to take risks and do not seem to feel as embarrassed or ashamed.

Gestalt physical process work is not just a cookbook of exercises to try when I have a child/adolescent in my office. Opening up the child natural movements requires being in "sync" with my client's internal dance. Only then can I collaborate with my client and develop experiments that push her boundaries of comfort and challenge her ability to experiment with newly discovered behaviors or ways of being in the world, (as for example, supporting a very shy child to take a risk and learn to speak up for herself).

Interventions that are used with physical process work can be schematically arranged along the Cycle of Awareness (Kepner, 1987; Tudor, 1991; Zinker, 1977). The Cycle of Awareness is a way of mapping the client's process of moving from Sensation, Awareness, into Action, Contact and Withdrawal from an experience. It is a frame for describing a completed unit of work either within the therapeutic session or across time as the client progresses. Impasses (blocks, stuck points) may occur anywhere along the cycle.

Besides the case of Connie, I will present examples and a range of interventions or approaches related to clients' various impasses on the Cycle of Experience.

Therapist as Body

By being an embodied presence, the therapist is a significant part of the field for the child/adolescent. Through the dynamic use of oneself as a body (being aware of one's breathing, musculature, physical affect), the therapist supports working with the whole child, and with being a whole therapist within the context of the therapeutic field. By being a body in the therapeutic field with the child and actively observing, mirroring, and joining the client's process, the therapist collaborates with awareness in changing the field. The newly created field enhances greater awareness and a more versatile range of choices and movement for the client.

Use of Self as Barometer

Physical process work is based upon the assumption that there are two living, breathing people in the session. Therefore, wherever the therapist's personal energy is focused, that is where he will direct attention. If the therapist is cognitively focused, asking questions and trying to figure out "why" the ten-year-old refuses to go to school, he will not be aware of his own bodily sensations to use them as a barometer. This involves the therapist checking in with what is being felt, what sensations are being experienced, how he or she is breathing, keeping grounded, and in one's own body. The process involves shuttling between monitoring these personal experiences and noticing the client's physical process. To try and notice the client's physical process without attending to one's own is a return to the self in isolation with the therapist as an observer, not as a dynamic part of the field.

Clear observations of the client's movement, breathing, walking and sitting, how she makes contact with toys or the therapist is invaluable information about the client's way of being in the room and the world. This knowledge will enhance the therapy. As an example, the therapist can observe, imitate with his body, and physically experiment with "trying on" the way a teenager may respond when she is angry and refusing to listen to an adult. The therapist may observe how his client holds her breath and tightens her shoulders as she refuses to listen to her mother. The therapist can imitate or mirror this behavior by holding his breath and tightening his shoulders. In doing this, the therapist is able to mirror back to the client how she behaves, join her in her experience, and share information with the client about what it feels like to breathe or hold herself in this way. This creates a shared ground of information to explore collaboratively.

Creative Adjustment to the Environment

The following is a descriptive example of a child's creative adjustment to support himself in a stressful life situation. Jamie's obvious method of holding, honoring, and dealing with his terror about his mother's debilitating disease assists me in appreciating his creative use of physicalization. My use of self as trying to embody his experience, both physically and emotionally, demonstrates the power of the technique of therapist use of self through mirroring and joining his experience.

"Like Mom"

Jamie entered the Headstart class today as he did everyday. He came with his little blue backpack on his back and dragging his right foot. No one noticed, as this was "just Jamie." It did not matter that the doctors said there was nothing wrong with his foot, leg, or spine. It did not matter that the teachers had spent weeks telling Jamie to stand up straight and to stop pretending. Jamie would just look at the teachers with his big blue eyes filling up with tears and quietly state," But I'm not doing it on purpose, my leg is just like my mom's." And indeed it was like hers. The difference was that Mrs. Miller had a degenerative bone disease, and her spine was really curved. She tried very hard *not* to drag her leg, but could not help it. Jamie could not either. At four and a half, his leg had been dragging most of his little life. Big people could yell, tell him to quit pretending, or laugh at him, but it did not matter. He was just like his mom!

In the beginning, I met Jamie outside of school everyday. At first, I merely copied or "tried on" (mirrored) his gait as he dragged himself to school. What I soon realized was that his right shoulder was raised, as was his right hip. This seemed partly due to his heavy backpack and partly due to the torque he was beginning to develop on the whole right side of his body. While walking with him I started to share my observations of what it felt like to drag my leg all the time. Jamie had been dragging his leg since he learned to walk at twelve months old. He could no longer feel the right side of his body at all. At first he just looked and stared at me as I dragged into school after him. The next day he was eager to see me and we dragged into school together.

As a Headstart Consultant, I had the opportunity to be in the classroom periodically during the day. This worked perfectly as I began to give Jamie feedback on my experience of dragging my leg all day. Typical of children this age, soon no one commented on me any more than they did Jamie. I told Jamie that I felt like a top that was all wound up and ready to spin. He thought that was funny, and I began to exaggerate my experience of being a "Jamie Top."

Soon Jamie looked forward to my mirroring his walk and movements, and he began trying to be a "Jamie Top" just like me. A bit later I began to put breathing and sounds to our top. We would exhale and moan as we slowly began to move our right frozen, uplifted shoulder to the right and down. I would exaggerate this movement and begin to include some torso and pelvic stretching to the movement. We slowly started to open up Jamie's right side.

Jamie loved to mirror and be mirrored (don't we all?). Gradually our interactive client/ therapist movements became more like a dance filled with shoulder, torso, and hip rotations, top sounds, and loud exhales. Once several other children joined our fun and we were all spinning and moving "Jamie Tops."

As with adult physical process work, it is important to integrate the physical process work within the context of the field of the child's experience. Gestalt work does not focus on the therapist's interpretation, but rather on the therapist's heightened awareness of the client's process and helping him or her own or discover unaware (disowned) parts of his or her self (Kepner, 1987). However, because of younger children's language limitations, there are times when the therapist may need to verbalize two or three different options for children to select from in the moment. In other instances a child will role-play or re-enact an experience without verbalizing anything. This is where the child therapist's keen observational skills are very important (Oaklander, 1985). Especially when trauma has occurred and the child is very young, there may be no accessible language. There may be only kinesthetic movements, body sensations, and jumbled memories (Bauer, 1996; Kepner, 1995).

As we began to physically release, unwind, and open up Jamie's right side, I began to share some of my observations of watching Jamie and his mom each morning. As we began to physically release, unwind, and open up Jamie's right side, I began to share some of my observations of watching Jamie and his mom each morning. While playing with Jamie I began to shuttle back and forth between my observation of his shoulders and legs, and then my own. I also began to add my experience of trying to feel my reactions if my mom could not carry me, or play ball like the other moms. "It would make me mad and sad if my mom could not lift me up and carry me like the other moms. How does it make you feel?" I ask. By beginning to fill in the context of Jamie's creative adjustment, I began to appreciate the complexity of his embedded field. I began to understand Jamie's larger experience. I could understand more about his hesitation in expressing any anger at the mom he loved so much, and his worry that she would become even sicker if he got mad.

Thus with our client/ therapist dance as "Jamie Tops," I gradually graded up the experiment to include physically opening his hips, shoulders, and legs. We gradually began to move our shoulders, twisting our sides and bellies, and shaking out our legs from the hips. As we shook our hips we shouted, "I love you mommy, and I'm sad and mad you are sick!" Soon we shook out all our mad feelings out of our legs so they wouldn't feel like rubber bands anymore. Over time Jamie and I were able to help him structurally begin to unwind his leg and his spine. We also found other ways for him to "hold or carry" his mother and feel his sadness that she couldn't carry him, or play ball with him. After increasing his sensation and awareness, Jamie began to straighten up and walk more erect on his own two feet.

Development of Client's Ground and Self Support

Body structure, the way the child/adolescent meets her environment, her awareness of her body, and her degree of self-support are all significant aspects of self-organization. The therapist may assist the client in claiming disconnected or disowned body parts or feelings that may be inhibited (retroflected) or desensitized. Physical process work can facilitate this by changing these fixed patterns. It can enhance greater fluidity in the client's natural pathway of expression and movement. The child takes ownership of his or her body, his or her feelings, and alternative ways of being in the world.

On Her Tiptoes

Nine-year-old Erin was referred to me because she kept trying to throw herself out of moving cars and jump on picket fences, in clear attempts to harm or even kill herself. She was bright, tall, very thin, and her energy felt like a hot electrical wire. Erin was grieving her aunt's death. Her aunt, who was very special to Erin, had died six months earlier.

When I looked at Erin I noticed that she did not walk, she bounced, jumped or cartwheeled everywhere she moved. When I asked her to move across the room, Erin walked on her tiptoes, hardly letting the heels of her feet touch the ground. Erin described herself as floating all over the place. This was how she moved across the floor in my office. The initial family pictures that she drew also had many floating heads with no bodies, legs or feet. Erin's sense of herself was not connected to the earth. Her physical process, thoughts, and drawings were of an ungrounded and disembodied field.

Erin embodied her ungroundedness. This was apparent in her high electric energy that spewed everywhere, in her continued impulsive acts to try to be near her aunt in heaven, and even in her inability to tie her own shoes. Her actions demonstrated her continued wish to try to leave this earthly plane.

Our work together focused on working to get Erin grounded in her own body. We worked to get her back into her legs and feet. First we tiptoed, then toe-heeled, then eventually stomped around the room together. Our large body movements evolved from pretending to be butterflies flitting around the room, to being panthers, and then elephants that stomped the ground. As Erin developed feet and no longer flitted or tiptoed around the room, she began to build more awareness and groundedness throughout her whole body. Erin's drawing began to have arms, legs, and bodies. Erin was able to support herself and acknowledge her physical connection to this earth. Finally she was able to sob and feel her grief over her aunt's death throughout her whole body.

Later Erin verbalized the fact that jumping from a moving car wouldn't take away the loss of her aunt. The reality was that she would also die and miss her mom, dad, and dogs. Soon Erin was drawing pictures for her aunt and sending them to her via balloon or prayer, rather than trying to be her own messenger.

If this child had been hospitalized, she probably would have been medicated and diagnosed as schizotypal, based on her behavior and self-report. By working with Erin's experience and process, we were both able to understand the meaning of her behavior. I helped empower her in her body and acknowledge her powerlessness over her aunt's death. This creative, vibrant child is now a typical teenager who has learned ways to channel her energy and utilize her whole body self in all her actions and behaviors. Erin now writes wonderful poetry, does gymnastics, and is in the gifted program at school. Through the provision of alternative forms of self-support and groundedness, Erin no longer has to react to her environment by flying off or tiptoeing around. She does not have to leave.

Sensation Formation

One of the basic approaches in beginning physical process with a child/adolescent is helping the client sense their bodily experience. Children/adolescents are often numb or deadened in parts of their body. Gradual increase in sensation helps the client develop support for self and contact with others. One method of doing this is to gradually increase breathing which gathers more oxygen to the blood stream and increases actual sensation. Teaching a client to do this develops her ability to experience her body/skin within herself and in relationship to others.

By gathering more energy and charge through this kind of breathing and movements, the child/adolescent actually has more energy for her body to use in different ways. This assists her in making contact with herself and increases her awareness of those around her. A subtle process of tightening and releasing muscle groups can also help the child develop sensation in her whole body. As one adolescent client reported, her body was no longer "something that just hung out below her neck." Her body actually had a form and a function for her, and it was hers.

The Plywood Gait

A fourteen-year-old came into my office with presenting problems of being depressed and not wanting to go to school. Her mother reported that Lisa seemed sad since her parent's divorce two years ago, but her behavior had gotten worse the last few months. When I first looked at Lisa, I saw a fairly neatly dressed teenager. What caught my attention was the way she held herself as she walked into the room and sat down. She walked as if she was a single piece of plywood. Lisa did not have a natural quality to her movement or a sense of ease in either her face or her gait. I noticed the tight and slightly extended muscles around her neck and jaw. As I observed her, I wondered what she might be holding in or retroflecting. Could it be anger?

I asked Lisa if she could feel her body at this moment. She said no, she didn't feel anything but, she knew she was mad at her mother right now. I asked her in a noncommittal voice (important in working with adolescents), "If you did feel, where might you guess you would hold your mad feelings?" "Maybe here or here" she stated, as she pointed to her chest and belly. " Okay, let's both put our hands on our own chests and bellies. Is this where you might feel it? Am I doing it right?" I ask. By collaborating, I was supporting Lisa in developing the experiment. This is especially important with adolescents, as they often need to feel in charge. I continued to grade up the experiment while making myself non-threatening by saying," I know this may be stupid, but bear with me. Let's both exaggerate our breath and breathe into our chests and bellies, into the places that you described as having some mad/hurt feelings."

By imitating (mirroring) and joining with her, I decreased her self-consciousness and we were able to experiment with increasing her awareness of herself and her actual body sensations. As a typical fourteen year old, Lisa tried the behavior twice and quit. I persisted by reporting my own sensations and awareness. "When I think about your mom or my own bossy mom, I'm aware my chest tightens and so does my belly." I continued to share my sensations and shuttle back and forth between mirroring her and reporting what I felt. "As I breathe into my chest and remember the story you just told me about your anger with having to clean your room, I realize it's hard for me to breathe into my chest. How about you?" Ever noncommittal and always curious, I supported the sleuth part of Lisa to stay with her awareness of body parts that may be holding her feelings.

As we breathed into our hands, chests, and bellies, I continued to share my own self-observations about my body sensations and feelings, mirror her behavior and make subtle observations about her breathing. Her breathing was shallow, not full. This was especially obvious when Lisa was talking about her mother or her parents' divorce. Lisa blamed her mother for her decision to get divorced and for the court order that she cannot live with her father.

Basic skills that were used with Lisa to develop body sensation and awareness included: directed observations, having Lisa report immediate sensations; being an embodied presence through self report (my experience when I model my body after hers); mirroring of behaviors; tightening and exaggerating the polarities (i.e., alternately exaggerate and tighten her jaw and neck, and then try to experience the feelings of the opposite direction and open wide and release her jaw, loosen her neck). Over time Lisa was able to feel much more sensation throughout her whole body.

Slowly, we developed more sensation language that Lisa could use when she started to feel angry with her mother. With observation and mirroring, I focused on her tightened jaw, braced shoulders, and shallow breathing. Her common statement of "whatever" with her swallowed anger about her mother could now be developed into observable data related to Lisa's body process. ("I tighten my jaw and brace my shoulders to numb out my feelings about you, Mother.") With my assistance, I encouraged Lisa to focus on her contact and relationship with her mother. We increased Lisa's awareness of the way she would tighten her jaw and neck and brace her whole body structure when she began to feel any anger with her mother. Gradually, Lisa became aware of the myriad feelings that she had shut down (retroflected) and numbed out in her body in order to adjust and accommodate for her unspoken rage and blame with her mother. Her intrapersonal physical adaptations assisted her in avoiding conflict on an interpersonal level.

Over time, Lisa was able to feel much more sensation throughout her whole body. We expanded experimentation to continue to develop further body sensation and awareness throughout her whole upper torso. Lisa's jaw, neck, shoulders, chest, and belly all looked tight and held firmly in place without much mobility.

After increasing sensation, Lisa was now able to use the Gestalt technique of polarities to further heighten her physical awareness. I asked Lisa to let the two body parts, her chest and her belly, have a dialogue with each other. Through subtle grading up of experimentation Lisa was able to say, "I tighten and brace when you yell at me about my dumb room. I really want to live with dad and have a room there!" In her chest, Lisa also carried the pain of the strained relationship with her mom. "I tighten and close my heart because I feel bad, and I don't like you to be mad at me." Gradually Lisa was able to carry on a dialogue between these two body parts that had both contained a lot of her overall body energy.

Since both her heart and her belly held so much emotional charge or energy, Lisa's creative adaptation had been to numb her body so she wouldn't feel either conflict. Thus, as is sometimes seen with children/adolescents, the presenting problems of underachievement at school or depressive behaviors are secondary symptoms of her more physicalized and embodied conflicts. Lisa was dealing with the intrapersonal conflict within herself and the interpersonal conflict between herself and her mother. ("I love <om and I'm also angry with her. And, I don't like being mad at her, or having her mad at me.")

Later, Lisa was able to further identify and feel her feelings. She was finally able to put them into action through language and movement. Lisa developed her own experiment using a pillow. First she would squeeze the pillow when she was angry (instead of her jaw and belly muscles), and then, breathe out to release her muscles, and hug the pillow. While doing this she also said, "I love you mom, and I don't want to fight. But, I'm angry you left dad, and you keep telling me what to do!" Lisa was now able to take deep breaths, expand her chest, and speak the previously unspeakable to her mother.

Over time, Lisa was able to begin to identify her own body cues when she started getting mad at her mom. She could begin to identify and feel herself tighten her jaw before she felt the knot in her stomach or felt her whole body tighten up. These concrete body cues helped Lisa remember to support herself through her breath, stay grounded and flexible in her body, and talk with her mother about sensitive issues right away.

Awareness Development–Body Structure

Body structure is a child/adolescent's fixed physical organization of self in the interpersonal field. What was once a creative adaptation or adjustment to the field has become formalized or frozen. Thus, body structure is frozen process; a fixed gestalt. After looking at the body structure of the child/adolescent and the way she contacts the environment, I continue to be aware of the client's overall pattern of making contact first with his or her self (intrapersonal) and/or the environment.

There are many aspects of the client's body structure that can be useful awareness. From a Gestalt perspective, I am not interested in labeling body structures (i.e., collapsed, rigid, swollen), but rather being aware of specific behavioral patterns that describe the child/adolescent's structure. Being aware of the development of a child's particular manner or stance of structuring himself helps me understand the form he or she learned to make and way in order to hold himself in the world, especially in times of crisis or stress. By appreciating the meanings of a child's structure, I gain awareness of alternative methods of assisting him or her in experimenting with other choices.

Briefly, four general aspects that I attend to include: alignment or posture; body mass; direction of tensions; and self-balance. Alignment or posture includes the child/adolescent's organization of his spine, head and neck, and attention to ways the child uses his or her pelvis and legs to the body. Body mass involves sensitivity to the type of body mass and awareness of how it is organized. Does the child have more mass in the upper or lower part of her body? What is the quality of his mass? Is it dense, stringy, elongated? Direction of tension involves focusing on any certain direction (inward, outward, up, down) that you see the child tensing or tightening in. The child may experience this tension as tightness or pain. Balance of the body structure involves observing how the child balances himself. Does he or she relax into the ground or grip the ground with his feet and tighten his or her arms? All these aspects of body structure can be useful starting points when assessing body structure (Clemmens, 1997; Keleman, 1985; Smith, 1985).

As a therapist, I continue to utilize the client's self reports and describe what I see, feel, and experience when I experiment and try to duplicate the walk or body structure of the client. By heightening the experiment of either exaggerating the stuckness, or doing the opposite by working the polarities, I am able to assist the child in experimenting with additional choices.

The child has developed a certain physical way of being in the world. This certain way of moving has served her well in the past. When the client habitually remains in this physical pattern her body becomes rigid, fixed like armor. Armoring is the process of developing a hardened, less sensitized area of physical experience. Armoring of sensitive areas serves as protection. It is a method of support, especially when the child feels no supports and must adapt herself to survive. Adolescents and children that have experienced frequent physical or sexual abuse or trauma quickly learn how to split off from their body and their awareness and no longer see, feel, or assimilate the environment.

The Cherry Popsicle

Gina, a reticent 15-year-old, learned very early in life how to "shut down" her system and not take in comfort, support, or the negativity that was all around her. Gina had an abusive, very disturbed mother. From the age of thirteen months on, Gina's mother kept both force feeding her and giving her enemas to make her "regular."

As I viewed this gaunt adolescent with severe features and a fairly rigid body structure, her history of conflicts with her environment (particularly her mother) was fairly observable. Gina had very constricted and developed jaw muscles and I could see the tautness of Gina's vagus nerves as they extended down her neck. When I visually followed her neck and shoulder lines, I saw her rigid, almost "perfect posture" and hardened shoulders. I also noticed not only her thin legs, but also the tightness, and rigidity in her hips as she walked. I noticed her staring at me between the two narrow slits of her eyes. As I observed her physical structure, I wondered why should she trust adults, whether here, at school, or at home? There had never been anyone there to help Gina in the past. What should or could change her experience now?

I joined with Gina and supported her non-trusting style of making contact with me. Instead of trying to "rip her off" as had been her experience with other adults, I congratulated her on her ability to " check me out" and other adults as well, to be smarter than her mother, and to stay alive growing up.

Over time we developed a somewhat trusting relationship. Then we were able to do several experiments in which I helped her slowly melt, like her favorite cherry popsicles, some of her hard veneer. One approach that was especially helpful with Gina involved me role playing or being her hard veneer. As I spoke from the tough shell part of her, Gina was able to let go and experience another part of herself. I was able to be her rigid outer shell and carry some of the protection for her, so she did not have to do it all by herself. By working this side of the polarity, Gina began to feel the terror and anxiety that she held in her pelvic and rectal area if she let herself soften and feel her vulnerability.

Slowly, Gina was able to begin to experience a wider range of feeling that she had kept locked away in her body. We gradually worked on Gina reclaiming her body as hers, not her mother's to force feed or intrude upon. Gently, like her melting popsicle, Gina was able to control and experience increased sensation and awareness throughout her whole body. Her fixed, more rigid body stance had held her in good stead in the past, but not as much now. Now, like a Popsicle that is not frozen solid, Gina was able to taste, feel, breath, and move on her own.

Body Structure as Creative Adaptation

Observations about a child or adolescent's body structure and the way in which he or she organizes the self constitute another very important avenue for assessment. When observing the child's physical body, I am not looking for a "right or wrong" type or appearance. Rather, I am observing the structure or exterior of the child/adolescent's system. Using a metaphor of architecture, what kind of house does this child/adolescent live in? Is he or she long, lean, and thin, or short, and more muscular, with his or her center of weight closer to the ground? Does he or she have well developed muscles or extra fat around his middle? Are there cultural, genetic facets of his or her looks, and/or might his or her physical structure serve as a protection, buffer to the outside world? Extra body weight and muscle are often, but not always, indications of a physical block. In other instances, genetic factors must be struggled with and accepted, despite pressures and wishes to be as tall or short as one's peer group.

Body image is frequently a significant issue for many adolescents. As I get to know my client, I am constantly observing to see if his or her body structure matches or stand out as being different from thoughts, feelings or behaviors of the child/adolescent. In other cases, an adolescent or child's body character has been impacted by stresses. Due to an adolescent's creative adjustments for self-support, he or she may gain weight, or lose weight, collapse his or her chest, or rigidify his or her body structure as a reaction to the environment. Using directed body awareness and experimentation, I collaborate with the adolescent/child to fully experience his or her body structure and physical image, and to try to experiment with alternative methods of moving in the world.

"Fire Thing:"
Undoing a Retroflection to Open the Whole System

Sam's story provides an example of observing a teenager's body structure, one that held extra weight to try to support this thirteen-year-old boy's inhibited grief and sadness over his father's death from cancer two years earlier. It had been a bitter battle for the whole family. Sam was the oldest of four children and he had been eleven years old when his dad was first diagnosed. Consequently, unrealistic physical and emotional responsibilities had been placed upon him.

Sam was a straight-A student, science club, and student council member at school. He was the overly responsible, oldest brother, and the perfect mother's son. He usually kept it together, but he began feeling depressed and seeing life as worthless. His weight gain of twenty-five pounds over two years and his minor suicidal ideation prompted Sam's mom to bring him in to see me.

Sam the Good Kid, continued to want to do it right, but his body could not handle the unexpressed feelings that he continued to carry around. When looking at him, I noticed his undefined baby face and the extra twenty-five pounds that he carried on his frame. The middle of his torso was fairly immobilized and shut down. Sam's overall physique reminded me of the cartoon character, Baby Huey. He seemed so pseudo-adult and so young at the same time. Despite the overly large center of his frame, Sam's hands, eyes, face, (all body parts that make contact with others) seemed diminished and very childlike. Although he had a big frame, his actions were inhibited, as were his movements, his voice, and even his handwriting. Initially he had very restricted handwriting and painting. His voice was soft and almost squeaky. My initial observation was that the outward expressions of Sam (his drawings, writings, painting, and movements) did not match the physical body and structure he lived in.

One of Sam's favorite activities was to do the *Fire Thing*. This involves writing down various feeling (i.e., hurts, worries, fears), squeezing them into a ball, and then burning the paper, and letting the feelings go as you take full breaths and exhales. By using written words, magazine pictures, and choices of big or small paper, Sam got a chance to physically move through and complete the process (cycles of experience) in the session. The following is an example of this process for Sam. At the point of Sensation he said, " I feel tightness in my chest." Moving to a more fuller awareness, Sam said and felt that the tightness in his chest meant "I'm mad my dad died." As Sam continued to mobilize his energy in the session, Sam wrote down words on a big piece of paper, and squeezed the words into several tight balls. While doing this we focused on squeezing all of the tightness out of his chest, into his arm muscles, and into the ball of paper. The point of contact occurred when Sam burned the paper up and expressed out loud his grief and anger over the loss of his dad. His withdrawal and integration occurred when he watched it burn, and focused on his exhale in his breath. I continued to ask Sam to pay attention to letting go of all his sad and mad feelings and letting go of his breath as they left his chest and his whole body.

The relationship over sessions can be seen, as the development of Sam's physical and emotional themes and corresponding skills evolved. Over time Sam went from tiny strips of paper or vague magazine pictures to choosing larger pieces of paper and larger, more specific magazine pictures. His writing got larger and less restricted as well. This process assisted him in making contact with his whole body and all of his feelings, not only in his head as headaches or thoughts of suicide. Instead, Sam was now able to express himself using his whole body. Previously, Sam had emotionally shut down, but he had continued to grow only by gaining weight in his efforts to support himself. When his contacts with others (his mom and dad) had been broken or strained, his only solutions had been to soothe himself through food, and try to do it right.

This expressive activity encouraged Sam to start to open up and express some of the feelings he had kept hidden for a long time. It helped him to verbalize and acknowledge his worries and anger, share feelings with a sympathetic adult, and squeeze feelings from his whole body.

By exaggerating the feelings to increase his sensitivity, Sam was able to shake his feelings out and let them go. We emphasized breathing out to expand his lungs and his capacity to let go feelings as he exhaled. While literally burning up the feelings written on his papers, he was able to acknowledge his own burned up feelings that his dad died. This experiment enabled Sam to send the feelings back to the universe. He did not have to hang on to them, or to hurt other people with them.

Our work together supported both his interpersonal and intrapersonal needs. I was able to encourage Sam to express some of his anger and grief. He no longer had to hide all of his feelings. On a physical level we opened up the natural pathway of his upper torso-shoulders to arms, then his legs, so he could feel his whole body. We added breathing and voice to help Sam feel his power, amid a tragedy where he was totally powerless. Sam was finally able to say, "I'm big and strong, and also sad and scared my dad died." His natural pathway of movement went back to his pelvis and abdomen, the area that Sam's overeating had tried to mask all these months. Sam felt sick to his stomach that his dad died and left him to be the "man of the house." He was just a kid and it was too much! Even if he overate, gained weight, and tried to restrict his needs (his movements, voice), he still could not do it. The weight of his grief and the extra responsibility of trying to fill his dad's shoes were too much. It was much more than the extra twenty-five pounds that he had gained!

The *Fire Thing* is a wonderful, concrete metaphor for Sam's anger and sadness. The repetition and power of ripping up and burning feelings and letting them go with his breath and movements made his present experience more real. By exaggerating his breathing and motions, Sam gained awareness of where he stored his feelings. This process of awareness development helped empower him. Sam's depression and suicidal feelings diminished. He was able to hold and own his real power as an adolescent, and not have to pretend to be the "man of the house." He did not have to be bigger (physically) or older than he was. Nor did he need to diminish his own needs for contact with others.

Sam physicalized and carried several contradictions or polarities in his body that were embedded within his field. By assisting him in gaining awareness of his body, I helped Sam gain awareness of some facets that must be accepted (death of his dad), and other facets that he has choices over (his degree of responsibility, his needs, his body).

Expressive Movement

Movement and expression always has a point of origin in the body. It is important to observe the pathway through which the movement flows. The pathway is the route by which energy moves in the body. All energy needs an outlet for expression. The natural direction of a movement is the habitual path for the discharge of body energy. There are points at which the child/adolescent's natural pathway inhibits, restricts, or modulates movements, based on how he or she experiences the field. This movement, or modulation in expression can become figural via tension, changes in breathing, flatulence, fatigue, or diminished energy to the whole system (Brennan, 1987; Kepner, 1994).

Father/Son Explosions: Working with the Whole Family System

The following is an example of working with a child within the context of his larger family field. As noted before, our behavior is experienced or demonstrated in relationship to others in our external field (i.e. school, peers. family). Within the context of Johnny's family system, living with his divorced father and having no contact with his mother, his behavior was not identified as a problem until Johnny went to school for the first time. His relatives saw him at home as being "his father's son," and not to be messed with by others. At school, his behavior was described as inappropriate, and a threat to other children.

Johnny was seven years old when he and his father first came to see me. Johnny had been in trouble at school for fighting, name-calling, and yelling at the teacher. The school had threatened to expel Johnny if he did not clean up his act. His dad did not want him to end up as he had, in Juvenile Detention five times before he was fourteen years old. Yet, despite fights at home, dad's threats of Johnny growing up and going to jail, and extreme punishments for weeks on end, Johnny kept acting out at school.

When I observed both father and son, I noticed many similarities. They both pranced and strutted when they walked into the room. Each interrupted and yelled at the other and both expressed their dissatisfaction with intense outbursts of anger. To understand Johnny, it was important to understand and experience him within the context of the whole field that he lived in at home. My work with Johnny included my intense work with his dad as well, to help support and change the whole family system. Behaviorally, I helped his father learn to develop an external structure for the household that was not either overly permissive (video games for six hours each Saturday) or punitive (no TV for three to six weeks at a time). The whole system needed to learn to develop moderation in its actions and affect. Neither father nor son had awareness of the consequences of his behavior (awareness part of the Cycle of Experience). Both frequently jumped from a sensation (usually intense and explosive) to action. Dad would be yelling and punishing, and Johnny would be kicking or hitting other children. They needed to increase their awareness of their sensations and feelings and learn alternative ways to deflect their immediate impulses. Both needed to learn some alternative ways to modulate their feelings and actions (retroflective techniques) to help them moderate their behavior and experiences. By helping them gain more of an embodied sense of themselves, both father and son learned concrete body cues and techniques to help them continue to change their behavior.

The following is the variety of experiments and physical process techniques that I employed with both father and son to help them gain more control and choice over their behavior. Since both of them had an impulsive, reactive style, it was important to begin with some large body movements to both focus and drain some of their energy. We initially began the session with ten-minute pillow fights. Dad had to be on his knees so their physical statures would be more equal. They could each select the size of pillow used. With a ten-minute free fight (high energetic charge) initially, each opened up their natural pathways of expression in a safe way while also connecting interpersonally in a manner that was productive and fun.

Later on we experimented with other methods of expressing frustration or aggression that were also safe and contained. Both Johnny and his father were encouraged to utilize other methods of large movement expression at home on a regular basis (pounding pillows, chopping wood, using a punching bag in their basement). We emphasized full body expression with all of these interventions. Full and complete inhale and exhale of breath and opening up of the whole lung area and rib cage were emphasized. With any of the large body movements, having a strong sense of his legs, hips and fluid movement up and down the child/dad's spine was emphasized, modeled and reinforced. The process of the action (i.e., how you hit the pillow, punch the bag) was focused upon equally with the affect of the task (i.e., dumping your anger here, not with the kids at school).

To assist Johnny at school, and his dad at work, we focused upon more subtle methods of self-modulation of affect and behavior. Early on I encouraged both of them to carry a box of 89 cent pencils with them at all times. When angry, frustrated and ready to "blow" each was supported to go to the bathroom and focus all of his intense feelings into the pencils. By strongly exhaling, making sounds and breaking each pencil into several pieces, the impulsive feelings could be channeled in a safe and contained manner. Later, the experiment was graded up to focus on using a squeeze-ball or a wad of paper in Johnny's pocket so he would not have to leave the classroom. We again emphasized squeezing all of his frustrations into the squeeze-ball and releasing them from his hand. The exaggeration of his exhale was done as well, but his sounds were to be quieter. As Johnny and his dad learned alternative techniques to use, Johnny was no longer getting sent to the principal's office on a regular basis.

While continuing to encourage large expressive movement and

high-energy release at home, we began to focus on more subtle experiments to use at school. These experiments provided Johnny with other concrete methods of gaining mastery over himself and his emotions and working within his environment. Johnny and his dad were encouraged to be actors and not always actively demonstrate or verbalize their displeasure with others. When angry or frustrated I taught them to tighten and squeeze their toes together and push the anger through their shoes and into the center of the earth. We experimented with Johnny squeezing his hands together to the count of ten and then imagining shooting fire out of his fingers into the universe so he would focus his anger and not get into trouble. We actively threw angry feelings away into the wastebaskets or into the plants in my office. The muscular exaggeration, tightening, and then release of his toes, feet, legs, arms, and fingers all assisted Johnny in energetically and physically releasing his feelings without exploding. Finally, we practiced the smaller, more subtle movements of learning to deepen, expand, and follow his breath to literally "blow away" his frustrations before they began to mount up. By imagining that his exhale was the spraying of bullets coming out of an Uzi machine-gun, Johnny learned to spray, flatten, and shred the teacher or kid in the class in fantasy without being yelled at or sent to the principal's office. This technique supported increased impulse control while also supporting Johnny to express his anger or frustrations in a very controlled and contained way.

Johnny loved the idea of seeing himself as an underground agent who can't "blow his cover," and not getting in trouble. Later, Johnny decided he didn't always need to kill others with his Breath-Uzi or with fire coming from his fingers. He could use these secret techniques to get rid of his feelings and stay out of trouble at school. Over time, Johnny was able to funnel a lot of his passion and excess energy into playing hockey and football, and drawing detailed imaginary pictures. Johnny's relationship with his father dramatically improved as well. Both have gained a wider range of options and have a greater sense of empowerment and choice for themselves in different environments.

Natural Movement Through Self-Expression

A client's natural movement, or the natural pathway of movement within the body is free flowing and includes the natural path that emotions would take from the center of the body outward to the contact places where the child/adolescent makes contact with his or her environment. In the emotions of deep grief or sadness, natural movement begins in the pelvis or abdomen. The natural pathway of movement for the client would be from the pelvis or abdomen up through the torso, shoulders, and neck. I might notice a break in energy or movement anywhere along the natural pathway, or at the points where the child/adolescent may make contact or connect with his or her environment. Thus, natural contact points would be through the eyes, face, or in movements in the arms. The following is an example of multiple breaks or blocks in Robert's natural pathway of expression. Use of large movements and then more subtle movements helped this child open up his or her whole contact style and way of being in the world.

Puppet Boy

Robert, or "Puppet boy," is an excellent example of held grief that blocks a child's natural pathway of expression. This five-year-old child was referred to me due to his Elective Mutism. This DSM-IV diagnosis describes a child that chooses not to speak, without having any physiological limitations or medical reasons for his inability to speak. Robert had been evaluated and he could talk, and would talk to children or at home. But, for four months he had refused to talk at the preschool he was attending.

When Robert was eighteen months old his mother had died of anorexia nervosa. Robert had been in the bed with her at the time. Robert became very sick and sad. In his effort to deal with his pain and anguish, Robert stopped having verbal contact with other adults.

Initially, I began to try to make contact with Robert using puppets. Through my silence I was joining Robert in his nonverbal world. I began to throw a ball back and forth between two puppets. After totally ignoring me for a while, Robert finally took a puppet. In silence, our puppets began to make contact through the ball. Gradually, I began to exaggerate my breathing as I threw and caught the ball. By throwing a ball and beginning to add breath, I upgraded the experiment. The upper body movements and breath work slowly began to open up Robert's natural pathway of movement through his upper torso, shoulders, and back. By adding more breath and beginning sounds (i.e., groans as my puppet missed the ball), our work expanded his awareness and his range of possibilities. We began to open up or unblock his inhibited (retroflected) vocal cords.

As we worked together, I always tried to slightly push the "comfort zone" of his experience without grading the experiment up too much. One day I found a large foam play box and threw it to Robert without the puppet on my hand. When I had tried to do this earlier, he had let the box fall to the ground. Then I had watched his eyes glaze over and he had retreated back into the safety of his own disconnected world. At that time Robert was not ready for that much direct contact with me. I had graded the experiment up too much. As with adult work, if it is the therapist's figure and not the client's, there will not be any focus or energy for the experience. This time he was ready for more interpersonal contact. Now he laughed and threw the big box back at me. We had made contact without the safety of the puppets. We continued to throw the box back and forth. And, as before, I graded the experiment up and began to add exaggerated breathing, groans, and other sounds, but still no words.

From a physical process viewpoint, we were opening up more whole body experiences for Robert. The box was almost as big as Robert. Hence, this play actually helped energize and sensitize not only his torso, arms, and shoulders, as before, but also his pelvis, abdomen, and legs. Our play with the box continued for several weeks. Gradually, Robert began to whisper one word to me in the session. I did not respond to him any differently than I had when we were in silence. When children are trying new behaviors and experimenting in areas that had previously been blocked, it is crucial for the therapist not to be overly intrusive or reactive. Hence, I contained my zealous reactions, and I continued to provide a non-threatening environment. Here, Robert's body could open up (unwind) and he could find his own natural pace.

One day, Robert came in and instead of throwing the box, he got under it and kicked it off of himself. He motioned for me to put the box back on him. I did. He rolled and kicked it off. This persisted in a repetitive fashion without words. Gradually, I began to exaggerate breathing and groans as he pushed, kicked and rolled out from under the box. Robert's movement through his cycle of experiences had developed and evolved from our sessions over time. Robert had finally developed enough sensation, had mobilized his energy physically, and he was now beginning to make contact with experiences that had been so traumatic over two and a half years ago. Robert kept pushing and kicking and rolling out from under the box over and over, faster and faster. This time Robert automatically used exaggerated breath, groans, and made deep sounds coming from his belly. Finally he began to cry and cry and say, "MA, MA, MA, MA, MA, MA."

I realized that his mother's body must have rolled over on him as she died. As compared to adults, children do not always have the cognitive awareness of what may be happening to them due to their age and development at the time. Thus, they may have the kinesthetic knowing and body memories that are held on a cellular level without the connected language that, as adults, we so frequently depend on (Bauer, 1996; van der Kolk, 1994).

Robert never could have told me that he remembered his mother rolling over on him. He could never verbalize his nonverbal terror about the experience. Yet, his body remembered, and his task was one of kinesthetic repetition and support to slowly open up his whole system. I helped provide Robert with enough energy and safety that he could re-experience this trauma, breathe, and cry through it. As I described to Robert what he may have seen and experienced with his mom's death, he was now able to begin to verbalize what was unspeakable when he was eighteen months old.

Physical process work enhanced Robert's natural movements and helped him unblock areas where he was rigidified, stuck, or frozen and opened up his natural physical pathways of expression and movement. By being sensitive and knowledgeable about body structure and the physiological process, I was able to help Robert recall his traumatic experience and develop new physical patterns based on his present needs and excitement. Now Robert can speak his truth and express anything he wants. His range of choice has been restored.

Conclusion

The previous case examples and descriptions of physical process work with children and adolescents are intended to help the reader try and experience this lively and rich way of working with clients. Physical process work is not an "add on" to Gestalt therapy, but a natural enlivened aspect of working with young clients in the present moment. They carry their histories with them in their walk, talk, stature, manner of breathing and making contact with their environment and with me as the therapist. By observing, imitating, mirroring and using myself as a barometer, I can enhance and enrich our clinical work together. As I share and serve as an extra set of eyes and ears in the session, I can help a young client experience a safe and open environment with an adult that will encourage taking risks and experimenting with different behaviors and ways of being in the world. I can help her experiment with increased sensation, awareness, and ownership of parts of herself that the child/adolescent may have never experienced or felt before.

Physical process work is especially advantageous with children and adolescents if they do not have access to use of language at different times in their life. Some young children may not have developed a language vocabulary, as was seen with the cases of Jamie or Robert. Due to trauma, others cannot describe their experiences as in the case examples of Erin, Connie, or Michael. With adolescents there are many times in their development when they do not have the awareness or words to describe all that is emerging in their body or their world, as described by the cases of Lisa, Gina, or Sam.

Physical process work also supports and provides outlets for healthy energy and aggression, as in the case example of Johnny and his dad. I continue to work with the child/adolescent and to support him to gain additional information about his own behavioral patterns and the way he organizes himself in his environment.

In the session, I continue to collaborate and *work with a person, not on a body*. My goal is not to fix or reshape someone physically. Rather our collaborative goal is one of ongoing dialogue to help the child/adolescent experience greater freedom, fluidity, and movement, both within herself and within her relationships and environments.

References

Bauer, P. (1996). What do infants recall of their lives? Memory for specific events by one-to two-year olds. *American Psychologist, 51*, 29-41.

Brennan, B. (1988). *Hands of light: A guide to healing through the human energy field.* Toronto: Bantam.

Clemmens, M. (1997). Unpublished lecture. Working with physical process training program. Gestalt Institute of Cleveland: Cleveland, OH.

Keleman, S. (1985). *Emotional anatomy.* Berkley, CA: Center Press.

Kepner, J. (1987). *Body process: A gestalt approach to working with the body in psychotherapy.* New York, NY: Gardner Press.

Kepner, J. (1994). Unpublished lecture. Working With Physical Process Training Program. Gestalt Institute of Cleveland: Cleveland, OH.

Kepner, J. (1995). *Healing tasks: Psychotherapy with adult survivors or childhood abuse.* San Francisco, CA: Jossey-Bass.

McConville, M. (1995). *Adolescence: Psychotherapy and the emergent self.* San Francisco, CA: Jossey-Bass.

Oaklander, V. (1978). *Windows to our children: A gestalt therapy approach to children and adolescents.* Moab, UT: Real People Press.

Oaklander, V. (1982). The relationship of gestalt therapy to children. *The Gestalt Journal, 5*, 64-74.

Oaklander, V. (1985). Unpublished lecture. Intensive training program in Gestalt therapy approach with children and adolescents. Center for Child Therapy and Adolescent Therapy: Hermosa Beach, CA.

Perls, F., Hefferline, R., & Goodman, P. (1951). *Gestalt therapy: Excitement and growth in the human personality.* New York, NY: W.W. Norton.

Smith, E. (1985). *The body in psychotherapy.* Jefferson, NC: McFarland.

Tudor, K. (1991). Integrating Gestalt in children's groups. *The British Gestalt Journal, 1*, 21-27.

van der Kolk, B. (1994). The body keeps the score: Memory and the evolving psychobiology of posttraumatic stress. *Harvard Review of Psychiatry, l*, 253-296.

Wheeler, G. (1991). *Gestalt reconsidered: A new approach to contact and resistance.* New York, NY: Gardner Press.

Zinker, J. (1977). *Creative process in Gestalt therapy.* New York, NY: Brunner/Mazel.

4

Integrating Gestalt in Children's Groups

Keith Tudor

Introduction

Children have been seen and heard–and written about–from the early days of psychotherapy: from Freud's work with "Little Hans" (through his father) at the turn of this century to the present (Freud, 1909/1977). However, theories of child development and particularly psychoanalytic practice with children, inherited from the grandfathers and grandmothers of that tradition, emphasize the pathological, disturbed and abnormal. Freud (1916/1973) wrote about the processes underlying early infant development in terms of defenses, fixations, envy and anxiety. Klein (1932) developed this further with her hypotheses of the "phase of maximal sadism" and the subsequent paranoid and depressive "positions." It was Winnicott (1965b) who was the first within the psychoanalytic tradition to reframe Freud's theories as "the positive process of maturation in the infancy and early childhood of the individual" (p. 9). It was also Winnicott, to the gratitude of many a parent whose parenting has been pathologized by professionals, who introduced the concept of "good-enough mothering." Erikson (1951/1965, 1968) also helps widen our understanding through his theory of psychosocial stages of development, suggesting eight stages of child and adult development in terms of tasks to solve or crises to resolve in order for there not to be a lag in a child's development and maturity. In children these are: Trust vs. Mistrust (0 - 18 months); Autonomy vs. Shame and Doubt (from 18 months to 3 years); Initiative vs. Guilt (from 3 to 7 years); Industry vs. Inferiority (from 7 to 12 years); and Identity vs. Identity Diffusion (from 12 years to maturity) (see Table 1).

The rich tradition of psychoanalytic child development theory and practice has been invaluable in contributing to our theoretical and clinical knowledge of psychological processes at work in both children and adults. Its theoretical foundation in the unconscious and emphasis on defenses, however, has led to a focus in working with children on the neurotic (occasionally psychotic), disordered, maladjusted and "problem" child. In this chapter the author promotes and develops the view that humanistic psychotherapy–which, following Maslow (1962), is regarded as epi-Freudian and epi-behavioristic ("epi" meaning "building upon")–has a more complete, realistic and positive approach to working with children than that of the psychoanalytic tradition alone.

Various schools within the humanistic tradition have built upon–and separated from–previous theories and conceptualizations of child development. Berne (1961/1975), the founder of Transactional Analysis· (TA), added the existentially healthy life position "I'm OK, You're OK" (I+, U+) to Klein's (1932) paranoid (I+, U-), depressive (I-, U+), and schizoid (I-, U-) positions. TA has a theoretical understanding of child development in terms of ego states and script formation and a number of concepts–such as protection, therapeutic potency and permission–which are of practical use in working with children (see Tudor, 1998). Gestalt and person-centered therapy are particularly close on their conceptualization of human development, both viewing the self as a process rather than a structure, developing fluidity in the context of the environmental field (see Perls, Hefferline, & Goodman, 1951/1973; Rogers, 1951). In describing behavior as "the goal-directed attempt of the organism to satisfy the experienced needs for actualization in the reality as perceived" (Rogers, 1959, p. 222), Rogers even uses the word gestalt to describe the human infant's interaction with its environment: in this he or she behaves "as an organized whole, as a gestalt" (ibid, 1959, p. 222). More recently, Gestalt therapists/theorists have contributed to a Gestalt understanding of child development (see Mackewn, 1991; Crocker, 1992), of attachment theory (Harris, 1996) and of self-psychology and the work of Stern (1985) (Friedman, 1992).

Drawing on these approaches within the humanistic tradition, the author suggests using the Gestalt "contact" cycle, both as a practical tool in working with children, particularly in groups, and as a theoretical framework for understanding phases of child development. In this work, the author thus takes an integrating view: that is, integrating elements of other psychotherapeutic approaches, notably TA, into a Gestalt perspective. This

Table 1
Using the Gestalt Cycle as an Organizing Framework for Child Development

PHASE OF GESTALT CYCLE	AGE	STAGES OF LIFE CYCLE *(Erikson, 1968)*	INTERRUPTION	INJUNCTION *(Goulding & Goulding, 1976)*	AFFIRMATION *(Levin, 1974)*	INTERVENTIONS, EXERCISES, & PLAY *(referred to in text)*
Sensation	0 to 6 months	Trust vs. Mistrust	Desensitization	Don't feel; don't exist	For being	"Feeling" corners, event/action statements, & questions
Awareness	6 to 18 months	Trust vs. Mistrust	Deflection	Don't know	For doing	Ego state faces *(Kleineweisse, 1980)*
Mobilization	18 months to 3 years	Autonomy vs. Shame & Doubt	Introjection	Don't think	For thinking; for feeling	Emotional literacy *(Steiner, 1984)*, problem solving, & role play
Action	3 to 7 years	Initiative vs. Guilt	Projection	Don't do; don't act	For power & identity	Role play & modeling
Contact	7 to 12 years	Industry vs. Inferiority	Retroflection	Don't make it	For structure	"Unfinished business," emotional literacy, fun, & play
Satisfaction	12 to 18 years	Identity vs. Identity/Role Confusion	Egotism	Don't enjoy	For sex; for separation	Appreciations
Withdrawal	18 years+	Intimacy vs. Isolation	Confluence	Don't let go	(For responsibility)	Letting go; good-byes

work is also part of the author's wider enquiry into promoting mental health and preventing mental and emotional ill health–as distinct from preventing mental illness (see Tudor, 1996).

Gestalt Therapy

Within the humanistic/existential tradition, philosophical assumptions rest on conceptions of the wholeness of human beings and their potential for autonomy and social responsibility. Maslow (1962) identifies two main emphases of existential psychology: "a radical stress on the concept of identity" and a "great stress on starting from experiential knowledge" (p. 9). Gestalt psychology may be regarded as epitomizing such existential stresses: "Gestalt practice represents a complete body of theory and technique which appears to use the major tenets of existentialism in the counseling and psychotherapeutic situation" (Clarkson, 1989, p.13). Clarkson summarizes and updates a number of "fundamentals" of the Gestalt approach, including: a dialogic therapeutic relationship; wholeness; the organismic tendency towards self-regulation; authenticity of the psychotherapist; respect for the integrity of defense and the challenge to change; the here-and-now; and the philosophical and ecological fact of "response-ability"–all of which may be applied to working and being with children whether therapeutically, educationally or socially.

Despite the wholeness of Gestalt psychology as a theory and practice, and with the exception of Oaklander's (1969/1988, 1982) notable contributions to the field, remarkably little has been written on working with children. Only one major article on working with children has appeared in The Gestalt Journal in nearly two decades–Shub (1981) and that focuses on methods and stages of intervention that are by no means unique to Gestalt psychotherapy. In Britain, Harris has written about the implications of attachment theory for Gestalt therapy (Harris, 1996), and of a single session with a bereaved fifteen-year-old client (Harris, 1994). In a process that is conceptually parallel to that of the clinical situation, the ground that is Gestalt psychology needs to be differentiated into and applied to the figure of work with children.

As with other schools within the humanistic/existential tradition, Gestalt psychotherapy emphasizes the movement towards health (and healthy self-regulation) and, in doing so, challenges a strictly medical model view of disease: symptom-diagnosis-cure.

The description of psychological health and disease is a simple

> one. It is a matter of the identification and alienations of the self: if a man [sic] identifies with his forming self, does not inhibit his own creative excitement and reaching towards the coming solution; and conversely, if he alienates what is not organically his own and therefore cannot be organically interesting, but rather disrupts the figure/background, then he is psychologically healthy (Perls, Hefferline, & Goodman, 1951/1973, p. 282).

It follows from this that for adults "no persisting desire can be regarded as infantile or illusory" (ibid, 1973, p. 347); and that for children the "maturing" developmental process is one of more or less contact and interruption to "inhibition" (Perls, 1947/1969) or frustration of contact at the contact boundary in the (self) organismic/environment field. It is, therefore as, if not more, important to identify healthy rather than neurotic processes. As Oaklander (1982) puts it: "all concepts, principles and theoretical discussions presented in the body of Gestalt literature available today can be related to child growth and development as well as to child pathology" (p. 64).

Oaklander also recognizes–as Rogers (1951) does–that "behaviors or symptoms are manifestations of a search for health" (Oaklander, 1982, p. 69) and that "behavior is basically the goal-directed attempt of the organism to satisfy its needs as experienced, in the field as perceived" (Rogers, 1951, p. 491). Thus, from a Gestalt and a person-centered perspective, "naughty," "bad," or "maladjusted" behavior is, more accurately and usefully, understood as an expression of the child's basic organismic motivational tendency. In this way, aggressive behavior may be understood precisely as aggression, that is: "everything that an organism does to initiate contact with its environment" (Perls, Hefferline, & Goodman, 1951/1973, p. 100-101). These humanistic approaches to the person are helpful in working with, for instance, children diagnosed and labeled as anti-social, with behavior problems and, most insidiously, having Attention Deficit/Hyperactivity Disorder (ADHD). Although ADHD is the subject of much controversy, my own experience of working with children is that, as a diagnosis (American Psychiatric Association, 1994), it is too readily applied, viewing and focusing on the "inattention" in the child rather than taking a systemic overview and assessment of the child in his or her phenomenological field, one which includes the family, school, community and culture.

Working with Children

As has been indicated, psychotherapeutic work with children has a long history, one of the key defining moments of which was the discovery of the importance of play. It was Klein (1932) who first saw that play could replace adults' free association as a medium of communication. However, it was Winnicott (1971, 1977/1989) who elaborated this aspect of working with children, seeing play taking place in the area between the child's inner and outer reality, and expressed through "transitional phenomena" or a "transitional object." Shmuckler & Friedman (1988) have connected personality theory and child development through play: "since play can be regarded as a central developmental process, it provides an important link between understanding healthy development and clinical process" (p. 82). As regards play therapy, Winnicott (1971) emphasizes the importance of play in itself and not for any interpretive value it may have for the therapist. While there are several good (re)sources for the therapist working with children–of which West's (1992) extremely thorough book on Child-Centered Play Therapy is a prime example–the ability to play and to be creative are essential personal and professional requirements for the therapist in this field.

Working with children also raises a number of issues additional to those under consideration when working with consenting adult clients: legal (see Jenkins, 1997), contractual (see Tudor, 1998), professional (in terms of further professional development and training), ethical, and practical. Most professional therapeutic training prepares the practitioner for working with individual adults and yet, post qualification, many therapists, particularly in the humanistic tradition, work with couples, groups, families, and children. In this respect, the psychoanalytic tradition is much more rigorous in its insistence on further specialist training for such specialist work–and on infant observation forming an essential part of an understanding of child development as the basis of working with adults and children; an argument I take up as regards clinical training in TA (Tudor, 1998). Campos (1988) highlights the ethical dilemma of working with children when they are returning to the same oppressive, parental/family environment and proposes "anti-injunctive" work with parents. Equally, in terms of the family dynamics and the parent/s' parenting skills, it is important that the therapist does not "take over" or undermine the parenting, or create an unhealthy dependence in the psychotherapeutic setting (see Winnicott, 1963/1965a). On this basis, all therapy may be viewed as family therapy. On the other hand, on the basis that an "enlightened, conscious witness" (Miller, 1991) is crucial in the face of unenlightened, unconscious or abusive parenting, it is argued that individual therapy with children is better than no therapy at all. In working with children (as with adults), it is important to provide a facilitating environment–in both practical and conceptual terms. Thus the physical environment needs to be suitable for a variety of play in terms of space (especially for a group), equipment (soft toys, drawing materials, sand, water, etc.), and boundaries. Thus, the fact that the workshops (described below) were not open to parents showed regard to the protective boundary around the children's space–as well as trust on the part of the parents/carers and the facilitators' trust in the children. In this respect, "children are our finest teachers. They already know how to grow, how to develop, how to learn, how to expand and discover... what is right for them and what is not right for them, what they need... All they (and the children within us) need is the space to do it" (Oaklander, 1969/1988, p. 324).

Working with Children in Groups

With rare exceptions, most therapeutic work with children takes place with the individual child, and there is only a small literature on group therapy with children (e.g., Gazda, 1978; Ginott, 1961/1994; Lennox, 1982; Slavson, 1950, 1952; West, 1992). However, there are good arguments for working with children in groups, particularly given the centrality of the therapeutic medium of play: "group play-therapy provides two media for catharsis, play and verbalization, so that each child can utilize the symbolic means of expression which best meet his need...the group accelerates the child's awareness of the permissiveness of the setting" (Ginott, 1961/1994, p. 7-8). Working with children in groups also has the advantage of peer group interaction, example and feedback. In a discussion of systemic assessment, Clarkson and Fish (1988) summarize the advantages and disadvantages of family, individual and group work with children in different contexts.

The inspiration and aspiration for the work described came firstly from a practical concern to put working with children more on the map within TA; and thus, for instance, to offer children at conferences a workshop on TA in their own right (as distinct from offering the parents creche/childcare facilities); in the events, many parents also wanted to attend the workshops! A second concern was a theoretical one to explore and develop concepts within TA and Gestalt psychotherapy for practical use in working with children. We began at a conference with a workshop attended by an international group of children with an age range of five to 14. Subsequently, we ran several workshops at conferences, a two-day group, and presented our work to adults at an education conference.

In initial presentations, specific material on "emotional literacy," which Steiner (1984) defines as knowing "both what it is that we are feeling and what the causes for our feelings are" (p. 165), was presented. We learned that as well as creating structure, we needed to be able to respond to issues and conflicts that came up in the less structured, "free" playtime the children wanted themselves. In fact, the most valuable "teaching" was elicited from interactions (transactions) in play, thus bearing out Winnicott's (1971) observation, made in the context of an individual child analysis, that "it is not possible for a child of this age (4 years) to get the meaning out of a game unless first of all the game is played and enjoyed. As a matter of principle, the analyst always allows the enjoyment to become established before the content of the play is used for interpretation" (p. 175). Campos (1986) regards play as an intervention in itself: "it is important to allow children to freely choose their play activity because such play serves as a permission structure where children can express their own feelings and needs in a positive setting" (p. 21).

In subsequent workshops we focused more and more on what the children themselves brought. Thus we explored issues about home (including how to deal with particular situations with regard to parents, siblings and family), school (similarly, in relation to peers, teachers, bullying, etc.), as well as issues of self-esteem and children's powerlessness. Whatever the content we aimed to create a "cooperative social environment" which Steiner (1984) describes as "an ideal ecology for the development of emotional literacy" (p. 167).

Working with Children in Groups: Contact and Interdependency

Later, we developed the practice of explaining to children the contact cycle–or, originally, the "cycle of the interdependency of organism and environment" (Perls, 1947/1969). (See Figure 1.) The "interruptions" to contact may also be considered in terms accessible to children (although they were not generally explained as such directly to the children with whom we worked) and are represented in Figure 3 (although it is recognized that any interruption to contact may occur at any phase) (also see Goulding & Goulding, 1976 and Figure 1).

Working with children in groups is described in terms of the phases of the "contact" cycle. While the examples quoted are neither exhaustive nor complete, and there is in practice an organismic ebb and flow between the phases, there was nevertheless a sense of development and movement through the cycle.

Sense/Feel

Although the more accurate translation for children of the sensation phase of the Gestalt cycle is sense and sensing, "sense" and especially "common sense" have pejorative connotations. Also, children have a less restricted (adulterated) relation to feelings that tend to be whole body, organismic sensations. In order to help children contact their feelings, on one workshop we created four "feeling corners:" happy, sad, frightened and angry. Each of these corners was represented by face drawings (developed from Kleineweise, 1980) and each equipped with furniture, toys and materials suitable for encouraging the children to "get in touch with" that particular feeling. Children were then invited to spend time in one or more of the corners of their choice, to explore their feelings and different ways of reacting to them. One question we asked the children at this phase was an action or "event/action" question, a development of the "feeling/action statement" (Steiner, 1984): for example, "When you tap your foot, what are you feeling? This also confronts passivity and passive behavior" (Schiff, et al., 1975).

Know

"Helping the child become aware of what he (and his organism) needs is the first vital step toward overcoming fragmentation and achieving integration" (Oaklander, 1982, p. 66). The "four corners" provide an experiential way for children both to feel and to know which feeling they are experiencing. At other times we used a more cognitive approach, using concepts developed in TA such as ego states, identifying "Feeling," "Thinking," and "Looking After" aspects of ourselves, using representational face drawings of different ego states (Kleineweise, 1980). We did this in a number of ways, depending on the age-range of the group. One popular experiment was to ask the children to say, draw or color in how they themselves feel when they are feeling, thinking or looking after. Sometimes we asked them "When you look like this..." (referring to the picture they had drawn), "How does your mum/dad look?" (asking the child to then choose or draw another picture). Campos (1986) implicitly warns against doing this kind of work with younger children as "they identify with their parents and lack a solid 'I' identity... Children will discount their feelings and needs to satisfy a needy parent" (p.19). Oaklander (1982) suggests, "deflection is probably the most common of the contact boundary disturbances manifested by children" (p. 68). As psychotherapists and childcare workers, appreciating the significance of developmental stages of the children with whom we work cannot be over-emphasized. During this phase in workshops the question is asked, "When do you feel... (angry, sad, etc.?)," thereby aiming to give children encouragement and support to know what they feel when they feel it. We also addressed individual and group process by asking "What do you think is happening now?"

Think

Working with children, this phase of the contact cycle is essentially about facilitating their thinking about what they can do–as a link between "Knowing" and "Doing" (the mobilization and action phases of the contact cycle). In this phase we helped children think through which options they themselves have in dealing with their own feelings as well as the environ-

Figure 1
The Gestalt Contact Cycle
(From Clarkson, 1989, p. 20)

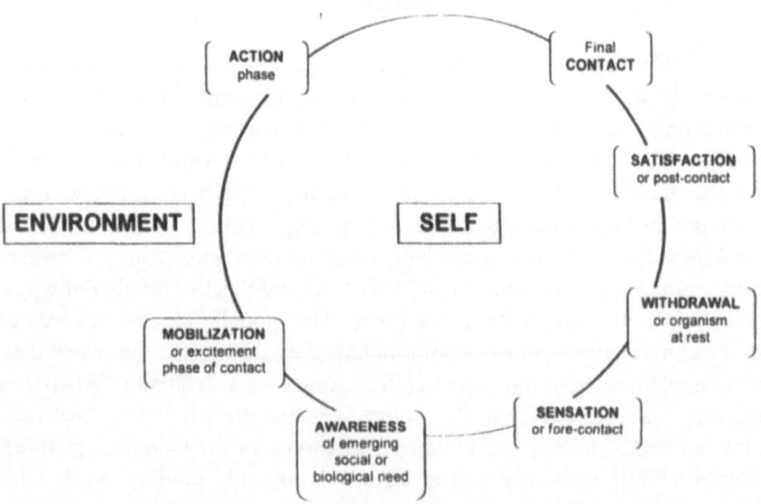

Figure 2
The Gestalt Contact Cycle for Children

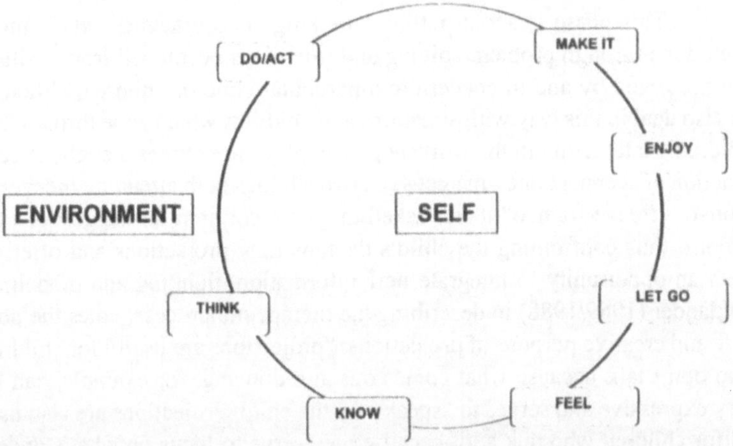

mental pressures they face. The ego/environment boundary (Perls, Hefferline & Goodman, 1951/1973) is interrupted by parental "shoulds" and "oughts." In this phase the children we worked with often needed to "check out" what is possible to think (and do) and what is possible to do in different contexts. What is OK to do here, in a safe, protective "cooperative social environment" may not be acceptable to do at home or in school. One group of boys expressed their incredulity when, in setting up a role-play and in response to their request, we told them that it would be all right for them to swear; having asked this and taken the permission, in the event they did not take up the option. The notion of different contexts, "realities" and frames of reference is a familiar one to children, particularly from around seven onwards, and is also a crucial one at the thinking phase. In this phase we were able to think through and (re)solve dilemmas on such issues as how to deal with relatives who demand a kiss, demanding younger brothers, and bullying at school. We explored these issues from a position of "How do you get what you want?" while maintaining two fundamentals of Gestalt: organismic self-regulation, together with individual and collective responsibility. Through our work with children I have become acutely aware of the immediate and wider societal context in which children are often immobilized in a powerless position. Clarkson (1988) suggests ways in which this creates ego state dilemmas in abused children.

Do/Act

This phase is about putting "thinking" into practice. This is most often done through problem-solving and role-plays developed from a situation presented by and of concern to a particular child or children, although we also deal in this way with situations and conflicts which arise through the children's interaction in the workshop or in play. Sometimes we rehearsed a situation or scene–at one time between two siblings both attending the workshop–or "freeze-framed" it and asked the other children for suggestions on options, thus confronting the child's de-activating projections and offering them an opportunity to integrate new information, thinking and modeling. Oaklander (1969/1988) in describing the therapeutic process, notes the positive and creative purpose of projections: "projections are useful for children who don't talk because what comes out in a drawing, for example, can be very expressive and serves to "speak" for the child. Projections are also useful for children who talk a lot because they serve to focus on what's underneath the talk" (p.193). In this phase, particularly, we noticed the children

Figure 3
The Gestalt Contact Cycle with Representational Examples of Interruptions
(With reference to Clarkson, 1989, p. 50).

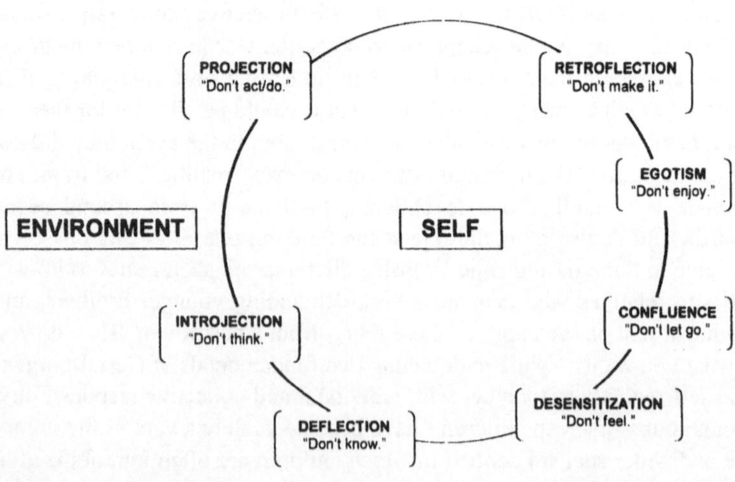

watch our modeling–an argument for co-leadership of such groups–and we acknowledged and supported new, experimental behavior. One of the common themes of such role-plays was that of children wanting and needing to learn how to defend and/or claim their own space. In our experience, the emotional and physical invasion of children from concerned over-parenting may be as common as neglect and needs to be recognized as abusive.

Make It

In this phase we again used Steiner's (1984) material on emotional literacy with the aim that the children would make full contact both with themselves and with others in their immediate environment. This contact and the emotional (and physical) organismic movement then involved confronting the interruption of retroflection, or turning in upon themselves. Perls (1947/1969) suggests that "the therapy of retroflections is simpler than the therapy of either repressions of projections... in retroflection… we can always deal with a conscious part... of the personality, which directs its activities against another part" (p. 221). Often in this phase we dealt with "unfinished business" between any of us. Near the end of a workshop or session, we had a chair on which each of the participants sits (or stands!) to receive acknowledgements and positive feedback from their peers and ourselves as group leaders. We also developed a lot of play and fun in this phase. One group culminated in dressing up and enacting a transformation scene for each child that symbolized their "journey' and change during the workshop. We also encouraged children to work out their own ways of making contact and in their own time. One 5-year-old spoke for the two days of a group through a totemic rubber man figure. Only near the end of the two days did he speak for himself when he said: "I liked this." This is what Campos (1988) refers to as "the totemic principle," one of four organizing principles he identifies in children's play.

Enjoy

In terms of the Gestalt cycle and our work with children, this phase is usually a moment (or few minutes) of enjoyment expressed by a child who has "made it" or achieved what he or she wanted in the previous phase. It is the beam of pure pleasure; it is the moment of realization that "I can do it" or "I did it;" it is the jump for joy at the end of a role-play in which a young girl has "discovered" (or contacted) a new way of expressing herself so that she can assert herself in her world; it is the moment when a child says "This is the best fun I've ever had!" It is a phase of intimacy with oneself and the environment: "contact, figure/background formation, is a mounting excitement, feelingful and concernful" (Perls, Hefferline & Goodman 1951/1973, p. 280). Any "intervention" at this (and the final) phase generally focused more on the process. We intervened at times to allow and encourage a pause–a time for appreciation and for enjoyment before moving on, for example–by saying to a child who is rushing on to the next activity, "Stop, pause, take a break." This is especially important in most North European and North American societies, and in an age of information overload, where we all too quickly seek the next peak experience without enjoying the last or present one.

Let Go

Similarly, in this phase it is important that interventions allow the children to experience the completion and closure of a particular cycle. Sometime when groups wanted to repeat a game or role-play, we saw this as an attempt to re-experience that particular sensation or enjoyment as a way of not letting go or ending. It is important that good endings are facilitated in order to confront the invitation to unhealthy confluence. Thus, at times during a workshop, after a particular interaction or event and near the end of a session, we built in a time for withdrawal. At one conference, at the end of the final session of a series of children's workshops we literally and physically laid out the Gestalt cycle for children with each phase as a stepping-stone and invited the children to jump from each phase to the next as they followed their own feeling(s) around the cycle. It was one of the most enjoyable, breathless, and feelingful moments of the entire conference, at the end of which we all collapsed in the middle of the circle in the middle of the lawn, literally and metaphorically representing the boundary between our self/selves and the environment. We then paused for some moments, moving from a state of satisfaction to withdrawal as we said goodbye.

A Complete Cycle

It is possible to identify and describe a complete cycle, indeed it is organismic to do so, developing from the initial phase when, for instance, a boy who had started off in the sad "feeling corner" moved to the "frightened corner" and curled up by himself (Feeling, Knowing). The therapist acknowledged that the boy was feeling frightened and that he knew that he felt frightened; the therapist then asked him to think about what else he could do (Thinking) other than curling up by himself. The boy responded by shaking and calling out (Doing) and, for a while, appeared more frightened (Making It/Contact). After a while, the therapist, responding to the child who had called out, asked him what he wanted. The boy put his arms up, reaching out to the therapist. The therapist asked him if he wanted a hug; the boy nodded and, while being hugged, smiled (Enjoying). The boy then stood up and, slightly apart from the therapist, paused for a moment (Letting Go), and looked back at him before resuming his place in the group.

> As her senses awaken, as she begins to know her body again, as she recognizes, accepts and expresses her buried feelings, as she learns to use her intellect to make choices, to verbalize her wants and needs and thoughts and ideas and to find ways to get her needs met, as she learns who she is and accepts who she is in her differentness from you and me, she will then find herself once again upon her rightful path of growth (Oaklander, 1982, p. 69).

The contact cycle may be seen in operation from any phase. However, if a client begins at a phase other than sensation they often have to be helped to retrace their steps to an earlier phase of the cycle; thus a client stuck at the Action phase may not have resolved the immobilizing introjections of the previous phase.

Conclusion

This chapter has reported ways of working with children in groups using Gestalt therapy and drawing on Transactional Analysis. In addition to being used on a micro level to describe, say, moments of a particular and precise sensation, the Gestalt contact cycle may also be used on a macro level as an organising framework for stages of child development. Table 1 reflects this, integrating the phases of the cycle with chronological ages and with Erikson's (1968) epigenetic stages of the life cycle, with injunctions and affirmations (from TA) and notes some of the interventions, exercises and play referred to in the description of working with children in groups.

Author's Note

The original article on which this chapter is based first appeared in the *British Gestalt Journal* in 1991 (Vol. 1, pp.21-27). This chapter was written in 1996-1997 since which time my own thinking and language have evolved. Today I would want to refer to more recent developments in child development and self-psychology and to emphasize the dialogic and co-creative aspects of the work.

Also, by my use of "we" and "our" in the text, I acknowledge the support and enthusiasm of my friend and colleague, Graeme Summers, with whom I ran the workshops from which I have drawn much of this material. I am also grateful to him for his contribution to the development of the Gestalt contact cycle for use with children and to Elana Leigh with whom we ran a two-day workshop for children.

References

American Psychiatric Association (1994). *Diagnostic and statistical manual of mental disorders, fourth edition.* Washington, DC: APA.

Berne, E. (1975). *Transactional analysis in psychotherapy.* London: Souvenir Press.

Campos, L. (1986). Empowering children: Primary prevention of script formation. *Transactional Analysis Journal, 16*, 16-23.

Campos, L. (1988). Empowering children II: Integrating protection into script prevention work. *Transactional Analysis Journal, 18*, 137-140.

Clarkson, P. (1988). Ego state dilemmas of abused children. *Transactional Analysis Journal, 18*, 85-93.

Clarkson, P. (1989). *Gestalt counselling in action.* London: Sage.

Clarkson, P., & Fish, S. (1988). Systemic assessment and treatment consideration in TA child psychotherapy. *Transactional Analysis Journal, 18*, 123-132.

Crocker, S. (1992). A philosophical framework for understanding developmental issues. Paper prepared for The Gestalt Journal's Annual Conference, Boston, MA.

Erikson, E. (1965). *Childhood and society.* Harmondsworth: Penguin.

Erikson, E. (1968). *Identity, youth and crisis.* New York, NY: W.W. Norton.

Freud, S. (1973). *Introductory lectures on psychoanalysis.* Harmondsworth: Penguin.

Freud, S. (1977). *Case histories 1: 'Dora' and 'Little Hans.'* Harmondsworth: Penguin.

Friedman, M.S. (1992). The infant research of Daniel Stern and its implications for gestalt therapy. Paper presented at The Gestalt Journal's Annual Conference, Boston, MA.

Gazda, G.M. (1978). *Group counseling: A developmental approach.* Boston, MA: Allyn and Bacon.

Ginott, H.G. (1994). *Group psychotherapy with children.* Northvale, NJ: Jason Aronson.

Goulding, R.S. & Goulding, M. (1976). Injunctions, decisions and redecisions. *Transactional Analysis Journal, 6*, 41-48.

Harris, N. (1994). A practical consideration: How many words do I need? A clinical vignette. *British Gestalt Journal, 3*, 114-116.

Harris, N. (1996). Attachment theory: Some implications for gestalt therapy. *British Gestalt Journal, 5*, 103-112.

Jenkins, P. (1997). *Counseling, psychotherapy and the law.* London: Sage.

Klein, M. (1932). *The pychoanalysis of children.* London: Hogarth Press.

Kleinewise, E. (1980). *Circle-face symbols.* Berlin: Institut fur Kommunikationstherapie.

Lennox, D. (1982). *Residential group therapy for children.* London: Tavistock.

Levin, P. (1974). *Becoming the way we are.* Menlo Park, CA: Trans Pubs.

Mackewn, J. (1991). Child development in early gestalt literature. Unpublished paper.

Maslow, A.H. (1962). *Towards a psychology of being.* New York, NY: Van Nostrand.

Miller, A. (1991). *Banished knowledge. Facing childhood injuries*, (L. Vennewitz, Trans.). London: Virago.

Oaklander, V. (1982). The relationship of gestalt therapy to children. *The Gestalt Journal, 5*, 64-74.

Oaklander, V. (1988). *Windows to our children: A gestalt approach to children and adolescents.* Highland, NY: The Center for Gestalt Development.

Perls, F.S. (1969). *Ego, hunger and aggression: The beginning of gestalt therapy.* New York, NY: Random House.

Perls, F.S., Hefferline, R.F., & Goodman, P. (1973). *Gestalt therapy: Excitement and growth in the human personality.* New York, NY:

Bantam Books.
Rogers, C.R. (1951). *Client-centered therapy*. London: Constable.
Rogers, C.R. (1959). A theory of therapy, personality, and interpersonal relationships, as developed in the client-centered framework. In S. Koch (Ed.), *Psychology: A study of science, vol. 3: Formulations of the person and the social context*, (pp.184-256). New York, NY: McGraw-Hill.
Schiff, A.W., Mellor, K., Schiff, E., Schiff, S., Richman, D., Fishman, J., Wolz, L., Fishman, C., & Momb, D. (1975). *Cathexis reader: Transactional analysis treatment of psychosis*. New York, NY: Harper & Row.
Shmuckler, D., & Friedman, M. (1988). The developmental function of play and its relevance for Transactional Analysis. *Transactional Analysis Journal, 18*, 80-84.
Shub, N. (1981). Psychotherapy in the classroom. *The Gestalt Journal, 4*, 47-56.
Slavson, S.R. (1950). *Analytic group psychotherapy with children, adolescents, and adults*. New York, NY: Columbia University Press.
Slavson, S.R. (1952). *Child psychotherapy*. New York, NY: Columbia University Press.
Steiner, C. (1984). Emotional literacy. *Transactional Analysis Journal, 14*, 162-173.
Stern, D. (1985). *The interpersonal world of the infant*. New York, NY: Basic Books.
Tudor, K. (1996). *Mental health promotion: Paradigms and practice*. London: Routledge.
Tudor, K. (1998). Working with the individual child in TA psychotherapy. Manuscript submitted for publication.
West, J. (1992). *Child-centered play therapy*. London: Edward Arnold.
Winnicott, D.W. (1965a). Dependence in infant-care, in child-care, and in the psycho-analytic setting. In M.M.R. Khan (Ed.), *The maturational processes and the facilitating environment* (pp. 249-259). London: Hogarth Press.
Winnicott, D.W. (1965b). *The maturational process and them facilitating environment*. London: Hogarth Press.
Winnicott, D:W. (1971). *Playing and reality*. Harmondsworth: Penguin.
Winnicott, D.W. (1989). *The piggle*. Harmondsworth: Penguin.

5

Compulsion and Curiosity: A Gestalt Approach to OCD

Gordon Wheeler

Like many 10-year-olds, Mark had a basketball hoop in his room, the freestanding kind with a backboard on a post, supported by a weighted pyramid base. And like many other kids his age, he was in the habit of shooting a few baskets at odd moments, especially before getting into bed at night. It was not unusual either that Mark liked to end on a good shot, and didn't like to quit until he had one. What was unusual was that in Mark's case this bedtime routine had somehow mushroomed into a lengthy and exacting ritual, which had to be accomplished in every last detail, or else there was no possible way he could settle down and get to sleep.

To begin with, the successful shot had to be a swish–that is, it had to go through without touching backboard or rim. Then it had to hit the floor and "die" (Mark's own word for it, meaning come to a stop) without at all touching the carpet that covered the room from the other end, where the bed was. This part was tricky, because if the ball came straight down on the pyramid base, it would naturally be deflected out into the carpet area, and an otherwise perfect shot would be ruined.

By the time Mark came to see me, this nightly ritual had grown into a full-scale ordeal that could take three hours or more a night. And they were three hours of torture for the family, with Mark in tears, his mother alternately yelling and crying, his father leaving the room and sometimes the house to manage his own anger and distress–even Mark's two sisters were beginning to be drawn in. Of the three therapists the family had consulted before they got to me, two had recommended he be taken straight to the Obsessive-Compulsive Disorder Clinic at a local teaching hospital for evaluation and medication, which is increasingly the treatment chosen for

OCD.[1]

What are we to make of "obsessive-compulsive" behavior? What does it mean when people repetitiously exhibit lengthy and stereotyped behavioral sequences that have to be performed in just a certain way and seem to make no sense to other people? And then what are we to do about it, what stance should we take? Are these behaviors the residue of unattached libidinal and aggressive energy, incompletely cathected/sublimated in the Oedipal crisis? (Few people would say so today, and yet our language for discussing these and other clinical problems remains extensively grounded in the classical psychodynamic model). Or are they dysfunctional past learning schedules that can now be altered for the better with reinforcement, and the behavior reshaped? Are they faulty belief systems? Perhaps a biochemical anomaly, which can be medicated away? Anxiety? If so, then what is anxiety, from a Gestalt or any other perspective?

Or does the problem lie rather in the family dynamic, the interpersonal "system," which may somehow be working to support the problem behavior and block change, in the service of something else? Is the family "undifferentiated," so that one person's moods and anxiety are somehow felt by others as their own–and if so, how does that happen? Or are we dealing here with a "fixed Gestalt"–and then what does that mean, and what do we do about it?

All of these possibilities (and some others) represent positions of major schools of therapy with regard to OCD. All of them plainly have some merit to them–even the classical psychodynamic, if we take it metaphorically enough, as Goodman (1977) did. And as Goodman liked to say, if all of us are looking at the "same animal," and all of us are sincere and none of us is crazy, then there must be some meaningful connection between and among our different ways of understanding these events (Perls, Hefferline & Goodman, 1951). What is that connection, and what is the particular Gestalt perspective on the problem? What does a Gestalt approach add to all the others, how does it differ–and most of all, how might it help us to contextualize and make sense of the sometimes bewildering array of other approaches? Because clearly if Gestalt, which bills itself as a "holistic" method, can fulfill its promise in this contextualizing way, then the "necessary eclecticism" forced on us by our patients can itself become a meaningful whole, and not just a menu of choices.

When I asked Mark what he thought his nighttime basketball activity meant, he said, not surprisingly, that he didn't know. "Well," I countered, "how about if I push you a little bit on that: when people feel like they have to do something just a certain way, and they're very upset if it doesn't work out, and they can't go on to the next thing, then a lot of times they say they feel very anxious about something. Would he say he felt anxious, say during the basketball routine, or during the day beforehand? "No," Mark replied, "I wouldn't say that."

But–I insisted–his parents were telling me he was very upset about *something* every night, and he himself said he couldn't possibly fall asleep until the task he had set for himself had been accomplished successfully: would he call that feeling anxiety, or nervousness, or what would he call it exactly? "Anxious, I guess," was Mark's somewhat grudging reply after another moment–maybe more as a way of managing me and my questions than anything else!

(Here I was reminded of 12-year-old Paul, who told me he'd decided to give up his presenting problem–a quite serious one of hurting himself with hard objects–because "it's just not worth it anymore if I have to come here and talk to you about it every time I do it." Not that he didn't want to come! He did, so he could "whip my butt" in our best-of-fifty Very Sorry tournament, where he was trailing badly at the moment, mostly because he played so unaggressively, and didn't pay any attention to my game, but only concentrated on his own. He just didn't want to have to talk about his "symptom," so he was giving it up to remove it as a possible topic. Was this therapy-as-punishment–or was it that Paul just didn't feel so much like hurting himself, now that he felt more empathic interest (from both of us) in himself and his subjective world? Or was it that he now had a better venue –the interpersonal field between us–for exploring/expressing aggression? Or all of the above? What we can say for sure is that the entry of another person, the therapist, into the subjective field of the problem somehow changed the problem, so that the patient organized his own field in some significantly different way).

With Mark, of course my aim at this early point was not to force him to parrot my terms–though I might be interested in pushing him, now or later, to try them on. On the contrary, I was delighted to see his resistance and then his sullenness–he was such a polite boy! To me, these things seemed to be positive signs for a productive relationship in the future, which might include some elements of conflict or struggle. For now, my hope was rather to begin mapping out the ground for what it was we were going to do together, what stance we were going to take up (together, if he would), toward his problems and his world. Specifically, I wanted to begin establishing the following things, which I also told him explicitly:

(1) that feelings matter, they are subtle and complex parts of ourselves that serve to orient us, to point us to where it is we want to go (or away from where we don't want to go). If we don't know our feelings, don't have a language of feeling, then we're operating without a compass, at least a big part of the time;

(2) that we get to know our feelings, develop and articulate and nuance that language, principally through kicking them around with another person, who takes an interest in our internal world;

(3) that behavior always has a meaning, or meanings, and that it is interesting, important, and very possible for us to figure out, together, what at least some of those meanings might be;

(4) and, finally, that for better or worse (or both), if we worked together then I was going to insist on being involved in some way, to some degree, in Mark's internal world (and here again was why it was important to begin getting some sense of Mark's capacity for resistance, which would be a crucial support for us in the work. If he couldn't resist the contact/influence of another person–which after all might be the nature of his problem in the first place–then we would first have to nurture and develop that capacity, before we could struggle together over other things, and he could wrest and own his own meanings).

Finally–and this part I did not try to say to Mark directly–in the Gestalt model there is an important sense in which all these four things–the language of feelings, the intersubjective exploration/construction of that language, the question of meaning, and the nature of the interpersonal field–are really the same thing, or aspects of the same thing. To understand this, we first need to back up and discuss the Gestalt notion of the concept/construct of self, and how that differs from the understanding of self and self-functions in other models.

Self-Process: A Gestalt View

Broadly speaking, in the Western tradition from the pre-Socratics through the Christian writers and on down through Freud, the self, or self-function, has been thought of as something purely internal, private, more or less equivalent to what we mean when we say "innermost self," the me known only to me–and perhaps to God. This last is significant, because "self" in this sense is very close, in the dominant tradition, to the term "soul"–that which is essential about a person, is ontologically real, and by definition (in that model) essentially and permanently separate and distinct from other selves. This is the monadic theory of self, articulated by Leibniz (1714) but actually characterizing the whole of the last three millennia in the West, at least in its dominant voices. The behavioral world yielded by this view is a billiard-ball world, where one "windowless monad," to use Leibniz's term, bounces blindly or "selfishly" off of the others–but all according to a divine plan, all for the best in the best of all possible worlds (this is the arbitrary or inorganic optimism satirized in Voltaire's *Candide.*) The glue of this universe, or for that matter of any society or any relationship within it, lies in the mind of God, not in any organic or inherent interconnectedness–or as we might say now, intersubjectivity–between and among individual people. Separate individuality is real; connectedness is only instrumental, and thus essentially illusory. Subtract God from the picture, and you are left with the world-view (and self-view) of the behavioral model, or of Nietzsche[2] or Freud, (each monadic self striving to act out its own monadic drive)–and, clearly, with the crisis of meaning that has characterized Western culture for the past century and more.

Of course, there has been a counter-tradition in the West, or various counter-traditions–chiefly the mystical tradition in its many variations, which typically have more closely paralleled the Eastern views of an underlying or supraindividual self. In these views it is connectedness that is essential and real, and separate individuality that is illusory. In the social/secular realm this tradition takes the form of the various communitarian movements which have been particularly strong in 19th and 20th-century America, and which very much influenced the Gestaltist, Paul Goodman (1947).

It was Goodman's particular achievement to attack the self problem in a way that refused to downgrade either pole of these two great broad streams of thinking–the individual and the collective–but rather insisted on retaining, even heightening, the creative tension between them. Indeed, he identified that tension itself, that "boundary," as the location and essence of the self-function, or as he would say, self-process (Perls, Hefferline & Goodman, 1951, p. 437). In retrospect, his achievement here is even more original and remarkable than it must have seemed at the time, even to him (since, as he liked to say–no doubt defiantly but also certainly sincerely–his formulations and observations were all "self-evident" and "obvious;" Perls, Hefferline & Goodman, 1951, pp. 269). That is, in his psychological formulations Goodman consistently harked back to the phenomenological–what it feels like, how it is for me–as the touchstone of theoretical rightness and usefulness, in sharp and obvious contradistinction to Freud (or, for that matter, behaviorism) who would say that the "patient," the person, is the last one we should ask, in establishing what is psychologically real. To Goodman it is always the contact that is real–the more or less satisfying resolution of the "external" world of resources, obstacles, perceived threats and sought-after goals, with the "internal" world, of felt needs and known desires, memories, aims, past learning and future hopes. It is this contact, this ongoing resolution (the best the person can manage with the world as she sees it, by definition) that is what Goodman (1951) called "creative adjustment," the operation of the self. That is, self and self-process or function are not coterminous with the "inner" world of the depth psychologists and Western philosophers–nor with the "external" world as the social psychologists would have it–but rather form a supraordinate or unifying function, which integrates the whole field from a subjective point of view. This is what makes Gestalt a holistic model, and this is what we mean when we say the Goodman Gestalt model relocates the self, to a position above the apparent dichotomy in the field, of inner and outer, private and public, even self (as privately conceived) and other.

But–and this is a point often neglected in the model–the articulation of this "inner" world, the world of feelings, desires, thoughts and fears, wishes, doubts, appetites and fantasies, is not an obvious thing we are born with, but is itself a developmental achievement, and at least as much as knowledge and exploration of the "external" world is learned and achieved over time, and by dint of considerable active energy and work. And more than this, even the skills and structures involved in getting to know one's internal subjective world, are themselves developmental achievements. That is, we aren't born knowing ourselves, or knowing how to know ourselves. All that too is learned, and the process by which it is learned is an intersubjective process. We learn how to be curious about ourselves, always and only through the benevolent, stimulating, empathic curiosity and interest of another person. As Winnicott puts it, the self of the infant exists first in the mother's eye (reading any intimate caretaker for mother here). It is through being treated as a self, which is to say as a being with a valid internal experience, or intersubjectively, that we learn to regard ourselves, and others, with this perspective, and with a firm sense of this reality. To the extent that this intersubjective process is impoverished or distorted in development, then the internal subjective world itself remains impoverished and unarticulated. And then the self-function, which is the ongoing integration of this world with the "outer" world, remains likewise impoverished, unarticulated, distorted in various ways and degrees.

It is in this sense that the Gestalt model is fundamentally and inherently an intersubjective model, by its nature and at its core. The relational perspective is not something "grafted on" to the model, in the way that the Self-in-Relationship model tries to do, over a fundamentally individualistic psychodynamic base (see for example the otherwise very interesting and fruitful work of the Stone Center in this regard, e.g., Surrey, 1985). Rather, relationality is given in the phenomenological premises of the Gestalt approach. When the patient enters therapy, it is always in some way because of a breakdown in self-process and self-function in this sense. This in turn means a breakdown or distortion or interruption in development–either currently, as in the case of a child, or in the past in the case of an adult (more rarely, an adult may seek therapy because of a transition or loss or other life event which is more or less purely a crisis in ongoing adult development, and not reflective of some past developmental trauma; this is rare because without that past trauma, that necessary compromise in natural development, the person will more likely find the intersubjective supports in her/his own informal relational network, without seeking a formal therapeutic support).

Put another way, the patient comes to therapy because she/he is *too alone* with his or her problem. What was Mark too alone with, I wondered? What fears or feelings were being held too closely and not welcomed, reflected, talked about, so that he could welcome and know and articulate them for himself, and thus incorporate them into his experience, in the full sense of that word (which is really another term for development: each one contains and implies the other)? His mother said that Mark had "lost his innocence" since entering fifth grade, which was in a middle school with older boys and bullies, entirely different in feeling from the more sheltered progressive private school where he had spent the previous four or five years, to all appearances very happily and successfully. Was this the stress (and note again that when we say stress, we mean a pressure that has to be borne alone, without support; it is the too-aloneness of it that makes it a stress, and not just a challenge)? But the family was talking about this, and working with it. I kept listening for something deeper, more embedded, in Mark's way of holding himself and approaching his world.

The Ground of the Story

When a child is brought to therapy, I'm always interested to know what was going on in the parent's lives when they were the same age the child is now. All of us live in a social field, and our belongingness, our lack of boundary between what is "us" and what is "not us" is just as real as our boundedness, our separate "individuality" (and note that individual means undivided, whole, not separated). These are the two poles of the Goodman self model–and the two poles of our experience, which is our integrating, if we can, these "inner" and "outer" aspects of ourselves. Just as there is a way in which we are always the same, ongoing person, there is a way in which we are a different person in a different field (just ask any child who goes back and forth between the homes of two divorced parents; many will tell you that it's not just the outer surroundings that change, but that they themselves are actually a different person, to some degree, in the two different worlds).

The age of ten, as it turned out, was a time of crisis in the lives of both of Mark's parents. For his mother, it marked the first of many hospitalizations for her own mother, in a lifelong history of depression. For Mark's father, ten meant the sudden (to him) death of his own mother from cirrhosis–a trauma which no one in the family then ever talked about, for many long years. I asked Mark, with his parents there, whether he thought his parents were any different lately, as he came into an age that had been so traumatic for them. Again, he said he didn't know, but this time he added a question: why did I want to know? Well, I said, at this point it's just an idea, but my idea is that if looking at him these days is reminding them of a lot of painful and anxious memories, and they're not talking about it that much–and then here he is, feeling anxious and not knowing why, well then, there might be some connection.

Mark's reply was that he didn't see how there could be one. Again, that was fine with me. To me what mattered was that he had asked the question. By asking the question he had agreed, provisionally, to have a conversation about these things, to be curious about them together. Conversation, literally, means a turning together, which is to say movement, with support, intersubjectively if you will, not alone. And movement with support in this sense, in the Gestalt view, is always in a constructive direction, always in the service of development, which is to say the direction of the growing and creative elaboration of the process of self-in-the-world.

Meanwhile, what to do about Mark's "symptom," the nighttime routine that was dominating family life (which would take what direction, without this structure?) I asked Mark what he knew about spells and rituals and good-luck charms–which turned out to be quite a lot. Athletes, chess players, politicians and gamblers–all are well-known for having lucky tokens and rituals they depend on to manage stress and anxiety, and Mark was familiar with a great many of them. In Gestalt, this non-pathological emphasis is important, because of the model's insistence that a "symptom" is/was a creative resolution which is no longer serving its function, or of which the secondary cost is too high (the "symptom" of substance abuse comes to mind, as a familiar example). To Mark I said that it seemed to me the problem here was not that he had bedtime routine or ritual, but that the thing wasn't working. Or better, maybe it was working in some senses (because Mark slept without further problems after each nightly workout, which may have served other family purposes as well)–but we might be able to figure out something together that would serve even better, and maybe at lower cost all around, once we understood more what it was he was trying to accomplish exactly, every evening with the basketball. Again Mark looked at me like we might not share common planetary origins, but he did assent to the idea, at least verbally, that we would explore the thing together.

Through the coming weeks we did this in a number of ways. The first had to do with what we might call "Mark bringing the problem to me." Since I couldn't be there in his room at night, to see just what was going on, we spent some time recreating his room in my office. Moving the chairs and sofa around, we marked off where the bed was, in relation to the basketball hoop (represented by a wastebasket), how far it was to the edge of the rug, how hard the shot was (I tried it repeatedly, with mixed results). At one point I offered the suggestion that the simplest solution to the whole thing would be to move the rug, so that more shots would count. This time, in place of the usual extraterrestrial look in my direction, Mark threw back his head and laughed–at the sheer outrageous simplicity of the idea. But what then emerged from all this spatial manipulation and exploration was a crucial realization for Mark: namely, that there were in fact already borderline cases, with regard to the swish, the backboard, the carpet edge, and that he was already making judgment calls, which varied from time to time and night to night. In other words, sometimes he was a more strict judge, harder on himself, than other times. From this it was only a short step to thinking about why that might be, what the variation in underlying feelings might be, from one time to another. In other words, parts of his experience–the affective and the behavioral–which had been split apart, now began to take up some relationship with each other–through the mediating interest of another person. And more–in an area of his life that felt like it was happening "to" him, he was beginning to discover bits and corners of agency and choice.

That was all a way of bringing the problem to me. A second mode we used to work on my being involved in his "symptom" and his world. We might call this "bring me to the problem." This we explored through the use of a journal. Since I couldn't actually be there at night to hear about these variations in feelings and severity, I told him, how about if he made a few notes, a sort of log, of how the bedtime routine went each night. That way he wouldn't forget what happened when. Then when we got together we could go over the log together and see what struck us. To begin with, I asked him just to note down how many minutes the whole basketball activity took each night, from start to head on the pillow, and–especially if that night was a long one, whether anything had happened that day that was difficult or upsetting, that might make it take longer to accomplish the work of the routine, whatever that might be (which after all, we were still far from having entirely clarified yet). And again, I didn't ask this expecting that he would come up with any simple one-to-one correspondence between day and evening, but rather to foster the general stance of checking for the feelings, insisting that behavior has meaning, and looking for possible connections between the two.

Mark took up this new activity with a will, and from the beginning wrote more than the assigned task. His first addition was just to record something about how strict he was with himself that night, which quickly led to our focusing special attention on any borderline cases–cases where he himself was aware of making that call, between an acceptable and an unacceptable last shot. Then, again following his initiative, I asked him always to include a note about how tense or anxious his parents seemed that night, in his experience. "Because you know," I told him at least once a week, "I have this theory that a lot of things we do, we do because of other people's feelings, not just our own."

"Yeah, I know you think that," Mark said to me after quite some weeks. "And I used to think that didn't make any sense at all. But now I'm not so sure."

The more the weeks sped by, the more the "figure" of the problem, which is to say the presenting symptom, fell off, to the point where I was concerned lest the figure disappear entirely, before we had understood the ground together (and in the Gestalt view it is that understanding together, not just a new behavioral experiment, which is transformational.) The part of Freud's work that has endured, after all, is the wealth of concrete clinical insights (as opposed to the metapsychological superstructure, which has not endured); prominent among these insights is the idea of symptom substitution. Again, in Gestalt language we would say that a change of figure is pointless, unless it is accompanied by a reorganization of ground, a different arrangement of perceptions and feelings about the inner and outer worlds of the subject, so that the "self itself" has new possibilities and new power.

In practice, this is a fine line. Of course we want to see the initial distress get better, to take pleasure in that with the patient–but without somehow conveying that there was something "wrong" or shameful about the person in the first place, that they were not good enough for us the way they were when they came in. (Though to be sure, there are times were we have to say a given behavior is not acceptable; this is part of the complexity of the fine line). To Mark I said that I thought it was great that his bedtime routine was working so much better for him now, that he was getting more of the benefit of it at less of a cost. When he spoke of maybe "trying to give it up now" altogether, I demurred mildly, saying, "Oh, after all, what's the hurry?" and "Remember, all that practice must be good for your basketball skills." Instead of giving it up, I suggested, why not play around some more with the rules of the thing–rules that he was coming more and more to experience as under his power as we paid attention together to his special role as Arbiter of Borderline Cases. What if we made an experiment in allowing a non-swish, say, or letting it go when the ball dribbled onto the rug?

And in the meantime, we weren't spending all our time on reading journals and moving furniture anymore. Part of the time we talked about his friends and his life at school, part of the time about his reading. Mark was a great fan of Jack London. The only London story I remembered, "To Build a Fire," turned out to be one of his favorites. This is the one about a man somewhere in the arctic who loses his last match, and realizes he will freeze to death before dawn without some heat source. His last hope is his dog, whose body he plans to use. Only the dog, somehow seeing murder in his master's eye, panics and runs off, and there the story ends. I couldn't help wondering what drew Mark to this harsh tale. Was it something wintry in his own landscape, maybe the nameless chill of his parents' withdrawal into themselves, as their own losses were reactivated? If so, we had at least worked on giving this chill a name, as their feeling world became a more open part of our discourse, both between the two of us and in the family in general.

And we played games. The function of structured games–board games and cards and the like–with latency age children is not generally well explained in the literature. Again, a Gestalt perspective is clarifying. The game, in the Gestalt view, is not just a pastime to keep the kid in the room, as is sometimes implied–nor, at this age, is it usually a mode of generating fantasy material, in the way of play therapy at an earlier stage of life. Rather, the game is an episode of contact in its own right, in the here and now with all the present issues and urgencies that implies, and with as much or as little passion as the people involved may bring to it. That is, the game is seen as a valid "slice of life" which can be analyzed and "played around with," figure and ground, like any other experience–only with the advantage of being lived in the present real relationship, and not just talked about. If the game has the right mix of structure and openness, luck and skill, movement and complexity, then it can call on many or all of the same strategies and feelings of any other life situation. Giving and taking, winning and losing, luck (and its inverse, shame), aggression and holding back, thinking clearly under pressure, taking care and trusting the other, opposition and alliance, defeating an adult (which may carry a range of dangers with it)–this is the stuff of living itself, with people. (I'm thinking now of 7-year-old Patty, who would not win at Go Fish. I asked her what she thought would happen to me if she really "slaughtered me" at cards: would I lie down and die? Explode? Hit somebody? Take drugs, like some adults she knew well? Eventually this became our great joke. If she beat me really badly I'd say well, I guess I'll just go take drugs now, or excuse me, I have to go hit somebody, or at least quit my job. And she would giggle and ask if I didn't think I was overdoing it just a little bit. Or if I won I might offer her my coffee, saying it was the only drug I had handy, and I knew she believed people had to take drugs if they had the least bit of stress. And she would shout, "No, they don't!" and look startled at the power of her own voice, and we'd both laugh).

And the choice of game is important. Some ten-year-olds can only play "baby games," where luck is everything and competency isn't in question. Twelve-year-old Bruce could only play blackjack with no betting, deal a hand, see who's higher, deal another one, for weeks on end. When I tried to introduce chips, he made it a rule that you take one chip from the bank when you win, but you don't give up anything if you lose. And the chips couldn't be stacked, presumably because that would make it too easy to tell who had more. It was a year before we were actually both putting up a stake, another six months till we could deal out seven-card stud, bet freely on every card, build a big pot and win or lose all. Bruce enjoyed discovering that I'm a rotten bluffer, whereas he had considerable untapped talent in that direction. But his biggest triumph ultimately came not from winning but from the day when I saw a chance to pull even in a board game tournament, and played ten minutes past the hour to try to make it happen. Bruce lost that game, but for the first time he didn't care, because he had gained a sense that I was invested in him, in a way that he now trusted somehow more than before.

Mark wasn't that eager to play a competitive board game at all, and when he did play, it was with reserve and seeming disinterest–in sharp contrast to the heat and passion of his isometric struggle with himself every night. When faced with a choice between advancing his game or setting mine back, he always chose the former, because the other way would be "mean." His preferred outcome, he told me, would be a draw. Next to that he preferred to win, but "just by a little." So that I wouldn't feel bad, I asked? I guess, was the answer. It certainly wasn't my goal to take away any of this quality of sensitivity and concern for the other person–especially now that I was hearing that his soccer game was becoming more hard-hitting and focused, with more open relish in the victories there when they came. I asked if he worried about the feelings of the losing team. "No," he answered thoughtfully, "I don't. Because they have each other."

The journal, meanwhile, was gradually replacing the basketball routine as a getting-down-to-sleep ritual. As the one got shorter, the other got longer. When Mark went out of town on a family visit, or after we went to an every-second-week schedule, he would mail the Xeroxed pages to me (because he didn't want to part with the journal itself: it now contained important parts of the self).

He still threw the ball at night, but almost any decent shot would count now–with intermittent exceptions, when he would suddenly be "hard on himself again," as he put it. These exceptions I tried always to greet with an "Oh good, that gives us another chance at understanding more about what makes some nights harder than others." I sort of regretted the rapid loss of the "problem," I told him–because of the window it offered us, into his world. Mark disagreed, sharply. And after all, as we both agreed, he was the doctor. Some eighteen weeks had passed since our first meeting–a total of fourteen sessions. Summer was coming. Now that he was able to sleep away from home, Mark was off to soccer camp, then a family vacation. We made a date to check in in the fall, which turned out to be the last time but once that I was to see him–at least so far.

Conclusions

Good patients make good therapists, as everyone who works with people knows. Mark's steady and fairly rapid improvement from such severe distress had everything to do with his history of having an involved, caring family who had provided many of the basic conditions for growth of the self, and were willing to work on those that might be missing. And no doubt something to do with his therapy as well, and the therapeutic stance of declining to pathologize his problem (and his solution), and of looking for health and growth. What the Gestalt model provided more specifically was a frame and a rationale for understanding Mark's distress in field/contextual and phenomenological terms–which is to say as a subjective agent among other subjective agents, and not in terms of drives, "objects," or behaviors detached from their meaning. That, and a guide to understanding the structure of experience itself (always an incomplete task), which leads in turn to some idea, at least, of where and how to go about supporting the unblocking and restoration of the natural contacting/organizing functions, which are the growing self in operation. And, finally and most importantly, the model's insistence that "understanding the structure of experience" is necessarily an interpersonal, intersubjective process: indeed, that that activity and intersubjectivity are one and the same thing.

Of course, a different patient would have needed different specific strategies, and certainly one without Mark's internal resources (which are the same as the structure of his family supports) would likely have needed a longer time, and much more structured therapeutic support, to develop/restore robust self-process ("develop" always being more difficult than "restore"). Indeed, the very idea of restoring rests on the presupposition of some stable, empathic/intersubjectively available person in the real world of the patient's history, whose interest and exchange provided the ground for self development up to the point of break or inhibition–the point which the idea of "restoration" aims back towards. Every school of therapy–and especially every school of work with children–knows this and tries in some way to take it into account, as with Winnicott's insistence that therapy has to be based on going back and reconnecting with the point or moment of "good-enough mothering," as he would put it, the point of good "object relations," and building from there (even if that point has to be in some sense invented; see for example discussion in Gustafson, 1986). In Gestalt we might express the same idea by saying that we are looking always for "lost voices of the self" (Lee, 1994), that place or time where the self process, which we have described here as the integration of our inner and outer worlds, was still proceeding without too much inhibition of either of these two experiential poles–and then where that "inner" world of, as Goodman (1951) would say, "authentic" self feelings and desires, was split off, suppressed, contained, or left too alone with itself, in silence. In Mark's case we might say simply that he had been left turning in too small a circle, trying somehow to work out in himself and on himself, things that could only be integrated and resolved constructively with other people. And that when we re-peopled his inner landscape–with the presence and empathic curiosity of the therapist, the reopened dialogue with his parents, even a warmer, more articulated voice from himself–then he found the resources to put the pieces together in a new way, that left new room for his inner world in the world, and for him to grow.

Mark's restoration of self endured. For some months after we stopped seeing each other he checked in, every month or so, always with a good report of some fresh milestones–a soccer trophy, a paper route, a trip out of town alone, with a friend's family. After that I didn't see him again for several years, and when we next ran into each other it was socially, and by chance. This was on the occasion of a "men's circle," a festivity thrown by a friend of mine to honor the passage into manhood of his 13-year-old son, who turned out to be a new school friend of Mark's. Our meeting was completely casual on the surface: after a warm handshake he paid no more and no less attention to me than to any other adult there, and I took my cue from him. This experience is a familiar one to those who work with children–as teachers, therapists, social workers, medical personnel: if your work is successful, they outgrow you, and for all the warm memories that may be there, when you meet later on they often find they have nothing to say. This only illustrates again the self in Gestalt perspective, as the integrator of past, present, and future, the inner and outer worlds and the lively "boundary" that demarcates and joins them at the same time. When one of these terms has changed and grown–the child's world of experience–then the "same" encounter yields a different self, even a sense of strangeness and shyness. This is as it should be. The adult caretaker remembers the child. The child remembers only the love, which he or she takes, and uses, and moves on.

Footnotes

1. By "OCD" here we are referring to behavior that meets the criteria of the DSM-IV for 300.30, Obsessive Compulsive Disorder (American Psychiatric Association, 1987). That is, the behavior pattern is repetitive and stereotyped, not "realistically" connected with the fears that provoke it, takes up "more than an hour a day," and is causing "marked distress" and/or interfering with the person's life and functioning. Clearly Mark met all the criteria for a 300.30 diagnosis.

2. The Nietzschean self-view is important here because it is so close to the Perlsian, which derives from it (through Nietzsche's disciple, Salomo Friedlaender (1871-1946), whom Perls identifies (1974) as his own philosophical mentor)–and so utterly different from the communitarian views of Goodman. Nietzsche's self as "will to power" is basically an internal drive model, very much like Freud's, with only the substitution of aggressive libido (later aggression and libido) for "power." Perls's own view, which permeates his writings, is of a self whose basic nature is a sort of aggressive self-assertion. In this way Perls remains closer to Nietzsche, and perhaps Adler, than to Freud, whose libido theory, while technically monadic, always tended more toward the relational. In sharp contrast, Goodman pictures a self and self-function whose basic goal is "getting along in the world," pragmatically and collaboratively, achieving some measure of satisfaction, self-expression, contact, and co-construction of meaning, always in a social context.

References

American Psychiatric Association (1987). *Diagnostic and statistical manual of mental disorders, fourth edition.* Washington, DC: American Psychiatric Association.

Goodman, P. (1947). *Communitas.* New York, NY: Random House.

Goodman, P. (1977). *Nature heals: The psychological essays of Paul Goodman.* New York, NY: Free Life Editions.

Gustafson, J. (1986). *The complex secret of brief psychotherapy.* New York, NY: W.W. Norton.

Lee, R. (1994). Couples' shame: The unaddressed issue. In S. Backman & G. Wheeler (Eds.), *On intimate ground: A gestalt approach to working with couples,* (pp. 262-290). San Francisco, CA: Jossey-Bass.

Leibniz, G. (1714). Monadology. In P. Wiener (Ed.), *Leibniz.* New York, NY: Charles Scribner's Sons.

Perls, F. (1969). *In and out the garbage pail.* Moab, UT: Real People Press.

Perls, F., Hefferline, R., & Goodman, P. (1951). *Gestalt therapy: Excitement and growth in the human personality.* New York, NY: Julian Press.

Surrey, J. (1985). *The "self-in-relation:" a theory of women's development.* Wellesley, MA: The Stone Center.

6

Janet Lederman and the Gazebo Park School

Eduardo Eizner

Located on the grounds of Esalen Institute on the Big Sur coast of California, the Gazebo School Park is a nursery school, a preschool, and a living sculpture where children can play and learn and live. Like any healthy environment, it is therapeutic without being "therapy."

The basic goals of the Gazebo are the goals of Gestalt therapy: to challenge teachers as well as children to become more aware of their existence, to make choices and to take responsibility for those choices (including the choice of unawareness), to view themselves as part of an environment and to take responsibility for that environment, to explore their world, to develop internal support, and to increase self-esteem and self-confidence through self-expression and aware relationship to others. In the safe environment of the Gazebo children are encouraged and allowed to make and take responsibility for their own mistakes as well as their own achievements, and to choose their own focus in the here and now context of their own lives.

At the Gazebo a child learns to be flexible and adapt quickly; every day in the school is different. At the same time there are certain touchstones of consistency that provide a background of safety and stability: the time, the park itself, and the teachers are the same from day to day. The children are not the same: not only is each child changing from day to day and week to week, but some children will be at the school long-term, while others may stay as little as a week, or a few weeks.

The structure and content of the days differ as well. In traditional nursery schools the days may be quite predictable, which can mean that a child is just going through the motions of the day, without heightening awareness or learning how to be flexible and take responsibility for choices. If the teachers create an environment where the child eats breakfast, lunch, and dinner at the same hour every day, and takes a one-hour siesta in the same bed after a meal, whether or not the child feels the need for a rest, then he or she will likely be confused and stressed out when faced with a break in that routine. Lederman's idea was rather to call on the child to be aware and choiceful, to learn to notice and use internal feelings and the external environment to explore and make aware choices in the real situation of the moment. In this way, she held, children would learn to operate and live well in many kinds of situations, with many different kinds of people.

The Gestalt Principles of Learning

The principles of the Gestalt model teach us that we are always orienting in a field of experience–toddlers as well as adults–so as to be in a position to address and solve problems and reach goals as they come up. Our fundamental cognitive strategy for orientation in a constantly changing field is the figure-ground process: the problem of greatest interest and concern to us at the moment is the foreground figure; the context or whole situation as we know it becomes background, which holds and contains the foreground figure, and can be drawn on as a resource at any time. When this process is working as it should, we experience an organic flow of figural needs and problems, which are manageable with the internal and external resources at hand. On the other hand, if we never learn to observe and notice and use the environment, or if we don't know what we feel and think and need, then our lives will be dull and unsatisfying, or chaotic and even destructive.

At Gazebo we start with the notion, which is neglected or denied in many school settings and teaching philosophies, that the child is always organizing and learning within a particular situation, where the struggle with the problem or learning task most of organic interest to the child, is foreground. In many traditional schools this whole notion is reversed: the assigned learning task is one thing, while the need and interest of the child, which is the area of greatest potential energy, is something else altogether. For example, when a small child at Gazebo comes to a stump and wants to crawl over it, the foreground figure is to get over that stump, within the context of the whole park, which includes the other people in it, as well as the child's own body and evolving capacities. Now, somebody can come along at that point to pick the child up and put him/her on the other side of the stump–or else to remove the child from that organically interesting problem and growth situation and present him/her with some other figure entirely (lunch, nap, preplanned teaching unit)–in which case the child learns nothing. Or worse, the child probably learns not to attend very much to interesting problems that arise organically, because they will be interrupted anyway. Soon what the child retains, if this keeps happening, is that rather than figuring out what you want and need, and how you might solve that, you can just stand in one place and cry until a grownup comes over, and takes over, thus short-circuiting the whole natural learning cycle, and gradually handicapping that child for full, healthy learning and living.

Children, like adults, are always learning something. This is because, as the Gestalt model shows, the perceptual/cognitive/emotional process of figure-ground formation is constant and involuntary: this is the child's neurological nature. The question is always, what is the child learning.

Gazebo and the Environment

Early childhood at Gazebo is a place to get dirty, to get clean, to get dirty again. Some skills are explicit, others hidden, awaiting discovery. Imagination is allowed to flourish with passion and humor. Children learn how to have ideas and make dreams come to life. Struggles become challenges. There is support for dreaming and support for doing. We do not hurry the child.

The physical setting of Gazebo Park School is in itself a major teaching tool. Minute by minute the child is obliged to master the environment. Moving through the park, he or she must pay attention as the earth changes textures and grades, as flowers and vegetables spring up where once there was open space. Science and math are everywhere; chemistry is in the wet sand box, at the worm farm, in the kitchen. The whole child is always involved in social, academic, and physical skills. Hands on, heads on, feet on, arms, legs, everything on, everything go–learning through a full-body experience (Lederman, 1969).

We begin with the real processes of living–first of all in our natural physical environment, close to nature and natural processes of birth and decay, recycling and regeneration. The Gazebo philosophy is an ecologically centered one that includes developmentally appropriate practice combining care and concern for the whole child with care and concern for the well being of the environment. Children learn to differentiate and recycle waste, and their vocabulary expands to include environmental concepts and language. It is the children who remember to put the compost buckets next to the lunch table, and to feed the worms. We compost all organic waste and leftovers. With the children we clean the pony poop out of the corral and put it in the compost bin, turn and water it to care for our friends the compost worms. We watch as slowly our leftovers transmute into rich food for plants. We mix this rich food into the soil and plant seeds in our garden. Patiently tending to the new seeds by watering and giving them space, we are rewarded as they push out of the earth and mature into beautiful flowers and vegetables that we can eat. We harvest the edible treasures and prepare them to eat at lunchtime. We compost whatever is not consumed. And the cycle continues. We stay in the moment and respond to what develops. When we use recyclable items, we gather them up, clean and prepare them, and take a field trip within Esalen Institute to deposit them in the receiving area. Questions come up and along the way we discuss what we are doing and why we are recycling with the children.

There are other daily jobs to be done, in addition to cleaning the corral, composting, tending the worms, and so on. We groom and feed all the animals, take care of the greenhouse and the gardens, clean up and order the internal structures. Whether or not the goat's water buckets have been cleaned and filled is an important part of our curriculum, as the children relate their own needs to those of other living creatures. Environmental education means that the emerging task becomes the curriculum, and is always honored. Children are generally free to choose and change activities as they wish; and yet with teacher guidance all the jobs get done.

Environmental ethics is at the core of this curriculum. Learning about the self and others is primary, and is integrated into an environment filled with opportunities to become aware of and bonded with nature. Getting to know a pony teaches respect for personal space as no other teacher can. Observing mama goat's pregnancy, nursing, and then stroking her babies and one day making cheese from her milk, places the child in the center of a living, organic cycle. Starting seeds in the garden teaches about time, and care-taking, and the reward of harvesting the results for lunch.

At lunchtime we begin to gather as a group, after washing hands, to sing songs, tell stories or share information, and then clean up together afterwards. Lunch is around noon, sometimes earlier and sometimes later. There is always finger-food available, and even small ones can feed themselves. Children are not reprimanded for being tired or not hungry at lunchtime; there is no compulsory playing, reading, eating, or napping time at the school. Within a safe environment children are free to choose what they want or need, at nearly any time.

Working, playing, eating and resting, being alone and being together, attending to one's own needs and the environment, taking care of the animals and the gardens and tending to the various real jobs–all this becomes a part of our daily routine and is an integral part of the emerging curriculum. Not once removed, not a lecture, but in the moment, moving with our needs and the needs of nature. It was Lederman's intention to reintroduce living into the learning process.

Early Childhood

Many different psychological theories address the importance of the first few years of life. Gazebo's philosophy is educational and preventive, where the early manifestations of symptomatic behaviors are handled from an existential approach. The Gestalt model rests on great faith in the underlying healthy process and organic drive for growth and health in the child. We understand symptoms and problematic behavior first of all as a matter of the young child not knowing her/his own needs, for lack of an environment that fosters this kind of learning. Our job at Gazebo is to provide those essential environmental conditions, where children can explore their own feelings, fantasies, and thoughts–as well as the environment itself –and through their own awareness unfold the necessary skills to deal with their own problems.

In practice everything depends on the age and developmental level of the young child. A little one six or nine months old can learn to crawl or walk in an open green space outside, and, while he is learning about garden, snails, animals, and grass, he is also learning about other people in the world, what his body can do by itself without anybody's help, with teachers there to support exploration and struggle by keeping the environment safe. In the community setting, Gazebo becomes a supportive/corrective family where no one demands that small children do certain things or put on a mask. Adults do not hover and impose their own agenda, as can happen even in well-intentioned families, particularly with an only child, where everybody focuses on the infant or toddler, who then never has an opportunity just to go where he or she wants, investigating and discovering life in his or her own way, at the pace that is natural to that child.

Children under two years old are also in a period of intensive learning about what their bodies can do, exploring and discovering climbing, running, playing, cooperating, and fighting. They are learning about their own aggression and their own emotions, in an environment where they are allowed to have and own their own emotions and aggression. If a child wants/needs to cry, he or she is allowed to do it, without anybody insisting that he or she stop. Often children are just expressing energy as they cry, without having the same stories adults have about why they are crying as they cry. A baby in particular needs to cry because that is what gets his or her nervous system back into balance as he or she moves organically through the day.

Small children at Gazebo are also learning about grownups other than their parents. They learn how it is to be without mommy and daddy, and then they learn how it is to be with them, and without their teachers and friends. The contrast supports awareness, as they learn about two different worlds, and how they can be successful in both. A little one may often decide it is more fun to be at school with friends than to be at home.

Children come to Gazebo at first with their parents, until they start recognizing their interests independently of their parents, and slowly move away from them. Often it seems that children are ready to explore the environment earlier than their parents are ready for them to leave. When parents feel insecure and dependent on the child, infants recognize that need and have a hard time separating from their caregivers. At Gazebo we encourage parents to express this ambivalence openly as they move toward separating from their children. Once the parents feel secure and comfortable, and have established a relationship of trust with the teachers and the environment of Gazebo themselves, they model and convey that trust to the child. The child then moves easily into exploring new relationships with the environment and the other children.

During the early days or weeks the parents are encouraged to participate in the life of the Gazebo, working alongside the children and teachers and establishing this sense of trust and friendship. When the parents witness and experience that their child is ready to move into the environment alone–even at a very early age–then they slowly become part of the background, with the guidance of the teachers, allowing more space for children to invest in the learning process at Gazebo. Once the child feels comfortable in the school and with the teachers, the parents move toward just dropping the child off, always writing their name and the time of arrival in the sign-in book, logging in the beginning of the child's day. As Janet Lederman wrote:

Children were more and more confined, encapsulated, and some incarcerated. The dreamer was punished, and the energetic labeled as in need of a "cure." Children were gradually not welcomed into the society. Isolation became a problem among teenagers, children protected out of life. We contained children in school, confusing learning and training. Some learned to be controlled; some fought their way out. Some spend a great deal of time looking for control in very bizarre ways.

There was a time when children learned from an early age by working alongside adults. They saw, they experienced, and they felt the abilities of experienced people. And then there were abuses to children, in sweatshops. Our solution was that children should not work: they are to go to school, come home, do more schoolwork, take out the garbage, set the table, and get allowances. What if children were integrated back into the working order of things? There is so much for us to learn from the young, and much for the young to learn from elders. Removing direct experience removes the ability to evaluate, reflect, and choose.

Many young people without these abilities follow strange paths to gain experience. Some children end up following tragic paths, with no ability to evaluate them; and parents who imagined they were doing all the right things end in grief and confusion. Experience relates to the self... the time has come to put the "self" path into a context that contains life. Nothing happens in a vacuum; we are always in relationship to an environment (Lederman, undated).

With these words, we can see the integration, through the living experiences at Gazebo, of Gestalt philosophy, environmental emphasis, and the learning needs of children beginning with infancy and early childhood. "Education" comes from family and society: learning comes from the child him or herself.

Gazebo and the Gestalt Ethos of Responsibility

Responsibility, as defined in the American Heritage Dictionary, means "being the source or cause of something. Involves personal accountability or ability to act without guidance or superior authority." Fritz Perls

(1969) added to this that responsibility means the "ability to respond," organically, meaningfully, in a way that integrates the self-needs and environmental awareness that we have been talking about here. On the basis of these two definitions, the Gazebo teacher supports each child's growing responsibility and responsible action, recognizing the uniqueness of each response to the challenge of personal, social, and environmental interactions.

For example, at Gazebo School Park, there is no way for a toddler to "fail." He or she cannot be too slow, too impatient, too sloppy, too active, or even too quiet and "dreamy." Some children learn by exploring everything actively, some by staying in one area for a long time. Some learn by touching every object, others by keeping familiar objects around them. Some are interested in pouring water carefully, others more interested in slopping it around. And all these proclivities change and balance out in time, given the right environmental conditions and support. Our children explore and interact from the first year of life, with little interference from teachers (safety and health issues of course always taking priority). We allow contact, cuddling time, time to push and pull and yell, disorder, confusion, chaos. I notice how excited Emilio, age one, becomes in the presence of Kesse, a six-month-old newcomer. Little babies want the space to explore and play with one another. Our society tends to keep babies away from interacting with other babies, instituting the beginnings of separation and isolation. Allowing babies to have experiences together in a safe environment is crucial for them to learn how to respond–to be responsible–to their own needs and wishes, and those of the other baby. These are the beginnings of the social awareness process, the recognition in the present moment of the kind of contact they would like to have, the taking of action to fulfill these aware needs–and then the noticing of the effects of their own behavior on the other person, and adjusting their behavior if those effects are not what they wanted. All this is the integration of self-needs, awareness, and responsibility in every sense.

Awareness and responsibility travel together. Children cannot learn to be responsible if they don't participate as choiceful agents in their own lives. Adults have a tendency to speak for their children, questioning or invalidating their experiences, not allowing risks and consequences. Then when the same parents are not around, the child may come to school and respond to challenging situations in a unique and creative fashion, showing both incredible abilities and great self-responsibility. Some children become aware that they don't like to be pushed or protected, and that they can move away from this kind of contact. Moving away is taking responsibility for themselves without taking a helpless, hopeless, and dependent attitude.

Our experience shows that when we allow free social exploration and "chaos," by the age of four children are "through" with that kind of contact and disorder. Spontaneously they look for more structure, want to learn to read, demonstrate interest in the computer area and the other more structured activities available to them. This kind of responsibility is more useful and solid, because the child owns it; it grows out of his or her own experience.

Children are encouraged to notice and reflect on what they are doing and experiencing, and then to choose either to remain with those feelings, or to modify the present experience. A typical example is the three-year-old who climbs up a tree and then won't get down by him/herself, proclaiming as an excuse that he or she "can't." At Gazebo a teacher, instead of just plucking the child down, will encourage the child to look around, pay attention to what is happening–"How did you get there? What steps did you use?"–and notice how he or she can find self-supports to get down. This allows, encourages, and challenges the child to develop self-responsibility.

Even earlier, children join in taking care of themselves, often before they can walk. When it is time to change a diaper, a teacher will change it, roll it up, and then hand it to the nine-month-old, who will crawl or walk to the trashcan and drop it in. From there, the child moves to a miniature sink to wash hands, learning in this playful way about self-responsibility.

As responsible beings, children act and react from their own experience. Acting out of their own unique personal experience, in a context of teachers who respect and trust their feelings, allows children to trust themselves, building confidence and responsibility. This experience begins with body sensations and feelings, which do not need external confirmation (though all too often they may be disconfirmed or just ignored by the adults around). At Gazebo, we encourage and support children to sense, feel and express themselves however they want, neither distracting them from their experience, nor moving to solve the problem for them. When a four-year-old says that he or she is cold, a teacher may reflect that statement, and encourage the child to think about doing something active with that body sensation: "I hear that you're cold–is there anything you want to do about it?" The feeling is accepted and validated, while the solution is left up to the child, within developmentally appropriate limits. If the child does not articulate feelings, the teachers watch for non-verbal cues, and make inquiries that patiently reflect and support the growing verbal expressiveness, which is a basic part of self-responsibility.

In talking with each other, teachers model the same attitudes for the children. We follow communications guidelines that emphasize:

- "I" instead of "you," "we," "they," and "it;"
- talking "to" rather than "about;"
- using "won't" instead of "can't;"
- using "and" instead of "but;"
- asking "how" and "what" instead of "why;"
- talking about "now" instead of back then or later
- describing rather than explaining;
- being specific and concrete as opposed to general and abstract.

It is amazing to see how fast quite small children learn to speak clearly for themselves in this environment, communicating responsibly with themselves, each other, and the environment itself.

Boundaries and Aggression

Many people will ask, "What about aggression? Are children free to bully and hurt other children?" The answer is that certainly we pay attention to physical safety, making sure at all times that if fighting occurs, we are close to the action to be sure that no weapons (teeth, nails, sticks or other hard objects) are involved. At the same time we believe that much problematic aggression is made worse by over-interference by adults, preventing all the children involved from experiencing the full interaction and learning both skills and self-responsibility.

Anyone who has observed young animals will have seen how every animal infant goes through a stage of rough-and-tumble with other infants. All of them wrestle, bait, provoke, fight–even scratch each other–as they learn their own powers and natural limits and consequences. Too often, little human beings have no chance to learn that kind of play, what it means and all that can be learned from it.

Children need to exercise their aggression in order to be fully alive. They need aggressive energy to bite into an apple, pull a potato or onion from the earth, play and work and accomplish things according to their own needs. Aggression is not a bad thing: it is the degree and misdirection of aggression that are concerns; and much of this misdirection comes from frustration of the child's natural directions and energy. We believe, as Lederman (1969) did, that if the human race would allow babies to live through that natural period of fighting and wrestling in a safe and healthy environment at the right developmental stage, the result will be less problematic aggression later on, not more. As early as the fourth and fifth year, we see a great increase in their own self-control over feelings and impulses, and their ability to use words to express necessary aggression.

All the energy children have and contain in their bodies needs to be played out, for them to develop their own natural pathways, inclinations, interests and talents. By putting children in a formal situation too early (and many day-care situations today are really quite structured), without room for expression of basic and primitive energy and feelings, we take away this natural unfolding and learning. As adults, to the extent that we suffered this kind of restriction and deprivation ourselves, we then tend to feel it is not safe to offer this environment and this expressiveness to children, who we feel "can't be trusted" with so much freedom. Instead, we have adults who are aggressively molding children's behavior and personalities. Then children learn quite a different kind of aggression, by reacting to or swallowing this aggressive frustration, and then exploding as soon as they are alone together, without supervision. Some children will by nature tend to withdraw from violent or controlling parents, while others will become violent themselves, all depending on the individual nature of each child.

In some cases aggressive instincts are controlled so early after birth that the parents never find out the nature of the particular being, who that individual child is and can become. Parents may not want the baby to cry, and may do everything possible to stop the expression of that much energy, whether by punishment, fear, manipulation or rewarding the child for not expressing. Later on in school all these tendencies are reinforced. At Gazebo, we emphasize the importance of recognizing each individual child's differences in aggressiveness and expression. Thus the child is supported to go out in the world later on better able to understand her/his own nature, and to take responsibility for owning and expressing her/his own feelings and impulses.

A fourteen-month-old walks around the school practicing some of his or her first words: *No!* and *Mine!* He or she has already been practicing limits at home with parents, communicating this information preverbally with body cues. Teachers and other children acknowledge and respect the child when he or she says no. When a child doesn't want to eat, we respect his or her decision. The teacher's trust in the child is a vital element for self-esteem. Children exercise taking charge, setting limits, making decisions in their growing process of becoming responsible leaders. "I am angry at you," says four-year-old Dakota to Trevor, when he doesn't want to play. Theron, aged five, facilitates an interaction between a three-year-old and a teacher, when the little boy comes to talk about a problem with another child. "Hey," says Trevor, "don't tell Dorothy [the teacher]. Go talk to Jovian [the other child]."

Children at the Gazebo learn about boundaries from day one. The boundaries that physically define the school area are made of hay bales no more than a foot high. Any one year old can crawl over those limits, and none of them ever do. We trust them, working with a fourteen-month-old who likes to play the edges until he learns that it is not safe to go outside. At Gazebo we have two absolute "no-no's." The first one is going outside the school area without a teacher. The second establishes the limits of how far we leave it up to them to work out their conflicts. We do allow children to fight over the hat they want. They push/pull and do anything they need to in order to take care of themselves; but weapons are not allowed in the school. We don't allow children to bring any kind of toy that represents a universally known weapon (plastic guns, knives, swords, etc). They can play war games in imagination, even stage fights and battles. But they may not hit each other with objects of any kind. These are the safety rules that contain the children and give them the security to exercise the maximum freedom, within these adult-established boundaries.

The animals at Gazebo teach boundaries without words, in a kind and gentle, sometimes forceful way. Pony rides and caring for the goats bring awareness to the children of how to treat other beings: if you don't pay attention to how the pony wants to be treated, he won't go. Everything counts, learning and boundaries are everywhere in the environment.

Teachers also have their own personal space, and their own personal boundaries. Adults at Gazebo don't overuse the word "no," so it never loses its power. It is very important to model clear and clean personal boundaries for the children. Teachers are encouraged to be congruent and consistent when they set a limit, respectfully describing what they saw, and pointing out the down side of the behavior. At times someone puts a child on time-out on the hay bales for a short period of time. It is important for children to recognize that teachers have non-abusive authority and power, and that ultimately they are in charge of safety. This knowledge is what allows the children to play, explore and take risks without carrying an overwhelming burden of worry about safety issues themselves.

Boundaries are also limits established by the children and any other individual that create a safe context for us to contact/relate to each other. Without encountering boundaries a two-year-old would not know what is appropriate and what is inapplicable in the school. Children at Gazebo learn that there are different boundaries for different environments, and different personal boundaries for different people: at school their verbal expression is unlimited, but this may well not be true at Grandmother's house.

With this safety and support, at Gazebo children learn to solve their own problems. There is always time allowed for that. Teachers give them all the time and space they need to struggle with something, being careful not to move in to help right away. Children have an opportunity to struggle, to solve something on their own and in their own way, and then to enjoy their success before going on to a new struggle. Two two-year-olds, Kodiak and Jasper, spend five minutes pulling, pushing and screaming at each other over a truck both of them want. As they struggle, a teacher gets down on ground level without interfering, as a presence to insure that the no-weapons rule is not broken. After the conflict is resolved (Kodiak walks away with the truck), the teacher sits by Jasper and supports him with a hand on his back, allowing space for full expression of his feelings. The scene ends with Jasper curled up in the teacher's lap for comfort. Jasper learns that he can survive a loss, and move on. He is finished with the situation, which is now a closed gestalt for him. Kodiak may decide that having the truck by himself is not as interesting as fighting for it was. Both boys learn something about the exercise of their own strength, and the experience of their own bodies and emotions. By the age of four, in our experience, neither boy will be involved often in this kind of scene. Without correction and "teaching," both will have learned to use words, not fists, in almost all of their dealings with others.

Emotion and Expression: The Story of Garret

Garret was born and raised in Los Angeles, arriving at Gazebo for a week when he was four-and-one-half-years old. The first day at school he was very upset, telling me he hated the Gazebo and everybody in it, and did not want to do anything. I listened to what he said as I kept raking the grounds, and asked him to tell me what things he hated most at the school. After spending at least ten minutes listing and describing everything he could name, he slowed down. I insisted he tell me more information, about the other things he hated. He went on for another ten minutes. At this point he told me he was bored, indicating movement to a more vulnerable, less defended place (from anger to being bored or at a loss). As I kept on raking and moving, he began to follow me. I went toward an area we call Magic Castle. Garret asked me what was magic about the castle. I just looked at him answering that I didn't know, maybe he could find that out on his own. So up Garret went. He climbed the wooden structure and asked me if he could say anything he wanted to. I told him I believed so, and that it was up to him. Garret's response was to say, "Shit, shit, shit!!!" hesitantly at first, and then louder and louder. Then, "Shit, fucking shit, OHHHH, big shit, fuck!!!!" over and over and over. For fifteen minutes Garret screamed non-stop, while I kept on raking. When he finally finished, he came back down and told me he liked the castle, that it really was magic.

That same day Garret went to his aunt's house, where he told her Gazebo was "really great," and that there was a castle there that was incredibly magic. His aunt asked him what was magic about the castle. "I'm sorry," Garret replied, "but I can't tell you the magic words I can say there."

Children need boundaries, and they need self-expression. The boundaries provided by the adults allow the children to feel safe and cared for, which provides the conditions for healthy expression and healthy development of self-confidence and self-esteem. Children have their own experiences and feelings, which they need to express in their own way. Strong among these emotions for young children are sadness and anger. If teachers attempt to change those experiences, telling the children what they should do and should feel, then they are trespassing on the children's boundaries. Rather, teachers at Gazebo describe what they see and share their own personal feelings. Certainly some behaviors are expected, such as joining in cleaning up the environment–which doesn't mean that a child can't have and share his opinion and feelings, negative or positive, about cleaning up. At Gazebo, we believe that this is the existential approach of teachers, and these are the environmental conditions, that support children's exploration of their emotions, beliefs, fantasies, and unfolding selves.

The Gazebo Faculty

Our own personal commitments and growthful learning as teachers at Gazebo include being respectful, sensitive, and caring. Gazebo teachers enjoy kids, and think they are funny. They can teach in a park or in a cave or anywhere, because their stance is to make it interesting by letting the kids explore and create out of whatever is available. Gazebo teachers are notable for their ability to make something out of nothing, which is the creative process itself.

Gazebo is not a finished idea, like an architect's drawing plans. Rather, we are constantly changing the idea and letting it evolve, within the direction of our basic evolving philosophy. A person from Brazil came along, and now we have Portuguese in the curriculum. The children are learning Portuguese songs, not from an American lesson, but from a real Brazilian who grew up with these songs and teaches them with passion. This is typical at Gazebo. There is always passion connected with the teachers, that passion which means being fully alive. We ask teachers to come in and share who they are. If they teach dance, we want someone who lives dancing, who loves to dance, a real teacher.

Teachers are modeling for children at every moment. Certain skills, like patience and sense of humor, are requisites for a Gazebo teacher. A base of self-confidence and self-esteem is fundamental. Genuine caring for children is demonstrated not just by awareness of them, but by self-awareness: admitting error, trusting ourselves, uncovering our own feelings, and being present in each moment we share with a child.

The members of the staff work as a family. As with the children, each individual brings a special expertise, a special talent, their own uniqueness in maintaining the balance of the whole, the equilibrium of the emotional/psychological ambience. This in turn provides a living model for one of the basic Gestalt postulates at Gazebo: the appreciation of differences. Through creating a family system the members relate freely and organically with each other, coming together and apart, agreeing and differing, living and loving in a shared farmhouse with cat, dog, and people who care.

In this ambience, without interpreting the child staff members can pay attention to and heighten awareness of both spoken and non-spoken aspects of communication, granting support and reinforcement when needed. Teachers are active listeners with their five bodily senses open and available, to themselves and others. They reflect on emotions and sensations and ideas, letting children know that they are heard and accepted, encouraging trust and expression of self. Each teacher has his or her own personality; each is unique. We don't relate in the same way. Some like to play games, some tell stories or make music. Some like intense activities while some prefer quiet ones. They appreciate and respect the curiosity of the child and the processes by which the child gathers information and creates experience. Teachers are there to provide the conditions that insure success and a sense accomplishment, which is critical at an early age. Their goal is to perceive the whole child and how his or her parts come together, in the creating of an integrated being–body, mind, heart and spirit.

Our staff at present consists of five core members that work full-time, and a part-time teacher who is a certified Red Cross trainer in first aid and CPR for children and adults; (in fact, all of our core teachers are trained in infant CPR and first aid, are registered with the state, and all have credits in early childhood education through Sonoma State University). In addition we have three full-time interns who live and work with us for periods of three months at a time. In each case what we look for in a teacher is the whole person, someone who will bring her/his own particular qualities, values, and background, which will make them an integral part of the school experience. As Lederman (undated) wrote:

> One of the most critical qualities of a teacher selected is that he/she be highly skilled and knowledgeable in the art and practice of survival on a day-to-day basis–teachers who have had to figure things out for themselves and who have benefited from their own experiences.

This is the art and practice of living, learning, and growing in an integrated way, which are what Gazebo and its Gestalt philosophy are all about.

References

Lederman, J. (1969). *Anger and the rocking chair: Gestalt awareness with children.* New York, NY: McGraw-Hill.

Lederman, J. (Undated). Gazebo school park. Unpublished manuscript.

Perls, F. (1969). *Gestalt therapy verbatim.* Moab, UT: Real People Press.

7

ADD: A Gestalt Perspective

Jay Kent-Ferraro & Gordon Wheeler

Six-year-old Dougie's acute distress was located for the moment in his teacher, who was, as she put it, "losing her marbles." "Oh, he's fine," she laughed ruefully on the phone, "it's me that's going out of my gourd. Every time I turn around, Dougie's someplace else. Today I passed out scissors and paper for a little multi-sensory exercise on the letter of the day–and before I'd finished Dougie's paper was cut up in little bits on the floor. Then at cracker time he still had his scissors, and he cut up the crackers all over the floor! If I send him to the nurse, he goes to the playground. If I send him to the office he goes to the nurse, and spends the day there. He does love the nurse, and she loves him, so that's good. Everybody loves Dougie, but what's going to become of him? And I have 24 other first-graders. Honestly, they should have kept him in kindergarten!"

Taylor, on the other hand, was 14, serious, "not a problem" in school–and deeply, deeply unhappy. In the therapy office he appeared moody and somewhat preoccupied, but not visibly more distractible or less focused than many of his age mates. When his father came in with him, however, the picture changed entirely, with the father scolding and railing at Taylor for being "lazy" and "completely unmotivated," while Taylor himself changed into almost a caricature of a textbook picture of ADHD, loud, disconnected, interrupting, constantly in motion, touching everything in the office, leaning back in his chair to the point of almost falling over, and generally not paying attention to anything that was said by anybody. If his dad had not come in with him that day, the therapist might well never have seen the behavior that had earned Taylor his clinical label, which he had carried now since second grade.

At 16, Chrissie seemed poised to bottom right on out of her last juvenile placement, on her way to the adult correctional system. "Borderline, Antisocial Personality Disorder, Conduct Disorder, Oppositional/Defiant Disorder"–with clinical labels like that filling her bulging file, Attention Deficit Disorder seemed almost a benign afterthought. Using her rage like a rapier, Chrissie was adept at drawing in staff and fellow inpatients alike, only to turn on them with devastating character attacks and brutal analyses of their various shortcomings. Her current placement-of-last-resort was her fifteenth in a two-year span that included five foster homes in three months alone–an eerie reenactment of her own parents' recurrent abandonment, leaving her again and again to suffer the sadly familiar tragedies of so many on the unit: sexual abuse, physical abuse and neglect, terminated pregnancies at pathetically young ages–and in her case, sole charge of four younger siblings. To teach Chrissie, deeply desensitized and boomeranging her way through her young life, how to focus attention on herself and her situation might almost seem cruel–if only there were another way to give her the tools to improve her own attentional process, and thus her life.

Scott's most pressing problems at the moment were legal ones. A quiet, unremarkable boy through most of his childhood, noted in school mostly for daydreaming with occasional flashes of literary talent, Scott had surprised everyone with a sudden arrest for petty drug trafficking, along with an older, tougher group of boys. Since he was now 16, he found himself in adult court, accumulating a record and in the hands of a savvy, street-wise parole officer, who was blowing the whistle on Scott's increasingly heavy marijuana use, which, it turned out, went back some five years without anybody's having much noticed. Scott's mother had taken off when he was "about three or four, something like that," in the words of his father, who maintained the lease on the apartment where Scott lived, but otherwise was not much more present himself. Perhaps surprisingly, Scott had never actually failed a course, which was probably why he had slipped through the cracks of the system for so long. "It's amazing," said his algebra teacher, "he's out of school a lot–I think he has a stack of blank permission forms at home signed by his dad. But he never misses a test, and I swear he can walk in here, sit down and make an 80 on material he's never seen before, didn't do the homework for, and didn't listen to when he was in class. And then he's basically a nice kid with a tough life–I hate to fail him." Scott was contemptuous/suspicious of any form of treatment, but luckily he thought of himself as a poet, and did have some interest in college, "to get out of here." It was the therapist's offer to show him some ways to "show everybody," (especially the drop-in, drop-out father) by changing all those C's and D's into B's and A's, that intrigued Scott and made him willing to make some preliminary contract for therapy.

What these four children and teenagers had in common, beyond their chaotic family histories and an uncommon level of inner misery (even Dougie was of course far from feeling "fine," as he ricocheted through the school day, bouncing off walls, people, and the press of his own developmental needs and goals) was a diagnosis of some form of "ADD"–Attention Deficit/Hyperactivity Disorder, Category 314 in the standard diagnostic handbook DSM-IV. But what is ADD? Is it one clinical disorder with a bewildering array of symptoms and forms–or is it rather a hodgepodge of different kinds of disturbances, grouped into a kind of "garbage pail" category, once a "diagnosis of last resort," now fast the way to becoming, if it is not already, the most common diagnostic label for children and adolescents in clinics and schools? And either way, what should our stance and our interventions be, as we work with these children, their teachers, and their families? To put the same question in language that is more in harmony with a Gestalt approach, how should we work with this population to support a richer, more satisfying unfolding of self for them, and not only for the comfort and managerial convenience of the other adults in their lives–when from the outside at least they often appear to be "under" or "randomly" motivated, with an organization of self and experience that seems to be as unclear and unsatisfying for them as it is for those around them.

This more phenomenological way of formulating the problem will be important to us here, because what we will be proposing in this article will be a somewhat different way of conceptualizing "ADD" in its many forms and presentations, in terms of a common feature of chronic and persistent difficulty in organizing the experiential/attentional field, so as to formulate, hold and realize figures and goals of potential interest and satisfaction. To do this we will rely on the fundamental Gestalt principles of an experience-near or phenomenologically-based point of view, together with a whole field perspective, one that views the child's inner world of subjective experience, outer world of reality constraints and conditions, and his or her developmental context of familial and environmental supports (or their absence) as an experiential whole, with the satisfying resolution of that whole field as both the activity of the self, and the material and the goal of development. In doing this we will be seeking not to replace or even displace the various familiar interventions for dealing with "ADD"–pharmacological, behavioral, family systems, milieu structuring, or even insight therapy–but rather to relate these and other methods and perspectives to each other, in a workable whole which can serve the clinician, teacher, parent, or other adult in the child's life, who after all is confronted with and at least potentially in contact with the child's whole subjective being. Thus it is to that whole subjective being, and its dynamic organization (which in Gestalt terms is the developing self of the child or adolescent) that we will turn.

First, however, as a preparation, we will spend some time here reviewing some basic terms and constructs, to familiarize or refamiliarize ourselves with the domain and features of "ADD," drawing on Barkley (1990), Levine (1994), and others, and also on the body of Gestalt work on the "cycle of experience," including especially the work of Root (1996), applying this model to the domain of attention deficit and related problems. From there we will move to a more clearly "Gestalt" way of understanding attentional process, recasting the Gestalt "cycle of experience" model somewhat as a "cycle of attention" model–a move which will lead us to schematize both the model and the problem in a different, more whole-field and phenomenological way, one that highlights in particular the dynamic issues of support in development, in self-experience, and in healthy functioning.

For convenience's sake, from here on in this discussion we will drop the quotation marks we have been using as a cautionary reminder, and simply make use of the popular term ADD, no quotes, at times interchangeably with the term ADHD, currently if somewhat contradictorily favored by the DSM–but still bearing always in mind that we do not mean to be designating a single "entity," much less a single cause of some single disorder.

(The contradiction in the latest DSM nomenclature lies in the fact that the primary form of "Attention Deficit/Hyperactivity Disorder, 314.00" is attention deficit without hyperactivity, which is the popularly defining characteristic of the disorder–again raising the question of whether we are dealing with a cluster of symptoms can be usefully grouped under one heading at all). On the contrary, as our discussion will show, we are firmly persuaded that almost all cases that are commonly included under this diagnostic category are multi-causal in an interactive way, the summative integration, importantly different in each individual case, of some combination of neurological vulnerability, possible bonding difficulty (which we emphatically do not assume from our field perspective to be "the mother's fault"), and ongoing environmental problems, which are themselves successively and dynamically integrated into and then as the emerging self-process of the developing child.

Let us begin, then, by examining some of these basic terms and constructs, with the aim of building a shared ground for the Gestalt analysis of attention and attentional problems to follow.

The Domain of ADHD: The Primary Constructs

Attention deficit/hyperactivity disorder (ADHD), as its name suggests, comprises a broad-based collection of highly diverse experiences and behaviors, all bearing on the child's ability to organize behavior over time, and manage or negotiate contextual demands for future performance. The domain of problems associated with the diagnosis ADHD (the most recent diagnostic label for this ever-evolving construct), is all those difficulties in children and adolescents (and now adults) having to do with serious disturbances in attention, impulse control, and poor management of activity level in relation to situation and goal (often "over-" but at times "underactivity"). The prevalence of this disturbance, at least as presently viewed in our culture, is quite high: approximately 3-5% of all children in the United States are currently diagnosed or estimated to be diagnosable with this disorder (DuPaul & Stoner, 1994). If this finding is valid, then we can safely assume that every classroom will contain, approximately and on average, one child reported as "having" ADHD, or symptoms currently grouped under this diagnosis. (To be sure, figures like these contain many hidden cultural biases, and must be viewed with extreme caution. It is well known, for example, that the incidence of ADHD varies inversely with socioeconomic status, which raises questions of a political, cultural, and racial-politics nature; see for example discussion in Borland & Hechtman, 1976).

In general, ADHD as a label is used to categorize difficulties in attention and activity level which are chronic in nature, occur across a variety of situations, and are present to a degree inappropriate for the child's age or developmental level, interfering with the child's ability to pay attention, inhibit impulses, and/or restrain or modulate/direct movement. Not surprisingly for such a sweeping collection of descriptors, children with ADHD are a heterogeneous population who display great variability in the degree and behavioral expression of their symptoms, the cross-situational pervasiveness of those symptoms, and the extent to which other disorders are also present (Barkley, 1990). ADHD, at this writing, is one of the most common if not the most common presenting clinical pictures of all the childhood disorders seen by mental health professionals, certainly the modal and perhaps the clear majority leader of all referral problems in school and mental health center or hospital clinical intakes.

Along with this diagnostic breadth and blurring, paradoxically or not, goes the tendency toward monocausalist thinking, with the pendulum currently far over on the side of "innate" or neurological, "hard-wired" explanations. What we gain in management efficiency (which is not necessarily treatment efficacy) by this reductionistic impulse, grouping large and diverse populations of children into broad and inclusive categories, we lose in phenomenological appreciation of the experience of any individual child. Attentional controls and modulation, after all, and all the subtle choice points and dynamic pressures that go into the life of any emergent figure or goal in a child's experience, make up a highly complex and idiosyncratic set of interactional processes which involve numerous interdependent variables.

Fundamentally, when we speak of ADD or ADHD, we are seeing or thinking of a breakdown in field organization and the capacity to sustain an energized figure/goal of interest, in the form of a want or need which the child identifies with in a sustained way, over time and across situational change. In everyday language we might say that the child "doesn't seem to know what he/she wants beyond the present moment," and/or "doesn't stick to it, doesn't carry it through." In more cognitive/behavioral language, we could characterize the same idea as an interruption of response modulation that seems to disrupt the executive functions mediating the space between environmental stimulus and the child's response. For good functioning (whether in terms of the child's own goals, or the goals of those around him/her), these executive functions need to be supporting complex self-regulation in the direction of some identifiable goal (or attentional figure) beyond the present instant; but there they do not seem to be operating in a useful way–again either for the goals of the adult environment, or for those of the growing child. Thus from a Gestalt perspective we are led right from the start to look beyond the issue of deficient neurobiological support only–i.e., the internal, "inborn deficit" explanation alone–to the wider question of personal, subjective field organization of and by the child, how the child makes use of past learning and structures to organize his or her experience now in a complex and ever-shifting environmental field. This kind of consideration then leads us on to whole-field and contextual questions such as what history and models of such structuring are available for the child, what figures of interest are likely to be realizable/achievable in that particular child's environment, what environmental conditions support or inhibit realization of those potential goals and interests, what skills and experience the child has for knowing and identifying with his or her own feelings, wants, and needs, the interpersonal and intersubjective history of reception of those inner feeling states in the child's developmental world, and so forth–all viewed here as entering dynamically into the particular phenomenological process and experience of this particular child, and coming out as felt awarenesses, intentions, wants, needs, desires, goals, and related components of subjectively organized experience.

To begin at least to appreciate these complex processes, we first need a language and nomenclature for this whole array of functions and stages which give rise to the creation of experience itself, a language which we find usefully in the work of Levine (1994), as he discusses the various attentional controls and processes identified as necessary to the formation and sustained investment in figures of attention, which the Gestalt model sees as key conceptual building blocks to an understanding to the creation of experience, and of the developing self.

Attentional Controls and Phenomenological Creation

Attention can be conceived of as a complex system of controls that support us to energize and regulate the boundary of contact between interior need and external possibilities, over time and across contexts. Levine (1994) offers a phenomenological description of the mechanisms involved in the regulation of attention, providing us with language to describe the interplay of processes required to move from sensation and arousal through mobilization (and focusing) of energy and sustained figural focus, to contact and boundary exchange and eventual need satisfaction–assuming that the process does unfold without dysfunctional interruptions, and was well-grounded to start with in some related processes of internal scanning, needs identification, and ongoing assessment of possibilities in a shifting environmental field. In other words, within the single word "attention" lies hidden a whole panoply of supportive, interactive processes–all of which together make the accomplishment of attention-to-satisfaction seem a daunting business indeed, whether to achieve or even just to talk meaningfully about.

This is where Levine's terminology, because it is experience-near and feels recognizable and commonsensical, is helpful to our discussion. Throughout this listing, our goal is not so much to give the reader (or ourselves) a complete dictionary, much less a permanent map, of all attentional process, as it is to give a sense of just how much is involved, how complex it all is, and how many points there are at which attentional processes are obviously susceptible to factors which are affective, interpersonal, environmental, interactive, and subjectively related to feelings like hope or confidence–as well as to underlying neurochemistry per se. It is with this aim in mind that we offer the following list of functions identified by Levine:

> First, mental energy control energizes our alertness and allows us to exert mental effort. This is the initial "fuel" needed for competency in achievement, productivity, and successfully modulated behavior. Several subsidiary functions are required for turning on, allocating, and maintaining an appropriate flow of attentional energy, all of which are required for the child to concentrate and be productive (again, whether in terms of our goals or her goals). The first of these promotes alertness, while the second has to do with the exertion of ongoing mental effort to modulate behavior in an organized and directional fashion.

Closely related are several attentional controls which assist in the processing of information. Collectively they function to create the experience of awareness and absorption of relevant information ongoingly, from moment to moment. Here again, Levine (1994) is helpful in languaging these seemingly abstract or ephemeral processes. We will identify five basic processing controls here. The first of these is saliency discrimination (what Gestaltist Kurt Lewin [1935] called "valence," or valuing), which helps distinguish what is important from what is not, allowing the child to filter out or ignore whatever is non-relevant for the moment. Plainly a deficit here, for whatever combination of reasons, is involved in at least many cases of ADD. The second is depth processing, which sees to it that incoming relevant information is processed with enough intensity to allow the material to stay in the mind. A third is mental activation, a control that turns on other necessary functions of the brain and utilizes the appropriate ground structures needed to interpret, relate, synthesize and make contextual sense of selected information. A fourth control, focal maintenance, keeps concentration going as long as needed–again an obviously sensitive point for our discussion here. Finally, satisfaction control determines continuously whether the current information or experience is satisfying to the individual, fulfilling his/her sense of his/her own needs. We agree with Levine in emphasizing the ongoingness of this function, which is not just an after-the-fact evaluation of experience (as a traditional Gestalt model, which we will discuss below, might seem to imply), but a necessarily continuous function which tells when and where to add energy as needed to attentional processes as we go along, depending on our changing estimation of how the whole process is going, and how much we are invested at the moment in the outcome.

Yet another group of attention controls has to do with the production of whole creations and behavioral activities. Collectively, these functions organize and structure complex behaviors that we produce in the movement toward an identifiable goal. Previewing enables a child to foresee or estimate alternative possibilities and assess potential outcomes that might be produced. Once an outcome is assessed we need actions or functions that support this directionality, while simultaneously inhibiting other actions and figural investments that are not wanted or needed at the time. Facilitation and inhibition work together to assist the child in modulating movement, "staying on task," as we often put it (and often hear it, as a complaint, from parents, teachers, and other adults in the child's life). As we shall see below, this function is particularly important in light of the current focus in ADD thinking and research on the issue of "behavioral disinhibition," the failure to inhibit what in Gestalt we would call "competing figures of attention," which will be discussed below. To complete this list of production functions, tempo control allows for this regulation of rate, pacing, and synchrony with the environment, while self-monitoring and reinforceability have to do with evaluating ourselves as we go along, estimating how effective our efforts are and learning ongoingly from feedback and experience.

In other words, the "life history" of an impulse, the process of following/ supporting an emerging figure into clear awareness and harnessing and sustaining sufficient energy to support direct actions in a complex and shifting interpersonal environment, is a sophisticated and challenging endeavor indeed, to a far greater degree than is often appreciated, either by therapists or by others who work with children in general. The same thing is true, we believe, of many Gestalt writers who have often shown a tendency to look at "figure formation" in a unitary or simplistic way–as it is of many writers on ADHD, who sometimes speak as if "attention" were one function, which is "organic" or inborn in nature, and either present or absent in some simple way that can be simply corrected by medication. Again, the point we wish to emphasize and build on here, and one which the Gestalt model is potentially well-equipped to address, is that the phenomena of attentional processes and the living out of a clear figure of need all the way to satisfaction or completion, involve the complex interaction of a number of processes, each of them with its own neurochemical dimensions, and each of them interacting not just with each other but with subjective organizational dynamics and relational context and history. Any and all of the boundaries and sub-boundaries between and among all these sub-processes, and all the field considerations and relationships outlined above, will mediate and co-structure the child's experience and thus her/his success or failure at forming and actualizing goals. By the same token, any and all of these boundaries may be the appropriate locus for intervention and support, which will be discussed below.

Primary Symptoms Associated with ADHD

ADHD children are often characterized as having chronic difficulties in the areas of inattention, inpulsivity, and overactivity. These problems are thought to occur quite early developmentally–again, to a degree inappropriate to their age, and across various contexts and situations. These disturbances disrupt these children's capacities to focus and sustain attention, modulate energy and impulses, and inhibit other movements in a way consistent with task demands. In this section we will summarize the primary constructs associated with the diagnostic category of ADHD itself, and make several conceptual distinctions to clarify the behavioral symptoms most often observed in these children.

Inattention

As we have seen, the whole notion of attention is a complex and multi-dimensional construct that can refer to difficulties anywhere in the areas of alertness, arousal, selectivity, sustained attention, distractibility, or span of attention, among others (Hale & Lewis, 1979). Research as well as common experience points especially to a core problem, for whatever combination of reasons, with sustaining productive involvement in tasks requiring ongoing attention over time (Douglas, 1983). This can be seen clearly in situations where children in free-play show limited interest, for example, in a single toy, or where their attention shifts rapidly from object to object, showing little commitment to any one in particular. Or the predicament of the school-age child who is required to do independent "seat work," homework, or some other chore–and who appears (to the adult observer) "lazy and unmotivated," apparently "uninterested" in tasks requiring sustained or repetitive involvement over time.

What does this mean from a phenomenological perspective, which is to say in terms of the child's own construction of experience, with all the functions and mechanisms that go into that construction? Barkley (1990) suggests that the problem here may not be simply one of heightened distractibility, or susceptibility to competing stimulation, so much as with diminished persistence and effort in responding to tasks that have either little intrinsic appeal, or minimal immediate consequences following completion. From a Gestalt point of view, we would say that there is too little support in the experiential field–either from internal self-supports, or from environmental sources–to carry the emergent figure through to completion. In practice this kind of factor will likely then appear in interaction with various other factors–all the ones mentioned above, as well as the whole area of behavioral disinhibition, to which we will turn next. What is important here, we believe, and what is supported by a Gestalt lens, is not to choose one single factor cause over another in understanding these complex dynamics, but rather to keep in mind the interplay of all these varying boundaries which point not merely to symptoms, but also to contact possibilities in the context of a field which contains both elements of challenge (task demands) and elements of support (particularly including potential supports not yet harnessed in addressing the problem).

Behavioral Disinhibition/Impulsivity

Added to the challenges of sustaining attention over time and across context, with all the questions of subjective motivation and the anatomy of attentional processes discussed above, are the problems associated with diminished capacity for modulating and inhibiting behavior in response to situational tasks and demands. These are all those problems that are grouped under the heading "impulsivity." This construct may be best described by noting what is seen and felt by others, in the presence of the ADHD child. Common descriptions include patterns of responding quite rapidly, without apparent consideration or planning, failing to follow instructions, missing salient information, "not listening," and/or not comprehending what is required in a particular task. Careless errors and diminished academic performance will often result, giving rise to "tag stories" which may become part of the self-definition of many of these children: "Dougie is always so careless;" "Scott never pays attention, never follows through, never finishes anything;" "Taylor does whatever he feels like without regard for my instructions;" "Julia is a real behavior problem, she's so oppositional all the time." Adults may characterize these kids as "taking the easy way out," "always trying to find a short-cut," or being, again, "lazy and unmotivated." Some may be seen as always "badgering" the parent or teacher, making "excessive demands," being self-centered or intolerant of others, having difficulty with cooperative play, and so on. These are the children, often, who always seem to be having difficulties with peers, with patterns of interrupting, showing no regard for others' feelings, blurting out answers, seeming rude or inconsiderate, violating others' personal space and boundaries, or otherwise ignoring the standard social mores for interpersonal behavior.

Some contemporary clinical studies suggest that in fact it is not so much inattention per se that is the defining hallmark or diagnostic differential of "attention deficit disorder," but rather this problem of behavioral disinhibition–the failure to inhibit behaviors that others find inappropriate and disturbing, and/or that lead away from task accomplishment (Barkley, 1990). What looks like random impulsivity, that is, may well rather be the converse, the failure to block and select among impulses, as other children might. Thus attentional problems per se may be in many cases secondary to a primary disorder of behavioral regulation and inhibition, rather than being themselves a primary, distinct deficit, apart from disinhibition of this kind. (But note too that even if this is true, we may still expect that interactive effects are very strong, and that improvement in attentional and attention-support processes will also support the "energy boundaries" of the present figure or goal, thus helping to inhibit competing impulses and figures).

Hyperactivity

The third primary characteristic of ADHD children is their excessive or developmentally inappropriate levels of activity overall, whether motoric or vocal. Again, these children are often seen as restless, fidgety, unable to sit still, and/or having generally high levels of unfocused and poorly directed energy, often not leading toward completion of any goal. They are "always on the go," "like the energizer bunny," "all over everything," "always making annoying noises," and so forth. From a Gestalt perspective again, what is important to note is the dynamically interactive relationship (or not) of activity per se, to intentionality of activity. In many cases it may not be so much the amount of activity per se that is problematic, as a certain random quality, not related to a clear figure or goal; this is the difference between a "high energy child" and one that we see as "impulsive." Again, the Gestalt clinician is drawn immediately to the question of initial figure formation, which in the Gestalt model is seen as key to healthy overall functioning: how does the child sense and know a need? does he/she identify it verbally, and identify/invest in and with it? If this process function and stage is missing, then everything that follows will be compromised, leading inevitably in many cases to a downward cycle of task failure, shame, lack of confidence, further compromise of the ability to invest a new figural goal with hope and energy, further task failure, and so on.

Numerous empirical studies do confirm this impressionistic picture of ADHD children, as more active, restless, and fidgety than other children, and less able to regulate activity level in relation to the particular qualities of the particular task or context at hand. Moreover, many studies suggest that a pervasiveness of these patterns across situation (home and school, for example) does separate ADHD from other diagnostic categories (Barkley, 1990). Taken together, these findings give us an image of the ADHD child, at least of the "hyperactive" type, as typically one with great available energy combined with insufficient awareness and focused ability to satisfy any clearly felt want or need. Again, Barkley (1990) suggests that these behavioral characteristics of hyperactivity and impulse disinhibition should be given greater weight in conceptualizing ADHD in distinction to other disorders, than should be given to inattention per se.

Our own persuasion is that these issues of relative priority and order of causation, which tend to come out of monocausalist models, will undergo more shifts yet before the clinical and conceptual dust settles on these questions. And when it does settle, we believe it will be in favor of a much more complex, whole-field, and interactive model of the type we are suggesting here, one that sees the problems of neurochemistry and clinical history, of environment and subjectivity and relational context, of reinforcement contingencies and all the various sub-stages of attentional process, and of behavior/energy level/goal formation/consequences as all much more highly recursive, much more mutually supportive (or mutually undermining), than is currently the fashion. It is for this reason that we favor a Gestalt, whole-field lens, as the most helpful theoretical base for organizing our thinking and experience in this difficult area.

Toward a Gestalt Model of Attentional Process

So far in this discussion we have been talking about ADHD mostly as viewed in the mainstream literature, with the idea of building, together with the reader, a common language and common picture of what the domain is of the problem we are dealing with, and what terms and constructs we need at least to refer to, in order to join in on current clinical and educational discourse in this area. At the same time, we have been making some reference to Gestalt perspectives and terms; and it is interesting and important to note just how close much of that mainstream discourse already is, to a Gestalt point of view on figure formation, sustained goal involvement, and needs satisfaction–particularly among writers such as Levine (1994), who treat the subject in both a process-analytical and an experience-near way. This is not surprising when we consider that cognitive/perceptual psychology today is saturated through and through with the language and perspectives of the Gestalt revolution in perceptual psychology that took place in the first half of this past century–a revolution and a tradition in which the Gestalt therapy model itself is of course deeply rooted, through the second half of the same century and right up to the present; see e.g., Perls, et al., 1951). Moreover, the Gestalt model of experience is itself a phenomenolgically-based mode–i.e., one based on the organization of subjective experience. Thus the "Cycle of Experience" model, which is prominent in Gestalt literature and practice in a number of domains and which outlines stages of sustained attention and movement toward a goal over time, is itself really an elaboration of a "commonsensical" approach to understanding the organization of experience and behavior. That is, in "experience near" terms, we survive in the world by meeting our felt needs in a shifting field, and to do that we must proceed in some basic way from self-awareness to needs identification ("figure formation"), environmental scanning, mobilization of energy and resources, the setting in motion of some action, the arrival/achievement or not of some usable goal, and some kind of evaluative, learning, or feedback process that enables us to know when we get there, and to correct as we go along. All this has to be in some way true, at least sketchily, for survival itself to be possible–and all of this is very close to both the anatomy of attentional process offered and reviewed by Levine, Barkley, and others, as well as to the various presentations of the Gestalt diagnostic rubric known variously as the "Cycle of Experience," "Contact Cycle," or just "Cycle" model (see discussion in Perls et al., 1951; Nevis, 1987; Wheeler, 1991; also Root, 1996, relating the cycle model to ADHD specifically).

What we aim to do here is recast this Gestalt model somewhat, and use it directly and discriminatively as a "Cycle of Attentional Process" model, building on the analytic anatomy of attentional functions offered by Levine (1994), as well as on the application of the cycle model to ADHD offered by Root (1996). Once we have done that much, we will go on to offer a revised version of the cycle model, reconsidered now as a whole-field model of conditions of support, internal and external, for the formation and realization of these attentional figures. Such a model, we hope, will serve to support the clinician or other adult working with the ADHD child or adolescent to make interventions in particular cases–interventions that are both more finely tuned, in terms of discriminative diagnosis of just where the attentional problems lie in that case, and at the same time more whole-field-based, in the sense of helping us to organize and mobilize an array of supports from different points in the experiential field of the child, in a more flexible, interactive, and integrative way.

To do all this, let us first turn briefly to a Gestalt view of attention itself, as we continue our development of a common language of Gestalt-based terms and concept/constructs for dealing with real ADHD kids, in their complex and subjective fields of living.

Attentional Process and the Gestalt Model

From its earliest beginnings almost a century ago now, the Gestalt model, which amounted to a complete revolution in the psychology of the times, was concerned with understanding the nature and processes of perception and cognition themselves–which is to say, the meaning and dynamics of attentional process. How is it that we focus on or attend to anything at all, differentiating that "something" from "everything else?" And then how do we hold and process these focal perceptions in some workable way to arrive at complex thinking, orientation, and ultimately problem-solving itself? After all, these questions and processes must be key to our very survival, as intensely social animals in a difficult and shifting field of life problems and challenges; and none of them seemed at all well accounted for under the older Associationist model, which was dominating perceptual research and theory at the time.

The effect of that first generation of Gestalt research was a transformation in our understanding of how seeing, noticing, and attending are organized, in the perceiving subject. Perception–the forming of an attentional figure in and out of a larger perceptual field–is not and cannot be a matter of just "adding up" discrete stimuli, as the Associationist/empiricist school had it. Rather, as the early Gestalt research seemed to demonstrate clearly, our perceptual/cognitive nature is to apprehend the world in "perceptual wholes" of understanding, clear, distinct, and relatively sharply-bounded "figures" which stand out from a background, and are subjectively experienced as having qualities of greater brightness, cohesion, interest, and "energy" or "pragnanz" (the early Gestaltists' word for "energy for going somewhere," a tendency to lead to the "next thing"), as contrasted with the background, or rest of the perceptual field, which tends to remain temporarily dull, undifferentiated, and without interest. Thus we hear the person we are talking to, and not the radio in the background, or the conversations of the other diners in the restaurant–at least until such time as the intensity or particular content of those "competing figures" becomes high enough to displace the figure we were attending to before (for a detailed discussion of early Gestalt perceptual work and its implications for later cognitive models, see Wheeler, 1991, Chapter 1).

In other words, we are "wired for attention;" it is our inborn nature, barring unusual personal trauma or neurological deficit, to select out and "bound off" a figure for sustained attention, and to exhibit some degree of selective inattention to other stimuli which are inevitably coming in at the same time–at least as long as they stay below a certain trigger threshold level, which may itself vary from one stimulus or situation to another. Combining these early Gestalt insights with an evolutionary perspective, we can see how something like this has to be true of us in some way, and that a pure associationist, one-stimulus-at-a-time model really couldn't account for all our behavior, or get us where we need to go in terms of sheer survival in the world. We are, after all, a low-instinct, high-learning species whose special adaptation is for flexibility and novelty in problem-solving, or what we call "creativity," across a wide range of environments (a way of expressing all those processes which the ADD child has trouble with), in contrast to many other species, who quickly die out when the environment changes. Moreover, our special life circumstance is high sociability, which is itself the consequence of physical vulnerability and a long dependent childhood, following birth at a much more immature stage than almost all other mammals. Shifting field, flexibility of response, high social learning–all these things dictate a neurological substructure which is adapted to metaprocesses of flexible yet cohesive field organization, the ability to integrate many stimuli into a quick, serviceable picture which enables us to take an action, solve a problem, and adjust that ongoing solution to shifting environmental conditions over time, on the way to the meeting of some need.

We are equipped, that is, to form a figure of attention related to some need, to hold that figure while we simultaneously evaluate it in relation to other needs and surrounding conditions, and sustain our attentional investment while we go through many substeps and supportive actions on the way to satisfying that need, at least well enough to survive and reproduce. Equipped, in other words, to organize and master all those subprocesses of the simple word "attention" presented by Levine (1994) and discussed in the preceding sections–barring some disturbance in that neurological substrate, and/or in all the complex learning processes implied in the word "master," at least some of which are detailed above.

Early Gestalt research was concentrated on relatively static, fairly artificial problems of fine perceptual discrimination or resolution of an ambiguous figure in the research lab, where subjective investment was fairly low, and other life issues and problems were pretty well kept out of the picture, as potential distractions from the study of "pure perception," which was still thought of as something apart from value, need states, and shifting external conditions. Still, even that first generation of researchers had noted that quality of attentional "pragnanz" mentioned above, that tendency of the percept to lead the subject somewhere, to move on some "next thing." Again, this fits with our picture of evolutionary utility, sketched briefly above. For the most part we don't "just attend," (though when things are quiet, inside us and out, we do go on with passive figure formation or "incidental learning," the elaborate machine of our perceptual apparatus in its "idling state"). Rather, if we are wired this way it is for a reason, and that reason is our incredibly flexible problem-solving ability itself, which is our special talent and our special need, as an individually defenseless, socially dependent species gifted for nothing in particular except this sociability and flexible creativity themselves (for further discussion, see for example Wheeler, 1996, 2000).

It was the second-generation gestaltist Lewin (1926, 1935) and his students, more than anyone else, who then took the model to this next level, out of the lab and into the "real life" world of problems, goals, needs, feelings and shifting conditions. Attentional perception and problem-solving, Lewin insisted, are not two different kinds of cognitive process and function: rather, all perception, all attention, is structurally and dynamically of a problem-solving nature. We resolve a chaotic field into a coherent, usable whole–and we do it in terms of our need, our goal state as subjectively experienced at the moment. The need, in Lewin's familiar dictum, organizes the field (see discussion in Wheeler, 1991; Marrow, 1964).

Attention, that is, is not separable from subjective, experiential issues of need, goal, and value–again a point which is brought out in the discussions by Barkley, Levine, and other writers on ADHD. Subjective factors of personal investment and the aimed-for goal are always in play, when we talk about attentional processes or attentional deficit. It is, to use a language reminiscent of another Gestaltist, Kurt Goldstein, the "whole organism" who pays attention, and not just the neurological aspect or substructure–a point which often seems to be overlooked, in "pure neurology" discussions of ADHD and related problems.

And how does the person move (and move back and forth) from figure formation or attention itself, to the accomplishment of some need that the whole attentional process is designed, potentially at least, to address? Again in a commonsensical way we can say that the process has to be something like that described by the ADHD writers above as they attempt to pull out and delineate the subprocesses of attention and goal realization, from their natural, functional holism: a movement, that is, from needs awareness to formation of some external figure of attention (a concrete destination or some imaged goal), the ongoing selection of stages or subgoals as intermediate figures along the way, the arousal and management of energy, the screening out of distractions, the organization of action in the field, leading hopefully to some satisfaction of the need. Each of these stages remains to be spelled out, of course; each is highly recursive, with movement back and forth in the management of enormously complex and changing internal processes and external realities; and each is obviously vulnerable to interruption or breakdown, with interactive "ripple effects" which, if chronic, will give us one or another of the symptom presentations we associate with the broad ADHD diagnostic category.

Toward a Gestalt Model of Attentional Process and Dysfunction–the "Cycle"

Fritz Perls, and later Paul Goodman, were deeply intrigued by the application of this more interactional, Gestalt field-contextual thinking, which they saw as providing more room for creative individuality than was found in the authoritarian, individually passive implications of the inherited Freudian constructs and categories that were the currency of clinical models of the times. The key issue, they were to argue in their 1951 collaboration *Gestalt Therapy: Excitement and Growth in the Human Personality*, was not libidinal cathexis, repression, and then either sublimation or symptom formation, but rather how the person makes creative contact in the world– i.e., how she/he organizes the self and mobilizes activity to meet important needs in living, as he/she experiences those important needs. Lewin had already moved to extend the Gestalt model beyond attentional perception of isolated figures to the question of mapping of whole contexts, whole fields of experience, with an eye to negotiating them to meet needs. Goldstein (1940), with whom Perls had worked briefly, had then moved further, in the direction of considering all the organizational and self-organizational questions of the accomplishment of complex goals involving a series of behaviors–which is to say, the issues of sustaining attention in a complex field over time, the same issue we find identified over and over as key in the symptomatology and treatment of ADHD. Goodman and Perls, in effect, moved toward taking the model all the way, to what we would call today a fully subjective constructivism, an emphasis on creativity of self-organization as the hallmark of the species, and of healthy attentional process in real life situation.

In his first book, Perls (1947) sketched this issue from a clinical point of view, outlining what he called the "metabolism cycle," six stages of progression from a resting state, to tension, awareness of a need, action, solution, and return to a quiet state. The Freudian, tension-reduction element of the outline is plain, but at the same time so is the attempt to move beyond "drive" to focus on the structure of awareness itself, which is the Gestalt issue of organizing attention in the field, and then taking action based in some way on that attentional figure. By 1951, Goodman and Perls were calling this same cycle "forecontact, contacting, final contact, post-contact" (Perls, et al., 1951, p. 471), but the accent now was more and more on the question of figure formation itself, the initial issue of attention to and identification with some need or desire, which sets the person and the process in motion. We might say that where the early attentional research of Wertheimer (1912) and his colleagues and students tended to look at perception and attention as a snapshot of a particular moment of figure or gestalt formation in isolation, the treatment by Goodman and Perls was more like a motion picture, the story or life history of an impulse and its vicissi-

Figure 1
The "Contact Cycle" or "Cycle of Experience"

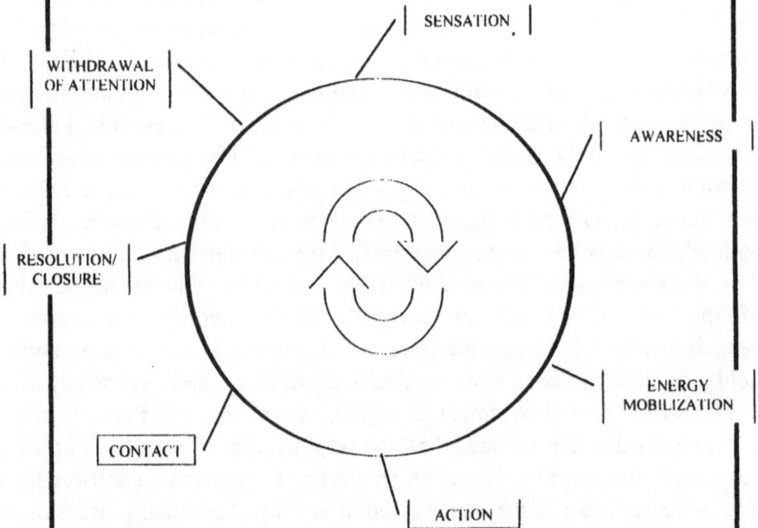

From E. Nevis, *Organizational Consulting*, GestaltPress 2001. Used by permission.

tudes over time, and in the contextual world. And from a clinical point of view, to paraphrase Eliot, between the conceiving of a thing and the doing of it, there can fall many a shadow–those shadows in this case being the disturbances and life difficulties we know as ADHD.

Subsequent Gestalt writers, particularly those associated with the "Cleveland School" of Gestalt therapy, then elaborated this cycle notion into a fully articulated tool for diagnosis, intervention, and teaching, calling it the "Cycle of Contact" or "Cycle of Experience" model, one version of which is given here in Figure 1 (for a variety of presentations of the Cycle, see e.g., Zinker, 1977, Nevis, 1987, or discussion in Wheeler, 1991).

The particular strength of this model lies in its usefulness for zeroing in on specific areas of problem or dysfunction at a concrete process level, and on a wide variety of levels of system–individual, couple, family, group, organizational, and so forth. That is, if a person or group of people is having trouble meeting goals and reaching satisfaction, we can observe that person or group in some slice of living process to see where exactly the dysfunction is showing up. Again as Lewin insisted, we are always engaged or potentially engaged in organizing to get somewhere, to accomplish or do something–and if that something is not going well, then we can use the model diagnostically to see just where the person is stopping or "leaving the cycle," thus never reaching the goal. Is the need or goal poorly imaged or articulated, so that no clear direction or purpose is laid down from the start (in which case a certain aimlessness and then dissatisfaction would have to be result)? Is there little or no mobilization of energy–and if so, then what is that about (which can lead, in therapy, to exploration of developmental inhibitions and prohibitions of the kind Perls and Freud were both so much concerned with)? Is the mounting energy and excitement somehow never mobilized (that is, focused and organized in a desired direction) and then carried forward into action–and again, is that just a personal or organizational habit, or is there a dynamic reason, a felt risk to taking that next step? What happens when "contact" ("full contact," in Goodman's sketch) is reached, if it is reached at all: does the person stay with it, finish, get the good out of it, learn from it–and if not, why not? Or does he/she tend to hold back at the last minute, and return to square one without any full accomplishment or experience? Finally, what happens in withdrawal/assimilation: is time taken to appreciate, learn, be impacted by the experience, integrate the learning or the gains and losses ("assimilate," in both Goodman's and Piaget's terms; see Chapter 10 in this volume). And does the person or group then question or confirm old assumptions usefully, so as to change and grow ("accommodate," again in Piagetian language)?

In each stage, characteristic defenses or "resistances" to the contact process can then be identified–again on the individual level, or as characteristics of a group or other social system (Polster & Polster, 1973; Zinker, 1977). Thus confluence, a basic lack of self-differentiation and sense of one's own ownership of needs and experience, might dampen the whole initial awareness process. Introjections (prohibitions and basic, unquestioned beliefs) might be blocking sensation of body needs and data, and awareness of certain desires and goals. Projection might be displacing these uncomfortable desires onto other people ("I don't have any bad wishes, but they wish to hurt/seduce/control me"). Retroflection would be a kind of reluctance to risk the move to action, habitually looking only to the self to satisfy, as well as possible, the needs of the self. Deflection might relieve all this cumulative discomfort by just switching focus altogether (a pattern directly reminiscent of ADD). And finally, moving around the cycle to full contact, egotism, Goodman's formulation for staying within the self boundary and thus avoiding a full meeting, a full giving of the self to the experience, might be a kind of last-minute retroflection, stopping just at the brink of full contact itself.

As a wide range of books and articles document, the Cycle model has proven useful as a diagnostic and heuristic tool across an extremely wide range of applications–not just in individual therapy, but in work with couples, families, small groups, and larger organizational settings (see for example Nevis, 1987; Zinker, 1994). Both common sense and problem-solving analysis support the idea that something like these stages will be necessary to go through, either reflectively or automatically, in order to reach any goal or manage or solve almost any imaginable situation or problem in living. And clinical experience and research (Woldt, 1998) do confirm that individuals and systems will often have characteristic distortions, at least in certain kinds of situations, where they will recurrently leave or inhibit the cycle at individually characteristic places, and with characteristic styles ("defenses" or "resistances"). Certain patterns of building or inhibiting a contact cycle may be broadly characteristic of certain cultures or groups, and others may tend to be characteristic of certain diagnostic categories (indeed, in a Gestalt process model those self-organizational patterns or "resistances" may be thought of as the diagnostic categories themselves; see e.g., Melnick & Nevis, 1992).

Relating the "Cycle" Model to ADD

Root (1996) has undertaken to relate this model to characteristic contact patterns of "ADD," emphasizing in particular disturbances and deficits in the first, or sensation/awareness phases of the cycle–and then to a lesser degree the failure to stay with "full contact" (which in any case we might expect to be compromised or not very attention-compelling, if the result of the cycle wasn't the payoff to a felt need in the first place). All or most of the eighteen symptoms listed in the DSM-IV as characterizing

ADHD in one or another of its forms, Root suggests, are indicative of or the same as a disturbance in sensation/awareness, including especially bodily sensation (p. 22). If the child (or adult) doesn't know how to register what he or she wants, needs, feels, beginning with body sensations, and/or doesn't stay long enough with these perceptions to "get grounded" in a particular direction toward some goal, then it is hardly surprising if everything that follows is problematic in a variety of ways. In this emphasis Root is in a sense joining the early Gestalt researchers, who emphasized "figure formation," how a person scans, attends to, organizes, and registers perceptions–in this case particularly those having to do with the person's own internal states and processes. This in turn leads him to consider interventions of the "delayed reaction training" type, such as Meichenbaum's (1999) program promoting reflection and goal awareness. That these programs, which have considerable face appeal, have not been shown to be consistently effective, Root suggests is due to their neglect of sensory experience (and, we would add, affective experience as well, which new research shows to be crucial in the organizing of cognition and intentionality, as the Gestalt model has long maintained; Damazio, 1994). "ADD" children, far from being hyper-reactive to internal stimuli as is commonly supposed, are actually tend to show arousal dysfunction, or hypo-reactivity to internal sensory information. Thus, Root reasons, it makes all the more sense to use sensory awareness training, which is an integral part of the overall awareness focus of Gestalt (along with meditation or other self-awareness enhancement training), to make this kind of slowing-down and taking-time-to-organize intervention more effective with the "ADD" child or adolescent (or, again, adult).

We find this line of thinking to be promising and persuasive. What we would like to add here, again, is our own conviction, growing out of all the research cited above as well as our own clinical experience, that not just the "sensation-awareness" or figure formation part of the contact cycle is implicated and crucial in ADD, and in attentional process in general, but the whole cycle as well, which represents all the equally important issues of the sustaining of figure across time and situation, the maintenance and management of attentional energy and attentional boundaries, if any important goal is actually going to be reached over time. To borrow a phrase from Freud, this is the anatomy and life history of "figure and its vicissitudes," all the things that can go wrong in the course of organizing impulses into meaningful intentions and goals, related in some useful way to a whole context of living: i.e., the very things the ADD child or adolescent is having trouble doing. The "vicissitudes" or mishaps of attentional figures on the way to realization then correspond both to the contact "interruptions" or "resistances" described in the Gestalt literature on the cycle model (see e.g., Polster & Polster, 1973), and to the various sub-functions and component processes of attention described by Levine above, and by numerous other writers on attention and ADHD.

In other words, what we are proposing is that the Cycle model, originally offered as a diagnostic diagram of needs satisfaction, can be usefully recast as a "Cycle of Attention" model, for use in the same way as a tool for the discriminative field diagnosis of ADD–a tool that is at once more exactly descriptive of the phenomenological functions and stages of attentional process, and more whole-field and phenomenologically oriented, in the sense of supporting our own attention, as clinicians and others, to issues and conditions beyond the purely individual or purely neurological emphases of so much writing in this field. These are the issues and conditions of field support (internal and external), which work for or against the forming and sustaining of attentional figures in the "real life" of the child, or for that matter of anyone.

Thus our first step here is to take the same Cycle diagram and relabel the progressive stages as the stages of attentional process and function, making use of the descriptive anatomy of attentional functions reviewed above. This picture is given in Figure 2.

Most of the terms and labels of Figure 2 are self-explanatory, or are explained above, in their earlier presentation in this chapter. Here we will comment on two descriptors in particular, from the Cycle of Attention: "identification with the figure of interest," and "maintaining/managing attentional boundaries." By "identification with the figure of interest," we mean the investment of self, and self-energy, in the attentional figure or goal. This is that sense of the goal becoming "my goal," a figure of interest that I want to have, achieve, arrive at. Here a whole raft of developmental capacities is implicated: the subjective sense of a stable "me" that supports and "has" or is my experiences; the experience of a personal history as an agent of wants and desires; an interpersonal, relational history and context that would underlie such a feeling of personal agency (see discussion of the intersubjective dimension of self-development in Chapter One in this volume); the capacity to remember and sustain that investment in a specific goal; the confidence that supports keeping that energy up; the capacity to modulate or "not run away with" that energy, to defer immediate outcome and gratification, and on and on. All of these are the supports from what we may call the "internal field" of a child's experience–though certainly each of

Figure 2
The Cycle of Attention

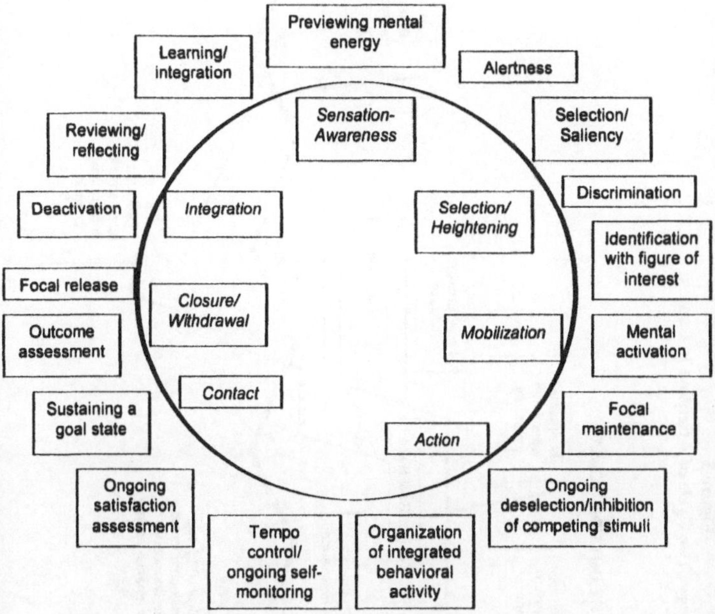

them has an interpersonal history and implicates more than "purely inner" factors such as inborn neurology. At the same time is the whole range of "outer field" supports that come into play here, the assumption of some stability in the outer context, enough safety to permit this kind of ongoing identification and focus.

This brief outline already gets us into issues of "maintaining/managing attentional boundaries," the second of the terms we want to explain here. For some clarification of what we mean by this, and how this notion may organize our whole thinking on ADD problems, let us turn to a different way of representing the "Cycle of Attention" model, one that looks at the same cycle-building experience more phenomenologically, more from the inside of the child's experience (rather than "objectively/analytically," in the way of the cycle as usually represented, without direct reference to context). This new presentation is given here in Figure 3.

In this version of the Cycle, which we are calling here the Cycle of Attention or "Cycle of Energy" version (because of the issue of the atten-

Figure 3
Cycle of Energy: The Cycle of Attention in Context

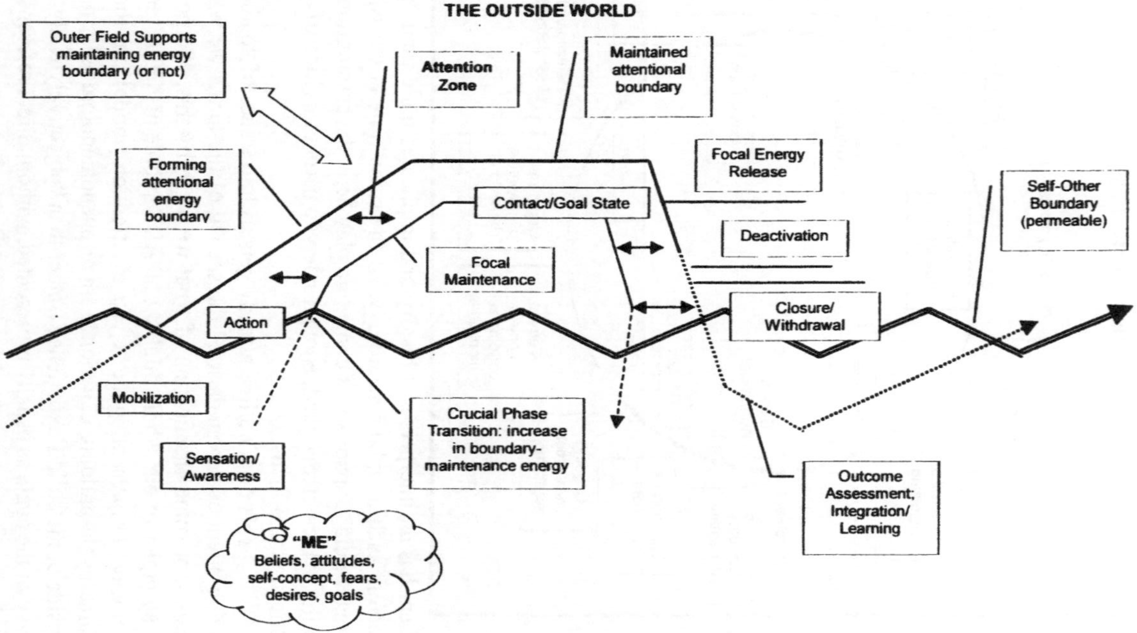

tional energy boundaries, which we want to focus on as crucial here), we begin with the inner world and experience of the child, adolescent, or adult, who approaches some life situation with a whole host of "things" already going on: inner feelings and needs, more or less clear, memories, goals, apprehensions and assumptions, and so on–as well as a whole ongoing range of percepts and beliefs about the outer world she/he is "looking out on," and trying to deal with in some way. Gradually, in some clear or unclear way, the person begins to mobilize in a particular direction, with all the problematics of that that have been discussed down through this essay. As this energy gathers and becomes more focused, at least in the "good-enough," productive case, there comes the moment of "breaking through" the internal/external self boundary, into activity that is manifest in the "outer field"–i.e., the world of other people, reactions, costs and contingencies and consequences.

This is a crucial moment in the cycle, a moment of qualitative shift that is not so singled out for focus in the older, "cycle in isolation" schematic as it is here. The shift here is the move from "just thinking" to "real world consequences"–the difference between desiring, say, to hit my little brother, and actually doing it (an experience whose organization is deeply dependent on whether or not the child has access to a "language of feelings"–see discussion in Chapter 5 in this volume). Plainly there is, or should be, a hesitation or potential hesitation at this transitional phase of the cycle–a pause which is often missing in ADD children; and here again we see the value of Root's focus on response delay, discussed above, through sensory awareness training, including the crucial step of putting language on sensation, in the service of that delay and of introducing choice into the previously unbroken flow of experience.

What we wish to add here, and what this version of the model helps us see, is the equally crucial issue of field supports, which come into play at every moment of the cycle, but particularly at this phase transitional moment, of going from "internal" to "external" experience. At each stage of the cycle, as we can see in this rendition, the issue is not just forward movement in isolation from context, but the maintaining of a boundary in the experiential field, between this activity, which is commanding a large part of the person's energy at the moment, and everything else, which is at least relatively deferred. It is this sustained difference of attentional focus that we are calling an "energy boundary," which is equivalent to an "attentional boundary." Actions, thoughts, impulses which contribute to moving us to the imagined goal have to be kept up and energized; behaviors, sensations, considerations that interfere have to be desensitized, de-energized, and not identified with for the moment: this is the behavioral inhibition and disinhibition referred to above. Without that inhibition–which is the same as the boundary we are depicting schematically here–the child's behavior looks and becomes random, impulsive, disorganized, or just meaningless, in the extreme case to the child him/herself, who cannot give us any usable accounting of it.

And the maintenance of this boundary requires support, at every stage and moment. By support, we mean any kind of available structure or process in the field of subjective experience–inner or outer–which serves to reinforce that "channel," that focalization of energy in an ongoing way toward some desired outcome. This can be neurological (a predisposition toward more "steady state" neural firings, without a lot of extraneous synapse activity that is so highly energized as to compete in an attentional way); personal/historical (that sense of confidence and good expectation that makes us "lean into" the goal direction, as opposed to chronically hesitating and holding back in apprehension); interpersonal, which would include present supportive or unsupportive people, helping the child to frame the task and organize the environment, as well as that history of attachment, reception, dialogue, and modeling which becomes internalized as the ground structure of present contact figures (again, see discussion of a Gestalt developmental perspective in Chapter One of this volume); or situational/environmental, in the sense of all those present external conditions that may help or interfere with the child's ability to stay with a single focus (including such serious contextual issues as violence in the home or community, insecurity about conditions of family life, worry about a dysfunctional parent, and so on).

All of these factors and more are in play ongoingly, as attention is sustained, or not, across changing situations and conditions all the time. And all of them are well and flexibly integrated, we believe, by this dynamic notion of field support–again, considering both the "inner field" of feelings, beliefs, attitudinal sets and neurological process, and the "outer field" of current real conditions, as subjectively present to and perceived by the child him/herself. All of these are real contingencies and dynamic, interactive factors in the "life history" of a figure of attention, from early figure-formation stages and on through sustaining, maintaining, and managing attentional energy and its boundaries in the complex and difficult field of living.

Successful intervention and treatment of attentional difficulties and dysfunction must always involve, we believe, attention to all these dimensions of the problem–a point which is borne out by research which shows, for example, that medication combined with psychotherapy (even a generalized psychotherapy which does not specifically take up the problem in this field-oriented way) is generally superior to medication alone, with ADHD diagnoses (Barkley, 1990). To take a look in a more concrete way what we mean by a "whole-field" approach to intervention, let us now turn briefly to our original four vignettes, representing just a few of the many types and presentations of this heterogeneous (yet meaningfully related) diagnostic category, to see how we might go about scanning the whole field of the problem for missing or inadequate supports, and what combinations of interventions might add up, synergistically and interactively, to an improvement in living for the child.

The Attentional Supports Model in Practice–Dougie

Six-year-old Dougie, who was driving his teacher "bananas," presented in the clinic with not just attentional dysfunction, but many signs of disordered thought process. After testing, the school psychologist was recommending immediate placement in a special classroom for seriously disturbed primary-level children in a different school. The therapist, who was a psych intern, was not so sure. Something in Dougie's personal contact, she felt, was more relational, more clear and "real" than testing alone suggested. Dougie's disordered communication and seemingly random verbal productions, which showed up so strongly on test questions, were better organized and more meaningful, more attentionally and interpersonally focused when they were "just talking." Couldn't it be, she hypothesized, that a certain pattern of random or "loose-association" speech production was a sort of anxiety reaction, a management strategy for deflecting challenge and getting through the pressure of anxiety-arousing questions and tasks, but not (or not yet, developmentally) a fixed pattern of dysfunctional organization, in figure formation and the sustaining of an interaction? Her supervisor agreed to let her make treatment interventions based on these ideas, keeping Dougie in his regular classroom for a time, but arranging for extra support for the times of day when he was feeling the most pressure.

Dougie's attentional focus seemed to "go to pieces" under the stress of task performance expectations. That is, he seemed more oriented if you didn't ask him, and more able to accomplish complex tasks if he set them up himself. On the level of internal supports for attention, he seemed to carry an assumptive set that the demands of another person were going to lead to some aversive or catastrophic situation, so that all his attention shifted to screening out or warding off dire consequences, with little or none left over for the original task itself. This set, combined no doubt with some vulnerability or "iffiness" of underlying neurological process, seemed to tip him over the edge into attentional dysfunction, behavioral impulsivity, hyperactivity, and chaotic thought process all at the same time. On his own, however, he was apparently capable of considerable complexity of behavioral sequence–coming home from the bus, letting himself in (if he had remembered his key, but a neighbor had another one and was in any case supposed to be monitoring his comings and goings for an hour till Dougie's mom got there), taking the shopping list from the countertop, going to the store, taking the money from the drawer, getting the items on the list (which he could read ideographically, in most cases), coming home with the correct change, and sometimes putting the items away–quite a lot, his therapist felt, for a six-year-old.

Leaving aside for the moment the question of whether a six-year-old should come and go by himself, which the therapist took up quite seriously with the mother (the neighbor, it seemed, was right across the foyer and really was on the job, leaving her door open and supervising Dougie closely, so that he actually was more at her house than his own for that hour; and neighborhood six-year-olds did commonly frequent the corner store alone, which was only two doors away)–the therapist focused on the issue of Dougie's underlying anxiety in general, and what happened in particular when an interpersonal demand was placed directly on him. In addition to expressive work, drawing and puppets and clay modeling, on family issues and fears, she also introduced more demand elements into their own play process. Dougie loved to play softball outside on the clinic lawn, using the trees as bases. Since there were only the two of them, they devised an elaborate team game of "leave on," whereby once Dougie got to, say, second base, then that "man" was left on base, as an imaginary runner who would advance only when forced by the runner behind him, while Dougie returned for another turn at bat, as long as the inning lasted. After each play, the therapist would insist that Dougie account for how the game stood at the moment–the relative score, the number of outs, strikes, balls, and so forth, plus how many "men" were on base, and exactly where they were, after the previous play. Some of Dougie's early responses, which the therapist noted in process notes, included:

"Uh, uh, uh, you eight, you four, strikes-balls-outs–I don't know I don't know, who cares leave me alone, (singing) take me out to the ball game." To which the therapist replied, "oh goodie, so I have eight and I have four, that means I have lots and lots and you don't have anything." "If you say so," said Dougie. "Well, you said so, so I'm winning and you're losing, way losing. I like this game," replied the therapist with a twinkle. It was the twinkle that tipped Dougie off, the therapist was convinced; and his capacity to catch that kind of contact nuance further convinced her that a thought disorder diagnosis was not helpful, in spite of the disordered speech.

"No," Dougie protested, seeming to hear a part of what had been said by a sort of delayed effect. "How come you're winning, if you struck out and I've got–I've got–how many do I got?"

"How many?" the therapist turned the question back on him.

"Three?" Dougie struggled.

"Well, let's count up," the therapist sat down on the grass.

"No," Dougie would almost plead, "just play."

"Can't do it, Dougie," the therapist was unrelenting. "I can't play if I'm all confused. I need to know where we stand. Now let's see–there was the time you hit that long one clear over the driveway–how many men were on base then?"

"One?" Dougie made an effort. "No, two!."

"Right, two, plus that was a homerun, so that's how many?"

"Three."

"Okay, right, now, were there any others?"

"Nope–I mean yes!" Dougie thundered. "The one you dropped!!" "So that makes–?"

"Four!! I got four," he pronounced.

"Right, you got four. And me?"

"Four," Dougie perseverated, losing focus again.

"Great!" the therapist got up, ready to play again. "I totally struck out, and now I've got four runs. I love it!"

"NO!" Dougie was angry now. "You got nothing. Nothing, nothing, nothing. You struck out!"

"Oh, right," the therapist sighed. "So what's the score?"

"YOU NOTHING. ME FOUR. FOUR TO NOTHING. NOW LET'S PLAY BALL!!!"

And so it went, baseball and drawings, puppets and baseball, week in and week out, rain and shine they were out on the lawn at least half of every weekly hour. And as the weeks went by, Dougie was settling down, wandering less and acting "you know, less like Dougie," his teacher reported, in school, more able to play with other kids after school in the neighborhood. He still had difficulty following directions given in a whole group, yet showed clear gains in complex instructions one-on-one.

There were other interventions. Dougie's father, divorced and seeming at times as "spacey" as his son, spoke constantly of moving to another state, seemingly for no particular reason. When the therapist told him that these constant vague plans and suggestions were undermining Dougie's progress, the father was angry, and felt "controlled"–but the remarks stopped, and Dougie settled down some more. In second grade he was evaluated by the pediatrician and recommended for Ritalin, which his mother refused to authorize. Still his progress continued, slowly. He continued to have difficulty finishing things, keeping track of some things, staying in his seat–yet now he was scoring around a year behind in school, in place of two to three years behind on standardized achievement tests (Dougie was actually answering test questions now, most of the time, instead of just fending them off). Perhaps his gains would have been greater with medication, perhaps not. By any behavioral standard he still qualified for an AD/HD diagnosis, yet he was learning, growing, settling into the life tasks and social relationships of a seven-to-eight year old. Disordered speech had disappeared entirely. He spoke now as if he were speaking to somebody, rather than throwing strings of words at some felt pressure–somebody who needed to receive something he needed to tell, something of him.

A couple of years later tragedy struck Dougie's family, in the form of violence and death. Many of his anxiety symptoms reappeared, grades plummeted, attentional skills went out the window, at least in the demand situations of fifth-grade academic classes. At this point Dougie (now Douglas) did enter a special class, and did accept a medication trial, which did seem to support his attentional process. And yet disordered thinking and speech–that quality of talking that seems to have come unmoored from any attentional goal or focus–did not reappear. He stayed in real contact with other people, including his therapist, and through that support, stayed in contact with himself, the real world of his almost unbearable internal thoughts and feelings. Grief work was intense and long–which is to say it was real, and in proportion to the enormity and the manner of the loss. With support, Dougie was still living his life, as opposed to skimming through it and warding it off; still growing, which in the end is what attentional process is all about.

The Attentional Supports Model in Practice–Chrissie*

*(*The "I" in the discussion that follows is Jay Kent-Ferraro.)*

We start with the working assumption that for Chrissie long abused and abandoned, desensitization and attentional defocusing clearly functioned in a self-protective, self-soothing way: needs which have gone painfully unsatisfied for a lifetime are finally not just unspoken, but unfelt within the skin. The result can be great organismic pressure, or "secondary gains," for moving into action impulsively and prematurely, together with a contact style organized around provocative anger and threatening rage, in a world of adults who have shown little persuasive capacity to hear and hold Chrissie's deeper longings, bitter disappointments, and felt terrors. In short, "an irritable and volatile kid who is impossible to get close to" (taken from notes in Chrissie's file). Given the toxic combination of extreme impulsivity, no doubt both organic and environmental in origin, together with rage and violence, possibilities seemed remote for Chrissie to experience and express parts of herself that were so wounded by abuse and neglect, and could only be healed now by real, sustained contact with others–the very thing she was least equipped to do.

Using our attentional cycle model, we can explore Chrissie's particular style of moving through the attentional cycle, looking for places where she might be available for contact within her idiosyncratic process. Wherever we can find such places, we can look for ways to support and expand them, with the goal of helping Chrissie move through the natural attentional cycle to a new kind of experience and resolution, one that can then serve as the incorporated ground for further new experience and new growth. In this way we hope to build on and use her natural organic potential to form and complete a healthy, growth-supporting self-process, which can then serve as a new learning model for a new kind of attentional experience in other areas. These are large goals, and again we do not mean to discount the importance of behavioral, milieu, relational, cognitive, insight, and neurological/chemical factors and interventions. Rather, we aim to integrate the diverse and sometimes disparate aspects of Chrissie's treatment and experience, into a unified figure of attention, and a better-supported personal process of knowing herself and forming and reaching her own goals.

Sensation, to begin with, is typically an explosive/implosive experience for Chrissie, one in which she cuts off or bypasses any "softer" feelings of sadness, hurt and grief in favor of rage and anger, which then play out in well-rehearsed, stereotypic sequences not clearly related to any positive attentional goal or figure. The result is not only organismic pressure for moving into impulsivity and premature action (in harmony with the least functional aspects of her underlying neurology), but a complete contact style organized around anger, in a context devoid of adults who could reliably receive and hold the validity of any other possible desires she might have formed. Thus while Chrissie experiences outrage and injustice, others around her are seeing "an irritable and volatile kid who is impossible to get close to," in the notes, again, of one of her many caseworkers in the past. In terms of our attentional cycle model, we would then say that almost the only internal figure she can support, by herself, is anger, which then cuts directly to fighting, skipping right over any healthy unfolding of the cycle progression, or any use of Levine's complex and interactive dimensions of attentional process as supports in moving toward any coherent desire or goal in the field. Since everyone around is then alienated, her inability to support other awarenesses and sensations, other desires and goals, is then confirmed and strengthened. The jerky, foreshortened attentional cycle which is her dominant contact style with herself and others, is then repeated over and over in a sad circle, with ever more serious consequences as time goes on.

This cycle began to play out one afternoon as usual in a focus group that was a regular part of Chrissie's inpatient program. She had had a difficult evening the day before, with several time-outs ending in a physical threat to a staff person and a physical fight with another girl. In group she began the brief "seduction" that often preceded her attacks on others: "I have something I want to work on (ingratiating smile)... I'm pissed off at the staff, and at Jenny, who reminds me of my mother when she used to abuse me." Her manner too was typical: lots of aroused energy, no particular focus, not addressing anyone in particular, seemingly cut off from the group. The ear-to-ear smile was in sharp contrast to glassy, puffy eyes that looked squeezed with the tension of holding back what I imagined must be rivers of tears, years and years of hurt and sadness.

The litany she began was familiar too: all the adults in her life who had failed her, staff who were inadequate and poorly trained, peers who were scapegoating her, she said (Chrissie knew all the jargon of years of failed treatment), for the failings of the whole program. The emotion seemed intense or at least noisy, yet seemed to keep her cut off, not connected, from others and herself alike. Whatever initial impulse or desire might have energized this attentional figure was long since lost, buried under the avalanche of accusations. The more she ranted, the more unfocused she seemed to become, interrupting others, reacting jumpily to noises from outside the room. We could say that having no felt grounding or direction, her attentional process had no clear boundaries, and the essential supportive function of deselecting other, competing stimuli, was completely missing.

As her experiential process continued to disorganize before our eyes, I moved, as the group therapist, to make myself a supportive attentional figure, stopping her, inviting her to slow down and breathe with me, inviting her to go back to her initial need, to say clearly what it was she was after, in volunteering to go first in group that afternoon. Her first reaction was to turn her irritation on me. The task I was proposing was "stupid" and "irrelevant"–signs to me of insufficient support in our field. I responded by offering her my intentionality, assuring her that my interest was in making her own need clearer, so we could try to meet it together in this community. (By this time the much-abused young ward staff were rolling their eyes. Jaundiced and wounded as they were from Chrissie's pattern of seduce/provoke/distance, they easily lost sight of the fact that a "manipulation" is at least an interpersonal bid, a focus on another person for a reason–and that behind that focus must lie some buried hope and need, probably as poorly known to the patient as to us at that point).

My own image at this point was of a sad little girl sitting alone at the end of a long sofa, her small knees hugged tightly to her chest, rocking slightly as if to soothe the small child she never had a chance to be. Her eyes, I imagined, looked out from her confusion and isolation with a hunger that she had no ability to organize, by herself, into any sustained figure of attention, need, desire. Quietly I shared this image with Chrissie, focusing on the tight muscles around the puffy eyes. I knew her anger a bit now, I told her–what about other parts as well? If we could know all the parts together, we'd stand a better chance of designing a change together, right here and now. "What if you could find out that inside you there is more to you than just this canyon of rage? Would that be interesting to you?" "Maybe," was her cautious reply, so I continued: "Chrissie, when I look into your face I see sadness, not anger. The anger may be the most familiar, but it's not what I'm seeing right now. What I see is enormous tightness around the eyes, arms that hold your knees so tight–"

The eyes began to twitch at this, then Chrissie's whole face flushed deep red, as she simultaneously rose to and fought against the experience of being seen by another human being. "Chrissie, do you find a place inside you that feels sad right now?" As I said this, her foot began to shake and the arms locked defiantly, as if to remobilize the familiar rage. "Would you be willing to close your eyes and focus on a sad space within? What does it look like? What color is it? What if you see it and touch it and breathe at the same time?" Tears were now pouring down her face. When I invited her to speak to me now from this new place, her response was, "I don't want to do this. It never does any good to cry–nobody cares anyway." The available support was not sufficient: her muscles began tightening even further as she fought to move away from the new feeling.

"Chrissie, have you seen the movie E.T.?" I broke in, to interrupt this familiar cycle. "Huh?" she was startled, then nodded. "Great," I went on, "here's my idea. You may be too alone to stay with this right now. How about if someone else from the group sat next to you, to be with you while you feel this sad place?"

"Oh no," suddenly Chrissie was focused and energized again, "no way is anybody touching me... forget it!" But I pushed on, still hoping to break an overlearned and dysfunctional attentional process cycle, possibly opening the way for a new experience: "Chrissie, remember in the movie when Elliot's heart was hurting, and E.T. took his finger, and just touched his friend's heart? I wonder if there's someone in the group you might be willing to let sit by you and just touch your finger with their finger while you work–just the finger." Chrissie nodded almost reluctantly, and extended a hand to Jennifer, sitting next to her. Once their fingertips just touched, the tears began flowing again, and soon she was sobbing deeply, then crying out to her mother, who was never there to hear the depths of her pain. From there, with constant checking and permission, Chrissie and Jennifer moved first to grasping hands, then to looking at each other, both in tears now–just looking. After some moments I asked Chrissie to focus again on her sadness, while still looking at Jennifer. She broke into a wide smile–while the tears continued to flow. While the two of them still clasped hands, the group turned to other work.

This was both an enormous experience for Chrissie, opening up a transformation of her life on the unit–and at the same time a tiny step in a long, long process. One experience of supported, sustained attention just to the very first stages of a whole attentional cycle did not of course give Chrissie a complete new way of contacting herself and the world. What it did do was to begin, for her and others, a process of regrounding an attention/action cycle in the experience of what is actually going on within, what the self can actually know of the self at a given moment, the longings and fears, feelings and wishes and goals that may actually be in there, as the essential starting place for a different kind of attentional process cycle, and ultimately a different kind of life. This is what we mean, in the end, by putting the subjective, experiencing child or adolescent back into the picture of ADD and the whole panoply of our interventions, to unify and integrate the experience in the only way that we can, given the terms and nature of our human attentional process. Clear expectations and limits and consequences continued to be important for Chrissie, as did pharmacological interventions at times, as well as special teaching/learning methods, the new kinds of relationships that began to be possible, the retelling of her story (as a feeling person now, and a survivor), milieu structure, and many other things. But none of these things can do the job, unless and until they are grounded in the subjective experience of feeling, knowing, and needing something meaningful to the self–and of finding from inside and outside the supportive structures and processes that are always necessary to sustain a significant attentional figure through its life history in a complex and shifting field of inner and outer conditions, other needs, other impulses, and perhaps most of all other people.

Conclusion

Our goals in this paper have been to present an overview of the issues of attentional process and "ADD" to the child and adolescent clinician or other helping professional–and at the same time to reframe and revision these issues and processes in the language and concepts of the Gestalt model of self-organization and experiential process. Outlining the primary constructs we need as a vocabulary for ADD and attentional process, we have drawn on the process terminology of Levine (1994), relating that body of work to the Gestalt model of experiential organization and needs satisfaction in a whole-field context and perspective. We reviewed the "Cycle" model as a Gestalt tool for diagnosing and analyzing problems in self-organization, recasting the model more contextually so that it becomes a "Cycle of Attention" schematic, with particular focus on the question of supports for attentional process in the field. Two more extended case vignettes then illustrated some of our ideas about application of these concepts and this model in a clinical setting.

In our work with "ADD" children and adolescents we return again and again to the questions we see as central to attentional function and dysfunction: how does the child or adolescent know and experience a want or a need? how is that experience organized from awareness to action, and how is support drawn and used from the whole field of inner and outer experience to sustain that attentional focus and bring a need to satisfaction and learning? what are the particular supports we need to find or supply, to facilitate these processes? and then how does the outcome of these processes, for well or ill, become organized meaningfully into the next and future ongoing cycle of awareness, attentional focus, and nourishing contact in the world?

The organization and sustaining of attention is the organization and management of energy in the field of living. In the end, our quality of life and of meaningful learning and growth depend on these processes. The Gestalt model we present here, we believe, offers support in the contextualizing and integrating of all our other processes, problems, and interventions in this difficult area, in the service of change and growth both for troubled children and adolescents and for their concerned, often confused and stressed caretakers alike.

References

Aylward, G.P. (1994). *Practitioner's guide to developmental and psychological testing*. New York, NY: Plenum Medical Book Co.

Barkley, R. (1990). *Attention deficit hyperactivity disorder: A handbook for diagnosis and treatment.* New York, NY: Guilford.

Borland, B.L., & Hechtman, H.K. (1976). Hyperactive boys and their brothers: A 25-year follow-up study. *Archives of General Psychiatry, 33*(6), 669-675.

Damazio, A. (1994). *Decartes's error: Emotion, reason, and the human brain.* New York, NY: Putnam.

Douglas, V.I. (1972). Stop, look and listen: The problem of sustained attention and impulse control in hyperactive and normal children. *Canadian Journal of Behavioral Science, 4*, 259-282.

DuPaul, G.J., & Stoner, G. (1994). ADHD in the schools: Assessment and intervention strategies. New York, NY: Guilford.

Exner, A. (1894). *Entwurf zu einer physiologischen Erklsrung der psychischen Erscheinungen (An approach to a physiological explanation of psychic appearances).* Vienna: Deutike.

Goldstein, K. (1940). *Human nature in the light of psychopathology*. Cambridge, MA: Harvard.

Hale, G.A., & Lewis, M. (eds). (1979). *Attention and cognitive development.* New York, NY: Perseus Books.

LeDoux, R. (1997). *The emotional brain.* New York, NY: Simon & Schuster.

Levine, M. (1994). *Educational care.* Cambridge, MA: Educators' Publishing Service.

Lewin, K. (1926). Vorsatz, Wille, Bedurfnis (Intention, Will, Need). *Psychologische Forschung,* 7, 330-385.

Lewin, K. (1935). *Principles of topological psychology*. New York, NY: McGraw-Hill.

Lewin, K. (1951). *Field theory in social science*. New York, NY: Harper.

Marrow, A. (1969). *The practical theorist: The life and work of Kurt Lewin.* New York, NY: Basic Books.

Meichenbaum, D. (1999). *Cognitive-behavioral modification: An integrated approach*. New York, NY: Perseus Books.

Melnick, J. & Nevis, S. (1992). *Diagnosis: The struggle for a meaningful paradigm*. In E. Nevis (Ed.), Gestalt therapy: perspectives & applcations, (pp. 57-78). Cambridge, MA: Gardner Press.

Nevis, E. (1987). *Organizational consulting: A gestalt approach*. New York, NY: Gardner Press.

Perls, F. (1947). *Ego, hunger & aggression*. London: Allen & Unwin.

Perls, F., Hefferline, R., & Goodman, P. (1951). *Gestalt therapy: Excitement and growth in the human personality*. New York, NY: Julian Press.

Polster, E. & Polster, M. (1973). *Gestalt therapy integrated: Contours of theory and practice*. New York, NY: Brunner/Mazel.

Real, T. (1996). *I don't want to talk about it: The hidden epidemic of male depression*. New York, NY: Scribner.

Root, R. (1996). The Gestalt Cycle of Experience as a theoretical framework for conceptualizing the attention deficit disorder. *Gestalt Journal, 19*(2), 9-50

Wertheimer, M. (1912). Experimentalle studien uber das sehen von bewegungen (Experimental studies in the perception of motion) . *Zeitschrift für Psychologie, 61*.

Wheeler, G. (1991). *Gestalt reconsidered: A new approach to contact and resistance*. New York, NY: Gardner Press.

Wheeler, G. (1994). The tasks of intimacy: Reflections on a gestalt approach to working with couples. In G. Wheeler & S. Backman, (Eds.), *On intimate ground: A gestalt approach to working with couples*, (pp. 31-59). San Francisco, CA: Jossey-Bass.

Wheeler, G. (1996). Self and shame: A new paradigm. In R. Lee & G. Wheeler, (Eds.), *The voice of shame: Silence and connection in psychotherapy*, (pp. 23-58). San Francisco, CA: Jossey-Bass.

Wheeler, G. (2000). *Beyond individualism: Toward a new understanding of self, relationship & experience*. Hillsdale, NJ: The Analytic Press/Gestalt Press.

Woldt, A. (1998). The gestalt contact styles questionnaires: Psychometrics, hermeneutics, and clinical applications. Paper presented at the Sixth European Conference on Gestalt Therapy, Palermo, Italy, October 2.

Zinker, J. (1977). *Creative process in gestalt therapy*. New York, NY: Brunner/Mazel.

Zinker, J. (1994). *In search of good form: A gestalt approach to working with couples and families*. San Francisco, CA: Jossey-Bass.

8

Healing Young, Wounded Hearts: Gestalt Group Therapy with Children of Divorce

Cynthia Reynolds & Ansel Woldt

Introduction

Children of divorce make up a sizable cross-section of the "underage" population who are often referred to school counselors and school psychologists, and/or brought to therapists in private practice or in community agencies. Just in the United States alone, since 1975, over one million children per year have experienced parental divorce (National Center for Health Statistics, 1995). However, the fact that divorce has become a normative experience for many children does not make it a normal or an easy experience to endure. Parental divorce is in the least, a difficult experience for most children and severely disturbing for many (Emery & Forehand, 1994).

Divorce has been described by various researchers of this topic as a stressful life event that increases the likelihood of inauspicious consequences for family members (Emery, 1982; Felner, Farber, & Primavera, 1980; Wallerstein & Kelly, 1979). Children are particularly vulnerable, given the probability that they will encounter multiple negative disruptions in family relationships, mental and physical health of family members, childcare, geographical mobility and economic status (Glass, 1991; Hetherington; Cox & Cox, 1985).

Research has consistently shown that children experience distress during the divorce process and that divorce is associated with a variety of short-term and long-term negative outcomes. Consequences (for the children) associated with parental divorce include increased acting out and aggression toward parents (Felner, Stolberg, & Cowen, 1975; Hetherington, Cox & Cox, 1979); increased moodiness, temper tantrums and school problems (Fulton, 1979); lowered academic and personal-social competencies (Guidubaldi & Perry, 1985); disruptions in both play and social interactions (Hetherington, Cox & Cox, 1978); twice as great a likelihood of referral for psychiatric treatment than those from intact families (Kalter & Rembar, 1981; Kelly & Wallerstein, 1976). Socio-emotional problems seem to be a result of an "interaction of familial, social, cultural, legal, economic and psychological systems with the experience and effects of divorce" (Guidubaldi, Perry, Cleminshaw & McLaughlin, 1983, p. 303).

The listing of empirical research findings on the negative results of divorce on children is compelling, but in many ways it fails to capture the full impact of the divorce process on the inner world of the child. Clinical interviews with children of divorce often reveal a depth of wounding that is both profound and moving to the adult listener. From the perspective of conducting Gestalt therapy with children, it is critical to be aware of their inner and outer world. Even more therapeutically important is the awareness of how they interact with their environment, what we commonly refer to as contact. As Isadore From and Michael Vincent Miller so clearly point out in their "Introduction" to The Center for Gestalt Development's edition of *Gestalt Therapy: Excitement and Growth in the Human Personality* (Perls, Hefferline & Goodman, 1994):

> Gestalt therapy... takes for its starting point something so obvious that our human and social sciences usually seem to overlook it: the exchange that goes on unceasingly between the human organism and its surrounding environment in all areas of life ties persona and world inextricably to one another. The world of Gestalt therapy is a busy world fairly humming with constant action and transaction, a place in continual flux. Within the flux, the experience of the "self" changes... it can take over the entire foreground of awareness... when one is in pain... during which time the self, in effect becomes the pain (p. xvii).

In our child therapy groups, the authors encourage the children to express their subjective experiences of pain associated with their parents' divorce through art. As a result, we have had the opportunity to observe numerous pictures created by these children. One symbol frequently drawn by later latency-age children to represent divorce is a broken or wounded heart, pierced by arrows, knives or lightning, with dripping blood and/or tears. Sometimes parents are included in the drawing, shown as staking their claim on a portion of the child's heart with an exclamation such as, "He's mine!" or "You can't have her!" Pictures depicting aggressive reactions toward adult figures are also common. The poignant ways children portray their feelings about divorce serve as useful metaphors in describing how therapists can assist them in the healing process. At some level, this means attending to and mending the fragments of the wounded heart. These pictures not only represent the pain of their experience, but also an aggressive response to their difficult life situation. From & Miller (1994) remind us, "For Gestalt therapy, aggression is by nature healthy and in the service of life" (p. xv).

This chapter continues with four sections. The first section contains a summary of Gestalt therapy theory, particularly regarding boundary processes, personal functioning, optimal/healthy development, coping styles and contact disturbances of children. The second section contains discussion of the impact of divorce on children from a Gestalt perspective. The third section contains information on the development and implementation of Gestalt group therapy techniques and procedures for children of divorce; derived from the authors' clinical experiences. The closing section includes a discussion of some implications of this work.

Gestalt Therapy Theory Applied to Children

Every approach to psychotherapy presupposes a view of human development, whether it is made clear or not–Gestalt therapy being no exception. Perls, Hefferline and Goodman (1951) advanced the view that sensing, excitement, contact, assimilation and individuation are primary processes in human development. The child grows and develops by assimilating what it needs from the environment.

> A couple of contemporary writers about Gestalt therapy say Gestalt is, above all, about the whole–smells, tastes, intuitions, the surrounding environment, the historical context, the planetary hologram. And all of these coexist like an excellent poem wherein which the artistry is never fully discovered, yet all the symbols and words, and cadences and shapes, interweave in a tapestry vibrating with life and tragedy and humour... Modern Gestalt aims for an integration of body, feelings and intellect, seeing the person's most basic needs within the context of the social envi-

ronment... [It is] theoretically an integrative approach to counseling rooted in an existential orientation (Clarkson, 1989, p. 1-2)

Carden (1992) summarizes Gestalt therapy as the "developmental outgrowth and creative assimilation of existential philosophy, phenomenology, psychoanalytic psychology, field theory, cybernetics, general systems theory and Gestalt psychology principles of perception and cognitive organization" (p. 57). This approach was originally introduced by Frederick Perls (with the adroit assistance of his wife Laura Perls, Ph.D.) in *Ego, Hunger, and Aggression* (1947) as "concentration therapy." Their ideas were based on their experience as psychoanalysts, that the most important process in psychotherapy sessions was the business of "focusing" in order to assist the patient with attending to the issue at hand. Their theory was soon thereafter renamed Gestalt therapy in what is often referred to as "the Bible of Gestalt Therapy" (Perls, Hefferline, & Goodman, 1951).

The theoretical aspects of Gestalt therapy have been expanded by many Gestalt therapists throughout the world; notable amongst them are Isadore From, Erving & Miriam Polster, Joseph Zinker, Gordon Wheeler, George & Judith Brown, and Violet Oaklander with her clinical applications to children and adolescents. Some of the recent contributors to theory building from outside the United States are Bertram and Johanna Muller in Germany, Jean-Marie Robine in France, Malcom Parlett and Petruska Clarkson in England, Ole Ry Nielsen in Denmark, Jean Gagnon in Canada, Miriam Sas de Guiter in Argentina, Jean Clark Juliano in Brazil, Anne Maclean in New Zealand, and Margherita Spagnuolo Lobb in Italy.

Central to the understanding of Gestalt therapy theory are a number of pivotal assumptions regarding the nature of human beings and their development. These assumptions are presented in terms of the population being discussed, namely, children. First, children are viewed as holistic beings whose bodies, emotions, thoughts, sensations and perceptions function inter-relatedly. This whole is more than and different from just being a sum of its parts. Second, the process of development is defined as the infant's progression from total reliance on environmental support to the child's optimal reliance on self-support. The neonate is completely dependent on the environment for survival, the confluence of which Paul Goodman regarded as the ground of absolute security (Perls, et al., 1951). As the child's sensorimotor functions and cognitive abilities mature, the child becomes more capable of securing, sustaining and satisfying his/her own wants and needs, and therefore more capable of self-support. In Gestalt theory this is referred to as "developing the competence for contacting"

(Lobb, 1996).

Development is characterized by an increased utilization of the Awareness and Action potentials. As a child's sensorimotor functions mature, increasing Awareness and Action are possible. Until these potentials are discovered and utilized by the developing child, they are seen as inoperative (Norton, 1980). Discovery and utilization of these potentialities are a progression of the interaction of the child's growing Awareness and Action capabilities. Developmental gaps are viewed as dysfunctions of this reciprocal relationship.

Human growth and development are motivated by the hunger instinct (Perls, et al., 1951). Aggression is the organismic representation of the hunger instinct, which explains the motivation for the discovery and utilization of the Action and Awareness potentials. Contrary to its psychoanalytic predecessor, Gestalt views aggression as a positive and necessary process for taking in and restructuring compatible aspects of the child's environment. The early influence of Otto Rank (1945) on Fritz Perls and Paul Goodman, although rarely acknowledged, is evident here with regard to the importance of the "Will" and its inherent relation to healthful aggression and learning. He conceived of an intimate, all-embracing link between each person and what surrounded him or her–referring to it as "the cosmic primal force" (p. 212). Rank's "Will" functioned as a "positive guiding organization and integration of self which utilizes creativity as well as inhibits and controls the instinctual drives" (p. 212). Further, his interpretation of the Freudian construct of defense mechanisms was called "Counter-Will," which is very similar to the concept of resistance in Gestalt therapy theory.

In Gestalt theory, the child engages in the learning situation when Awareness and Action processes are not immediately available to resolve or master a situation, at which point the child experiences disequilibrium or tension and mobilizes energy to recreate and finish the activity. Perls (1947) theorized that the hunger instinct motivates the child to interact with the environment in such a way that the field can be organized, the right response discovered and the gestalten closed (at least temporarily). This aggressive response develops previously under-developed and undeveloped Awareness and Action capabilities.

Children are viewed in the context of their environment and cannot be understood outside of the interaction/interplay of "figure" and "ground." Children develop in relation to their environment. The environment is seen to gradually expand as the child matures. This expansion typically progresses from the primary care provider to an organized environmental field. As children develop, they function in response to the figure/ground interplay and their naturalistic processes (referred to as organismic self-regulation) constantly striving for homeostatic balance.

Additional Gestalt therapy principles for better understanding childhood and child behavior include the belief that children only experience themselves in the present. The past is experienced as memory and the future as anticipation, both of which can only be experienced in the now. Children are capable of being aware of their sensations, thoughts, emotions and perceptions. They are intrinsically neither good nor bad. Each child's purpose in life is to actualize his or her inborn potential. Children are seen as being capable of proactivity, determining their own responses to external and proprioceptive stimuli, not simply reacting to stimuli. Through self-awareness, children are capable of choice and can be responsible for their behavior. Learning to assume responsibility for their choices and behavior, and the consequences thereof, is central.

Gestalt therapy theory of personality views the child as a self-regulating entity that maintains himself or herself by fulfilling acknowledged needs through establishing contact with his or her environment. Organismic self-regulation is seen as the ability to run smoothly, to stay in balance and to maintain homeostasis. The authors acknowledge this as subscribing more to Fritz Perls' "intrapsychic" model that is based on the premise:

> ...that all life and all behavior are governed by the process which scientists call homeostasis, and which the layman calls adaptation. The homeostatic process is the process by which the organism maintains its equilibrium and therefore its health under varying conditions. Homeostasis is thus the process by which the organism satisfies its needs. Since its needs are many, and each need upsets the equilibrium, the homeostatic process goes on all the time. All life is characterized by this continuing play of balance and imbalance in the organism... When the homeostatic process fails to some degree, when the organism remains in a state of disequilibrium for too long a time and is unable to satisfy its needs, it is sick. When the homeostatic process fails, the organism dies (Perls, 1973, p. 4).

In addressing the dynamics of personal and interpersonal functioning in organizations, Merry and Brown (1987) describe the homeostasis process as follows:

> A need arises within the organism and the organism contacts the

> environment to satisfy the need. When the need has been satisfied, the organism returns to its steady state until another need arises. Alternatively, a change occurs in the environment, disturbing or arousing the organism. The organism takes action to deal with the change and returns to its steady state. In both cases some change, internal or external, creates a stress that can only be alleviated by the organism taking action in contact with its environment. A way of seeing this process is that of self-regulation, in which a changing organism interacting with a changing environment is constantly maintaining a steady state of adjustment. The homeostatic process can also be viewed as one of closing the gestalt (p. 181).

Perls (1973) reiterates, "We might call the homeostatic process the process of self-regulation, the process by which the organism interacts with its environment (p. 5). Of course this functions the same in children as in other human beings, where we see the process of maintaining balance, organismic self-regulation and homeostasis being accomplished in a cyclic manner. The child first becomes aware of a need (figure) that impacts his/her equilibrium (ground); the child then moves to make contact within the self, environment and/or other in order to satisfy that need. The child returns to a state of balance/homeostasis when his/her need is either met or another satisfactory alternative is discovered.

In his diagram of the Gestalt Homeostasis Cycle, Woldt (1993, see Figure 1) depicts the various processes involved in seeking and maintaining homeostasis. Gestalt therapy theory defines psychological health as the consistently self-enhancing flow of contact with internal aspects of the child (intrajacent contact) and/or between the child and his or her environment (circumjacent contact). Psychological non-health is defined as the consistently self-defeating disruptions in the flow of contact among inner aspects of the child (intrajacence) and/or between the child and his/her environment (circumjacence). Thus, the behavioral choices of the child can range from conscious and aware choices that are creatively spontaneous with a modulating flow in response to the variety of figures surfacing from ground, to unconscious, unaware and defensively rigid mechanistic adjustments to environmental and personal demands. The healthier process is one of creatively adjusting compared to the less healthy type of contact that is in defense of the ego and often a staid adjustment (Perls, 1973).

Woldt's Gestalt Homeostasis Cycle shows a detailed elaboration of the cycle of experience that contains both the intrajacent and circumjacent

Figure 1:
Woldt's Gestalt Homeostasis Cycle

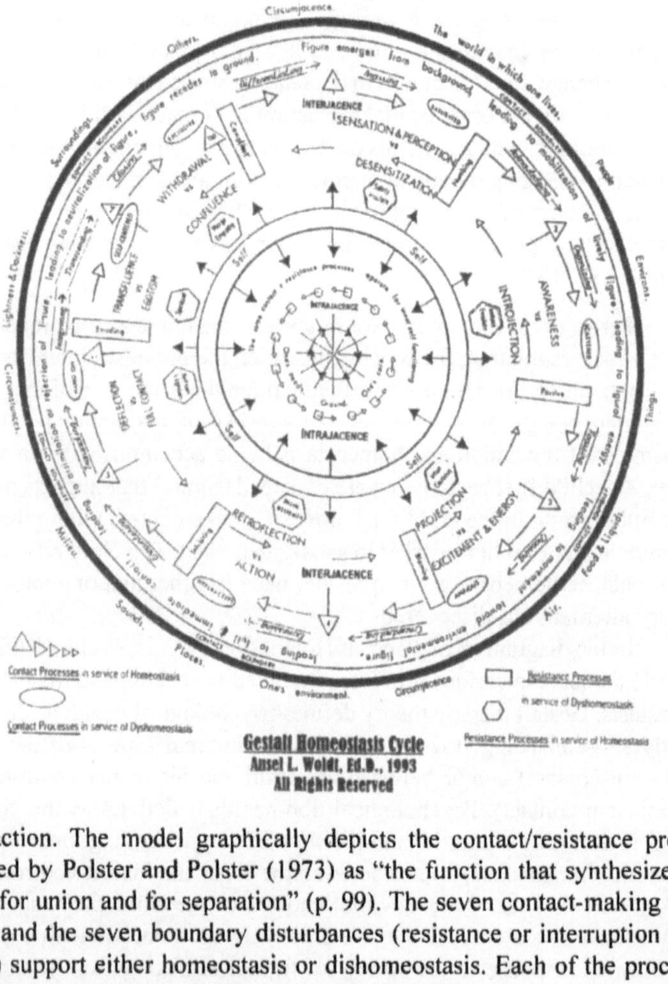

interaction. The model graphically depicts the contact/resistance process defined by Polster and Polster (1973) as "the function that synthesizes the need for union and for separation" (p. 99). The seven contact-making functions and the seven boundary disturbances (resistance or interruption functions) support either homeostasis or dishomeostasis. Each of the processes functions at either the aware or unaware level, conscious and unconscious, and can result in validating and invalidating experiences.

As depicted in the Gestalt Homeostasis Cycle, the contact/resistance process begins with a primary awakening of Sensation and Perception within the child to an external or internal stimulus. As the child focuses on the stimulus by experiencing it effectively and cognitively, a "figure" emerges from the "ground" and Awareness of feelings and possible choices develops. As the meaning of the figure is experienced and realized, a fuller sense of choice becomes available to the child and if this awareness is sufficiently supported, Excitement and Energy are mobilized to either meet the need or respond to the demand of the environment. Mobilization moves naturally toward engagement. The transformation of energy into Action and Contact results in a fuller engagement and encounter between the child and his/her environment to satisfy the need or meet the demand. Intrajacent or circumjacent Contact progresses to facilitate the child's restructuring and processing of the experience. As the contact evolves to the extent that the need is met or resolved, Assimilation of the experience by the child occurs. Awareness of completion and satisfaction urges the child toward Differentiation and Closure leading toward Withdrawal and "zero contact" (Mraz, 1990; Woldt & Ingersoll, 1991). The child then becomes available for movement into another cycle around a new figure.

At any point in the contact/resistance process, the child or his/her environment can interrupt the flow of the present experience. Within the Cycle of Experience seven major interruptive functions or boundary disturbances operate, which in general are referred to as styles of resistance. Fritz Perls (1973) addressed this in the following terms: "Human nature is organized into patterns or wholes that are experienced by the individual in these terms and that can only be understood as a function of the pattern of wholes of which it is made" (p. 3-4). This principle is derived from Gestalt psychology that focuses on the individual's ability to organize isolated concepts through the perceptual process into meaningful wholes rather than perceive them as isolated or unrelated. Conceptualizing this principle as underlying the concept of personality traits or personal styles, helps in understanding these interactive dynamics, processes and styles of making and disrupting the internal and external flow of contact at the boundaries where a child meets both self and environment.

Through the dynamic boundary process of Desensitization the child slows down, or even shuts down/off, the sensation, perception and/or proprioception functions, essentially disrupting or blocking both internal and external stimuli from affecting his/her sensations and emotions. The boundary process called Introjection refers to the "swallowing whole" of certain beliefs, attitudes, expectations or forms of information from the environment by the child, such that he or she becomes rule-bound. The material–ideas, values, matter and/or ways of behaving–then does not become assimilated as an integrated part of organismic functioning of the child. The boundary process called Projection is a disowned aspect of self that is attributed to others or some aspect of the child's environment. An example of unhealthful projecting is when a child cannot accept his/her own thoughts and/or feelings (which are likely to be experienced as disturbing) and instead attributes them to others or to the environment and then experiences the thoughts and feelings as being directed toward him or her by them or it, rather than the other way around. The dynamic process called Retroflection involves difficulty for a child to express outwardly the impulse or desire to act or express thoughts, ideas and feelings, as well as difficulty in receiving potential support or nurturance from one's environs. What the child would prefer to receive from or do to the environment, the child instead provides for or does to him or herself. The retroflective child redirects action inward and attempts to do unto him/herself what s/he would likely do or say to the other/environs to interact and/or destructure the event and thus proceed to make final contact. Being bashful, fearful, shy, guilt-prone and ashamed are inherent factors that support this inhibiting response and make expression and reception difficult. The dynamic process called Deflection is the redirection of action and the veering away from direct contact. While it functions to disrupt contact in various phases of the homeostasis cycle, its primary adaptation by children is to prevent their excitement from flowing into final contact and to avoid committing to full contact and integration with self (intrapsychic) and the other/environs. The deflective child is likely to use humor and withdrawal inappropriately and engage in behavior that is indirect, vague, off center or off the mark. Once the basic conditions for final/full contact have been made, a child's Egotism can disrupt final contact. This dynamic is egocentric, a self-serving ego-syntonic process wherein the child "holds on" or "holds out," paying more attention to his/her identity and boundaries than to the other/environs. The egotistical child finds the process of joining to be uncomfortable and may even be "confluent phobic" (Swanson, 1988, 1989). The dynamic process called Confluence, similar to the concept of enmeshment in the rhetoric of family therapy, is an unbounded merging of aspects of self with the other/environs. The confluent child blunts individuation, lacks appreciation of individual differences, wants everyone to like and appreciate him/her, appreciates non-discrimination and avoids differentiation from his/her environment.

Gestalt therapists consider contact/resistance styles to be response patterns that develop within the context of the child's most meaningful relationships (Kepner, 1982; Oaklander, 1978). The child's openness to or interruption of contact at any point in the Homeostasis Cycle is likely the most adaptive response possible given the situational context in the child's life. However, as the child's here-and-now life field changes, the same behavioral responses may become maladaptive. "As contact/resistance processes evolve into contact/resistance styles, they change from figure to ground (i.e., aware to unaware)" (Carden, 1993, p. 70). Thus, the child's lack of awareness and ability to choose responses at different points of the Homeostasis Cycle would be considered to be less healthy.

This lack of awareness and ability to choose responses at different points of the cycle may cause a child to display a number of different symptoms. The symptoms that cause a child to be brought into therapy usually indicate a lack of integration (Carroll, 1995), boundary disturbances (Ownby, 1983) and/or an impaired sense of self (Oaklander, 1982).

In *The Pinocchio Syndrome: Path to Wholeness*, Felicia Carroll (1995) likens the process of therapy to the one Pinocchio experiences on his journey from wooden puppet to real little boy. Many symptoms can indicate a lack of integration. These symptoms may be behavioral, affective, interpersonal, or a combination of these which reveal inner conflicts or fragmentation of the child's personality and contribute a woodenness or artificiality within the developmental process. Without therapeutic intervention, the child becomes much like a glued together puppet in his/her world, rather than a living being.

Ray Ownby (1983) contends that the therapeutic intervention with a child is guided by the therapist's awareness of the disturbance of contact boundary between him/her and the child in the here-and-now. The principal resistances Ownby observed being manifested by the children he saw as a school psychologist were confluence, projection, introjection, retroflection and deflection.

Gestalt therapists attempt to place the child in progressively better contact with what he or she is experiencing at the moment. Growth occurs through the present actuality of contact in a supportive and experimental environment, as for example, the counseling group. Since actuality will include the child's resistances to contact with the therapist, resistance will be assimilated. Both Oaklander and Ownby remind therapists of the importance of making our counseling explicitly grounded in and consistent with theory. Oaklander (1982) also insists that a good sense of self is a prerequisite for making good contact with others and the environment – an important consideration for anyone pursuing a career as therapist. This is inherent in the training of Gestalt therapists who are required to have their own therapy.

The tools of contact identified by Polster & Polster (1973) are looking, talking, touching, listening, moving, smelling and tasting. Children who are in trouble are unable to make good use of one or more of the contact functions in relating to adults in their lives, to other children, to school and to their environment in general. Before contact functions can be used effectively, the tools of contact need to be developed and operating in a manner that provides for awareness of process and content.

Oaklander (1992) considers the primary goals of Gestalt child therapy as being to help the child gain self-support, self-acceptance, self-nurturance and integration. As the child accepts all the aspects of the self without judgment, growth occurs. As the child brings out darker aspects of the self into contact with the nurturing self, the child experiences integration.

The Impact of Divorce from a Gestalt Perspective

There are a number of ways that divorce disrupts the heart of the child's development, causing boundary disturbances, impaired sense of self, lack of integration and developmental gaps. Divorce and its resulting stress upset the equilibrium of the figure/ground flux as well as the homeostasis process. This inevitably impacts on the heart, mind and psyche or soul of the developmental process.

Human development is viewed as a process involving movement from total environmental support (complete confluence in the womb) to optimal self-support (an interdependent adult able to ask for help when needed). The infant arrives in the world in a state of total dependence and vulnerability. The caretaker/family must provide all of the basic needs (food, water, shelter, medical care, clothing, love, security) to insure survival. The caretaker/family is figural in the early years of the child's life. The maturation process involves separation and individuation from the confluence of the initial state. As the child begins to actualize his or her potential through the mastery of basic developmental tasks, the family slowly, but gradually fades from figure to ground as non-verbal communication, crawling, walking, talking, feeding self, reading, writing, etc. take on more form and become figural for the child to more effectively interact with the environment. The family, as a stable and loving support system, vacillates between figure and ground as the child continues to mature and develop. Even when not figural, the family provides a ground of support and love that can be called upon when needed by the child.

Divorce, with all of its related stresses, disturbs this natural flux between figure and ground. It becomes extremely difficult for a child to maintain as figural common childhood academic, social, physical and psychological tasks when worries about family push for prominence. Focusing attention on learning double digit subtraction is a momentous task when a child is worried about who will be taking care of him/her, whether there will be enough money for the bills, or if there will be another terrible fight when Dad comes to pick him or her up on Friday. Learning how to kick a goal in soccer or ride a bike may not be figural when a child is unsure about with whom and where he or she will be living next month. An extended period of the stresses of divorce may cause the child to be preoccupied with parental discord, losing ability and energy to focus or make figural the many basic childhood tasks, resulting in gaps in development. This intrusion into the natural flux of figure/ground in the child's life strikes at the very heart of development, preventing the child from being able to integrate both childhood tasks as well as aspects of the self.

Divorce is a significant life stressor that disrupts the balance (homeostasis) of a child's life requiring coping efforts to maintain stability. The coping processes, which are a part of Gestalt therapy theory, involve the successful completion of the Gestalt cycle of experience. According to Gestalt therapy theory, the cycle of experience is one's attempt to be in balance with the environment or homeostasis (Perls, et. al., 1951; Latner, 1973; Zinker, 1977).

Woldt's (1993) Gestalt Homeostasis Cycle (Figure 1) depicts the intrajacent and circumjacent interactive processes. These contact-making and resisting/interrupting functions create and maintain the equilibrium of the child, thus preserving personal homeostasis. They also create and maintain disequilibrium of the organism, diminishing personal experience by interrupting healthy interaction within one's self and with the environment. Creative use of the resistance/interruption functions may represent the best adjustment given the situational context in the child's life. However, as the child's here-and-now life-field changes, applying the same responses that were used in an earlier similar situation may be maladaptive, invalidating or non-nurturing. For example, a deflection strategy that works to prevent a fight between sparring parents may not work as well when used at school in the middle of a teacher-directed classroom activity where there is heated debate. In the meantime, over-reliance and habitual use of contacting and interrupting processes may evolve into contact resistance styles, personality traits and/or character structure. The more habitual a style becomes, the more it changes from figure to ground and from an aware to unaware coping process. That lack of awareness and inability to choose is seen as less than optimal nurturing, but the necessary and functional way to cope with the emerging situation.

When subjected to frequent parental shouting matches, the child may begin to "tune out" or "shut down" the sensation/perception of the sight and sound, essentially blocking the stimuli. This desensitization function serves a useful purpose of protecting the child from an ugly and disturbing scene. When this desensitization is used to block other stimuli, such as the sounds and sights of traffic when crossing the street or the coach's instructions, it may be non-nurturing or even harmful to the child.

Divorcing parents have been known to engage in character assassination, dredging up every offensive behavior possible. The child, wanting to please and assuage the offended parent, may "swallow whole," or introject, those attitudes about the so-called offensive parent, failing to weigh and select those facts as true or false. Habitual use of this resistance style may lead to development of a very gullible trait or character formation, leaving the child unaware of his or her own attitudes, as well as preventing him or her from benefiting from the positive qualities of that parent.

A child may not be able to own his/her own anger about the divorce because of fearing the loss of his/her parent's acceptance and love. The child may then project that anger upon teachers, principals, counselor and other children at school. It is not unusual that children of divorce are heard saying such things as, "They're all out to get me," or "They don't like me," or "They're picking on me." All of these quotes have elements of unfinished angry business in them which indicates a disowned impulse to want to hate, hurt or disagree with the other. Again, this process may become hardened over time into a defensive personality trait, so that the child is unable to mobilize that anger into more constructive uses, and relies on projection as a defensive process.

Being forced into a custody schedule determined by lawyers, judges, referees and dissolution moderators may not be the best arrangement for the child. Just keeping quiet about it and doing as they are told may reduce much tension for children during transitions of visitation. Some children, rather than striking out at the environment, turn their anger and frustration inward (retroflecting it). Over time this can result in a variety of somatic complaints such as sore throat, stomachache, nausea, headaches, sore muscles, lower back pain and colitis.

When returning home after a weekend with Dad, Mom may pump the child for personal information about Dad's life. The child may choose to deflect by changing the subject or mumbling an "I don't know." These responses can be clever and useful adaptations that avoid being disloyal to Dad and/or insubordinate to Mom. However, using these same processes at school when called on by the teacher may not bring the expected relief the child may desire.

The child may choose to cope with the divorce as a "spectator" of his/her own life, an ego-centered but creative adaptation that might serve him or her well initially. Continued use of this resistance style of egotism may prevent the assimilation and growth necessary for the child to move on with life after his/her parents' divorce is settled. This style of coping appears to be particularly problematic later on when there are stepparents, stepsiblings, half-brothers and half-sisters entering the family.

One way in which parenting differs in a single parent family is the lack of a significant other for partnership and companionship. The child often serves that function, blurring the traditional boundaries between parent and child. This confluence, or unbounded merging of aspects of the child with the parent, which is also known as parentification and enmeshment, can rob a child of the usual or normal opportunities to individuate from parental figures and to differentiate from their protective environment.

Thus, the unaware and unchoiceful use of resistant and interruptive functions by the child to cope with the disequilibrium caused by the stress of divorce can also hit at the heart of the child's development. Part of the task of the Gestalt child therapist in working with children of divorce is to facilitate the awareness and choicefulness of these processes on the part of the children. Another task of the therapist is to educate parents about the negative impact of their own behavior on the child, thus lessening the degree and number of wounds to the child's heart.

There is a vast amount of literature available to parents regarding helpful and unhelpful actions during and after divorce. The following is a list of thirteen damaging parental behaviors that we have called the "Dirty Baker's Dozen" (there being 13), often discussed in by children in group and individual therapy:

- physical violence to the other parent, the child, siblings, a pet or household items;
- verbal threats made by one parent to the other parent or to the child;
- not allowing the child to enjoy positive contact with the other parent, his/her family members or the stepfamily;
- forcing the child to choose sides–one parent over the other;

- making the child feel guilty for loving the other parent;
- using the child as a messenger or spy;
- disparaging remarks about the other parent or his/her family;
- broken promises;
- relying on the child for support that should be provided by another adult;
- failure to apply a reasonable consistency in child rearing practices;
- attempting to buy the child's affection or loyalty;
- failing to provide needed financial or emotional support to punish the other parent;
- abandoning the child.

These behaviors by parents are viewed by children of divorce as the knives, arrows and lightning that strike at the very heart of their development. Coping with the stresses of divorce is a challenging task for children, one that can be made less difficult by parents who agree to forgo ongoing hostilities for the sake of their child's development.

Group Strategies for Children of Divorce

Group interventions are particularly effective for children of divorce. Two of the most problematic beliefs common to children of divorce are that they think they are the only person going through this crisis and that they are afraid what their peers think about the fact their parents are divorced. Group experience with other children of divorce mitigates those misconceptions. Children of the ages of 9 to 12 are also developmentally more ready for group interventions as they move from a more sensorial to abstract level cognitively and from relative dependence to greater independence emotionally and socially. The influence of peers begins to be figural in their lives.

The main goal of the group is to facilitate awareness, choice and responsibility of the members. Objectives are: to develop an understanding and appreciation of the divorce process and its various stages; to facilitate awareness, expression and acceptance of the various divorce-related feelings; to develop a safe and nurturing environment; to practice clear, direct and responsible communication; to examine the choice of responses to divorce situations; and to develop a playful group camaraderie.

The school is an ideal setting for divorce groups for a several reasons. From the child's point of view, the school represents a neutral territory–safe and removed from the usual sources of parental conflict. The child does not have to depend on one parent or the other for transportation to group. The child has time to assimilate learnings from the group before parental grilling begins.

From the school counselor's point of view, there are often 30% to 40% or more of the children in the school from divorced families, so there are many potential clients. It is also possible that the school counselor can witness the impact of interventions on the child at school, academically, socially and emotionally. Many parents are more willing to allow their child to participate in a free, educational activity than a costly, agency-based intervention.

The ideal size for a divorce group for later latency-aged children (ages 9 to 12) ranges between 5-8 students. A co-facilitator is recommended with more than four students. It is important to have a meeting room where the group will not be interrupted or overheard. The length of in-school group sessions is dependent in large part upon the school's schedule of classes, lunch and recess–typically 30 to 45 minutes per week for 6 to 10 weeks.

It works well for the counselor to meet in classrooms with all members of the class present to discuss the offering of group experiences for children of divorce. Interested children can choose to sign up and to have written information about the timing and purpose of the group sent home to the parents. Letters to parents include an explanation and permission forms. Parents are encouraged to call the counselor with any questions or suggestions. It is advisable for the counselor to meet individually with participants before the first group session to screen out children who may benefit more from individual counseling.

It is well for the group leader to come to the group with a plan, while being fully prepared and able to deviate from that plan to work with what emerges from the group, with willingness both to experiment creatively and to experience deeply the feelings of the group. The leader should be able to operate in a flexible manner at three levels of intervention: (1) as a therapist at the intrapersonal level, (2) as a facilitator at the interpersonal level, and (3) as a consultant at the group or system level. The process of Gestalt groups is present-focused in the here-and-now as the focal point at which to initiate meaningful interaction/contact. Attention to and comment on the counselor's own awareness of both verbal and nonverbal interactions and resistances to contact are important to the group's fruitfulness. Both types of communication should be the focus of facilitative interventions. It is also important that the leader encourages and model responsible, clear and direct communication. The leader must accept children where they are and work from that point on, not try to have them be something or act like someone they are not.

A typical group may include children whose parents were just divorced along with children whose parents have been divorced many years. This heterogeneous grouping is both helpful and important to the healing process. Those just going through their parents' divorce can see that other children have survived the divorce process and are flourishing. Children with more post divorce experience feel empowered as mentors to the less experienced participants.

Setting structure or ground rules for the group helps children benefit from the group process. By providing this necessary foundation, energy can be focused on the work at hand. Depending on the style of the facilitator, rules can be leader-directed or participant-selected. Regardless of how the rules are originated, it is important that all members agree to abide by them. A written and signed contract, delineating rights and responsibilities sometimes enhances group management, particularly for children or counselors who have difficulty with ambiguity. Creating an agreement can also provide hope, if not assurance, for members who are fearful of trusting; after all, they have all, in some manner, personally experienced a "broken trust" in their parents' divorce.

It is well to begin each group session with a checking-in procedure and a warm-up activity which focuses in some fashion on present awareness of self, awareness of the group's process or unfinished business from the previous session. The middle or work section of each session involves an activity, experiment or experience often emanating from an issue that surfaced in the warm-up. Working in depth with this emergent need or process is where the bulk of healing work is accomplished in the group. If all goes as planned, the final segment of each group session ends with an activity promoting closure, sometimes as simple as expressing a thank you to someone who touched you today, singing a song together, or a group hug.

Several activities, planned or spontaneous, can be included in the middle segment of the group session. For counselors/therapists with experience and confidence in their therapeutic artistry, it may be possible to create an experiment based on emergent data, to process the "what and how" of present group behavior and/or to use "Gestalt rounds/exaggeration" to build on a member's figural statement. For less confident counselors who are inexperienced with the flow of group dynamics and group process, activities such as drawing, art, bibliotherapy, a videotape, lecturettes, discussion, a board game and psychodrama are useful. Art can include drawing, painting, charcoal, clay sculptures and collages which utilize prompts such as:

> *"My Feelings About Divorce;"*
> *"The Best or Worst Thing About Divorce;"*
> *"What Every Parent Should Know About a Hurting Heart;"*
> and *"How I Found Out About My Parents' Divorce."*

Lecturettes might include such leads as:

> *"Understanding the Stages of Divorce;"*
> *"Learning How to Create and Use Support Systems;"*
> and *"Adjusting to Changes I Never Asked For or Wanted."*

Psychodrama enactments of the different games that children of divorce play such as:

> *"I Spy;"*
> *"I'll Go Live With X (parent);"*
> *"My Ping-Pong Game;"*
> *"But Mom Lets Me ______;"*
> *"Dad Always Buys Me ______;"*
> *"You Spent My Child Support;"*
> *"Let's Watch Mom and Dad Fight;"*
> and *"Why I Forget My Homework."*

These are extremely effective in encouraging awareness, acceptance, expression and assimilation of children's feelings related to divorce.

The most frequent positive outcome for children cited by both the children and their parents is that they learned they are not alone and that other children have gone through similar or even worse situations and survived. In addition, even though the child's environment may not have improved or changed, the child has more awareness of choice of possible responses and coping processes, and thus feels more centered, empowered and supported. Having a safe place away from both parents and being surrounded by kindred spirits where they are free to feel, say and express what has been repressed, as well as being supported to be spontaneous in their expressions and to say or enact what seeks expression as it emerges is essential to their healing process. This work demonstrates clearly how children can learn self-nurturance in a supportive community of peers with a facilitative and therapeutic counselor.

Implications and Conclusion

The small group setting provides an atmosphere where children can heal and begin the process of mastering the psychological tasks necessary to assimilate their parents' divorce and move on with living and growing up (Wallerstein, 1980). By listening to others and self-reflection, children are better able to understand their parents' divorce at a deeper level. Surrounded by fellow survivors of parental divorce, these children discover the importance of strategic withdrawal from the divorce battleground and how not to rely on the same coping strategies in other contacts with adults. Expressive activities help to deal with the loss, anger and guilt, thus removing many of the arrows, knives and bolts of lightning so poignantly depicted in their drawings. Witnessing other children who are further along the path to divorce recovery, while imbuing a sense of permanence of the divorce, also carries with it a sense of hope for the child's future.

Ernest Hemingway's statement in *A Farewell to Arms* applies well to the strengths that develop from this type of counseling and therapy. Hemmingway said, "The world breaks everyone and afterward many are strong at the broken places." Gestalt therapy theory provides a useful framework for understanding how the hearts of children of divorce are broken and Gestalt group approaches for children of divorce provide an opportunity to make strong once again those wounded places of the heart.

References

Carden, A.D. (1993). Characteristics of men in a diversion treatment program for spousal abuse/violence: A gestalt/ecological perspective. Unpublished doctoral dissertation, Kent State University, Kent, OH.

Carroll, F. (1995). The Pinocchio syndrome: Path to wholeness. Unpublished manuscript, Santa Barbara, CA.

Clarkson, P. (1989). *Gestalt counselling in action*. London: Sage.

Emery, R.E. (1982). Interpersonal conflict and the children of discord and divorce. *Psychological Bulletin, 92*, 310-330.

Emery, R.E., & Forehand, R. (1994). Parental divorce and children's well-being: A focus on resilience. In R.J. Haggerty, L.R. Sherrod, N. Garmezy, & M. Rutter (Eds.), *Stress, risk, and resilience in children and adolescents: Processes, mechanisms, and interventions*, (pp. 64-99). Cambridge, MA: Cambridge University Press.

Felner, R.D., Farber, S.S., & Primavera, J. (1980). Children of divorce, stressful life events, and transitions: A frame-work for preventive efforts. In R.H. Price, R.F. Ketter, B.C. Bader, & J. Monahan (Eds.), *Prevention in mental health: Research policy and practice*, (pp. 81-108). Beverly Hills, CA: Sage.

Felner, R.D., Stolberg, A.L., & Cowen, E.L. (1975). Crisis events and school mental health referral patterns of young children. *Journal of Consulting and Clinical Psychology, 43*, 305-310.

From, I., & Miller, M.V. (1994). Introduction. In *Gestalt therapy: Excitement and growth in the human personality*, F. Perls, R. Hefferline & P. Goodman. Highland, NY: Center for Gestalt Development.

Fulton, J.A. (1979). Parental reports of children's post-divorce adjustment. *Journal of Social Issues, 35*, 126-139.

Glass, L.S. (1990). Ethnicity and treatment schedule: A study of the children of divorce intervention program. Unpublished doctoral dissertation, Fuller Theological Seminary, Pasadena, CA.

Guidubaldi, J., Cleminshaw, H., & Perry, J. (1985). The relationship of parental divorce to health status of parents and children. In J.E. Zink, D.I. Wagner, & C.A. Mahler (Eds.), *Health promotion in the schools: nnovative approaches to facilitating physical and emotional well-being*, (pp. 73-88). New York, NY: Haworth Press.

Guidubaldi, J., Perry, J., Cleminshaw, H., & McLoughlin, C. (1983), The impact of parental divorce on children: Report of the nationwide NASP study. *School Psychology Review, 12*, 300-323.

Hess, R.D., & Camara, K.A. (1979). Post-divorce family relationships a s mediating factors in the consequences of divorce for children. *Journal of Social Issues, 35*(4), 79-98.

Hetherington, E.M., Cox, M., & Cox, R. (1978). The aftermath of divorce. In J.H. Stevens, Jr. & M. Matthews (Eds.), *Mother/child, father/child relationships*, (pp. 146-176). National Association for the Education of Young Children, Washington, D.C.

Hetherington, E.M. (1985). Long-term effects of divorce and remarriage on the adjustment of children. *Journal of the American Academy of Child Psychiatry, 25*(5), 518-530.

Kalter, N., & Rembar, J. (1981). *The significance of a child's age at the time of divorce. American Journal of Orthopsychiatry, 46*(1), 20-34.

Kelly, J.B., & Wallerstein J.S. (1976). The effects of parental divorce: Experiences of the child in early latency. *American Journal of Orthopsychiatry, 46*(1), 20-34.

Kepner, J.I. (1982). Questionnaire measurement of personality styles from the theory of gestalt therapy. Unpublished doctoral dissertation. Kent State University, Kent, OH.

Latner, J. (1973). *The Gestalt therapy book.* New York, NY: Julian Press.

Lobb, M.S. (1996). The moon is made of cheese: Understand-ing and treating seriously disturbed patients based on gestalt therapy's theory of development. Paper presented at The Gestalt Journal Conference: A Global Vision–Taking Gestalt Therapy into the 21st Century, Boston, MA.

Mraz, T.J. (1990). A study of the validity of the gestalt person ality theory of homeostasis and the gestalt personal homeostasis inventory-revised. Unpublished doctoral dissertation, Kent State University, Kent, OH.

National Center for Health Statistics (July 20, 1995). Births, marriages, divorce, and deaths for January 1995. *Monthly Vital Statistics Report, 44*(1). Hyattsville, MD: Public Health Service.

Norton, R.F. (1980). Toward a gestalt theory of child development. Unpublished doctoral dissertation, California School of Professional Psychology, Fresno, CA.

Oaklander, V. (1978). *Windows to our children: A gestalt approach to working with children and adolescents*. Moab, UT: Real People Press.

Oaklander, V. (1982). The relationship of gestalt therapy to children. *The Gestalt Journal, 5*(1), 64-74.

Oaklander, V. (1992). Gestalt therapy with children: Working with anger and introjects. In E.C. Nevis (Ed.), *Gestalt therapy: Perspectives and applications*, (pp. 263-284). New York, NY: Gardner Press.

Ownby, R.L. (1983). Gestalt therapy with children. *The Gestalt Journal, 6*(2), 51-58.

Perls, F. (1947). *Ego, hunger, and aggression.* London: Allen & Unwin.

Perls, F. (1973). *The gestalt approach and eye-witness to therapy*. New

York, NY: Bantam Books.

Perls, F., Hefferline, R F., & Goodman, P. (1951). *Gestalt ther apy: Excitement and growth in the human personality*. New York, NY: Dell.

Perls, F., Hefferline, R F., & Goodman, P. (1994). *Gestalt ther apy: Excitement and growth in the human personality*. Highland, NY: Center for Gestalt Development.

Polster, E., & Polster, M. (1973). *Gestalt therapy integrated*. New York, NY: Brunner/Mazel.

Rank, O. (1945). *Will therapy*. New York, NY: Alfred A. Knopf.

Swanson, J. (1988). Boundary processes and boundary states. *The Gestalt Journal, 11*(2), 5-24.

Swanson, J. (1989). In response: Another look at revising gestalt boundary theory. *The Gestalt Journal, 12*(1), 69-80.

Wallerstein, J.S., & Blakeslee, S. (1989). *Second chances: Men, women, and children a decade after divorce*. New York, NY: Ticknor & Fields.

Wallerstein, J.S., & Kelly, J.B. (1979). Children and divorce: A review. *Social Work, 24*, 468-475.

Wheeler, G. (1991). *Gestalt reconsidered: A new approach to contact and resistance*. New York, NY: Gardner Press.

Woldt, A.L. (1993). The gestalt homeostasis cycle. Unpublish ed figure, Kent, OH.

Woldt, A.L. & Ingersoll, R.E. (1991). Where in the "yang" has the "yin" gone in gestalt therapy? *The British Gestalt Journal, 2*, 1-9.

Zinker, J. (1977). *Creative process in gestalt therapy*. New York, NY: Brunner/Mazel.

Part III:

Perspectives and New Directions

9

Between Parent and Child: The Power of Shame

Gordon Wheeler

Feelings of shame and their dynamic role in human interaction and process are among the most poorly understood of all the emotions and, until quite in recent years anyway, among the least attended to as well, both clinically and in everyday relational life. In a sense this is odd, since all of us know shame only all too well, from personal experiences–that painful sense of exposure, rejection, or inadequacy that can gnaw at us, make us want to hide or disappear from scrutiny when the self we feel and know is suddenly (or chronically) unacceptable, to a world where we want and need desperately to belong and grow. There is something curious, to say the least, in the fact that feelings this intense and acute, this personally disorganizing in the way they can suddenly cut to the bone of our sense of ourselves and our personal worth, have been so overlooked, underestimated, and at times denied, down through most of the past century or so of clinical and psychological study.

At the same time, from a Gestalt point of view, this neglect and misunderstanding are not accidental, but stem necessarily from the terms and limitations of our most basic cultural and clinical paradigms, which is to say our long-dominant Western ideology of individualism and autonomy. This ideology, which posits that the individual exists in some essential sense apart from, and prior to relationship and context, has set particular limits and blinders on our traditional conceptions of human nature and interpersonal relationships, especially where the lifelong importance of our connections with others is concerned. If the self is conceived as it traditionally has been in the West, as fundamentally separate from other selves and striving for ever-greater autonomy through the course of personal and even cultural development, then plainly shame, which is the affect par excellence of interpersonal sensitivity and relational reaction, will be difficult to address in any clarifying way–and may tend to disappear from view altogether, or at best be classified as marginal and/or pathological by definition. That is, in these terms shame seems to be something aberrant, something to be ashamed of, not a natural dimension of our emotional makeup and our connection with people, to be considered and analyzed along with other basic ground conditions of contact–such as power, cultural context, and gender, for example. Certainly this pathologizing of shame has tended to be the case with the long-dominant psychoanalytic model, with its hyper-individualist biases, where shame was pictured (if it was seen at all) as an emotion of infantile dependency and fusion, characteristic of pre-Oedipal children, women, "primitive" cultures, and any other individuals or groups who had not achieved fully mature autonomy and independence from the social field (see discussion in Lee, 1995; Wheeler, 1996; and Wheeler & Jones, 1996).

Given this broad background, it is perhaps not surprising that until quite recently, even such discussions of shame as could be found in clinical literature still seemed to shy away from those areas where intimate relational process was most centrally involved (and where shame, as an emotion of relational vulnerability, would seem to be most directly implicated)–which is to say, the inner workings and dynamics of family life, intimate couples' relations, and the subjective processes and experiences of child development (all those areas, that is, where the terms of the individualist self model are least helpful, and fit most poorly with lived experience). Such areas in general, and particularly parent-child relations, have tended to be seen as governed by instinctive drives and attachments (psychoanalytic theory), reinforcement contingencies (the behavioral model), power (feminist perspectives, and also the "back in control" movements in parent education), and all the various role, rule, and authority perspectives of some of the wide array of systemic schools of thought. All of these perspectives, to be sure, can make a real and valuable contribution to our understanding of close relational process in general, and parent-child relations in particular; and yet all of them seem to leave something out, to focus on these intimate and powerful life experiences from the outside, missing the feel of strong desires and fears about goal and outcome which we subjectively experience as the driving forces organizing our behavior. This something is found again, we believe, in the crucial phenomenological dimension emphasized in the Gestalt contact model, with its focus on the organization of experience and the resolution of a coherent whole of perception, cognition, affect, and behavior–resolved in terms of goal and meaning. It is this phenomenological, "experience-near" dimension, we believe, which holds the key to understanding and to intervention, and which is itself supported by the clearer picture of shame which is offered by the Gestalt model.

On a more affective level, there is a large and important literature of bonding and bonding effects in child development and family life (see for example Bowlby, 1969; Ainsworth 1979)–but hardly any corresponding treatment at all of shame in parent-child relations, even though internalized shame as we understand it from a Gestalt field perspective is the direct converse of good bonding, and the inevitable result of disturbances in bonding processes between parent and child (a set of points which will be developed at some length below). And yet we have come to believe, over the course of a number of years of clinical study, that shame plays a crucial, often hidden role in nearly every difficult interaction or breakdown of parent-child relations–and even more critically, that our understanding of stress and crisis in parenting and parent-child process is necessarily incomplete and often misleading, without the clarifying perspective provided by clear attention to the dynamic role of shame in family life.

To illustrate and explain what we mean by these points we will first take a look, briefly, at the (non-clinical) psychological tradition which has dealt extensively with shame and shame dynamics, which is the tradition of affect theory, deriving first from Darwin and then extensively elaborated in this century by Sylvan Tomkins (e.g., 1963), Gershen Kaufman (1989), and others. As we will see, this tradition, which is fundamentally contextual, social, and communication-based, has many direct affinities with the Gestalt field perspective on "contact," the intersubjective construction of experience. From there we will explore–again briefly–how a Gestalt view of these issues can integrate the insights of affect theory and clinical tradition, yielding a model that can guide our understanding and interventions in difficult moments of parent-child interaction, for ourselves and our clients. And with that discussion as a ground, we will turn to an exploration of shame in parent-child relations through an experiential exercise, and application of the model to actual case material of problematic patterns and moments in parent-child life, drawn from our patients and from our own experience.

Shame in the Affect Theory Tradition

The psychological tradition which has paid the most, and the most productive, attention to shame experiences and shame dynamics, interestingly enough, is a perspective which has developed outside clinical literature per se, with curiously little cross-fertilization between the two domains. This is the tradition of affect theory, a body of work rooted ultimately in Darwinian thinking, and resting on a small set of psychological/evolutionary observations and propositions elaborated by Darwin himself in his classic 1872 work, *The Expression of the Emotions in Man and Animals*. These propositions, along with the general, quite distinctive flavor of affect theory as a line of thought, may be summarized as follows:

(1) As individually defenseless members of a species evolving and living in social colonies, human beings have need of a highly active and elaborate system of rapid communication for group signaling and survival.

(2) Specifically, the information and reactions carried by certain "affect clusters" having to do with safety, danger, group cohesion or other urgent social survival messages cannot wait for verbal explanation, but need to be communicated and understood almost instantaneously. Examples would be fear, joy, excitement, anger, sadness, discouragement–and the emotional cluster Darwin calls "self-attention-shame-shyness"–which he understands as that continuum of affect we experience as shrinking, pulling back, not being "up to" the encounter at hand.

(3) These affect clusters, together with their characteristic signals (facial expression, posture, gesture), are universal and inborn. Darwin further assumed that the relatively hairless human face had evolved to communicate these urgent messages of affective information rapidly across a visual distance, and to a whole group at once (thus the emphasis of his title, *The Expression of the Emotions...*). Therefore, he reasoned, these signals must be fairly consistent and stable across cultural differences; populations that evolve to be "prewired" for recognition of these urgent signals will have a plain survival advantage, over those that have to invent and teach all this from scratch to each new member. To test out these assumptions he set up an intriguing field experiment. Using photographs which subjects in Britain would readily identify as expressing the various affect clusters (again, anger, joy, fear, pride, shame, disgust, and so on), he then had these same photographs shown to field anthropologists as well as to members of African tribes and other "primitive" cultures. This elegant and quite path breaking bit of ethnographic research was never statistically quantified in the modern way, but Darwin was satisfied that the assumptions were validated by the results, and that various affect clusters as represented by characteristic facial expression were readily identifiable cross-culturally. Thus he concluded that the affects he had identified were indeed universal and universally under-

stood in a fairly consistent way.

In our own century Darwin's work has been taken up and extended by Sylvan Tomkins and his followers, with particular emphasis on the special role of shame in emotional dynamics and life. To Tomkins, as to Darwin, shame is the affect of shrinking away or holding back, the whole cluster of feelings that arise when we sense that what we want to do, or are in the middle of doing, or have just done, is not well-received or not acceptable in the social field, or perhaps that we are going to fall short of the expectations of others in some way. Thus we find shame always paired with other affects–particularly the affect cluster of "excitement-joy," but also at times with others, whenever we are in a position to feel exposed, wanting or trying or being expected to do something that is going to result in our "looking bad" in the eyes of others. At a common sense level this pairing of shame with other affects makes sense once we think about it: it is most of all in states of desire or expectation (our own or others') that we are most vulnerable to judgment, rejection, or falling short in some way. If my impulse or desire is sexual, say (or angry, or playful, or selfish, or whatever is judged inadequate or unacceptable by my group), then feelings of anticipated shame can actually function to protect me from a dangerous loss of approval, affection, or belongingness in the "real" world of relationships with others.

This is the functional side of shame, much emphasized by affect theorists, which is not the way we usually think of an emotion most of us experience as unbearably negative. Still, it is natural that a perspective grounded in evolutionary thinking would be looking for the functional aspect of any universal behavior or process pattern, and clearly advantages will accrue to the group if the members are susceptible to feelings like these, which should function to bring individuals into some relative harmony with the whole. (And Darwin, remember, was concerned with the evolution and survival of populations and groups–not just the primacy of the "fittest individual," as some of the politically conservative "social Darwinists" among his followers have long misinterpreted him as meaning).

As Tomkins, Kaufmann, and other contemporary writers on affect theory have pointed out, this perspective gives shame a special status among the affects. Whereas the other affects tend in general to direct us motorically in the outer world (roughly, "toward" in anger or excitement/joy, "away from" in fear, perhaps "up" in pride and "down" in grief, and so on), shame functions more as a governor on the energy and intensity of the other affects themselves. That is, I may feel fear and want to run away, but anticipated shame and shaming may undercut that impulse. Likewise with, say, sexual excitement: I may feel moved to go toward the stimulating other person, but if he or she is the "wrong" person–perhaps even the "wrong" gender, in the values of my group–then shame may hold me back (and again, may protect me from seriously bad consequences). Or I may be overwhelmed with feelings of hopelessness and resignation in the face of some daunting task, but fear of being shamed for failure may make me try again.

Thus, shame emerges as what Tomkins calls a "regulator affect," mediating and modulating the actions I'm energized to do, or not do, by the other affects I'm feeling. The trouble comes, of course, with my human and Gestalt tendency, equally inborn, to learn, generalize, make a meaningful whole where and as I can, and then apply that learning and those generalizations as the context of some future problem-solving challenge. In clinical tradition, this is the whole area of "internalization"–whether in the classical sense of superego and transference, or just the everyday sense of any learning from experience or generalized belief, examined or unexamined. As the behaviorists put it, I am forever associating or pairing one thing with another, even though many of these pairings are "superstitious," and do not or need not transfer to the new situation. In the more complex terms of the Gestalt model, this tendency to generalize and form beliefs in the first place is understood as the most fundamental characteristic of human process, and most basic tenet of the model: it is my "human nature," the thing, as a human being, that I cannot not do. I can deconstruct it, critique it, challenge it, experiment with it and test it out–indeed, this is what psychotherapy is all about. But I can never stop doing it, because this is what I am "prewired" for, as a low-instinct, problem-solving, social being; that is, mapping the whole field into a meaningful contextual gestalt in the service of practical problem-solving is literally what I am "born to do."

Well and good, but putting these various insights together, it is easy to see how the problem in human relations is not shame or shaming per se (these, again, are natural individual/social processes), but internalized shame–learned in the past under conditions of more or less extreme duress and dependency, and then carried within as a complex experiential schema, which becomes activated, or threatens to activate, whenever I'm faced with any experience that makes me feel exposed, inadequate, undervalued, rejected, inappropriate, or unsafe in this personal, something-wrong-with-me way. In the extreme, a high level of internalized shame (which is the residue of high use of punitive shaming and other aversive relational behavior in a damaging childhood, long ago) can make me jumpy and reactive, liable to respond to the first flicker of these feelings with some strong countering gesture; (anger, counter-shaming, even rage or violence–or alternatively a dulling of the feeling, through depression, self-medication with drugs, or sexual or other acting out to escape the feelings).

This is because strong feelings of sustained shame are unbearable, and are impossible to stay with, in the absence of powerful, countervailing support. Again, this is something we know, personally and clinically, but which is difficult to understand or explain, from a purely individualist point of view. That is, if our basic nature is to be separate and independent (at least after a period of childhood dependency which we should naturally outgrow), then how can it be that shame has the power it has–whether to support social cohesion, as Darwin and the affect theorists emphasized, or to cripple us and/or throw us into destructive reaction patterns, as we know it can do with fragile and "poorly-structured" personalities (and here again, our contention would be that "poorly-structured" or "borderline," a high level of internalized shame, and a history of abusive shame and shaming, are really all ways of saying the same thing)? Why don't we just "rise above" these inner feelings and the opinions of others alike, "listen to ourselves," and ignore new or old messages from a shaming environment?

The answer, from a Gestalt point of view, is because that's not what self and self-process mean, or how they work. In the Gestalt perspective, based as it is on the construction of meaningful wholes in the field of experience, we understand "self" as the process of integrating the whole experiential field, "external" as well as "internal," into a livable, workable whole, which enables me to act, live, understand, and move on or grow. Thus in this view, which we would argue is much closer to lived, felt experience than is the pure individualist model, "self" and "others" are not really separate at all, experientially, but are parts of the same unified field, integrated through self-process. "I" and "you" are distinct as experiences, to be sure–but not separate or separable, in living self-process. The one implies and contain the other, subjectively: we are.

And thus, I cannot "just ignore" my social field. Indeed, opposing the people around me, standing up for something I believe in (which is a crucial capacity and a part of creative living), are things I can do only by feeling the support and connection of some *other* group (what social psychologists call a "reference group"), to supply that meaningful connectedness in the field which I always need, by the very terms of my nature. That is, in a Gestalt view, "independence" is never "autonomy," but is always a more complex form of interdependence in the field, now integrated in a new and more complex way so as to be more independent of immediate time and place. We "stand against" by calling to mind other values, other groups we feel a connection with; just as we bear feelings of rejection, inadequacy, and loss of felt connection, in the end, only by making a similar kind of appeal, implicitly or explicitly, to supportive connection and validation with and through other competencies, other affirmations, other connections in the field, which we cannot live (or cannot live well) without.

To bring these various points full circle, we can say that in Gestalt, we understand shame as the affect of an important loss of connectedness in the field (again, see discussion in Lee, 1995). Our life has to do with "making contact"–finding and making meaningful wholes of perception, feeling and action that bring our inner world of needs and desires into some satisfying resolution with the outer world of resources, including principally other people. This is survival–again, what we are "wired" to do. "Self" is our name for that integrative process, the ongoing creative union of the field, in ways that support my living and growing as well as I can. A significant break in that field–a loss of receptiveness in some important area–threatens not just my practical well-being but my reliable feeling of self cohesion and self-process as well–and must be addressed, for good or ill, in one way or another (there are many perspectives on shame, and many models; but none of them suggest that serious shame feelings can just be ignored–all of them recognize that it is simply not in our makeup to do that). To put Tomkins' affect-theory insight into Gestalt terms, we could say that shame modulates contact (again, see discussion in Lee, 1995 or Wheeler & Jones, 1995). In other words, shame is always with us–as a potential, as anticipation, or as an immediate feeling. And to the extent that a damaging past has been internalized and carried over in the form of powerful beliefs and expectations, many of them negative, shaping and limiting our present contact process, then shame becomes a time bomb, a sort of depth explosive that can go off at any time, whenever current signals and events act to release old "shame triggers" from the past–sometimes with grave, even tragic consequences.

Between Parent and Child: Shame in Parent/Child Relations

But how do feelings of shame and shame dynamics enter into parent-child interactions–particularly difficult or problematic interactions, ones that erupt into crisis, or break down into distance, alienation, recrimination and self-reproach? To explore these questions, we have sometimes used an exercise of the following general type, with some variation depending on the makeup and interest of the particular group joining us in the exploration. As the reader, you may choose to take pen and paper or laptop and do the exercise yourself as we go along, or else just to participate by following the responses of others, some of which will be included in the discussion below. Here are the instructions we give:

> *Close your eyes, go inside, and let your mind play over some painful or difficult memories–memories of a difficult or "bad" parent-child interaction which you were part of, in one way or another. It may be one specific interaction, or it may be a type of problem situation that happens over and over. Either way, make it as concrete and specific as you can. Picture what happened, and pay special attention to how you were feeling: what was the overall feeling tone, and how did you feel in your body? What did you say to yourself, during the interaction and after? Are you still troubled now by anything you regret, out of that scene? What did you hope for? Do you think it can change? How do you wish it would have gone, or would go now or in the future? And again with each question, pay attention to what feelings come up, as you play over the scene in your mind.*

Write your scene down, in a few sentences or phrases. Use the present tense, to make it more immediate. Be sure to include some of the feeling tones and words that come to you, along with the dominant feeling and dominant longing you are left with, from those memories.

Once the group has had a chance to write for a few minutes–and once the furious intensity of the writing has begun to slack off–then we ask people to turn to a neighbor, or pick a partner, and just tell that person however much of the experience they are comfortable sharing. If any part of the actual details feels too private to share with a stranger, we tell them, then just skip over the concrete events and concentrate on sharing the feelings they had at the time, and the feelings they are left with now, some time later. This point is very important to us–both out of respect in general for the privacy of people's experience and the importance of their making intentional choices about what to share, and even more, because we believe that we are opening up and stepping into a terrain of shame with these questions; and shame, in our view, has of all the emotions the greatest potential to trigger decompensation of our usual personality supports and organization, and outbursts of self- or other-destructive behavior, in gross or subtle form (including at the milder and less visible end, for example, lengthy and obsessive private bouts of punitive and undermining self-recrimination).

Once the pace of writing lessens, a mood of heavy silence usually settles over the room, as if people are lost in thought, in unhappy terrain. Then when we invite people to share with each other, typically the room bursts into noise and an equal intensity of energy, now directed outward instead of inward. These patterns make up the first of the interesting results of the exploration. First of all, there is the fact that out of some hundreds of people who have joined us in these explorations of quite difficult memories in one form or another, we've never had a single person whose response was that she/he just "couldn't relate to the question," "couldn't think of an example," or "just wasn't interested." Apparently we all carry these memories, together with the ability to access them, at times, only all too easily.

Second, it is worth noting that even though we leave the choice open, it is fairly exceptional that anyone calls up and writes about a memory of him/herself in the child's role. Most participants–including people who do not have children of their own–tend to choose a difficult interaction where they themselves were in the parental role (often freely adapting the word "parent," quite reasonably, to include child-raising and childcare activities they may have been involved in, personally or professionally, without being the literal parent of the child). This is perhaps surprising, given that all of us can remember at least some painful and difficult moments from childhood, that many such moments do include a conscious element of shame, shaming, or feeling inadequate in some way, and that shame in its nature has a way of lingering, and burning in memory even when recalled years after the event. Of course, it may be in part that the difficult parenting moments are just more recent, and more urgent in our current lives, as pressing problems to be worked on. Our own feeling, however, is somewhat different: we suspect, rather, that what is so pressing about the painful parenting moments is the fact (often confirmed spontaneously by participants) that they often have not been shared before, or shared deeply in feeling terms–and that this fact itself, this privacy and reticence, has a great deal to do with shame. The child felt shame then, perhaps, back in the time of the painful interaction or event–but it may not be shameful to recall that now; and maybe for this reason the event may well have been retold and shared with others by now–a retelling which itself mitigates shame, in our view. Again, in the Gestalt terms developed above, shame has to do with disconnection, in some important and threatening way–with not being able, or confident, to command/inspire the involvement and acceptance we know we need, and indeed cannot thrive and grow without. Thus shame leads to isolation (to cover the shameful cause of the disconnect), and tends to become a vicious circle: the very sharing which would potentially relieve the shame, by knitting up connection with the listener, may tend not to happen because of the anticipation of the opposite–which is to say, more disapproval, judgment, inadequacy, rejection, and shame.

Significantly, no one we know of has ever yet availed him/herself of the option of not telling the events to a partner at all, but just mentioning the feelings without any concrete details (though certainly some people may have edited the events in the retelling–a kind of contact modulation we would wholeheartedly support). Apparently there is something about a group where "everybody is in the same boat" (as in a 12-step or other recovery group, for example) which supports people to share difficult or unflattering things about themselves, no doubt in the hope that the resonance and understanding received will outweigh the judgment and disconnection we may all at times fear.

Next we usually ask the participants to share out in the group to "share out" with the whole room. Here again, we make a point of telling people it is not the specific details of the events that we want, but the feeling tones and emotional memories, both from the time of the interaction itself, and the ones that came up in the remembering and writing, before the sharing with a partner. Again, we do this because we do not want to invite a level of exposure, in front of a roomful of strangers, which may be hard to support afterwards. However, some sharing of concrete events does spontaneously occur in the process, or in the discussion that follows, which sometimes includes explicit consultation and problem solving on the dyad or group level. Here are some examples of the kinds of stories people tell–some taken from these discussions, and some from parent consultation in a clinical setting. All of the examples have been altered biographically, preserving the structure of the problem and the feelings, but protecting the identity of the respondents:

> *My problem is that I get so angry, and then I lash out–not physically, but verbally. And I hate it when I do that–I hate myself. It's like I can see that I'm hurting Rachel, but I can't help it. It happens most of all at bedtimes, when she keeps getting up and getting up, and it keeps getting later and later. And I get mixed up, because I'm not sure if it's not Michael I'm really mad at, because he's no help. He's been gone all day, while I've been with Rachel, and now what I really want is some time alone with an adult–with him. But he just indulges her, and tucks her back in, and tells her another story–forever. And I feel sort of powerless, and lonely,*

and I'm not sure what I feel–helpless, mostly sort of a weak feeling in my body and guilty, with Rachel.

This is every day, right now. This sounds funny, but my problem is, my son won't get dressed in the morning. I mean he flat won't. It's a disaster. And it's my job–I'm supposed to get him ready for school, because my wife picks him up. And she's very cool about it, she just says it's his problem, let him go in his pajamas. But you can't do that–I mean, he has to wear something! And he's not a toddler–he's almost 8 years old. So I try to hurry him up, and make it a game, and promise him something, then I try to bribe him, and then I get stern–nothing works. We all end up shouting–my wife too,–and he's in tears, and we're all late to work, late to school. And I feel–well, I feel embarrassed about it, to tell you the truth. I think maybe he should be in therapy–or I should–or we all should. I mean, this is something people should be able to do, right?–get dressed in the morning. I feel like a total failure, and it's over something so trivial. How do people do this?

My daughter gets in these monster fights with my wife, or my wife does with my daughter, I don't know how they start, but the thing is, my wife gets to a certain point, and then she appeals to me. "You make her go to bed," or "You make her be polite–I can't." I mean, I think parents should support each other, and step in for each other when the other one has lost it, and all that–but the trouble is, by the time I get her, she's already a basket case, they're yelling at each other, more like sisters really (my daughter is 12), and what am I supposed to do? So I come on like the heavy, and then I'm the bad guy, and of course it doesn't really help, and everybody is glaring at everybody, and the younger ones are scurrying around getting out of the way–but I wonder what they're learning, for their own adolescence. I feel torn, mostly–and I'm not sure between what, exactly, but it's a feeling of being torn, almost physically.

My problem is the whining. I'm a single parent–I just can't take it. I know it's my problem, I know my reaction is exaggerated. But I don't know how exaggerated–I mean, I don't know how much whining is okay, like at mealtimes. I don't like this; I don't want that. I should handle it rationally, be cool, tough love, this is dinner, take it or leave it, but I don't–first I twist myself around trying to please them–because I feel bad about the divorce, I know–but then I think what about me? If I had whined like that, my mother would have slapped me. I do feel angry about it–but something else too, something more hopeless. It just feels hopeless. And yet–overall, we're pretty happy, and they're doing well. I really don't understand the whole thing. I just know it feels really bad.

If we then ask people to share out the feelings and feeling tones from vignettes like these, what we get is the whole gamut of the imaginable negative emotions, and constellations of emotion: anger, hurt, helplessness, rage, impotence, loneliness, resentment, discouragement, disappointment, sometimes embarrassment, inadequacy, guilt, in some cases fear, explosiveness, desertion, anxiety, sadness, flatness, fatigue, even grief, at the seeming death of a dream or fantasy, of what having children would be like, and how it would all be different from one's own childhood. The most positive term we're likely to get here is a kind of rueful humor, the kind of wry self-compassion a person may feel in contemplating the reality of his own frustrations and disappointments, in contrast to his hopes and dreams.

Next, we sometimes ask for a comparative list, of how it felt to be telling the story to a partner, and hearing their partner's story, here in the exercise now. The contrast is not surprising, but is still striking all the same. Warm, accepted, self-accepting, understood, supported, relieved, teary, lighter, more energized, hopeful, less alone, inspired–even equipped with new ideas for solving the problem, or at least handling it differently. And all this is from just telling the vignette to a stranger, with no intention or instruction of facilitating any major change, much less a problem-solving session!

Curiously (or perhaps not so curiously, as we become more familiar with the dynamics of this fugitive and deceptive emotion), one word we hardly ever get on the first list is shame. And yet the list is always full of loaded feeling terms that seem to circle around the missing term: helpless, hopeless, weak, inadequate, judged, failing, even embarrassed or exposed. In our view this absence speaks to the kind of social taboo surrounding the term shame itself, and the full experience of the cluster of feelings it connotes. Again, in our dominant individualist ideology, shame itself is shameful; to admit this shameful feeling, even to oneself, is to admit weakness, inadequacy, dependency–in a word, all the things that make it seem unlikely that we'll be seen as worthy of connecting or reconnecting with, or in other words unlikely that the shame itself will be repaired. And thus shame hides, as each of us tries to manage or deny alone, what can only be repaired and restored in relationship, under particular conditions of trust and support.

To explore this further, we sometimes ask participants to go back to their story, first perhaps alone and then with the same partner, and retell it entirely in terms of feelings of shame. We do this not because we think shame is the only thing people are "really feeling" here (shame, remember, always accompanies other emotions)–and certainly not with the idea of telling people what they "should feel" (whatever that might mean)–but rather in the spirit of an experiment, trying on a new behavior and framing, in the service of a new experience, to see where that experience then fits for the person, and where and how it may modify her understanding of her own feelings and experiential process. Because this framing may feel awkward or unfamiliar (or shaming), we ask the partners to act as a coach, asking at each part of the vignette: "In what way did you/might you/could you possibly feel a feeling of shame here or some related feeling at this point in the story?"

Thus in the first vignette above in going back to the initial phrase, "I get so mad," the storyteller's partner would ask: "In what way do you feel ashamed of that, what is shameful about getting so mad at your daughter?" In this case, the answer was immediate, and already suggested in the next statement, "I hate myself:" "I'm ashamed of getting so angry at her, she's just a little girl, and really he's almost encouraging her (to keep getting up). I feel like a bad person, a bad mother, I should be able to control my feelings–or at least to understand them, not just take them out on her!" So far the material was not surprising to the participant, but the next part felt much newer to her, and threw quite a different light on her own reactions. To the part about "Michael is no help" (and the question, how might that be shameful, to you), she first felt angry, then hurt and alone–and then an overwhelmingly flooding sense of shame. "What's wrong with me," she lamented, "that he doesn't want to be with me in the evening? Of course he wants to see Rachel–so do I–but by this time we've had three or four hours with Rachel. And this part isn't exactly quality time, just hopping up every fifteen minutes to tuck her back in bed. We could be having a glass of wine, talking, reading aloud to each other, making love–anything. And I want that–why doesn't he? Why doesn't he need it? I just feel completely worthless to him, and undesirable. Maybe sexually, but more as a person, like my company is not worth anything to him, not something he needs. That's why I get so enraged at Rachel–and at Michael. It isn't jealousy, I've asked and asked myself that. That's not it. It's shame–not that he's paying attention to her, but just that he has no interest in any special time for me. Like he doesn't want that anymore, doesn't want me anymore. No interest, and no need." By this time she was crying softly, in the arms of her exercise partner, who was crying too. Looking around the room, we could see that they weren't the only ones with tears in their eyes. If shame is contagious, as it famously is, then the relief all of us feel when we finally, for once, can unburden ourselves of this most solitary of feelings is equally universal, and moving in various ways to us all.

This example could stand for many. In the second and third vignettes above, each of them a father facing a difficult problem in the general area of "discipline," both of the narrators had already begun to frame the problem as one of inadequacy. In the first of the two–the little boy who wouldn't get dressed–the shame feelings that came more clearly to light were plainly gender-keyed. Mothers all over the land are somehow getting their children to school with clothes on, this man told himself (and us)–so why can't I, a father, do it? Probably children don't feel as close to their fathers, and don't want to do what they ask, don't want to make life easy for them, they way they do for their mothers. Probably there's something missing in my makeup, as a man, some deep emotional deficiency, that creates a gap in the relationship, so my little boy just doesn't care. And I don't want to go to my wife for help–because that would just make it true, and there I'd be, stuck in my own inadequacy as a man, and my own shame."

Likewise the next vignette, where the father telling the story felt challenged–and found wanting–in his authority as a father, and as a man. Just as in his own family of origin, when the mother couldn't handle some "discipline problem," she handed it on to the father. And his own father had always handled it, then and there, no nonsense and no backtalk, end of story and no appeal. Just the words, "I'm going to tell your father," had been enough to solve the problem–as long as we agree that "the problem" was the "discipline issue" of the moment, which certainly disappeared from view–"but at what a cost," this participant recounted, "at what a cost." The cost of course was the relationship between father and child, which was "distant–no, make that nonexistent."

This father didn't want to repeat that, and hadn't repeated it. And yet he still carried unaware feelings of shame about not being "man enough" to command that kind of authority and respect. In this case, just posing the question in terms of shame was enough to change the felt terms of the issue significantly. "But I don't want that kind of 'respect,'" he protested–against himself, his father, wherever those messages were coming from, that a "real man" would inspire instant obedience based, presumably, on fear. "That isn't respect, really–and it sure isn't relationship!" This was one of those moments where we bracketed the discussion for a moment of group consultation and problem-solving–both as a learning exercise, to show how the experiment of framing the feelings of the parent-child interaction as shame might lead to a new frame and a new behavioral solution, and also because when a problematic problem emerges out into the open like this that is clearly dystonic with the rest of the person's feelings, style, and values, then oftentimes "single-trial" learning is possible and effective, with only a very brief intervention. What is respect, really, the group asked him? "Dialogue"–was the swift answer. "When two people–parent and child, say–really talk and listen to each other, that's real respect. The other kind–'discipline'–is just phony." From this it was only a couple of brief steps to designing a new reply to his wife when these crises occurred, and she appealed to him to solve them. Roughly the response he developed and rehearsed in the group went something like this: "I want to back you up (to his wife), and I certainly support the idea that she (the 12-year-old) should listen and speak to you with respect. But I can't solve this thing at this moment for you because right now neither one of you is listening to the other one. We all have to listen to each other–me too–and if there's any way I can support that right now, I want to do it. Like maybe each of you could tell your perspective to me right now, and the other one could just listen. If there's an issue of safety or your homework or your jobs in there (this to the daughter again), then you know I'm going to back up your mother a hundred per cent. But if it's an issue of not hearing each other out, then we're all in it together, and I'm supporting everybody."

It is only fair to say that to some in the group this sounded "wimpy," while to others it sounded "provocative." That's part of the value of groups. The important thing was–to this man it sounded right, it fit with his values and his style, and it fit his feelings, once he had gotten in touch with and worked through his own out-of-touch feelings of shame about the "wimp" issue itself, which were what was getting in the way of his finding his own path and his own voice. To those who said "wimpy," he replied, firmly and feelingly, that on the contrary, he felt strong in his beliefs, about dialogue with children, and proud of his relationships with all his family–and above all fed up with being driven by his own shame issues on that very topic, of trying to "be a man" in a way that he neither felt nor believed in. To those who said "provocative," on the other hand, he said he could see their point, that his wife might feel abandoned in mid-crisis, and that in response to that warning he would talk to her about it ahead of time, let her know that he was no longer going to step in in that way, and ask her input, about how he could make it plain in the moment that he was supporting her as a parent, while supporting both of them as family members with feelings to tell, and the right to tell them. (While they were at it, the group took care of the problem in vignette #2 as well. "I can solve that for you," said a mother of six. "It's great to get in touch with your feelings about all this, and I hope you do get over the idea that mothers have some secret ingredient you don't have, when all we really have is the bond that comes from holding them when they're upset and nursing them when they're sick, which are things I'm sure you do too. So take a look at that. But as far as your clothes problem goes, here's what you do: dress him the night before. I know it sounds crazy, but believe me it works. Some kids can't make decisions in the morning–it's too hard, they're worried about the day, or whatever. It's nothing to do with you, it's him and the day he's facing. Maybe his teacher is hard on him, or maybe the other kids are hard to get in with–you know, shame issues. And what do they wear anyway, at that age?–sweat pants and tee shirts, that's all mine ever wore; things that look exactly the same whether you sleep in them or not. Just have him change his underwear at night, and put on whatever he likes, and next morning you're all set." At last report, some months later, both solutions were in place, and both situations much improved).

The final vignette, the single mom with the whiney, picky-eater kids, was somewhat different. What this woman got in touch with, once we posed the problem in terms of shame feelings, was a massive feeling of being unappreciated, together with equally massive feelings of shameful insignificance which echoed back for her to earliest childhood, her two failed marriages, and out into other relationships in her current life. "I work so hard for them," she said softly, "and they don't appreciate it. How could they–they have no idea, I've protected them from all that. Their father contributes nothing, I'm at work all day, and all they can do is bitch about dinner. I feel like whining too–I'm whining now!–only there's nobody for me to whine to. It's like I don't matter"–this last part was almost a whisper. There was silence around the room, until we asked if there was anyone else there who could relate to those feelings, of not mattering, not counting like other people, of taking care of the world while your own feelings are not taken seriously. Slowly–still in silence–hands began to go up around the room, till finally most of the hands were up. We asked then how she felt, just seeing the hands and faces. "Warm," was the reply, "and light and accepted."

It felt important to us that in this case we did not make a space for solutions, or encourage the group to offer consultation on how to deal with unappreciative children, picky eaters, whatever. Not that any group of parents is not full of good and useful ideas–as we've already seen in the examples above! Rather, our concern is that with deep issues of internalized shame, especially as the feelings are first being contacted, "helping" and "fixing" are distancing, even hierarchical moves, when what is needed is close emotional connection, to restore the person's own self-confidence and creative problem-solving capacities. Even worse, distancing of this kind, from acute feelings of worthlessness and shame, may be felt an experience of further shaming–since the shame feelings themselves, to repeat, are probably experienced as shameful, and other people's move to distance themselves from the discomfort of my extreme shame, may well be felt as a move· away from a shameful person, who is myself.

In each of these cases, the experiment of reframing the vignette as a story of shame proved clarifying to storyteller and audience alike, and served to open up a new dimension of buried feelings and hidden dynamics that considerations of problem-solving, strategy, role, power issues, and even deep feelings of anger or hurt and lonely disappointment did not completely bring to light. And, in each case, what was needed first of all was an experience of being-with, in the present moment of the telling–of feeling and bearing a sense of inadequacy and judgment, of absence or withdrawal of support, that may be simply overwhelming if felt alone. A Gestalt understanding of shame, remember, emphasizes the importance of the disconnect in the social field–a rupture which, if significant enough, is felt as a rupture in self-cohesiveness and self-process themselves (again, for a very clear exposition of these ideas in theoretical terms, see Lee, 1995). Thus it is not surprising to find, in this view, that the first and most urgent need, in healing and transforming deeply internalized shame, is an experience of knitting up that rupture, an experience of feeling and bearing shame together. Not "this is how you could fix that,"–at least, not at first–but "I too know that feeling, and how hard it is to bear." This applies to the group members with each other–and to all of us as therapists, caretakers, and/or parents as well. Fixing is likely to be felt as shaming, unless and until it has first been preceded by an experience of "just being there," and letting the person know that he/she is not alone in these feelings, which always threaten to take us into a sinking place of isolation, compensation through anger or denial, or some other lonely form of what psychoanalysis calls "acting out." All of these are ultimately ways of trying to manage in isolation, what can only be held and lived in a new way if it is held and lived in the company of other people.

Parenting in our individualistic, community-thin culture can be a terribly lonely experience; and loneliness, as a Gestalt field model of experience helps us to see more clearly, is inherently linked with shame. And shame itself is shameful, by the very terms of the individualist ideology we are so steeped in, in our culture, our own early and later experiences, and our inherited clinical models. Thus we have the ingredients of a pernicious circle, where isolation leads to shame, which is hidden and often only leads to more isolation, possibly fueling a destructive parenting dynamic of increasing inadequacy, and increasingly desperate or panicky attempts to heal the breach in the field of connectedness, and restore some sense of self as a worthwhile person, supported in an essential field of belonging–essential because without that sense, self-cohesion is impossible or at best impaired.

The only way to break this vicious circle, we believe, is with support–itself a shame-tinged concept in our dependency-phobic culture. It is this charged and difficult field, in our view, that must be lived in together with our clients, if our interventions to help problem parents (or just parents with problems) stabilize and reconnect are to be successful. We find the Gestalt model an essential map in negotiating this tricky field, so full of blind alleys and land mines that are the hidden sediment of our hyper-individualistic culture. When we receive our patients' and clients' experience, explore it without first aiming to correct it, and introduce a vocabulary of shame to name feelings that are often inaccessible or taboo, then we begin a joining that can spread through the field, offering some new ground of connection to ourselves and all of our children.

References

Ainsworth, M. (1979). Attachment as related to mother-infant interaction. In J. Rosenblatt, et al., (Eds.), *Advances in the study of behavior.* New York, NY: Academic Press.

Bowlby, J. (1969). *Attachment and loss.* New York, NY: Basic Books.

Darwin, C. (1872). *The expression of the emotions in man and animals.* London: John Murray.

Kaufman, G. (1989). *Shame: The power of caring.* Rochester, VT: Schenckman.

Lee, R. (1995). Gestalt and shame: The foundation for clearer understanding of field dynamics. *British Gestalt Journal, 4*(1), 14-22.

Tomkins, S. (1962). *Affect, imagery and consciousness, volume two.* New York, NY: Springer.

Wheeler, G. (1995). Self and shame. *British Gestalt Journal, 4*(2), 29-36.

Wheeler, G., & Jones, D.E. (1996). Finding our sons: A male-male gestalt. In R. Lee & G. Wheeler (Eds.), *The voice of shame: Silence and connection in psychotherapy*, (pp. 61-99). San Francisco, CA: Jossey-Bass.

10

Confluent/Constructivist Treatment of Children with Learning/Behavior Disorders

Joan A. Benevento

As a result of new research findings regarding the principles of learning, child development, cognitive psychology, and developmental psychopathology, psychology, and special education have shown gradual but persistent changes in their philosophies. These disciplines are now giving serious consideration to the creation and refinement of new intervention models for children and youths whose normal growth and development has gone awry (Sadler & Whimbey, 1985; Poplin, 1988).

The concepts of Gestalt therapy (Perls, 1947, 1969, 1973; Perls, Hefferline, & Goodman, 1951) and genetic epistemology (Piaget, 1968, 1970, 1971, 1972) have contributed to the many reconceptualizations in mental health and learning theory. Since the mid-1970s, as separate strands of thought, these theories have been used in the evaluation and remediation of the problems presented by children with learning/behavior disorders (Gelfand & Peterson, 1985).

Each has offered a set of propositions that give a phenomenological account of the processing of psychological development and a developmental explanation of behavior. Both theories deal with a psychological unfolding that is anchored in biological/sensorimotor roots and governed by the interaction between the individual child and his or her environment. Both consider behavior to be active, meaning-making adaptation that is built upon a sequence of emerging capacities. The child is viewed as an active processor of his or her own experiential data and relationships, who, at his or her level of maturity and comprehension, differentiates and restructures his or her self and the environment. It is from the specific organization of the child's subjective existence that ontological truths derive (Jacobs, 1992).

The growing awareness and wider acceptance of these constructs used to explain behavior have resulted in more focus on the importance of developmental changes in the learning process (Meltzer, 1993; Reid, 1988).

Confluent/Constructivist Treatment

The Gestalt therapy view of human behavior as reflecting biological processes, interpersonal experiences, and self-regulation shares a strong common ground with Piagetian consideration of human behavior as a reflection of physiological maturation, physical experience, social experience, and equilibration. A synthesis of the two can provide a cogent theoretical explanation of maladaptive behavior and knowledge acquisition and a sound foundation for psycho-educational treatment. The term confluent/constructivist treatment has been chosen in defining and interpreting this synthesis (Perls, et al, 1951; Piaget, 1974).

What follows is a description of how these similarities can be woven into a coherent, comprehensive treatment model that better facilitates the diagnosis and intervention of certain clinical conditions that occur in children who suffer deprivation of, and/or disruption in, their normal growth processes.

Gestalt therapy adopts the concepts of organismic self-regulation and the dynamic of chronically unfulfilled needs in the form of pathological Gestalten pushing into conscious awareness. For Perls, knowledge is the flowing together of the motoric, affective, and cognitive elements in a learning situation. The areas to be focused on are body awareness, development of positive self-concept, healthy interpersonal communication, adaptive decision-making, rational thinking, and values clarification. The most significant aim of psycho-educational treatment is fostering a positive self-image (Kelly, 1972; Brown, 1971).

Perls (1979) assumes that the basic human functions are orientation and manipulation. These functions demonstrate a process involving disturbances that upset the organismic equilibrium and actions that attempt to regain the equilibrium. It is through figure/background formation that a connection between orientation and manipulation is achieved. Development is facilitated by integration and arrested by dissociations.

Confluent education gives immediate justification for an interactional basis for treatment strategies by holding to the following beliefs that: (1) the cognitive content of the situation and the skills related to that content represent the environment, and (2) the affective dimension is the child's response to that environment. The purpose of confluent education is to recognize the legitimacy of affective goals, principally those stemming from fundamental human concerns, and to place these goals within the disciplined context of a total curriculum soundly constructed, effectively taught, properly sequenced, and carefully evaluated (Shiflett, 1975, p.127).

> ...as a maxim for child education: the child does not want affection, it even hates being suffocated with it. The child wants facilitation, that is, opportunity and assistance for his development (Perls, 1979, p. 12).

Kelly (1972) identifies five categories of a teaching/learning approach based on Gestalt principles: (1) sensory awareness, brought about through activities that finely tune decoding skills; (2) education-in-feeling, enhanced by techniques for releasing and expressing emotions; (3) body learning, advanced through activities to develop awareness of the interdependence of affect and body; (4) education-in-purpose, brought about by activities to help the child clarify his or her values and objectives (e.g., language, conceptual thought, and volition); and (5) the learning encounter, enhanced by marrying the emotions with the body and the intellect.

Piaget's genetic epistemology translates into constructivist education that holds that reality is arrived at through a dynamic interaction between each child and his or her environment. Piaget defines knowledge acquisition as the constant construction (or reconstruction) of a motor, cognitive, and affective structure that integrates one's experiences into meaningful gestalts (Kamii, 1975). Cognitive structures are developed, refined, and transformed by the processes of structural organization and self-regulation (Sigel, et al., 1981). What Piaget brings to a discussion of emotional factors in learning is a sense that feelings are natural accompaniments to, and not foreign intruders in, the intellectual endeavor. His approach indicates that working and playing with feelings is part and parcel of symbolic development (Cowan, 1978). Adaptation is seen as arising from the child's ability to make meaning of the interaction of his or her internal and external environments. A child's adaptive ability can be determined by knowing how he privately composes his or her experiences (Kegan, 1980).

Piaget explains developmental changes as happening through maturational processes stimulated by self-directed exploratory experiences. The child actively seeks stimulation and problem solutions that in turn promote mental growth (Gelfand & Peterson, 1985).

Common Conceptualizations

Underlying both Perls's Gestalt therapy and Piaget's genetic epistemology are the five powerful and major concepts of figure/ground relationships, self-regulation, contact, awareness, and experimentation.

Figure/ground relationships–Figure/ground formation is a basic tenet of any structuralistic, holistic philosophy. All parts of the organism are seen as being dynamically interrelated and each part can be understood only in relation to the other parts.

Gestalt therapy works from the premise that "figure" is the focus of interest and "ground" is the setting or context. The dynamic interplay between figure and ground is of great significance because the same ground may give rise to different figures, or the details of a given figure may themselves become ground as a more refined image emerges as figure.

In a like manner, a strong Piagetian theme holds that there are field effects or immediate interactions among elements perceived simultaneously in their mutual relations. Any element in the center of a perceptual (or cognitive) field is by this very fact overestimated, whereas the elements noncentered are devalued in relation to it, the overestimations or underestimations being proportional to the sizes of the elements considered.

Self-Regulation–The true theoretical core and the propelling force of both Perls and Piaget's thinking is the concept of organismic self-regulation, i.e., self-correction, accomplished by the self's functioning in the organism-environmental field. Both hold that the incentive for adaptation requires a balance between intrinsic factors and experiential factors. The organism is striving for the maintenance of a balance that is continually disturbed by its needs, and regained through their gratification or elimination. Equilibration is the process of intrinsic (self) regulation that balances assimilatory and accommodatory processes; compensates for external and internal disturbances (internal or external to a particular structure); and makes possible the development of more complex, hierarchically integrated operational structures (Perls, 1947, 1969; Perls, Hefferline, & Goodman, 1951; Piaget, 1968, 1972, 1973, 1976, 1981).

Self-regulation stresses the idea that the system is always in some sort of controlled tension. Piaget (1968) uses the terms assimilation and accommodation to describe the processes and results of self-regulation.

Assimilation is the integration of external elements into evolving or existing internal structures. It actively transforms what the child incorporates, blending the world to fit the child's existing structures. On the other hand, accommodation is the modification of the assimilating structure that is changed by the elements it encounters. It is, therefore, blending the child s structures to fit the world.

The child's existing cognitive structures are the means by which he uses assimilation and accommodation. Within any stage even if the child may be overly prominent in one function, he will eventually find some contradictions. This will cause the child to construct a new structure that resolves or compensates for the contradiction. The transformations signify attempts at integration among structures, as well as assimilation-accommodation interaction with the environment (Breslow, 1988).

It is from an imbalance of assimilation and accommodation that emotions emerge serving as an energizing force. This energizing force combines with cognition to cause the child to focus interest on specific objects and/or events in the environment. Affect helps to regulate a child's actions and determine his or her value systems. It influences the way in which a child avoids or approaches objects and/or events. It can accelerate, retard, or prevent how a child learns by influencing the rate of knowledge acquisition (Piaget, 1981).

Growth demands that the child has both assimilation and accommodation. Conceptually it is possible for assimilation to become instances of accommodation that in turn become departure points for further assimilation. Closure or conservation lies behind all assimilation; indefinite openness of choice, behind every accommodation (Furth, 1987).

These two drives working together motivate the child to maintain and develop him or herself. The closure tendency aims at keeping the child in balance with his or her environment. Connected to the equilibrium of a logical structure, it implies self-direction. Closed logical structures allow mental operations to move in any direction and return to the starting point. It is a necessary base for expansion, the second drive, which aims at the formation of new structures at a higher level of functioning. These two tendencies represent a developmental sequence that is valid for all areas and at all stages of development. The sequence follows accordingly: (1) conservation; (2) expansion; (3) disturbance; (4) compensation; (5) reconstruction; and (6) conservation (Furth, 1987).

Perls uses similar concepts. For him, the child is a unique system of needs that is self-regulatory if not disturbed in its process. All movement, all thought, or all emotion responds to a need. There is a need when something, either outside the child or within him or her, is changed. Behavior has to be adjusted as a function of this change. A need is always a manifestation of disequilibrium. The organism grows by assimilating what it needs at any given moment from the environment. What is taken in is destructured and parts are selectively transformed and absorbed. What has been assimilated reforms the contact boundaries and becomes part of the self-regulatory process. Every new accommodation is conditioned by existing assimilations.

The confluent/constructivist position holds that self-regulation refers to the natural development of such crucial cognitive milestones as object permanence, symbolic formation, conservation, and decentration (Piaget, 1972, 1973, 1981). Healthy self regulation allows these cognitive milestones to be experienced without triggering the psychological defenses, as described by Perls (1947, 1969, 1973), of confluence, introjection, projection, retroflection and deflection. That is, if they are allowed unimpaired growth, are not rushed to completion, and/or destroyed, good figure formation arises. A dialogue, free from fixated thinking and compartmentalization, is allowed to flow between the child's perspective and that of others (Latner, 1986).

Contact–Contact boundaries serve as the meeting places between the self and the environment where all psychological growth occurs. They are the points where the child either attempts to fit the environment to meet his or her internal structures or adapts his or her structures to the environmental pressures. The contact process itself is evolving, spiraling, and developing.

The child initially makes accidental contacts with objects located in his or her physical space. Gradually, he or she learns to reenact the movements that produce these contacts. Intellectual development results as the child makes changes in his or her behaviors. He or she seeks a balance between pressures from the environment and his or her efforts to change the environment (Perls, Hefferline, & Goodman, 1951; Piaget, 1970).

According to Piagetian thought, a child faced with particular problem first tries to solve it by assimilation, i.e., by attempting to use whatever knowledge or strategies he has available. When faced with a contradiction, the child's schemes of assimilation are no longer adequate and a state of disequilibrium results. Piaget (1970) describes three types of contact with the environment. The first, exercise, refers to the child's physical or mental activities that do not lead to any new knowledge (accommodation). At this level, if the child is aware of any contradiction, he will ignore the problem. Or, if aware but not sure if the new information really belongs in his or her established structures, he or she may form a new category of just the contradiction. Secondly, the child can make contact by what Piaget refers to as experience proper. However, this new knowledge is concerned only with discovery of properties and affirmations or, what is. The child is not aware of polarities, but does attempt to integrate the new information by changing his or her structures. The possibilities for his or her responding are extended. In the final type of contact, the child's reflection on his or her activities themselves leads to the discovery of negations or polarities. This involves an anticipation of a possible transformation and leads to an easy accommodation of structures to a variety of new information.

From a Gestalt therapy framework, ego boundaries serve as the places of contact. Experiencing the ego boundaries can be described from several vantage points. Sensations and movement help to provide the child with subject-object separation at body boundaries. Then, learning through an awareness of appropriate and inappropriate ways of demonstrating behavior and feelings leads the child to separate his or her emotions from those of others, and to establish contact points called expressive boundaries. As the child develops awareness of his or her habitual behaviors, and of his or her unwillingness and/or inability to try a new behavior or feeling, he or she comes to realize familiarity boundaries. The child also gradually learns how he or she avoids contact, that is, he or she develops exposure boundaries through an awareness of his or her reluctance to be observed and/or recognized, and of how he or she tries to avoids being so (Polster & Polster, 1973). Disturbances at the contact boundary are characterized by two things: (1) rigidity rather than movement, and (2) the absence of awareness rather than the ability to discriminate.

Awareness–Awareness is the process of being attuned to the most important elements in an individual-environment field with full psychomotor, affective, cognitive, and motivational support. It allows the child to respond to a given situation in a fashion appropriate to his or her needs and to the possibilities of the situation. As the child approaches rational consciousness, he or she arrives at an accurate awareness of his or her real nature as a person, his or her natural and social environments, and his or her connection to the outside world. A rationally conscious child is one whose perceptions are accurate and who has the ability to act on his or her accurate understanding of reality (Werner, 1982). For Piaget, awareness is the only basis of knowledge and communication and serves as the source of connections of meaning-making systems (Tenzer, 1983).

As a function of attention and concentration, awareness brings into the open all internal and disowned parts of the personality as well as external bodily senses and movements and the external environment itself. Awareness, especially of resistances and conflicts, aids in differentiating the functions of the organism–body, emotions, and thinking–and in taking responsibility for their functioning. It occurs when figure and ground do not form into a clear gestalt. Unmet needs, clamoring for attention at the point where nourishment or toxicity is possible, help to develop awareness.

Awareness evolves in a sequential fashion through the elaboration of the assimilatory function. The process begins with an initial need that results in systematic searching. At this point, there is no independence of what is searched for. The need is merely an extension of the child. As the need becomes stronger and the search increases, a dim awareness causes an adjustment to the concrete situation. Repetition of behavior aids in a separation of assimilation and accommodation.

Following this is an active search, but the searched-for-object is connected with the action. The need and the search are not yet separated. The search may be successful but the child may fail to transfer. He or she acts as if the object owes its existence to the action.

At the final stage the search is marked by an opening up to the outside world. The object of the search becomes the center of interest of its own (Swanson, 1988). Yontef (1988) provides a developmental sequence of awareness and awareness work. At first, there is the level of simple awareness during which the child is not conscious of the awareness process, being aware, or of his or her relationship with others. After this, he or she becomes aware of awareness, that is, of his or her own avoidant and resistant tendencies. This brings the child to the next level that is characterized by an awareness of the conditions and behaviors that lead to awareness and avoidance. Lastly comes the level of phenomenological awareness that results in the knowledge that there are always multiple realities. The child at this level can use repeated observations to achieve insight into the actual workings of a situation.

Following Piaget, Tenzer (1983) describes the process of insight in terms of stages. Insight cannot develop unless the child shows some degree of affect, sense of an experienced need, maturation, active involvement, and intentionality. These prerequisites characterize the initial stage of insight development. During stage two, the child still does not have insight, but his or her behaviors seem to be halfway between an unconscious state and awareness of them. At stage three, the child has greater reciprocity with the outside environment and can become involved in exploring the implication of his or her behavior. Next, the child develops a greater degree of self-observation. Insight can be generalized, i.e., what has been learned in previous stages is now incorporated into different aspects of the child's behavior. Finally, at the level of integration, the insight becomes the source of progress as well as the point for a reorganization of a great number of behaviors. This is not unlike the achievement of a new Gestalt. The child sees him or herself differently.

Experimentation–The experiment is the vital mechanism of integrated adaptation. It is an exploratory task, a trial, or a special observation made to discover something unknown or to establish some suggested or known truth. In short, it facilitates meaning making. Through the experiment, the child expands his or her capacity for accommodating to new perspectives rather than assimilating them unchanged into preexisting modes of thought. The experiment leads the child to an awareness of inconsistencies (1) in his or her perceptions, (2) between what he or she experiences and what he or she knows must be reality, (3) between what he or she feels and thinks, and (4) between what he or she does and says about what he or she is doing. It can be used to counter the deadlock the child may be facing by his or her inability to decentrate or his or her inability to assimilate and accommodate adaptively (Perls, Hefferline, and Goodman, 1951; Piaget, 1981).

Subject-Object Separation

Subject-object separation on each level of development is imperative for the establishment of reality. Each level demands that a whole new course of subject-object separation be run in order for equilibrium to be achieved.

Development begins with organismic/sensorimotor behavior during which the child engages in movement to find solutions to problems. Movement is the primary building block of true knowledge. The child lacks knowledge outside his or her actions and establishes subject-object separation through the construction of closure of actions. There is a progressive awareness of the self as the agent of its own actions. With an emerging awareness of his or her own activities, an infant organizes his or her actions by coordinating and differentiating them into practical acts of intelligence which Piaget (1981) considers a logic of action. These actions are later organized into semilogical structures and preoperatory systems through the use of symbolic functions.

As the child begins to solve problems through symbolic functioning, defined as internal representation or thinking, he establishes a subject-object separation through the construction of closure of symbols. The child cannot only evolve a mental image, but he can also internally imagine a series of actions with that image without motorically acting on it. With an emerging awareness of his or her own symbol usage, the child organizes them by coordinating and differentiating them into a logic of the symbolic functions. The child gradually comes to recognize the self as the agent of his symbols and representations. However, at this stage he or she is restricted to static imagery and to his or her own perspective. Using his or her perspective as the ultimate standard, he has little ability in anticipating how things might appear to someone else. As thought develops through the medium of symbolic functions, they continue to evolve into concrete operations.

The concrete operational child can engage in logical manipulation of part-whole (figure/ground) relationships. He establishes subject-object separation through the construction of closure of the rules that govern these relationships. This provides a framework for logical transformations of thoughts and feelings. With these newly acquired cognitive skills the child is no longer fooled in problems that involve conflicts between logic and perception. The child comes to recognize the self as the agent of his or her own rules/transformations. These transformations are carried out primarily through the function of conservation that leads the child to acquire a sense of the perspective of others. Through mastery of conservation, he can now attend to all aspects of a transformation and can see correspondences between various transformed states, that is, figure-ground relationships. This signifies thought reversibility. Now, being able to anticipate what will happen to an object or person under various conditions, the child appreciates that an object or person can at once have different roles. One remaining problem is that the child has difficulty applying these logical abilities in non-concrete situations (Inhelder & Piaget, 1964). Eventually, in normal growth and development, the concrete operations become the formal hypothetical-deductive characteristics of adolescent thought.

The formal operational child establishes subject-object separation through the construction of closure of logical cognitive systems that provide a framework for hypothetical thought. The child gradually comes to recognize the self as the agent of his or her own thinking (value) system. Hypothetical thought provides the criteria that can lead to rational objectivity. At this most developed level the child becomes capable of applying logical thought to all classes of verbal and emotional problems in all time/space variations. He is convinced simply by the power of the word (Rosen, 1991). (See Appendix A.)

Children with Learning/Behavior Disorders

Children with psychomotor, affective, and cognitive disorders manifest special difficulties with the abovementioned processes. In Piaget's terms, these children consistently show structural delays in at least four important conceptual abilities: (1) object permanence; (2) symbolic formation; (3) conservation; and (4) egocentrism. Perls would describe them as suffering from deficiencies in modes of self/environmental contact, either being invested too much in the self or too much in the environment. Attending to these difficulties can bring the child with learning/behavior disorders closer to his or her own reality.

These children can so alienate themselves, or be so alienated from their self-processes, that awareness of self and/or environment is minimized. They can experience negative attitudes, feelings of rejection, low self-esteem, lack of personal initiative, and discouragement. Any or all of these symptoms can interfere with self-regulating and prosocial processes (Elias & Maher, 1983).

In comparison to non-disordered children, those with disorders often show inadequate:

- body awareness and coordination;
- sensory systems that consistently and correctly register information;
- attention span;
- memory skills;
- understanding of non-verbal situations;
- temperament/environment match;
- powers of abstract thinking;
- predictable, cooperative, prosocial behaviors;
- ability to consistently stay on-task;
- ability to consistently use effective social contact attempts.

The child's particular abilities and knowledge base interact with environmental/situational demands and continually change throughout the developmental process. In the case of a learning/behavior problem, a mismatch occurs between the child s learning style and skills and the task demands. This child often lacks the ability to access his or her knowledge base spontaneously and automatically and to coordinate his or her skills, processes and attributes effectively. Helping the child discover his or her own assimilatory and accommodatory patterns of behavior and how he coordinates these functions across domains promotes changes in the child's thinking and feelings.

Dysfunctions in Assimilation and Accommodation

The mechanisms of assimilation and accommodation are believed to operate at all developmental levels. They create and modify structures. If accommodation and assimilation are present in all activity, their ratio may vary, and only the more or less stable equilibrium that may exist between them characterizes a complete act of intelligence (Perls, Hefferline, & Goodman, 1951; Piaget, 1968).

The concepts of assimilation and accommodation have been applied to the affective domain. Structural deficits may result from a strong and maladaptive predominance of either assimilation or accommodation. For example, imperviousness to environmental feedback can be seen as maladaption in the form of over-assimilation while over-conformity and over-responsiveness to the environment is considered maladaption in the form of over-accommodation. The behavior of some learning/behavior-disordered children may have pervasive assimilative or accommodative styles (Breslow, 1988).

Any dysfunction of these mechanisms might therefore contribute to either a lack of attainment of the age-appropriate structures or an asynchrony in their balance. Or, a strong and non-adaptive predominance of either assimilation-over-accommodation or accommodation-over-assimilation may exist. Finally, functional imbalance may result from the child's difficulties in coordinating reasoning across different areas of knowledge (Gordon, 1988).

Over-assimilation–Perserverating on a stance to the point of over-assimilation blocks adaptation to reality and hinders the development of psychological structures. In an over-assimilative frame of reference, a child is unable to tolerate likeness. There is surrender to an overvalued autonomy and self-sufficiency. Such a child is isolated and taken over by self in order to maintain separation. He or she demands rigidly closed boundaries that are experienced as a safe refuge from invasion. He or she is unable to tolerate neediness that he sees as weakness. Such a child avoids what he or she experiences as being swallowed up and taken over by others (Swanson, 1988). The child may withdraw or refuse to elaborate on his or her own reactions to situations involving others. This may be manifested in the child's elaboration of personal feelings without the consideration of the alternative perspectives.

Over-assimilation is apparent when the child insists on the acceptance and accuracy of personal interpretations of interpersonal problems; consistently blames others; and has difficulty with modifying interpretations of him or herself or of others by considering different viewpoints (Gordon, 1988). This resistance to contact at any price, results in a loss of the other. The characteristics of an object are not accounted for. The child centers on his or her own actions and his or her own viewpoint resulting in egocentrism. At an extreme pathological degree, behavior may be seen as autistic.

In over-assimilation the child resists integrating particular experiences into a higher-order system. An earlier developed structure is used even though a more developed structure exists and becomes encapsulated. The encapsulations are dependent upon the developmental level of the earlier structures to which they are associated and they:

> ...can be more physical (based on magical thinking, focused on the body-self and images of bodily survival during physical separation), concrete-action oriented (based on a view of the self as an agent that acts on the world or needs to manipulate the world deceptively to achieve need gratification), or psychological (a state where feelings are expressed in symbolic form around identification with others) (Noam, 1988, p.108).

Over-accommodation–In over-accommodation, the child cannot tolerate difference. He or she demands and moves toward likeness with the environment. Surrendering to sameness, the child uses a hanging on mode of contact even at the possibility of a loss of self. He or she risks being swallowed up and taken over by others in order to maintain a connection (Swanson, 1988). Dependent conformity to, and/or a denial of personal interpretations of the environment may interfere with the creative modification of internal structures. This withdrawal, through the refusal or inability to expand upon personal reactions to environmental situations, represents the over-accommodative position (Gordon, 1988).

Over-accommodation is manifested in either a maladaptive conformity to the environment or a denial of personal interpretations of events and may prevent the creative modification of structures. There may be withdrawing behavior, which is the refusal or inability to elaborate ones own reactions to situations involving others or to elaborate personal feelings (Gordon, 1988). The characteristics of the self are not accounted for. The child centers on the actions and viewpoints of others, resulting in other-centeredness. The course of perception, cognition, action or affect is directed by an external structure. If this is incorporated into a child's internal structure, it will shape experience and behavior. This imitative stance is similar to rote knowledge and is not apt to result in reconstruction that allows for further accommodation. Contact is non-existent, weak, or faulty since merging and a loss of boundary occur through behaviors that are fluid, permeable, and dissolving (Swanson, 1988). At an extreme pathological degree, behavior may be seen as schizophrenic (Furth, 1987).

Healthy contact offers free options from logical alternatives. There is awareness and no loss of ego-functions to unawareness (Davidove, 1988). On the other hand, Smith (1988) defines psychopathology as any pattern of habitual self-interruption in the contact/withdrawal cycles (p. 40). Self-interruptions can come in the form of blocked excitement or blocked action; colluded awareness by introjection, projection, confluence, deflection, or retroflection. It can be manifested in self-absorbing attempts to influence the environment while not allowing any other object to be an influence.

When the child's ability to engage the environment becomes dysfunctional, he becomes stuck at or near one of the poles of contact or withdrawal. Unhealthy or dysfunctional contact involves chronic conditions of too much or too little contact with the environment (Crocker, 1992).

Confluence–Confluence exemplifies an over-accommodative boundary stance. There is too much of the environment residing in the organism and an absence of experiencing the other as different from the self. With the inability to differentiate between him or herself and the environment, the child feels as if he or she is the entire field or the field is entirely him or her. There are no definitively established ego boundaries. In addition, the child experiences no separation from self-as subject and self-as-object. Part-whole relationships are blurred. With no sense of object permanence, space, time, or causality, there is no distinction between assimilation and accommodation (Brown & Merry, 1985; Davidove, 1988; Latner, 1982). Confluence within the same boundary leads to childhood schizophrenia and psychosis; and away from the same boundary, to autism.

Introjection–Introjection is an attempt to avoid assimilation (Latner, 1982). It can be understood as a process in which the child has taken in information but has not assimilated it into his or her system. His or her internal structures are altered to fit the environment before they become a truly absorbed part. The introjected action, emotion, or value is taken into the child's system in such a way that it is not genuinely his or hers. The child justifies as normal what is in reality unassimilated and metaphorically experienced as an alien body. However, even though it is actually unassimilated, the child will resist its dislodgement. He or she gives up his or her point of view and does not reverse the demands the environment makes. The child will not act aggressively upon the environment to extract what is needed. Authority will not be questioned (Smith, 1988). The boundary of the environment is somehow moved into the self (Brown & Merry, 1985). The environment can be described as an overpowering permanent object. Space, time, and causality are determined from outward to inward. There is salience of the norm(s) of the other.

According to Smith (1988), there is no self-other confusion in introjection. Confusion does, however, lie in ownership of a need, emotion, or value. Introjection indicates a state of inadequacy and confused awareness concerning the self as a perceiving agent. The self-as-subject, takes in too much of the environment, while the self-as-object, acts "as if" (a pseudo-assimilation). The child over-accommodates.

Retroflection–Retroflection indicates that some function that was originally intended to be directed from the child into the environment somehow was redirected back toward the child. Attempts to change the environment are thwarted and the intended energy is turned back against the child (Brown & Merry, 1985). The child acts as if a part of him or herself is in the environment. He treats this part as he or she would like to treat the environment. In retroflected interaction, the needed environmental object is not present for satisfaction. The child gives up any attempt to influence the environment. He or she reinvests his or her energy into the intrapersonal system and becomes divided (Latner, 1982).

In retroflection part of the organism is made the environment of another part of the organism (Davidove, 1988). It can be compared to having two permanent objects and two viewpoints within the same system. In one intrapersonal boundary system, the child has self-as-subject assimilating and self-as -object accommodating. The assimilation and accommodation both take place within the ego boundary, not at the ego boundaries. There is a negating, holding back, or balancing of the impulse tension by additional, opposing sensorimotor tension. Activity at the contact boundary is seriously diminished. Introspection, intellectualization, and withdrawal are characteristics of the child who uses retroflection as a defense. He often feels chronic fatigue and tension.

Projection–The child who projects does not distinguish clearly between the internal and external worlds. There is an overextension into the environment. The child attributes to the environment those personality characteristics with which he or she cannot identify. An action, emotion, or idea that actually belongs to the child's own personality, but is not experienced as such, is attributed to the environment, and is then experienced as being directed toward him or her. It is the tendency of the child to hold the environment responsible for what should be attributed to him or herself (Brown & Merry, 1985). The intent of putting some part of him or herself into the environment is to exclude that part from awareness (Latner, 1982). The projector places parts of him or herself into the immediate environment and often feels assailed by those same characteristics in those around him or her. Authority is held in suspicion and is often questioned (Smith, 1988).

With his or her ego boundaries having been moved out into the environment, the child often feels split or empty in his feeling and behaviors (Brown & Merry, 1985). Causality is often reversed and can be described as coming from inward to outward and back again. Projection indicates a state of confused awareness concerning the self as perceiving agent. There is a state of division in the same intrapersonal system. The self-as-subject, rather than assimilating the unwanted and/or unrecognized parts of him or herself, ascribes them to the environment and then assimilates them as self-as-object. The child can experience actor/acted upon, real self/ideal self, partial object/whole object splits.

Deflection–Deflection exemplifies a state in which contact with the environment is made on a hit-or miss basis. The child either does not invest enough energy to get a reasonable return or he or she invests it without focus and it scatters and evaporates. The child winds up depleted with a dulled awareness and a lack of perceptual sharpness (Smith, 1988).

Deflection finds the child diverting responses from their intended targets and expressing them elsewhere in the environment. Any figure, prevented from taking its most coherent form, is rushed to completion, closed and destroyed (Latner, 1982). The child who deflects often attempts to diffuse contact through the overuse of humor, abstract generalization, and questions rather than statements. There is a significant inconsistent pattern of assimilation and accommodation (Frew, 1986).

The child must experience sufficient exposure to situations in which he or she can assimilate and accommodate. Without much opportunity to encounter other persons' points of view, he or she may be hindered in the ability to modify his or her own personal viewpoint. Or, he or she may not have much occasion to use his or her already formed ideas. In either case, cognitive development may be hindered (Gordon, 1988).

Treatment

A purposeful, integrated intervention strategy approach maintains that the transactional relationship among cognition, affect, and motor behaviors presents a critical need for the clinician to consider the situational, cultural, and ecological variables of the individual child. It strives to ensure that each child achieves that amount of integration that facilitates his or her further development. The overall objective is the development of self-regulated learners (Graham & Harris, 1993). This is no less true for children who experience developmental delays.

Knowledge of the functional requirements of various stages of development provides an appreciation of the demands placed upon the child at each age, and clearly shows how developmental disorders can present particular compromises at each stage. When the spectrum of difficulties of learning/behavior disorders is seen from a developmental perspective, there are special implications for treatment and prevention (Saxe, Cross, & Silverman, 1988).

Since all developmental stages involve promoting and balancing assimilation and accommodation across different domains of knowledge and emotions, the ability to coordinate judgments from all the different domains can facilitate the making of more adaptive life decisions (Gordon, 1988).

In working with the learning/behavior disordered child important foci to be considered are:

(1) how disruptions and delays in development affect the domains of information processing;

(2) how clinicians can help the child with learning/behavior disorders integrate the different levels of processing into the construction of adaptive experiences;

(3) how positive change in one behavioral domain can bring about positive change in another (Goldberg et al., 1983).

Essentially cognitive structures arise from the child's making his or her own meaning of the intrapersonal and interpersonal worlds. Therefore, activities of the child must have primary treatment emphasis. In order to enhance optimal immediate adaptation and future cognitive and emotional maturity, the child must learn to envision alternatives, evaluate alternatives, engage in perspective taking, and reason according to his or her current developmental level (Gordon, 1988).

Meaning-making is always a constructivist activity guided by the inner logic of the child's achieved developmental level and transformed by interactions with others. Changes in reality result from an understanding of behavior that, in turn, come from the conscious awareness of conflict or contradiction. Inner conflicts are, for the most part, reliable in the sense that they can be trusted to be attempts at self-regulation. If inner conflicts are brought into awareness, they can be incorporated with existing information for conflict resolution. Conflicts should not be dissolved, but resolved (Werner, 1982).

In order to know objects and/or events, the child must act upon them, and therefore transform them. He must displace, connect, take apart, and reassemble them. At times, what a child knows and what he reports he is doing is not in accord with what he actually does. If these discrepancies become of interest to him, he may try to make sense of them. Because of this awareness, he may search for new ways to understand and regulate his or her behavior, ways that are subject to conscious control. The most effective form of self-observation is to have the child describe what he or she is doing doing it. Even though such self-observations may be inaccurate, the child nevertheless focuses attention on what would otherwise be automatic behavior. Stopping to think about what he or she is doing may cause an opening of a crack that leads the child to an exploration of a cognitive gap and a heightened level of awareness (Piaget, 1976).

Any comprehensive treatment paradigm founded upon the principles of Gestalt therapy and genetic epistemology necessarily concerns itself with (1) the body's sensations and actions; (2) affect as well as cognition in an attempt to inculcate and foster positive interpersonal relations; (3) here and now awareness; and (4) assimilation/accommodation balance. Such an approach would provide a child with the best chance of experiencing all kinds of important motor-cognitive-affective connections in order to help him or her begin to separate him or herself from the environment.

A confluent/constructivist approach for a learning/behavior disordered child, would design strategies specifically to:

(1) Evaluate the child in terms of limitations and distortions in his

or her awareness of reality and then strive to bring these limitations and distortions to a closer approximation of reality. What a child needs to become aware of is the real nature of him or herself, his or her relationships, and his or her environment. Awareness techniques make possible the discovery, or recovery, of ego skills.

(2) Encourage the child to transform the organizational structures he or she has already developed. By permitting the child him or herself to decide which figure he or she would like to attend to, the clinician can assume that existing related organizations are being engaged. By requiring the child to use the figures in the appropriate context, the clinician can elicit a wide range of responses (Giordano, 1981).

(3) Inquire if, and how, any learning and/or behavior disorder interferes with self-regulation. Does a learning/behavior disorder interrupt the systematic functioning of the developmental milestones and contribute to the formation of the mechanisms of confluence, introjection, retroflection, projection, and deflection? Is there limited interaction or contact with others? (Latner, 1986)

(4) Foster within the child the integration of polar opposites through centering, as well as through accepting, rather than analyzing, experiences.

(5) Determine the direction of any pathologic imbalance between assimilation and accommodation so that the non-dominant function can evolve. As a counterbalance to the imbalance, tipped in either direction, the clinician must first encourage the child to engage in activities that focus on the non-dominant functional mechanism. Treatment must be flexible enough to adopt either an assimilative or accommodative stress.

Therefore, the clinician working with a learning/behavior disordered child must learn how to help him or her: (1) conceptualize his or her behavior as a search for meaning; (2) monitor his or her comprehension to ensure that meaning indeed is derived; (3) engage him or her in strategic behavior to bring meaning to behavior when there has been a break in comprehension; and (4) modify his or her choice of strategies to meet the various demands of adaptation.

Both Perls and Piaget offer approaches that strive to get children to obtain closure from the "cause" rather than the "victim" position. Piaget's theory points out the dynamic changes in cognitive self-regulation associated with specific developmental phases while Perls's theory points out the dynamic changes in emotional self-regulation associated with specific awareness phases. The integration of the two theories does not diminish or eliminate the principles of either one. Rather it can be used to more comprehensively inform the choice of intervention.

References

Breslow, L., (Ed.). (1988). Possibilities and pitfalls in clinical application of cognitive-developmental theory. *New Directions for Child Development, 39*, 147-164.

Brown, G. (1971). *Human teaching for human learning: An introduction to confluent education*. New York, NY: Viking Press.

Brown, G., & Merry, U. (1985). Neurotic mechanisms applied to organizations. *The Gestalt Journal, 8*, 49-85.

Cicchetti, D. (1984). The emergence of developmental psychopathology. *Child Development, 55*, 1-7.

Cowan, P. A. (1978). *Piaget with feeling: Cognitive, social, and emotional dimensions*. New York, NY: Holt, Rinehart and Winston.

Crocker, S. (1992). A philosophical framework for understand ing developmental issues. Paper presented at the 14th annual meeting of The Theory and Practice of Gestalt Therapy, Boston, MA.

Davidove, D. (1988). Exhibitionism in disarray. *The Gestalt Journal, 11*, 61-80.

Elias, M., & Maher, C. (1983). Social and affective development of children: A programmatic. *Exceptional Children, 49*, 339-346.

Furth, H. (1987). *Knowledge as desire: An essay on Freud and Piaget*. New York, NY: Columbia Press.

Frew, J. (1986). The functions and patterns of occurrence of contact styles during the developmental phases of the Gestalt group. *The Gestalt Journal, 8*, 55-60.

Gelfand, D., & Peterson, L. (1985). *Child development and psychopathology*. Beverly Hills, CA: Sage.

Giordano, G. (1981). The re-emergence of Gestalt psychology and implications for reading readiness. *Journal of Learning Disabilities, 14*, 121-123.

Goldberg, A., Sprafkin, R., Gershaw, J., & Klien, P. (1983). Structured learning: A psychoeducational approach for teaching social competencies. *Behavioral Disorders, 8*, 161-170.

Gordon, D. (1988). Formal operations and interpersonal and affective disturbances in adolescents. *New Directions for Child Development, 39*, 51-73.

Graham, S., & Harris, K. (1993). Teaching writing strategies to students with learning disabilities: Issues and recommendation. In L. Meltzer (Ed.), *Strategy assessment and instruction for students with learning disabilities: From theory to practice*, (pp. 271-292). Austin, TX: PRO-ED.

Inhelder, B., & Piaget, J. (1964). *The early growth of logic in the child.* London: Routledge & Kegan Paul.

Inouye, D., & Jacobs, L. (1992). Insights from psychoanalytic self-psychology and intersubjectivity theory for Gestalt therapists. *The Gestalt Journal, 15*, 25-60.

Kamii, C. (1975). One intelligence indivisible. *Young Children, 30*, 228-238.

Kegan, R. (1980), Making meaning: The constructive-developmental approach to persons and practice. *Personnel and Guidance Journal, 58*, 373-380.

Kelly, C. R. (1972). *The new education.* Santa Monica, CA: Interscience Research Institute.

Latner, J. (1982). The thresher of time: On love and freedom in Gestalt therapy. *The Gestalt Journal, 5*, 20-38.

Latner, J. (1986). Spelling out structures. *The Gestalt Journal, 9*, 23-29.

Meltzer, J., (Ed.). (1993). *Strategy assessment and instruction for students with learning disabilities: From theory to practice.* Austin, TX: Pro-Ed.

Noam, G. (1988). A constructivist approach to developmental psychopathology. *New Directions for Child Development, 39*, 90-121.

Perls, F. (1947). *Ego, hunger and aggression: The beginnings of gestalt therapy.* New York, NY: Vintage Books.

Perls, F. (1969). *Gestalt therapy verbatim.* Moab, UT: Real People Press.

Perls, F. (1973). *The gestalt approach and eye witness to therapy.* Palo Alto, CA: Science and Behavioral Books.

Perls, F. (1979). Planned psychotherapy. *The Gestalt Journal, 2*, 4-23.

Perls, F., Hefferline, R., & Goodman, P. (1951). *Gestalt therapy: Excitement and growth in the human personality.* New York, NY: Dell.

Piaget, J. (1968). *Six psychological studies.* New York, NY: Vintage Books.

Piaget, J. (1970a). *Main trends in psychology.* London: George Allen & Unwin Ltd.

Piaget, J. (1970b). *Structuralism.* New York, NY: Basic Books.

Piaget, J. (1971a). *Biology and knowledge.* Chicago, IL: University of Chicago Press.

Piaget, J. (1971b). Piaget's theory. In P.H. Mussen (Ed.), *Carmichael's man-*

ual of child psychology, third edition, (pp. 702-733). New York, NY: John Wiley & Sons.

Piaget, J. (1972). Intellectual evolution from adolescence to adulthood. *Human Development, 15*, 1-12.

Piaget, J. (1973). *The child and reality: Problems of genetic epistemology*, A. Rosin (Trans.). New York, NY: Grossman.

Piaget, J. (1974). *Development des qualities chez l'enfant*. London: Routledge & Kegan Paul.

Piaget, J. (1976). *The grasp of consciousness: Action and concept in the young child*. Cambridge, MA: Harvard University Press.

Piaget, J. (1981). *Intelligence and affectivity: Their relationship during child development*. Palo Alto, CA: University of California Press.

Piaget, J. (1981). *The psychology of intelligence*. Totowa, NJ: Littlefield, Adams & Co.

Piaget, J., & Garcia, R. (1991). *Toward a logic of meaning*. Hillsdale, NJ: Lawrence Erlbaum.

Polster, E., & Polster, M. (1973). *Gestalt therapy integrated*. New York, NY: Brunner/Mazel.

Poplin, M. (1988). The reductionist fallacy in learning disabilities: Replicating the past by reducing the present. *Journal of Learning Disabilities, 21*, 389-400.

Reid, D. (1988). Reflections on the pragmatics of a paradigm shift. *Journal of Learning Disabilities, 21*, 417-420.

Rosen, H. (1991). Constructivism, personality, psychopathology, and psychology. In D. P. Keating & H. Rosen (Eds.), *Constructivistic perspectives on developmental psychopathology and atypical development*, (pp. 149-172). Hillsdale, NJ: Lawrence Erlbaum.

Sadler, W., & Whimbey, A. (1985). A holistic approach to improving thinking skills. *Phi Delta Kappan, 67*, 199-203.

Saxe, L., Cross, T., & Silverman, N. (1988). Children's mental health: The gap between what we know and what we do. *American Psychologist, 43*, 800-807.

Seltzer, L. (1984). The role of paradox in Gestalt theory. *The Gestalt Journal, 7*, 31-42.

Shiflett, J. (1975). Beyond vibration teaching: research and curriculum development in confluent education. In G. Brown (Ed.), *The live classroom: Innovation through confluent education and gestalt*, (pp. 121-131). New York, NY: Penguin Press.

Sigel, I., Brodzinsky, D., & Golinkoff, R. (1981). *New directions in*

Piagetian theory and practice. Hillsdale, NJ: Lawrence Erlbaum.

Smith, E. (1988). Self-interruptions in the rhythm of contact and withdrawal. *The Gestalt Journal, 11*, 37-58.

Swanson, J. (1988). Boundary processes and boundary states. *The Gestalt Journal, 11*, 5-24.

Tenzer, A. (1983). Piaget and psychoanalysis: Some reflections on insight. *Contemporary Psychoanalysis, 19*, 126-136.

Werner, H. (1982), *Cognitive therapy: A humanistic approach.* New York, NY: Free Press

Yontef, G. (1988). Comments on boundary processes and boundary states. *The Gestalt Journal, 11*, 25-36.

Appendix A

Guidelines for Assessing Behaviors at the Various Piagetian Stages

1. Sensorimotor

To what extent and in what way does the child:

a. have any recognition of him or herself and his or her actions?
b. experience any sense of separation of his or her actions from him or herself?
c. have any recognition of others and their actions?
d. experience any sense that others see themselves as being separate from their own actions?
e. select actions from his or her repertoire?
f. incorporate received actions into his or her repertoire?
g. see objects as sharing a common physical space?
h. use available objects as means to achieve a goal?
i. understand spatial arrangements among objects located in his or her immediate physical surround?
j. understand spatial arrangements among objects moving through familiar space?
k. cause a reoccurrence of various events and thus reveal

his or her concept of the cause of these events?
l. have evocative memory; i.e., permanent object?

2. Preoperational

To what extent and in what way does the child:

a. have any recognition of him or herself and his or her symbols?
b. experience any sense of separation of his symbols from him or herself?
c. have any recognition of others and their symbols?
d. experience any sense that other see themselves as being separate from their symbols?
e. select symbols from his or her repertoire?
f. incorporate received symbols into his or her repertoire?
g. see symbols as sharing a common psychological space?
h. use available symbols as means to achieve a goal?
i. understand sequential mental arrangements among symbols located in his or her immediate psychological surround?
j. understand sequential mental arrangements among symbols moving through familiar psychological space?
k. cause a reoccurrence of various symbols and thus reveal his or her concept of the cause and sequence of these symbols and what they represent?
l. differentiate between symbols and their referents?
m. differentiate between his or her self-created symbols and reality?

3. Concrete Operational

To what extent and in what way does the child:

a. have any recognition of him or herself and his or her knowledge of part/whole relationships?
b. experience any sense of separation of his or her knowledge of part/whole relationships from him or herself?
c. have any recognition of others and their knowledge of

part/whole relationships?

d. experience any sense that other see themselves as being separate from their knowledge of part/whole relationships?

e. select knowledge of part/whole relationships from his or her repertoire?

f. incorporate received knowledge of part/whole relationships into his or her repertoire?

g. see part/whole relationships as sharing a common psychological space?

h. transform available knowledge of part/whole relationships as means to achieve a goal?

i. understand simultaneous transformations among part/whole relationships located in his or her immediate psychological surround?

j. understand simultaneous transformations among part/whole relationships moving through familiar psychological space?

k. cause a reoccurrence of various part/whole relationships and thus reveal his or her concept of the cause and interactions of these part/whole relationships?

l. combine and recombine parts without distorting the parts or the whole?

m. have a value hierarchy by which he can evaluate how his or her own behaviors play a role in his situations?

n. can take mental detours or alternate routes to the same goal?

o. see the others viewpoint in a two-person situation?

4. Formal Operational

To what extent and in what way does the child:

a. have any recognition of him or herself and his or her ideational systems?

b. experience any sense of separation of his or her ideational systems from him or herself?

c. have any recognition of others and their ideational systems?

d. experience any sense that others see themselves as being separate from their own ideational systems?
e. select ideational systems from his or her repertoire?
f. incorporate received ideational systems into his or her repertoire?
g. see ideational systems as sharing a common psychological space?
h. use available ideational systems as means to achieve a goal?
i. understand mental arrangements among ideational systems located in his or her immediate psychology surround?
j. understand mental arrangements among ideational systems moving through familiar psychological space? (Comparison of ideational systems?)
k. cause a reoccurrence of various ideational systems and thus reveal his or her concept of the cause and relationship of these ideational systems?
l. arrange elements in an ideational system in such a way as to systematically test all possible combinations?
m. coordinate two ideational systems rather than two variables or relationships?
n. distinguish each party's point of view from that of a third person; i.e., be an impartial spectator in a two-person situation?
o. think about his or her own ideational systems?
p. see him or herself in an infinite variety of possibilities?
q. see himself as having a balanced ideational system?

11

A Gestalt Developmental Model for Working with Young Children

Steven Wexberg

As a pediatrician, I have been trained to be supportive and diagnostically oriented. My interventions are often prescriptive and focused, designed to suggest to patients and their parents what actions I feel will yield a fairly rapid resolution of their presenting problem. As a Gestalt therapist, I have been trained to observe process and to share my observations and my curiosity about what I see. If these observations are communicated in a supportive and contactful manner, the clients' changed awarenesses will support their contacting their environment in a more functional manner, thereby meeting their needs more fully.

Thus there are some striking differences in my posture and interventions between these two settings–and yet some fundamental similarities as well. As a pediatrician I am very goal-oriented, and many of these goals are quite specific. As a therapist I am aware of goals for my clients and myself, but my stance is much more process-oriented, as befits the larger goal of supporting the client's developing self-process. Specific goals are less clearly defined, and the path toward these new ways of functioning is much less predictable, at times circuitous.

In both situations, however, I am acutely aware that most of the time the healing or growing that is to occur happens primarily because of the orientation of the clients: their innate tendencies generally move them toward health. A child with fever and diarrhea tends to sleep more and eat less. These changes make it easier for her body to repair itself. A psychotherapy client tends to become curious about what isn't working for him, when this curiosity is supported in the therapy session. If these healthful tendencies are clearly identified and supported, the individual's healing will likely be more expedient and complete. My role in both situations is to augment and support these inherent processes.

In this chapter, I try to blend useful aspects from both of these backgrounds in order to present an approach to early childhood development that is both practical and grounded in Gestalt theory. To illustrate these points, I will be using specific examples from the process of toilet training, to translate theory into a practical approach. In the process, I will share a way of looking at human development in general that uses the Gestalt Contact Cycle model as its template.

Long before the advent of psychotherapy and psychological theories, human beings were successfully navigating the range of developmental tasks before them as they grew to adulthood. They learn to take in nutrients, to become mobile, to make relationships, and find a productive place in the context of a family and a community. They observe their environment, taking in information that enables them to change, survive, and become more independent while continuing to meet their needs, both on their own and with others. Later on, people discover or invent ways to move through adulthood, support the continuation of their species, and ultimately approach a time of waning vitality and death. At any point in time, in order to satisfy a particular need a person creates a "best possible solution" given her context and what she perceives as available to her. This holds true whether we are talking about an infant trying to get food (when crying and rooting are all he can muster), or a single parent of four trying to make ends meet and hold together a family.

This developmental journey through life does not occur in isolation. Gestalt theory emphasizes that each and every developmental progression occurs within a context. Neither the individual nor the environment exists in isolation. As a person evolves, so does the field of which he is a part. To assess a person's development adequately, one must look at that individual with a broad enough lens to take in the whole picture: individual and his environment. At every point in a person's life there exists a developmental field which incorporates who he is, the developmental tasks he has accomplished, tasks on the horizon, his temperament, where he lives, who is in his immediate world, others' wants and needs, as well as all the needs of the individual and the needs, demands, constraints, and resources of the environment. Any human's development is a product of the creative integration necessary to balance these simultaneous needs and conditions. These two dimensions, self and environment (including social environment), together create the field. With growth come change and a new balance of the entire field. We have evolved in such a way that the ability to evolve, to creatively adapt, is itself part of our intrinsic being. In Gestalt theory this is the basic principle and process of organismic self-regulation and growth. This process, juxtaposed with the fundamental drive of the child, adolescent, or adult to master new and larger realms of living as part of a field, becomes the foundation for a Gestalt developmental model.

If unimpeded by her environment or intrinsic disabilities, a child's development will move forward of its own accord in a productive and healthful manner. Suppose a particular infant does not like to be on her stomach. Her parents may ask me, "Do we have to place her on her stomach? Will she learn to roll over even if we don't put her in that position, which she doesn't like?" She absolutely will! You couldn't stop her short of tying her down. Barring severe physical disability, all children will learn by themselves to roll over–and they don't stop there. Most children, for instance, toward the end of their first year of life, develop a preference for feeding themselves, often refusing or even "rebelling" if a parent continues trying to feed them. As this occurs the entire field shifts. The child is no longer a "spoon-fed baby;" the parent no longer the "spoon feeder," and who they are to each other takes on new meaning.

The field does support or interrupt, to varying degrees, particular developmental paths. But individuals are not dependent on their environment to instill in them a basic need to "meet the world" in a progressively more complex manner. All children will find some way to continue forward on their developmental journey. They are not dependent on their parents or their surroundings for their fundamental developmental drive, but only for the interactive arena within which it unfolds. In most situations it is not necessary as parents (or therapists) to teach youngsters how to develop. On the contrary, what is generally needed is merely the space and support to "do their thing." If as adults we can have faith in their inborn process, and respect their individual differences, we can then offer appropriate support as we "sit back" and lovingly provide input to shape their environment in the direction of responding to their specific needs.

The Contact Cycle

Based on Gestalt theory, the "Contact Cycle," or "Cycle of

Experience Model" (Figure 1), offers one highly useful lens for articulating the process by which an individual attempts to meet his needs through contact and interaction with and in his environment (see Figure 1; see also discussion in Nevis, 1987, as well as in Zinker, 1994). To illustrate how the model works, consider the prototypical case of satisfying the basic, recurrent, universal need to take in nutrients from the environment.

As I sit as my desk writing, there is a gurgling or grumbling in my belly that is perhaps the first sign of hunger. Initially, these stirrings occur without my necessarily being aware of them. As they cross the threshold into awareness, these sensations constitute the "raw data" of my experience. Gradually they reach an intensity that permits them to interfere with other ongoing processes (thinking, writing): awareness crystallizes into a "figure," which stands out from the background of my ongoing experience. This process of organization of sensory data is then the next stage in the cycle, that of figure formation or full awareness. After awareness, depending on conditions and competing needs, may come energy mobilization, the segment of the cycle where I invest energy to process, respond to, and get a sense of what I am going to do with my awareness. Am I going to put aside my work and go eat, or will I perhaps try to ignore my hunger for a time, in order to continue writing.

Once energy is mobilized and a decision is made, I am in a position to move toward action. This action, which may be getting up, going downstairs, and making myself a sandwich, is directed toward meeting the need that initiated the particular cycle. Contact itself is then the part of the cycle when there is a direct meeting between self and environment. In this situation full contact comes when I eat the sandwich. After contact neither my environment nor I am the same as before the interaction.

Contact is followed by a decrease of tension, now that the need driving that particular cycle has been met. This relaxation occurs during the resolution/closure phase of the cycle and leads into the withdrawal/assimilation phase, during which the contact experience likely loses its immediate pertinence, and fades into the background. In addition to withdrawing from and assimilating the previous contact, the individual now becomes more available for a subsequent sensation, and the start of a new cycle. In this example, this part of the cycle will include the literal assimilation (digestion and absorption) of the sandwich. Having satisfied this nutritional need I now begin to be aware of other sensations, which may be driving the next cycle: perhaps a slight tension in my stomach or chest, as I consider that my work deadline is coming closer. Healthy functioning depends on being able to move through cycles in this way, creating and destroying figures with relative ease and clarity, balancing and integrating one with another, neither skipping nor progressing through stages too quickly, nor getting too stuck along the way.

Of course, this example is both and over-simplified and idealized, in the sense of unfolding without any of the conflict and contextual issues that may go with the resolution of larger, more complex needs and desires (or even, for a good number of people, with eating and food itself). Still, as an analytic and diagnostic tool, the model offers both theoretical and practical insight into all the developmental and contact processes and episodes of our unfolding lives. Contact, in this sense, means an organismic coming together around any relevant boundary, or point of difference in the field. This may be an interpersonal boundary (as between parent and child, or my client or patient and me), or an intrapersonal boundary (as between that part of me which is loving and patient with my own children, and that part which

Figure 1
The "Contact Cycle" or "Cycle of Experience"

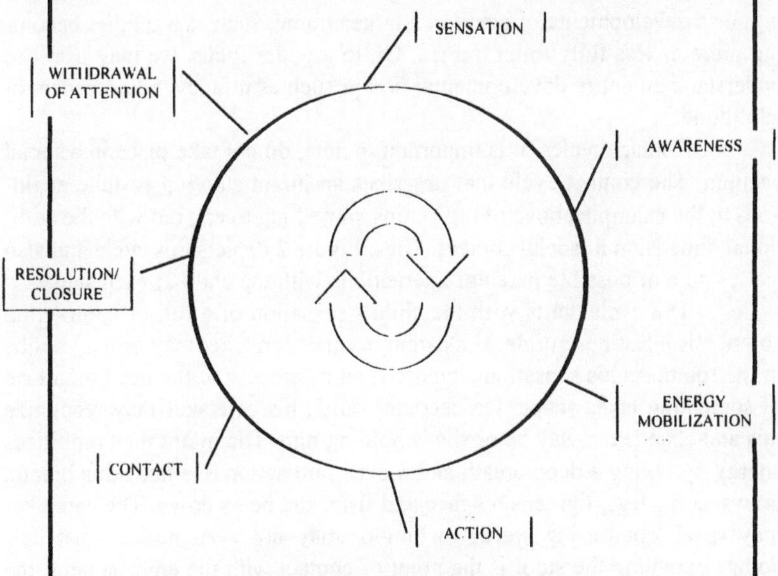

From E. Nevis, *Organizational Consulting*, GestaltPress 2001. Used by permission.

may be exhausted, burnt out, and ready for this bedtime ritual to be over now!) I can conceive an inter-visceral boundary within a child, for example one whose intestinal system is full and muscularly ready to evacuate, and her psyche that is hesitant, perhaps afraid it may hurt to have a bowel movement. I may experience a temporal boundary between who I am (and what my experience is) at a particular point in time, and who I am a moment, a month, a year later. The boundary may be between fields that are concrete (my nuclear family and my extended family, say), or ones less easily delineated such as the child's developmental readiness and status today and her position a month from now. In all cases our experience is organized around these felt, relevant boundaries or differences in the field; and our survival and development proceed by the process of contact, the resolution of these differences into an integrated process of living and growth. Any significant interaction, action, process or even thought will include and integrate numerous contact boundaries of this sort, at many different levels.

All the cycles are initiated by some organismic need; without some sense of need, the organism simply does not mobilize and organize to act and to live. Often it is instructive to identify the particular need or needs driving a cycle, as well as the process and stages by which it plays out. The cycle may be used to extract and study a particular act, such as infant stooling, or a developmental process in a larger frame, such as a toddler becoming more or less fully toilet trained. Or, in a wider focus, we may use it to understand an entire developmental period such as infancy, adolescence, or adulthood.

Contact cycles, it is important to note, do not take place in a social vacuum. The contact cycle that describes an infant stooling is quite analogous to the example above of me getting something to eat, but with the additional dimension of social context. Thus, Figure 2 depicts this cycle and also makes note of possible parental interactions with the child at each stage.

The cycle starts with the child's sensation of a full or contracting colon. His intestines gurgle. His parent or other caretaker may or may not be in the room. As his sensations intensify, an awareness of the need to get rid of something takes shape. He becomes quiet; his caretaker may recognize this and change the way he or she is holding him. The infant then mobilizes energy by taking a deep breath and moves into action. He holds his breath, draws up his legs, tightens his face and fists, and bears down. The caretaker may speak comforting words to him–or may not even notice what he's doing. Expelling the stool is the point of contact with the environment: the infant soils his diaper. The adult is then available to change him–or not, partly depending on the availability of wider societal support for adults taking care of infants and children (and here we see the adult-child dyad itself contextualized by the larger social field).

After stooling, resolution is marked by a lessening of tension, a feeling of relief and a sense of well being for the child. Perhaps the adult picks him up to cuddle. During assimilation the previous experience becomes part of his history (ground) and he becomes available to whatever the next need-fulfilling cycle may be (nursing, crying, listening to a bird outside the window, etc.). The child is alert and looking around; the adult holds him and mimics his cooing, or sets him up with toys or possibly the TV. The baby progresses along his own contact cycle, but the environment's response impacts his experience.

Let's use the same Cycle model to follow the developmental process of a toddler learning to toilet train, as her mother and father are simultaneously learning to be the parents of a "potty-trained" child. In this wider situation we will track the infant's cycle together with the parents' parallel cycle. From the toddler's perspective the cycle begins, again, with the sensation of a full or contracting colon, plus the vague sense that there may be something new on the horizon. As the adult notices the infant becoming focused and quiet (or smells the gas discharge), he or she may be quite aware of a feeling of being fed up with diaper changes (parent's sensation/awareness). Perhaps he or she also feels some excitement, knowing that before long the baby will be toilet trained–or shame at being reminded that all his or her friends' kids are already out of diapers.

The child progresses to awareness: "The poop is ready to come out –mom and dad poop in the potty–they want me to poop in the potty," even that "Poop feels yucky in my diaper." Meanwhile, it dawns on the parent that the youngster has been waking up from naps dry, the start of preschool is just a few months away, and "Oh my God, I've never done this toilet training stuff before!" moves her toward a place of energy mobilization that is more elaborate than when the child was an infant. The child must retroflect–hold back–her urge to stool if she is going to move successfully toward the actions of getting an adult to take off her diaper, making her way to the potty, sitting and straining, and so forth. On the parent's side, mobilizing energy for the adult may take the form of getting advice from family and friends, checking out a toilet training book, buying a potty chair and/or speaking with a partner about how this process is supposed to happen. Parents may also engage in supportive actions of role modeling the use of the toilet, reading potty books to the toddler, and sharing their pleasure when the child shows an interest in the potty.

Next comes contact with the environment: in this case, stooling in the potty. The full contact experience at this point is deeply interpersonal, not merely mechanically somatic, not a matter of just stooling, but of managing and modulating intrapersonal and interpersonal boundaries in a more developmentally advanced manner. This yields a richer and more self-defining experience. In the best case, a parent is right there, supporting the accomplishment and sharing the pride.

The resolution phase now includes a feeling of relief, lessening of tension both physical and interpersonal, and a sense of pride in what she has done. She is now a "toilet kid," not a "diaper kid." Her parents are now the parents of a toilet-trained youngster; no longer are they "diaper changers." In other words, everyone involved how has a somewhat different identity. Parents too experience a lessening of tension as they savor their "success" and feel relief knowing that a major impediment to preschool or daycare entry is behind them.

Withdrawal/assimilation from this learning process (and every contact cycle is potentially a learning process) includes integrating a new sense of self into the child's ground and once again readying oneself for whatever the next developmental need (codetermined by the child and the environment) may be: perhaps learning to ride a tricycle or sing the alphabet. For parents, withdrawal may include putting away the changing table, paying more attention to school options and choices (if any), perhaps giving advice to other parents and feeling more secure in their parental roles. Depending on how the process has gone, parents may also reflect on issues like pressure, support, and the particular personality of their particular child–reflections that may serve them well in other, even more daunting developmental challenges that lie ahead, for their child and for themselves.

Again, at each stage it is the interplay that is crucial, between the child and his "environment" (i.e., principally the other people around, who are themselves carriers of wider social norms and attitudes about toilet training). Are those people respectful or teasing, indulgent or impatient, supportive or pressuring, hovering or neglectful? What happens when the child has an accident as part of integrating his accomplishments during closure? Is this tolerated? And then do adults permit him time and space for internal processing during withdrawal, or are they in a hurry toward the next milestone? Every child is "preprogrammed" for growth, but the type of support that is present or absent in his surroundings greatly shapes and impacts his evolving process and sense of self.

Finally, who is this new person, who has these new capacities? Who are her parents now; and what is the new interaction between them? What happens in moving from one significant developmental cycle to another is not merely the acquisition of a new skill, but actually a shift in who the child is–and thus in who all the other people are, to some degree, around her? She, in conjunction with her environment, now becomes a new "developmental field."

Resistance

Healthy functioning is the ability to create and destructure important figures of contact with fluidity and ease. Historically, impediments to cycle completion were often considered "resistances" to contact, in much the same way that early psychoanalysis considered "resistance to analysis" as something the patient must get over, rather than as part of the essence of the therapeutic relationship. Wheeler (1991) has demonstrated how these so-called "resistances" are actually categories or dynamic dimensions of the contact process itself. Without some use of projection, introjection, confluence, retroflection, deflection, and so on, there would be no contact at all (just as we saw above how retroflection was directly involved in the child's choiceful movement toward the more complex level of contact resolution which toileting involves). The process of learning to modulate contact in this way is itself a necessary set of developmental tasks, without which human development would not be able to progress beyond an extremely rudimentary level.

Contact modulation in this sense occurs at all stages of the cycle, and is particularly pertinent in supporting the child and the field through the "pregnant" energy mobilization stage of the cycle, when the field is in heavy transition. Previous ways of being are being dismantled in order to make way for the new ways yet to be created–and this is true not just for the child but for the parents, who may be rushing development at a sensitive time for their own reasons, or possibly retarding it, reluctant to see their baby grow up and out. Parents too must deflect, retroflect, project, and so on, as they attempt to meet the child and create a field that can support all of them as well as possible.

This in turn speaks to the crucial need for a foundation of trust and support between a child and his parents. As the child moves along any developmental contact cycle, there is a point at which he contemplates, approaches, and initiates a new action. Again, at this point he is actually trying out a new way of being, creating a new self (and destructuring an old one). In order to do this, the child must give up some of his sense of self and security, for the risky time of transition to new stability. As anyone knows who has started a new job, school, relationship, or even sport or other skill, this can be a time of great vulnerability. This vulnerability, along with the ambivalence and excitement that accompany it, demand a context of a supportive and trustworthy environment. Without it, the result has to be some degree of stress and developmental compromise.

Figure 2
Contact Cycle of Infant Stooling With Possible Adult Interactions/Supports, and Possible Wider Field Support

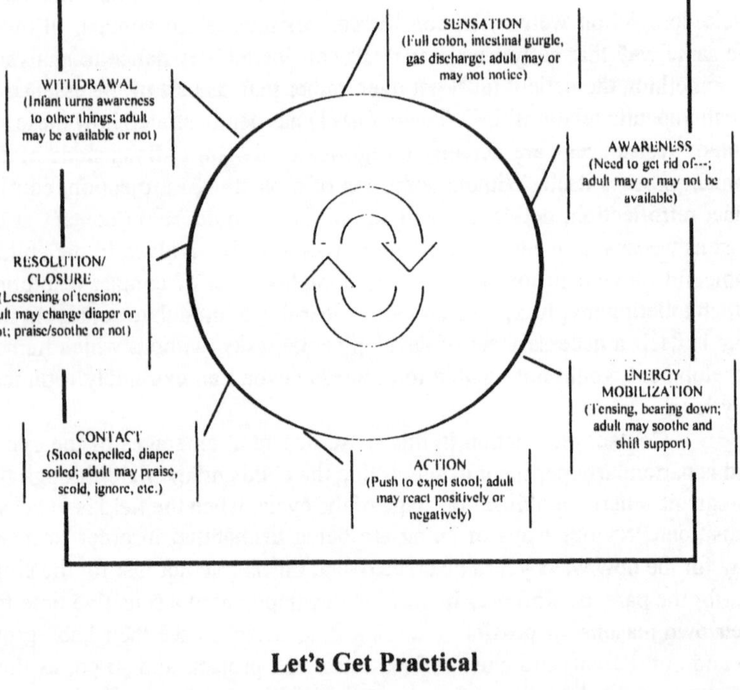

Let's Get Practical

Now let us look at how this translates into a practical approach for working with young children (and their parents) around this issue. I counsel parents on a variety of developmental and behavioral issues with regard to their toddlers. Of these, among their most frequent and urgent concerns are about sleeping through the night, tantrums–and toileting. The most useful insight I share with them, on all these issues, is this: "The most important thing at this time in your child's life is to have your attention. It is even more important to him than having your love (however heartfelt that may be in your own mind and private being)." This statement highlights the fundamental importance of contact.

With this said, my advice to parents in anticipation of toilet training is intended to provide a structure to lessen anxiety and increase the opportunity for support of the process in the field. Seven main points are now offered.

1. Readiness

The most important starting point is the child's readiness. When she/he is ready, it will happen. Signs of readiness for toilet training generally include the ability to walk, a basic understanding that others do poop and pee in certain places and not others, an ability to recognize her own process of elimination (such as by signaling when she has a soiled diaper), and demonstrating that she is able to interrupt her spontaneous response when the urge to stool or void arises (waking up from naps dry, or going to another room for privacy in order to have a bowel movement in diapers).

2. Vocabulary

Use clear words to describe things (poop, pee, wet, dry, etc.), so that it is easier for the child to communicate his needs. Part of the reason for this is so that the child can get the adult's assistance in taking of his diaper, opening the bathroom door, and so on. Enhancing a child's vocabulary makes him more able to support himself and get support from others.

3. Role modeling

Children at this age are exquisite mimics. They actively "try on" the behaviors they see around them in order to support the evolution of a new identity with greater differentiation. Where possible, the greatest potency often comes through modeling on a contemporary or slightly older child. (Indeed, parents of several offspring often report that they never did toilet train the youngest one(s), because "They just took after the older ones, and did what they did").

4. Books

This is another way for the child to try on what isn't yet integrated. Through the creative use of projection the youngster can identify with the toddler in the book, picture what the process must be like, and imagine his or herself doing it. This kind of projective or imaginary contact amounts to "grading down" the task, practicing it at a moderated level, before tackling the "real thing."

5. Be pleased

Share your experience of pleasure as your child moves in the desired direction. Over-praising or gushing can "take the experience away" from the child, making it more yours than his. Similarly, inauthentic praise will likely be confusing, and do more harm than good. Remember, it is the reality and quality of the whole communication (including body language and "fuming") that determines how impactful the contact is for the child.

6. A very important caution,
again: Don't want it too much!

This is the most important instruction, after observing for the child's readiness. If progress through toilet training is going to get derailed, this is the most likely place where it will happen. The task of becoming a "toilet kid" as opposed to staying a "diaper kid" takes place in large part at an inter-visceral boundary. The brain and gut must be in full contact to achieve this milestone. When a parent gets too involved, the primary contact boundary shifts from the intrapersonal to the interpersonal. Instead of the interpersonal boundary serving as a structure and background support ("my parents will like this, I'll be a big girl"), the intensity at the interpersonal level interferes, taking needed attention and awareness away from the crucial intrapersonal cues. Either over-strictness or over-praise may distort the developmental process in this way.

7. Decrease diaper time

Make diaper changing "just taking care of business," and not a primary moment in the day for face-to-face contact and communication. Instead, be sure to find another time for that cuddling and close playful contact. For stressed, overly busy, under-supported parents this may be a challenge, but it is one that will pay off in increased available time and energy for the parent and for the parent-child dyad.

When Things Go Awry

Now I would like to take a look at interventions aimed at righting things when the toilet training process goes awry. Generally, as the discussion above would indicate, the most important and effective intervention for getting the child back on track is to get the parents out of the process as much as possible. As stated earlier, this particular developmental task is highly dependent on the child's ability to attend to an intrapersonal contact boundary, with the interpersonal boundary in the supportive background. Parental over-involvement reverses this natural order of priority. By having the parents disengage from the process, the child is more likely to reconnect with her own visceral processes and reestablish her own developmental pathway.

Thus, the first step is to educate and reassure the parents. Letting them know that what is happening is quite common and even age appropriate can lessen their anxiety and bolster their faith in the child's own developmental abilities. I emphasize to them that the most important ingredient for success is the child's own interest in the process. As the adults feel more comfortable with this notion and less responsible for the child's actions, it becomes easier for them to sit back.

I suggest that they have a one-time conversation with the youngster, letting him know that they realize they've been reminding (or nagging) him a lot about the toilet, and now they have faith that he'll work this out on his own when he's ready. ("And I bet it won't be long, because you're such a big boy now.") After that they can relax and follow the guidelines given above.

This by itself usually results in resolution of the problem, when the intervention is made fairly early on. If the tension has been going on for awhile, or is part of a more generalized power struggle between parent and child, it is likely that the pattern of push/resist is already relatively fixed in the child's (and the system's) ground, and has become part of her self-gestalt. In this case, what are needed is a more thorough destructuring and restructuring process between/within the child and the social environment. Normal developmental ambivalence has been magnified and polarized, generally with the parents representing one pole and the child the other; additional interventions are likely to be necessary to support the system toward new action.

Probably the most commonly used technique at this point is the familiar sticker chart or those famous M&Ms. These give the child a sensationally pleasing contact experience, while generally including a more or less explicit contract: "You sit on the potty, you get an M&M. Poop in the potty, you get five." As Wheeler points out (in the present volume), this type of contract is helpful in supporting the child and parent to disengage from each other where the engagement has become stereotyped and counter-developmental, in deflecting the contact from the toileting issue per se, and thus in making a charged boundary less destructively potent. As the adults implement the contract it is important that they not dwell on it or repeatedly remind the youngster about the prize awaiting her (much less assign "negative points" for failure, or mix this reward system up with any other issue, which only serves to reinstate the power issue). What makes behavior modification work, when it does work, is contact modification. In most situations these simple interventions and a little time are all that are needed to get the youngster (and the parents) back on track.

As a pediatrician, I am likely to hear about toilet training difficulties earlier on than most therapists, and therefore may be able to make small interventions early, which yield large results. However, if the power struggles around toileting have been particularly intense or protracted (the situation when therapists may most often be called in), it may be necessary to remove the parents more completely from the interaction. This can be done by having the therapist become the person with whom the child discusses all issues relating to toileting. Most often the parents are relieved (if not ecstatic) to hand over the reins to the counselor. With support they can lessen their sense of responsibility and failure, as well as any fear that they may have traumatized the child for life.

On some occasions though, a parent may have great difficulty taking him or herself out of the loop. In these situations, in addition to sessions with the child, it may be necessary for the therapist to work separately with the parent(s) to further explore their feelings around separating from their child, giving up control, toileting concerns, or other personal issues that become relevant. This is awareness-building with regard to the parent's cycle.

When working with the child, the therapist should let him or her know from the very beginning that the reason they are getting together is to help him or her with toilet training, and that the child will be reporting back to the therapist at their weekly sessions. By way of taking a history from the parents and spending time with the youngster, one can get a sense of how big or small the incremental steps of developmental change need to be. The goal is to come up with a plan that makes success attainable for the child without creating too much anxiety. This is fostered by establishing a sense of safety and trust for the child in the sessions, which is engendered by the therapist's recognizing that there are good reasons for whatever toileting habits may have evolved, by not feeling an urgency to "fix" the child (even though the parents may well feel that urgency), and by having faith in the youngster's ability to succeed. This boils down to respecting the child, and who he or she is as an individual.

In most situations a sticker chart (an aid in modulating contact) is particularly useful in supporting the youngster to initiate a change in behavior. A key element in encouraging a change of behavior is the ability to grade up or down, as needed what is expected of the child, finding a way for him or her to succeed one step at a time while moving toward the ultimate goal. Grading down may mean the chance to earn a sticker for stooling in the diaper (or pants) while in the bathroom, a sticker for just sitting on the toilet, one for straining on the toilet, and perhaps a special one for actually stooling in the toilet. For most small children having a potty chair on the floor (where they can firmly plant their feet) as an alternative to the "big" toilet is a way of grading down the risk. A child who usually stools in the squatting position may find squatting with his or her feet on the floor or even on the toilet seat is a more approachable option than sitting on the adult-sized toilet.

In addition to addressing these issues through sticker charts, answering questions and educating the youngster using drawings and explanations of the digestive system may also be helpful in demystifying the process. This supports the child to be in contact with the actual process of elimination rather than some fantasized version. Much of the work of relationship-building in therapy which permits the child to diffuse his or her distress around stooling happens in the context of contactful play, using whatever techniques the therapist feels most comfortable with, such as puppets, sand tables, or drawings. Always, the aim is to meet the child where she/he is.

Although quite rare, an underlying medical condition can cause constipation that then precipitates or aggravates the toileting difficulties. (More often it is the child's diet, perhaps together with the child's own tension or ambivalence that initiates the constipation). Therefore, it is important that a medical practitioner who can also oversee any medical interventions indicated evaluate the child. Stool softeners, dietary changes, and in quite rare situations, an enema may be important if the struggle has resulted in chronic constipation or painful defecation. It is often helpful simply to have the child sit on the toilet after meals (a time when intestinal contractions are likely), in order to help resensitize him or her to his or her own visceral process. Children in this situation have often become quite desensitized to their own intestinal activity. All of these interventions are aimed at bringing the child into greater contact with his or her physiologic and developmental tendencies, and lessening contact with other distracting figures.

The Contact Cycle as a Template for Development in General

In addition to using the contact cycle model to track relatively short term processes like those of an infant stooling or a toddler toilet training, we can also apply it to the longer term process of human development over a lifetime. In diagramming a contact process, it is often helpful to identify the underlying need driving the cycle.

A fundamental need underlying most human behavior is survival itself. Of greatest importance for immediate and ultimate survival of any individual is the ability to distinguish self and other, in a context of relatedness. Without this distinction, survival of self could not be experientially discriminated from the survival of anything else, nor could it be integrated into the relational context that is also essential for survival. I believe that the process of human development is driven to a large extent by a need for self-definition in this sense, thereby permitting survival and continued evolution. In order to self-define, one must be able to be in contact at a boundary with some "other;" hence the fundamental importance of contact. Being able to interact in a more complex manner at a greater array of boundaries heightens one's sense of self, and may even be used as a definition of personal growth or human development.

A contact cycle that describes human development across a lifespan begins, as any cycle does, with sensation. What an infant knows of herself or her environment comes to her through her senses. Because in many ways infants are relatively undeveloped, it has been common to misinterpret their limited behavioral repertoire as a manifestation of passivity, confluence, or lack of awareness (blank slates, waiting to be written on). The truth is, their powers of discriminatory sensation are wondrous. A newborn baby placed on his mother's abdomen immediately after birth will scoot himself up toward his mother's breasts to nurse. If one of the mother's nipples has previously been washed, the newborn will consistently seek, find, and suckle at the unwashed nipple.

Infants are fundamentally grounded in their sensations: this is a time when a child's sense of "what is" could be stated as "I know what I can see, hear, smell, touch and taste." She is in a process of developing concrete knowledge of herself and her environment. When hungry, infants cry until fed. When their colon is distended, they fuss and strain until they stool. When comfortable again, they nestle for even greater contact. They have a limited repertoire of actions, but those they do have are focused on meeting their needs by contacting with sensation. It is through these sensationally oriented experiences that they learn about themselves and their environment. Infants and young children learn about trust, safety, and who they (and the world) are by being held, rocked, and sung to–or not.

Later on, in later childhood and early adolescence, sensations are less often the primary figure. Building fuller awareness is not a principal developmental task. The child takes in more of self and environment, and develops a sense of self that is not immediately dependent on primary sensations. She becomes able to integrate experiences that are not concretely present. This is the time of life when abstract thinking becomes possible and youngsters begin to become aware of subtleties in themselves and the world around them. Not everything is black and white anymore; there are lots of grays. Parents and adults are no longer all-knowing. Along with this shift of perspective comes the development of interiority, the sense of an inner life that is not directly dependent on outer events and actions.

As the young person moves through adolescence and young adulthood he enters the time of life that developmentally corresponds to the energy mobilization state of the contact cycle. This is a critical time in the development of the individual, a time of a major paradigm shift when he has moved from defining himself primarily in the context of family, toward broader peer, societal, and ultimately world (or universal) contexts. If we view the process of human development as an ongoing evolution of self-definition in relationship, it is easy to see why adolescence and young adulthood are often so tumultuous. The individual is moving from defining himself in terms of a primary point of reference that was environmental, to one in which that primary reference is contact with himself (and not merely a physical or external self, but an internal, non-tangible self or experiential self). In addition, his body has undergone tremendous changes: even physically, he is a different self. Thus this stage of development may be marked at first by a diminished sense of self, and a heightening of the question, "Who am I?"–a hallmark refrain of this time of life. Coincident with all this comes the marked ambivalence which often characterizes the energy mobilization part of the contact cycle, with the resulting abundant use of contact modulations (projection, introjection, deflection, egotism, and so on), which mark the adolescent years.

As the process continues, the young adult manages this developmental ambivalence, navigates energy mobilization toward commitments of various kinds, and moves ahead into the action part of the lifecycle. This is the part that for many people characterizes much of our adult lives. We are actively involved in doing, being, producing, problem solving, managing, and "living." This is a time of our lives when who we are may often be experienced as a reflection of what we are doing. Our sense of self may be as a procreator/protector, a parent/nurturer, a breadwinner, an artist, a professional–or often a conglomeration of many of these roles and activities. This is the time of life when one can easily become "all action." If who I am is defined by what I am doing, this is the perfect stage of life to become a "do-aholic."

And with and after action comes contact, the part of the lifecycle when the need that drives the contact process gets met, when the contact is consummated. If the driving need of human existence is self-definition, this is the time of life when an individual is involved in bringing some completion to the process of personal integration. One's sense of self is beginning to gel; a person "hits stride" and "knows who she is." This time of life carries a lessening of tension, as one's personal boundaries no longer need to be so energetically mobilized; greater intimacy is possible, with oneself and with others. What others may think of her becomes less pertinent to the person. Greater self-acceptance and a more relaxed worldview become attainable without needing to distance from or be confluent with others.

For many people this transition can be as ambivalence-laden as are the teenage years. Just as the teenager must be willing to destructure his sense of self in order to move on and evolve into a "new" self, so an older adult during this time needs to de-energize or even dismantle his boundaries, to continue further with the process of interiority and meaning-making that has its roots in adolescence and before. This evolution may often be experienced at least in part in a spiritual context. A "loss of self" may be experienced, perhaps to the point of acute vulnerability, along with the awareness of one's own forthcoming death. The heightened contact with one's own mortality, together with this lessening of habitual self-boundaries, may constitute a sort of "double whammy" on individual security and stability. As a result, many people may find themselves teetering once again on a developmental cusp, between fortifying and letting go of ego boundaries, rigidifying or relaxing into new and increased contact between self and the universe. Ironically, losses and illnesses–one's own and those of others–may prompt many people to become unstuck at this stage, less ego-oriented or defended, more contactful and ultimately more available for the next transition and developmental stage.

Resolution is marked by a further lessening of tension, a sense of well being and satisfaction, and the beginning of savoring one's own lifetime history. This is a time, ideally, of taking pleasure in who one is and has been, and feeling regret about parts of oneself that did not develop as fully as was hoped or planned for earlier in life–or wished for now. Pleased or displeased, as this stage progresses there is an experience of integration of one's sense of self, a new perspective, a time of making meaning of one's life, recognizing and affirming one's lifelong themes and tasks, and increased clarity in seeing oneself in the larger contexts of family, community, world, and the universe.

Finally, after resolution comes assimilation, or withdrawal, a process of turning away from one's individual, corporeal life and saying goodbye. The lifelong task of greater self-knowledge and definition is no longer figural. The task now is to clear one's slate in preparation for the complementary component of this stage: making oneself available for the unknown cycle that lies ahead.

All this is the individual lifecycle, in large focus. Within these stages, of course, all the stages are occurring all the time, both in the background of this larger cycle and as components of all the smaller cycles of contact that make up our lives. At the same time, there exists the complementary cyclic process of the world at large, and the entire individual lifecycles of the people around us. Societies and cultures have cycles of their own, which contain and contextualize individual lives, impacting our particular developmental journeys and relative abilities to be open to sensation, capable of awareness, able to bear energy mobilization, utilitarian in action, vulnerable to contact, accepting of resolution, and peaceful in withdrawal.

Conclusion

People are by nature interdependent, developmentally driven

beings. Gestalt theory's focus on context and process make it a highly useful model for addressing issues of human development. Fundamental to working successfully with children, or people of any age, is the ability to establish safe and respectful contact with them, and a sincere appreciation of the whole field of which they are a part. This field includes their historical, cultural, family, and environmental contexts.

In order to communicate this respect, it is of primary importance to recognize that even though there may be logjams and distortions in their process, and apparent dysfunctions in their interactions, all individuals and systems are functioning as they are for some historically valid reasons. A "best possible solution," given the constraints and level of awareness at the time, has already evolved to support survival, and where possible, growth. Times of developmental change, of the emergence of new capacities or new environmental demands, are those times which call for a new solution, a new creative adjustment. This is true whether the new capacity/demand is toilet-training, entering school, entering puberty, leaving home, or any of the other new challenges or transitions we have touched on in this article. Challenge becomes stress–and stress may rigidify into a dysfunctional or "fixed gestalt" pattern–when there is not sufficient environmental and self-support to meet the new task with a new and larger resolution of capacity and self-definition. As parents, therapists, and others who work with children, when we can provide some of that needed developmental support, we will have contributed to the growth and creation of a new "best possible solution" for our children, our clients, and ourselves, and a new and richer set of connections for all of us.

References

Nevis, E. (1987). *Organizational consulting: A gestalt approach.* New York, NY: Gardner Press.

Zinker, J. (1994). *In search of good form: A gestalt approach to working with couples and families.* San Francisco, CA: Jossey-Bass.

12

The Pinocchio Syndrome—Path to Wholeness: Gestalt Therapy with Children and Adolescents

Felicia Carroll

The story *Pinocchio* holds for all of us a very important theme, the theme of moving from the experience of brokenness and being fragmented to wholeness and aliveness. This is not only a psychological theme; it's a spiritual theme. It's a theme that holds the imagination, the longings and the desires of humanity. Stories and myths of all cultures from the earliest of times explore the awareness of an essential sense of loss and a longing to return to a place of wholeness and unity within ourselves and in relationship with others; to quote T.S. Eliot, "to return to the place where we started and to know it for the first time." Pinocchio speaks to our longing, not just in adults, but to the organismic longing in children as well.

The story is, in essence, a folktale. Carlos Collodi, an Italian journalist and government official, started writing a series of stories for children titled *The Adventures of Pinocchio*, which was published in book form in 1883 and sold a million copies in Italy alone. It has become a classic. There is power in this story that we can continue to look into at many levels.

As the story opens, Pinocchio is at the beginning of his life. We meet him as a broken figure, a piece of wood. He is being chopped up for various reasons. One of the things I think is important in the story, if we look at it metaphorically, is that the essence of the wood cries out not to be hurt. Yet from "birth," every character that comes in contact with Pinocchio does just that. The story begins with the wounding of Pinocchio. There is the trauma; there is the lack of attunement. The wood is to be something else. Pinocchio comes into the world as a wounded figure. Again, I want you to think of this in terms of children. I don't think any of us gets out of childhood without some kind of wounding.

In childhood we begin to lose ourselves, our essential process of being who we are, and there is often little support for our developmental needs. We come into the world out of the desires of our parents (many of us, not always, but many of us) and that was true for Pinocchio as well. That is, Gepetto wants a puppet. He is not longing for a real boy. He wants a puppet that does what he wants it to do. He wants a puppet that will dance and do somersaults and do all sorts of things to entertain Gepetto.

So, Pinocchio comes into the world wounded and out of the narcissistic need of Gepetto–his creator, his father. Pinocchio comes into being in order to meet his father's need to have a puppet to entertain him–to be the child the father wants him to be. He is not affirmed for himself. As soon as he arrives (is shaped), however, he immediately takes exception with all of this. I call this first stage of the story of Pinocchio, "the wounded child." This is the Pinocchio who is described by his behaviors as being "a bad boy." We can come up with all kinds of diagnoses from the DSM-IV for Pinocchio–conduct disorder, impulse disorders, and attention deficit with hyperactivity. We would have a heyday just diagnosing Pinocchio according to these conventional labels. Simply, we see a child who is out of contact with himself (faulty sense of self) and out of connection with his world. In his efforts to protect himself and to find himself, not to be a puppet, to discover and to be himself, this very attempt to be himself is what gets him into trouble, and the story unfolds.

In order to be himself, not his father's puppet, what does Pinocchio do? He breaks contact, he runs away. The tension in the story begins–his running away is the beginning of his journey back. He loses his resources, he loses the Other, he loses relationship. And the kind of relationships that Pinocchio ends up having are usually relationships in which he is mistreated; relationships in which he is taken advantage of. He is gullible; he is woodenheaded, as he is often called in this story. He cannot get even his basic needs met, organismic needs of hunger and of sleep. No one will help him. They all think he is just one of those kids on the street who is begging. When he comes home, he is hungry, he is tired, and he falls asleep. Because it is a cold and wet night, Pinocchio puts his feet up next to the fire, and while he is asleep his feet burn and he doesn't know it. The next morning, when Gepetto calls to try to get Pinocchio to let him in, Pinocchio stumbles and falls because he has no feet. He loses his own footing. He has lost balance. He falls.

This is an image of a desensitized child. Many of us see children who have lost a sense of their bodies. They don't have a body orientation with the world, and Pinocchio doesn't either.

This is the first part of the story. It is this child who is wounded, shamed, out of contact with himself, out of relationship with the Other, with himself, with his own body, and completely at a loss as to purposeful interaction with others in terms of getting his needs met and discovering who he is in relationship with the environmental Other and Internal Otherness.

The second part of the story is interesting for me because things begin to change for Pinocchio just at the moment when he is considered to be most lost. Pinocchio meets a fox and a cat who are posing as beggars. They are trying to get money out of Pinocchio. He has come into five gold pieces in his journey, and he is trying to get back to his father to give him these gold pieces. But he runs into the cat and the fox, and they are trying to "outfox" him, outsmart him, so he will lose his money to them. They tell him there is a field of miracles, and if he will go and bury his money in this field of miracles a tree will come overnight bearing all kinds of gold coins, and his five gold pieces can turn into a million gold pieces, or something like that, overnight. Pinocchio first wonders about this, but then he goes for the possibility of being wildly rich, and of course loses his money. He runs away, and again they catch up with him, this time disguised as assassins. They catch Pinocchio and hang him from a tree, hoping that his money will fall out of his mouth. This is the ultimate constriction and Pinocchio loses breath. He is completely cut off. He stops breathing.

Just at the moment we think Pinocchio is about to die, someone sees him, and this is the Blue Fairy. This is the section of the story in which Pinocchio begins the journey toward himself–toward wholeness. His relationship with the Blue Fairy continues throughout the rest of the story, although it goes through many transformations: (1) child, (2) sister, (3) mother, and (4) friend. This is the first relationship that Pinocchio has had with someone who sees him, who cares about him, who accepts him for who he is. The Blue Fairy not only sees him for who he is and accepts him, but also sees him for who he can be, a real boy. It is through this relationship with the Blue Fairy that Pinocchio has the first inkling and the first thought of becoming real. Up until this time he has just been a puppet who has been trying to get away from anyone and everyone.

The Blue Fairy cares. She brings him in from the hanging tree and is concerned about whether or not he is dead or alive. She brings in the wisest physicians that she can possibly find to help her make the decision, is he dead or alive. The physicians, a crow, an owl, and a cricket determine that he is alive, but Pinocchio's response to their discovery, to this being, reveals his shame. His recognition of shame comes in response to the words of the cricket. Unlike the Walt Disney version where Jiminy Cricket is the helpmate, in the original Italian story the cricket is a harsh critic. "This is a bad boy, he doesn't mind his father, he is running away," the cricket says to the Blue Fairy. It is the cricket, when Pinocchio is lying on his deathbed, which says, "Oh, I know this boy. This is a puppet, he runs away. He does all of these horrible things," and Pinocchio cries in shame. This is the first time Pinocchio cries out in recognition of his own brokenness and of being exposed/seen by others. Through this experience and through the Blue Fairy's acceptance, not rejection, Pinocchio begins to respond to her.

As the story continues, the Blue Fairy holds out the possibility of Pinocchio becoming a real boy. It is not a smooth road. We see the resistance come up. The Blue Fairy beckons him and encourages him to reconnect with his father. Gepetto is seen as being the Other and there is need for belonging to something, someone. Our own longings are evoked. We now begin to see that this is a possibility for Pinocchio. We wonder what is going to happen. We don't know. The Blue Fairy does not know.

Throughout this part of the story, Pinocchio doesn't lose his connection with the Blue Fairy. I am seeing this as an important part of the therapeutic relationship, that the relationship is there and it is through that relationship that the child moves and comes and goes, not immediately being transformed into something wonderful. The process of building self-support, learning about one's self, takes much time. The child in therapy continues the behavioral and emotional patterns that "got him into trouble;" that have brought him into treatment.

Every once in awhile he comes back and reconnects with the Blue Fairy, and each time he is at a different level of relationship with her. In fact, she develops from being a fairy and being dead herself into becoming a more "real" figure for Pinocchio. They transform together throughout their relationship.

The Blue Fairy part of the story represents the therapeutic relationship and some of the things that go on in this relationship. This relationship is not always a smooth road, as we know. Sometimes the therapy is one step forward and two steps back. Clearly, the Fairy experiences this with Pinocchio.

Pinocchio gradually moves out to the edges of himself as the story progresses. He goes out to the cliffs and looks out over the sea. From there he sees his father in a boat. Gepetto is looking for Pinocchio. He is out in the depths of the sea in the middle of a storm. There is not enough self-support or environmental support for Pinocchio to go into the sea and he leaves the cliffs. He loses sight of his father once again. Pinocchio returns to the Fairy and visits with her. He tells her that he has seen his father. Gepetto is in the midst of a storm, in the midst of a massive sea. At her encouragement, Pinocchio returns again to the cliffs and yet he is still uncertain about going out into that great and turbulent sea.

It is here that Pinocchio meets Lampwick. It is here that he is beckoned to Playland where there is the promise of no problems. There, he is told, everything is play. This is the ultimate temptation. He does not have to face the uncertainty of those depths. He tries to find another way, and Lampwick certainly holds the possibility of getting out of all the demands of growth, of becoming real altogether. And so, Pinocchio joins with Lampwick. We all know what happens. Pinocchio finds himself a donkey, a mule, an ass, a fool in some sense, but learning a lot of lessons as he does so.

Ironically, in a fateful turn of events, Pinocchio is thrown into the sea. His new owner of the little donkey wants his skin to make a drum. He is on the verge of death. Then, once again, something happens in his life to take him forward.

I think this is grace; we don't always know what it is that brings about these "miraculous" circumstances in our life. It's like something seems to happen, and we wonder, how did the right circumstances occur, the right things happen. It is not magic. It is grace; something outside of our own doing takes place. Such an experience happens when Pinocchio is thrown into the sea with a stone around his neck. He is being drowned because the man who has purchased this little donkey wants to use his skin to make a drum. All the small fishes in the sea come and start eating the flesh away from the little donkey, and as they do that they expose the figure of Pinocchio within the flesh of the donkey. When the man pulls up what he thinks is the drowned donkey, there's Pinocchio on the rope. Pinocchio explains to him his whole story of how he met Lampwick, and about all the children who are now donkeys. As he tells this story, his owner becomes irate at his loss. Immediately, without thinking, Pinocchio throws himself into the sea.

In the next section of the story Pinocchio finds himself descending into the depths of the sea. This, to me, is the essential process in growth, transformation, and psychotherapy. This part of the story is what I call the "Monstro experience." That's Disney's word for the whale. In the Italian version, Collodi writes about a huge shark. Disney chose a whale and called it Monstro; Collodi called the shark, Attila. I like Monstro better. It captures the immensity of this experience. Pinocchio confronts the great fish in spite of all his fears at being faced with this enormous being. He gets sucked into its belly. Pinocchio awakes in the darkness of the belly of the whale.

We recognize this story as a familiar one in the literature of transformation, for instance, Jonah and the whale. There are many characters in stories, heroes and heroines, who are swallowed up by monsters. This experience of being swallowed up into something that is bigger than oneself is the beginning of facing something within oneself. In surrendering to the depths of one's self, comes the possibility of transformation to become a new being, of becoming who we are.

Oftentimes this process of transformation is a part of the therapy process with children that is not dealt with adequately. Maybe it is because we don't want children to have to go into these depths; we don't want them to have to face Monstro, to face the torment of their own inner conflicts, to look at the disowned parts, the pain of self-hatred, the shame and self-loathing that is there.

Pinocchio finds himself in Monstro, the "realm of introjects." What does Pinocchio find when he goes inside? He finds whole ships. He finds all sorts of things that have literally been swallowed whole that are just sitting inside the stomach or in the interior of this being, which we recognize as a metaphor for his inner life, his sense of self.

However, in this time of descent and emergence, we see something different about Pinocchio that was not present at the beginning of the story. He is supporting himself in this experience. There are still signs of his anxieties, of his fear, but there is now focus, there is intention. There is now a sense of "what am I going to do with this?"–a conscious awareness of choice. He is in contact with this experience rather than moving away from himself or attacking the external world. He is now present with himself. It is inside this experience that Pinocchio discovers the most amazing thing and the most unlikely of all things: the introject of his father. There, Gepetto sits (whole and complete) at a table with a lighted candle writing, a man who found himself within the belly of the whale in his recyclical search for Pinocchio. Finally, they have come together. They meet and join together in order to get out of their predicament. They have to work together. Gepetto is also different. He leans on Pinocchio, not saying to him, "You have to do this" or "You are a bad and ungrateful son." Pinocchio initiates, Pinocchio takes agency here, not being a puppet but an agent in his life. He says to Gepetto, "Don't worry, father, we'll find a way out of this." Gepetto points out that their resources are depleted. The last little bit of candle is all that is left, and if they don't get out soon they will be in complete darkness. They have to work together to get out of this situation. Pinocchio says, "Follow me, I'll lead us out." (Pinocchio has learned many things in finding his father. He knows the way out.) Quite a change from the Pinocchio who has been running away from his father and demanding of his father that he be taken care of. Gepetto trusts Pinocchio; they hold hands and together begin the journey out of the belly of the whale. It is again not an easy road out. But to make a long story short, they finally come to the mouth of the whale where they must face the formidable teeth.

This part of the story, this part of the therapeutic process, is an aggressive part of the restorative process that requires the child to chew the introjected material. He has to experience again these beliefs about the self and the concomitant shame and self-hatred that are residing in his or her belly realness.

Pinocchio and Gepetto have to face the teeth, and they are indeed terrifyingly large and sharp. Collodi gives them a way out. In Disney's version, they start a fire, and it is all very dramatic. However, Collodi describes Atilla as an old shark who has asthma, and when he is asleep he sleeps with his mouth open. In this way, they are able to get out. In the story, Pinocchio suddenly realizes that the whale's mouth is open. Isn't this true of our own journeys? Sometimes we think the next step is too frightening, too demanding, and then we realize that the way is open. Pinocchio looks out of the whale's mouth and sees the stars in the night sky, and exclaims, "We can just walk out!" So the jailed are released. They walk out and dive into the water. As they are swimming they both tire. Gepetto gasps, "Oh, Pinocchio, I can't swim!" Pinocchio tells him not to worry about it. Throughout this journey Pinocchio has learned that he has much resourcefulness inside of himself. He assures his father, "Don't worry, I can swim." First of all, he's light, he's wooden, he can float. "I'll carry you. Get on my back." Pinocchio swims and carries Gepetto. He gets tired and begins to wonder if he can make it. He feels discouraged. "Can I make it?" he worries. Then he begins to use some of the other external resources that are now available to him. Another character, a tuna fish, shows up and Pinocchio and Gepetto climb on the back of the fish, and the fish takes them to the final goal of land and puts them on the shore. Both Gepetto and Pinocchio rest on the shore. This is the end of the most important part of the story; what I call "Monstro, the Realm of the Introjects."

That is not the end of the story, however, as we all well know. In therapy too, even though we have chewed, we have taken in, and are now free of the unassimilated introjects, we also know that in terms of the therapeutic process there is a period of assimilation, of carrying the new experience of self into our lives. Well, this is certainly true in the story of Pinocchio. He doesn't become a real boy immediately.

Pinocchio and Gepetto go onto the land and there is a period of time when Pinocchio actually lets go of the idea of realness. It is no longer a goal in his life. It recedes into the ground of his life. It's not figure for him. What does become figure for him are the new relationships in his life, his sense of the other, his connections. There is a healthy interdependency developing in Pinocchio's life. He cares for Other, especially his father, and he gets on with the day-to-dayness of life; doing the chores, going to school, learning what he has to learn. There is an ease about Pinocchio. We don't see the things that we saw in the beginning. He is comfortable in being who he is.

One of the persons that he recognizes in his new home is his old friend, Lampwick, who is still a donkey. He sees Lampwick and recognizes him even though he is a donkey. Pinocchio sees that his friend is dying because he has been so mistreated and so worn down in his work as a donkey. This is a poignant moment. Pinocchio cries, deeply wanting to help his friend and not to have Lampwick die in this way. We can feel the genuine grief of this loss in Pinocchio. There is the beauty of an emotional life in him. He cares, he cries, he laughs, he is competent, he is tired, etc.

As the story continues, news comes to Pinocchio that the Blue Fairy is quite ill and does not have the resources to provide for herself. Pinocchio has two shillings that he's earned in his daily work. What he wants to do with his savings is buy some new clothes for himself. But, when the word comes to him about the Blue Fairy, he gives her messenger the two shillings and says, "Take these, and I will send regularly as much as I can so that she can be cared for." In his gift of two shillings, you see his ability to give of himself to the other, to be concerned which is hallmark of a rich emotional life. In this awareness of himself and of others, and a sense of connection with his life, we begin to see Pinocchio's life unfolding naturally.

In therapeutic terms, this story is a metaphor of the integrative process. I am talking about integration as a process towards wholeness, towards completeness, aliveness, realness. What I want to stress is what I am calling the Monstro experience in terms of therapy with children. As I said earlier, many of us hesitate; we're kind of like Pinocchio in that we would like to go into the Playland. We would like the therapy to be a pleasant experience for kids. Somehow we want this to be an experience without much pain or discomfort. We would like children to be able to get on with their lives, be happy, and go on. Well, Pinocchio tried that. And that is what clients want. You invite them into the impasse; you're standing on the precipice, just as Pinocchio was. You look out over those cliffs, and my God, who want to go out there! Certainly, children don't want to, and certainly as therapists we don't. We say, but you're so young, you don't need to jump into those depths. But they do have to. How do we do that in the therapy process? How do we help children go into the belly of the whale and have these experiences? And, as importantly, how do we support ourselves as clinicians in helping them do this? Oftentimes we try to truncate this process. We try not to go into it. For some reason we think this is not good. Who wants to face self-hatred? Who wants to have a child talk about how they hate themselves? Who wants to experience the pain of shame? Who wants to look at this? Yet, without that there is no possibility for wholeness. The introjects stay in the belly of the child and stay as unfinished business and come up again. They become the adults who are sitting in our offices saying, "I feel bad about myself." The origins of that are in childhood. And we see it in our clients.

This is the integrative work of therapy. The reason I do that is because we are clearly asking the child to face a part of himself that he had disowned, a part of himself that he is saying "No" to. And this is what we see ourselves struggling with. It is precisely these disowned parts, these disowned aspects of self that we have to face and take into ourselves as a part of who we are. Before children, adolescents, and adults as we know can do this, there are certain things that have to be in place. (1) The therapeutic relationship has to be in place. There has to be support in that relationship, there has to be a therapeutic alliance, good contact between the child and the therapist. (2) It also means that the child has to have self-support through breath, and good development of self-function, and the ability to see and to use all of themselves that is available. So all of this we are assuming is taking place in the therapeutic process at this time. (3) There needs to be a sense of self, who I am and who I am not, a sense of self-other. We see this in how all of this develops in the story of Pinocchio. Pinocchio does this; he jumps into the depths with much self-support available to him. 4) Another thing that has to be in place is a familiarity with the realm of emotions. The child needs to be familiar with anger, sadness, joy, grief, and the whole realm of experience. Now, those readers who have done work with Violet Oaklander or trained with her are familiar with her work and understand that she has a particular process or way of working that develops these functions within the person. Of course, that's all part of what we are talking about as an integrative process. It is laying the groundwork, and each step in and of itself, is essential and important.

All these capacities are in place, and all of that is the foundation for this "Monstro experience," the realm of introjects, the integrative work, which means taking the child into the world where they hate themselves, to face the parts of themselves they don't like, and parts of themselves that make them mad, the parts of themselves that hold the feeling that I'm bad, the sources of shame, I'm unwanted, I'm unloved, I'm not pretty, I'm stupid, I'm clumsy. These are the fundamental introjects that mold a life; that limit, constrict, that set all these other resistances to contact in motion. It's these beliefs–what I call the self-gestalts, these beliefs that are who I am. When we work in treatment with adults, we might explore where all this came from. And it doesn't mean someone said, "You're unlovable." There are constrictions of self, these beliefs out of our experience of self-other. When we are talking about the construction of meaning, the organization of experience, children are constantly organizing their own experience of self and saying who they are, and that organization certainly comes out of the field, their relationship with others, peers, family, school, church, you name it. And they do that with very limited developmental capacities to assimilate their experiences.

The first thing that has to be present between the therapist and the child is recognition that there are parts of the self that the child does not like. This will become evident over time. The therapist doesn't always jump on it the first thing. You begin to gather these understandings, like the Blue Fairy, and you begin to open up the possibility that there might be something more to do with this, by the way you receive the child's feelings and accept them. The sense of being accepted that the child must experience in the relationship is very, very important. So, first there is the recognition of the existence of the disowned aspects of the self; then the carefully listening to and hearing about these parts that the child does not like.

I began to hear it in the case of one of my Pinocchias–someone I called Jonelle–in a chapter I wrote for another book. Jonelle was a child who seemed, throughout her childhood, to have difficulty with making connections and being in relationships. Her family was disturbed; she was the child of a mixed marriage. That, in itself, created important conditions in her life. In terms of looking at the field and the context of a child's life, she was struggling in the world she was in, the white world. In my story she is Hispanic. Jonelle was a child who was constantly struggling with these worlds and herself and trying to organize herself in these two experiences.

Early in her life she began to get the feeling there was something wrong with her. This came up early in her work because she felt this was her mother's attitude towards her. "You always feel like I'm the one who's at fault, I'm the one who's bad." At age four, her mother who was Hispanic, remarried a white man. Her stepfather did not accept her as an interracial, bicultural child. The story of this lack of acceptance was a very dramatic story. Jonelle's mother entered into an agreement as part of her marriage contract with the stepfather, who never wanted children, that he would never have to have anything to do with Jonelle. Jonelle could never understand why this man would not respond to her. In fact, he was so rigid about not participating in her life that when something would come up he would not talk directly to her. Even if she were in the room he would talk to her mother about her. Then this would go through the mother to the daughter. It was literally driving Jonelle nuts. She dealt with it and never understood because she didn't know about this agreement until a family session in which there was much rage expressed by Jonelle towards her stepfather. You can just imagine the rage she felt. Finally, in the session, the mother intervened. In the third or fourth family session that we had, her mother disclosed the agreement. It was just stunning when the mother turned to her daughter and told her what their agreement was. It certainly was one of those turning points in treatment. A lot of things fell into place, we were able to move forward, and things changed. But this young girl had introjected so many things about herself that were so deep within her sense of self. The belief that she was unwanted and unlovable was deep inside of her. Her self-hatred that had come out of the family situation was very strong in her. How that got played out in terms of symptoms and her relationships with others, as we can all imagine, was very tragic for her life.

The first part of the work with Jonelle was building self-support, working with the family, hearing these experiences, hearing her say things about herself indicating that she was unwanted, and comments such as, "I'm bad," or "There's something wrong with me." She would phrase this very globally; the sense that there was "something wrong with me" which is something children do. This is an egocentric way of interpreting or organizing experience: "It's me, I must be the cause" of all of this that's going on in the world.

In the course of treatment we were hearing all of these things. But towards the end of her work we could begin to identify these aspects, these parts of herself, and we finally got down to what was this final thing with her which was what she called "Flaw." She always felt there was something wrong with her, she was flawed in some way, and this was the part of herself she began to identify.

Another aspect of this, as in Step Two, is, rather than saying "I hate myself," or whatever children tend to say in a global way to move from general statements to the specific parts of self, they say very general global things. We want to help them become specific so we can work. We ask, "Can you give me an example?" "Did that happen this week?" or whatever. You ask children to say, rather than I hate myself, I don't like myself, or I'm a horrible, miserable person, to tell you what part of yourself don't you like, or what part of you is unlovable, what makes you think that? Or how did that happen? Not in a way that says, "Oh, that's not true," or "How could you feel that way?" or "I just think you're a wonderful human being." I mean, sometimes we want to do that, to reassure, doing a lot of things that encourage our young clients to go into what I'm calling the Playland experience. Rather than encouraging them to go deeper into the introject. In this process, we ask them to tell us about these unliked parts of self. With Jonelle it was the Flaw that she represented as a black spider.

It is important to ask a child to elaborate on those parts of themselves. It could be making a clay figure of that part. Or, it could be, in terms of Jonelle, talking about the spider and how she chose this puppet, how this was like her, how she experienced herself. Or, we can just simply ask children to choose a puppet or make a drawing of this part. This step begins to externalize the experience of self. We externalize the experience, we objectify it, it becomes something that's out here so that now we can see and talk about it. This helps the child to experience this part of themselves and to relate to themselves.

The next step of this process is sometimes difficult for therapists. We don't want to take children into these experiences of self because we have to ask them to express towards the figure what they feel, and this is self-hatred. "I hate it, I don't like you, why are you here?"; all the things that adults feel towards the self, children do too. "Why did I do it!" Carlos says. "It makes me mad, I don't like you when I do that." "Why do you do this? I wish you wouldn't do it." It doesn't have to be catharsis for the child to say,

"I don't like you. I don't want you to do this." The expression of anger and self-hatred is essential.

For Jonelle, because we had done the emotional expression work, there was a safety between us to express anger. So she said to her spider, "I don't like you." She took it off her hands, and said, "I don't like you," and she squeezed it, and she threw it.

What is happening here is again the release of something that goes on internally all the time; the strong level of self-attack. So we work with the child as they express their anger, their rage. We are not putting something there that is not already there. We are allowing the expression of the existing feeling toward the self. It's the belief and the feelings about the self. To encourage the child to do this and to express these feelings is contrary to our tendency to want to say, "Oh there, there, there, you're okay." The Blue Fairy didn't say that to Pinocchio. The self-rejecting feelings have to be expressed, and the self-rejection has to be fully available for the child to be able to move and for there to be energy for the self-acceptance (which is also present if our theory holds).

What has to occur next in terms of this experience, in terms of digesting and chewing these things, is to begin to look at the disowned part and begin to develop what might be called reframing and reorganization of the self. That can be represented through identifying a polarity of the self-rejection. With younger children it can be a fairy godmother. It can be a person in their life or they can go back and talk to the younger parts of self from what they understand now (as Violet did with Carlos). The self-accepting self is a part of the self that can at least look at the despicable self.

With Jonelle, as she sat there holding the spider puppet, I began to propose to her that this Flaw, this feeling of not being "wantable" was the feeling of a much younger part of herself. I began to talk to Jonelle about the Flaw, and I described to her a little girl (and I don't tell her it's herself), "who wanted very much to be loved and cared for by her mom and dad, but they argued all the time. Then, one day her dad left. Her mom was scared and alone, and the little girl was confused. She did her best to understand what and why all these things were happening, but because she was so little it was not possible for her to figure everything out. So she did what all kids do. She decided all these things were happening because she was bad. Many other things happened to her in preschool, which made her feel bad about herself. And then her mom remarried, but her stepfather didn't seem to like her, and her dad was far away and she didn't see him much."

As I talked very softly to Jonelle she began to cry quietly, not sobbing. She recognized herself in my story so we didn't have to make that explicit. I went on. "The little girl kept trying to understand and kept coming up with the same answer, 'I'm bad. Something is wrong with me.'"

With this, Jonelle was quiet. She held the spider puppet, then she put it back in the basket with the other puppets, and that was the end of the session.

At the next session Jonelle came in, sat down, looked at me and said, "It wasn't my fault." I said to her, "Jonelle, would you get a puppet out of the basket that understands the Flaw? You know, maybe like a fairy godmother." She picked up a princess puppet and then we began. So I said to her, "If this is the Fairy Godmother who could understand the Flaw and knows about the Flaw, what is it the Fairy Godmother would say to her?" She said, "It wasn't your fault, you were just a little kid, they were the grown-ups." She said this as the Fairy Godmother to the Spider puppet. I was amazed. I quietly said, "Jonelle, could you have the Fairy Godmother say something like this: "Even though you sometimes feel unwanted, I love you." She did. She said, "Even though you feel unwanted, and like you, Flaw, I love you." Well, we talked about how it felt for her to say this. Then I talked about how she could continue to do this kind of thing in her own life. I asked, "Is there anyone in your life right now, Jonelle, who accepts you, flaw and all?" Well, there was someone in her life, which was her equestrian coach. So I just simply brought that to her awareness. She went out, and I would like you to know that, as with Pinocchio, there was a qualitative difference about Jonelle from that point on. From time to time we would talk about this notion of her self-acceptance, but her life just seemed to unfold. She became softer; she became happier in the sessions, the family was laughing; there was more going on in her life; there was less conflict with her friends at school, she was riding well, she was entering competitions. Over the next few months or so I could see this change in this young girl.

The final step in this process is owning the process. For instance, with Jonelle, at some point I took the Fairy Godmother puppet from her and said, "Jonelle, can you say that to the Flaw, that even though you feel unwanted sometimes and you feel flawed, I love you?" Then, lastly, Jonelle as Jonelle says it to herself. That begins her capacity to see herself and accept herself. This is integration, taking in the flawed and unwanted part and being able to nurture and care for herself and be who she is which includes her feelings of being unwanted and unwantable. This is where the alchemy of therapy takes place–a new being emerges. This process is very moving. I'm always touched. There is a part of me that wants to reach out and embrace, but I have to hold that impulse back because the embrace has to come from the child to the child, not from me. My embrace is my presence and my being there.

As in the story of Pinocchio, acceptance and self-nurturance are the key. What has happened between Pinocchio and the Blue Fairy is that he heard she was not doing well and he sent his money, his only money, to her. That evening Pinocchio worked late because he was trying to earn money, support himself in his own life, and now he wanted to give something more to the Blue Fairy, and also Gepetto. So he worked late. He went to bed and fell asleep. As he slept he dreamed he saw the Fairy, lovely and smiling, who gave him a kiss, saying, "Brave Pinocchio, in return for your good heart I forgive all your past misdeeds." (This is the self-nurturing; this is the acceptance. I forgive myself all my past misdeeds.) And then the dream ended, and Pinocchio awoke, full of amazement. You can imagine how astonished he was when he saw that he was no longer a puppet, but a real boy just like other boys. He looked around. Instead of the straw walls of the cottage he saw a lovely room simply though beautifully furnished and papered. Here was the revival of sensation and the vibrancy of life. He jumped out of bed and found a pretty new suit, a new cap, and a pair of boots as pretty as a picture. When he was dressed he put his hands in his pockets and found there a little ivory purse, on which these words were written, "The Blue Fairy returns Pinocchio's two shillings and thanks him for his good heart." He opened the purse. Instead of two silver shillings there were 20 gold pieces inside. Then he looked in the mirror, but he could not recognize himself. Instead of the usual reflection of a wooden puppet he saw the expressive intelligent face of a good-looking boy with brown hair and blue eyes, who looked contented and full of joy.